NEB

BUJA'S DIARY

D1235142

BUJA'S DIARY

SEYEONG O

NBM ComicsLit

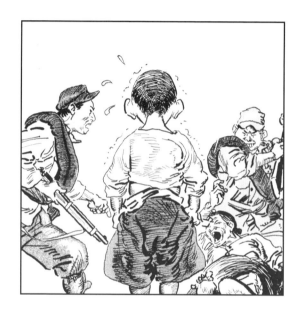

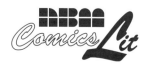

ISBN 10: 1-56163-448-4
ISBN 13: 978-1-56163-448-4
© 2001 by Seyeong O
Originally published in Korea by Words & Images Publishing Company
Translated by Moon-ok Lee & Nicholas Duvernay (Yohan Lee)
Pusan National University, School of Graduate Studies
This book is published with the support of the Korea Literature Translation Institute in
commemoration of Korea being the Guest of Honor at the Frankfurt Book Fair 2005.
Printed in Singapore.

Library of Congress Cataloging-in-Publication Data

O, Se-yong, 1955-
  [Puja ui kurim ilgi. English]
  Buja's diary / Seyeong O.
    p. cm.
  ISBN 1-56163-448-4 (pbk. : alk. paper)
  1. Korea (South)--Social life and customs--Fiction. I. Title.

PL992.58.S28P8513 2005
895.7'35--dc22

                                                                2005050519

Comicslit is an imprint
and trademark of

NANTIER · BEALL · MINOUSTCHINE
Publishing inc.
new york

TABLE OF CONTENTS

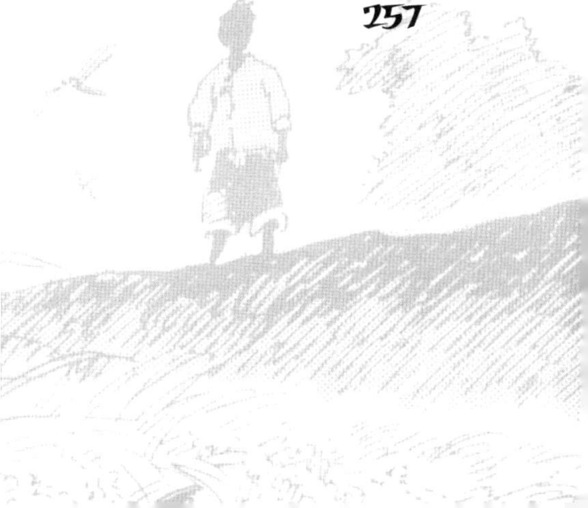

Other Asian Tales:
Songs of our Ancestors
by Patrick Atangan
The Yellow Jar (Japan)
Silk Tapestry (China)
Tree of Love (India)
hardcovers in full color, $12.95 each.

Add $3 P&H first item $1 each additional.

Write for our complete catalog
of over 200 graphic novels:
NBM
555 8th Ave., Suite 1202
New York, NY 10018
www.nbmpublishing.com

SILK TAPESTRY
AND OTHER CHINESE FOLKTALES

SONGS OF OUR ANCESTORS
VOLUME III
PATRICK ATANGAN
TREE OF LOVE

THE
YELLOW-JAR
TWO-TALES-FROM-JAPANESE-TRADITION
VOLUME I
PATRICK-ATANGAN
P-CRAIG-RUSSELL

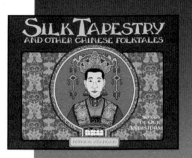

THE LITTLE ALLEY WATCHER

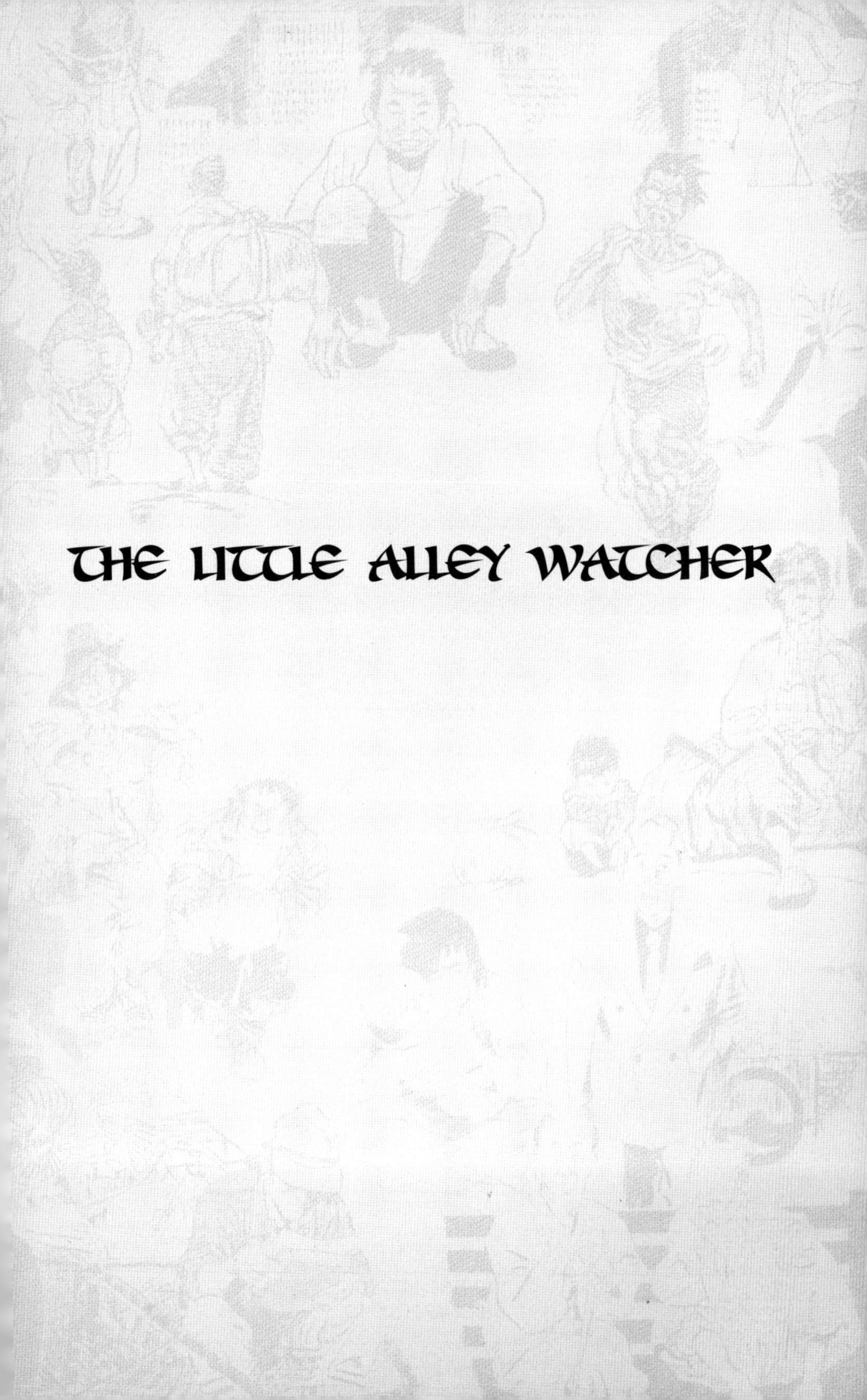

OH SE-YOUNG
DECEMBER 1990

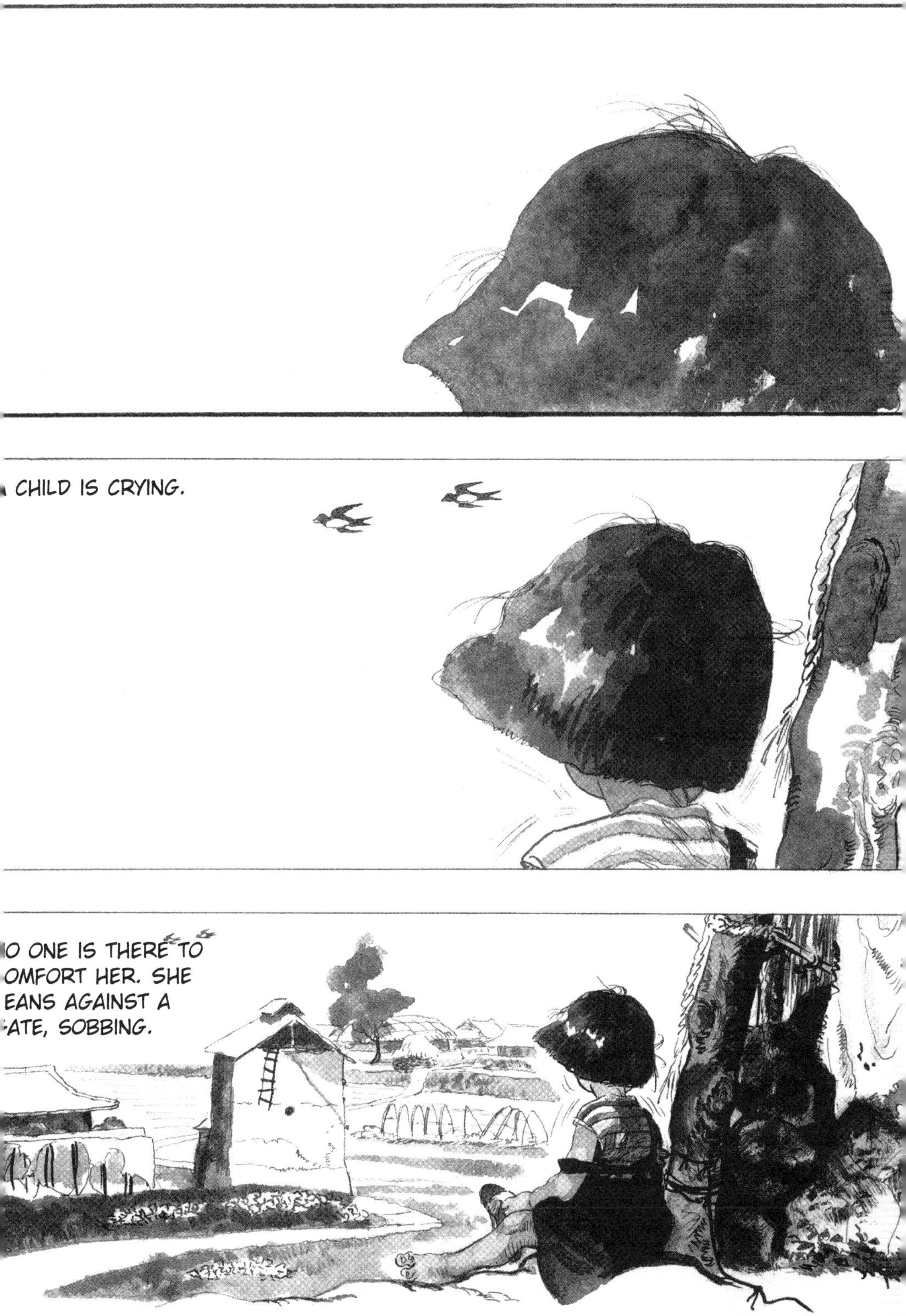
CHILD IS CRYING.
O ONE IS THERE TO
OMFORT HER. SHE
EANS AGAINST A
ATE, SOBBING.

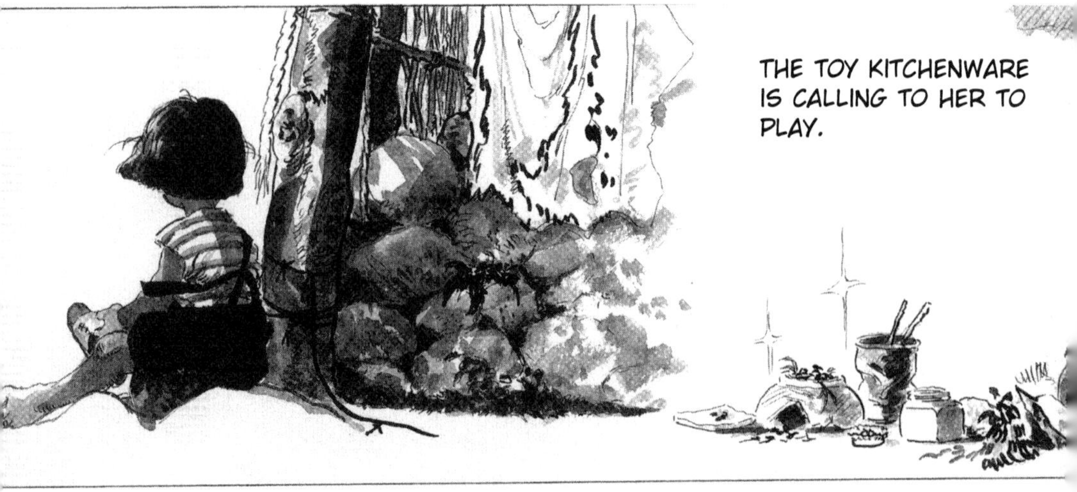
THE TOY KITCHENWARE IS CALLING TO HER TO PLAY.

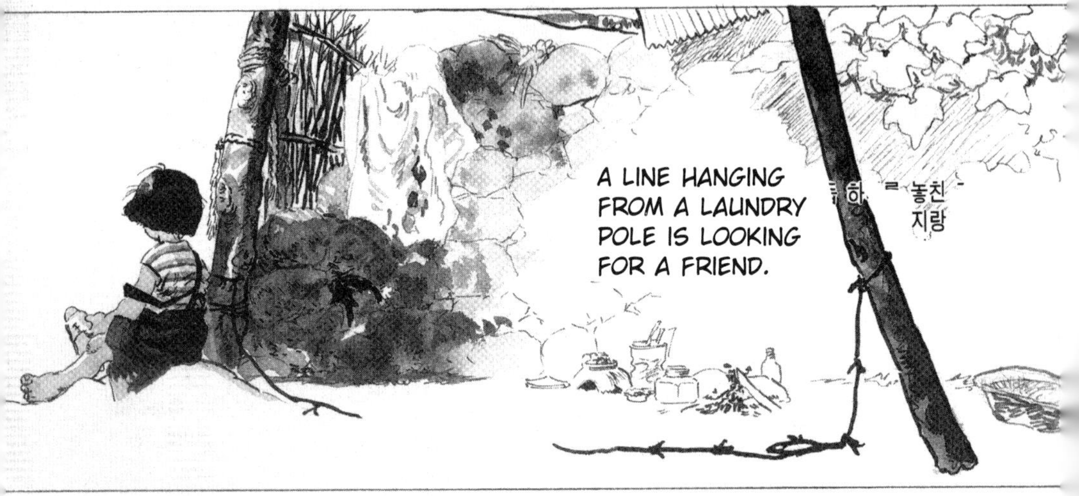
A LINE HANGING FROM A LAUNDRY POLE IS LOOKING FOR A FRIEND.
놓친
지랑

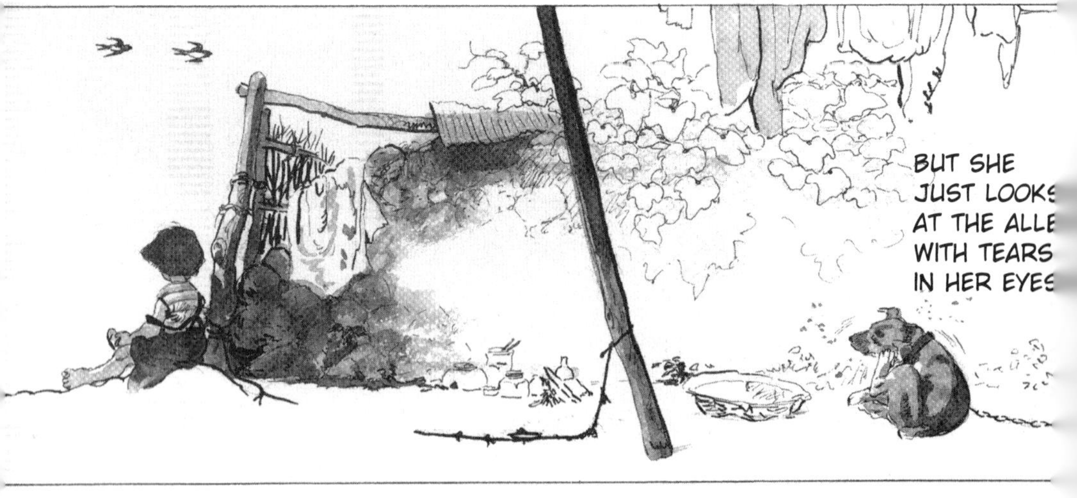
BUT SHE JUST LOOKS AT THE ALLE WITH TEARS IN HER EYES

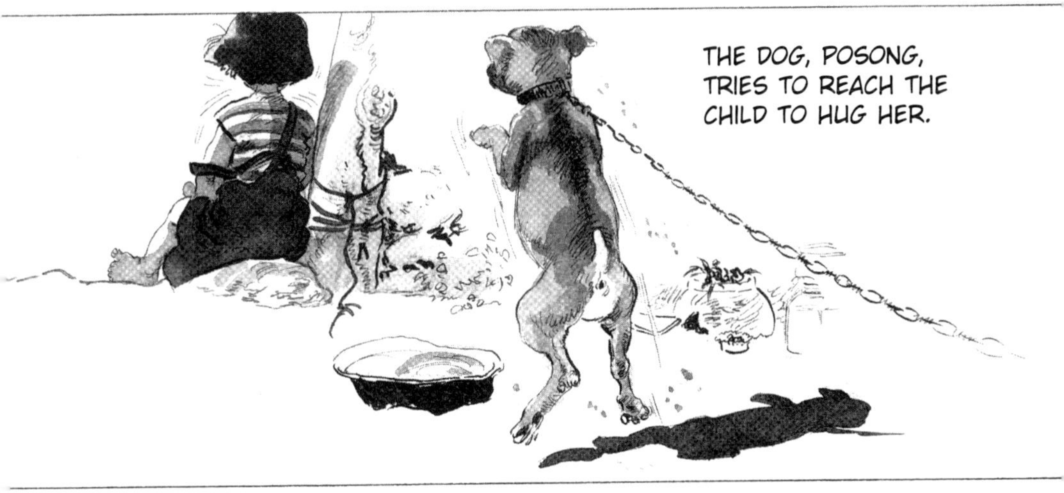
THE DOG, POSONG, TRIES TO REACH THE CHILD TO HUG HER.

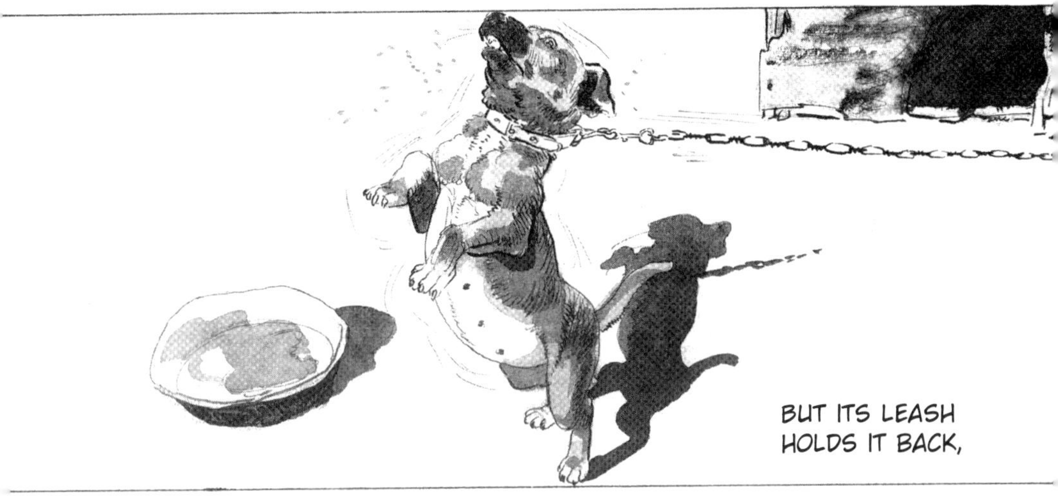
BUT ITS LEASH HOLDS IT BACK,

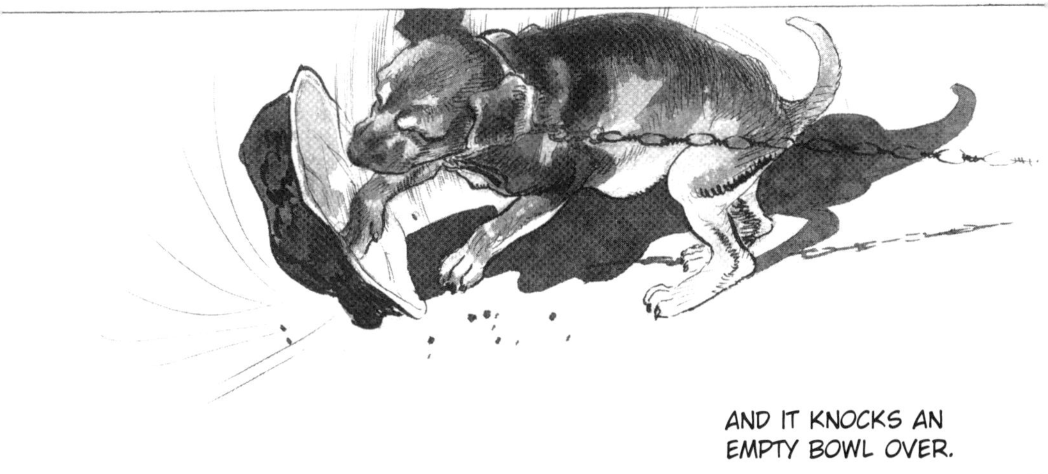
AND IT KNOCKS AN EMPTY BOWL OVER.

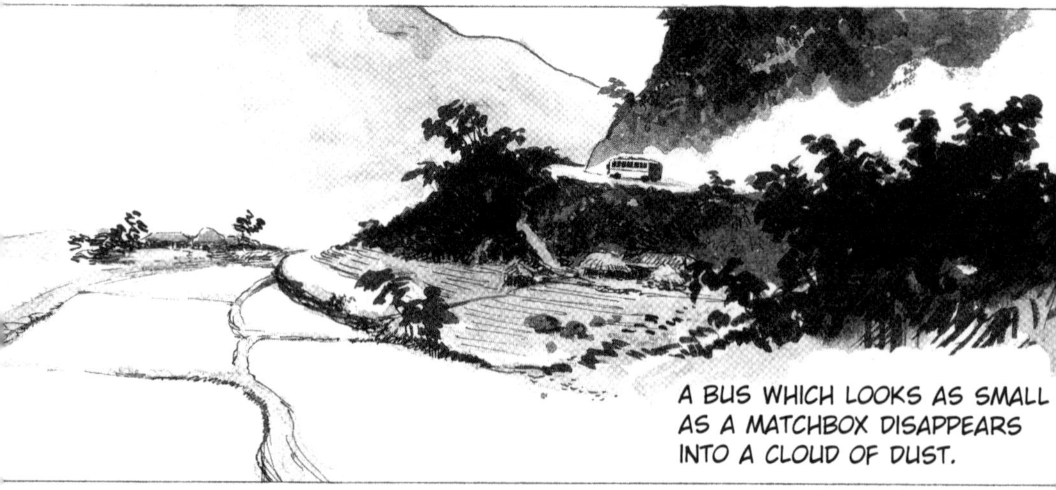
A BUS WHICH LOOKS AS SMALL AS A MATCHBOX DISAPPEARS INTO A CLOUD OF DUST.

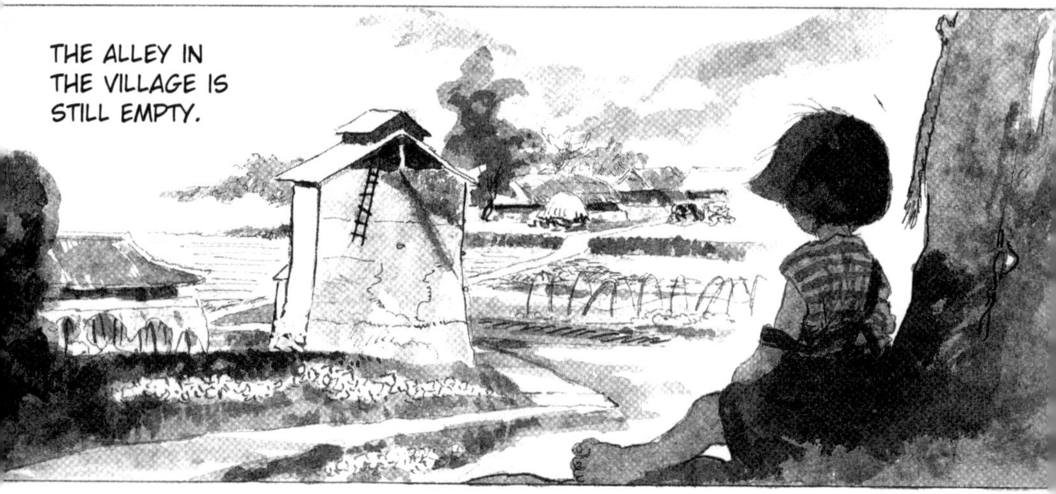
THE ALLEY IN THE VILLAGE IS STILL EMPTY.

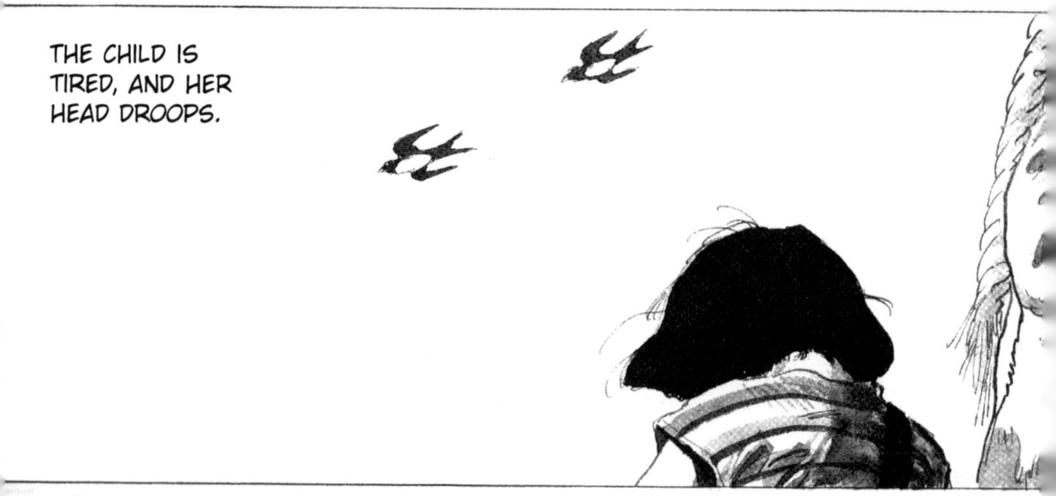
THE CHILD IS TIRED, AND HER HEAD DROOPS.

A SWEATING ANT
DRAGS ITS LOAD.

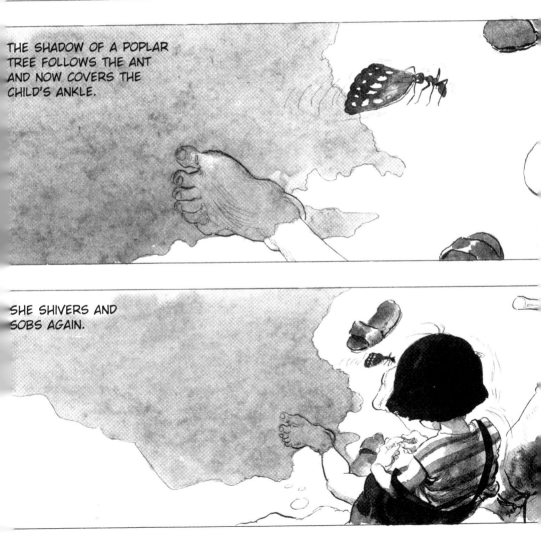

THE SHADOW OF A POPLAR
TREE FOLLOWS THE ANT
AND NOW COVERS THE
CHILD'S ANKLE.

SHE SHIVERS AND
SOBS AGAIN.

13

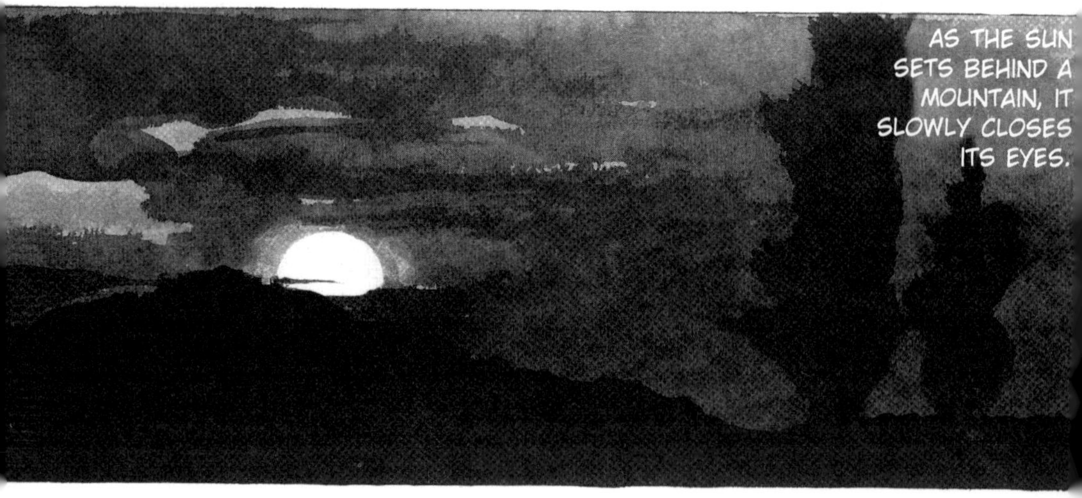
AS THE SUN SETS BEHIND A MOUNTAIN, IT SLOWLY CLOSES ITS EYES.

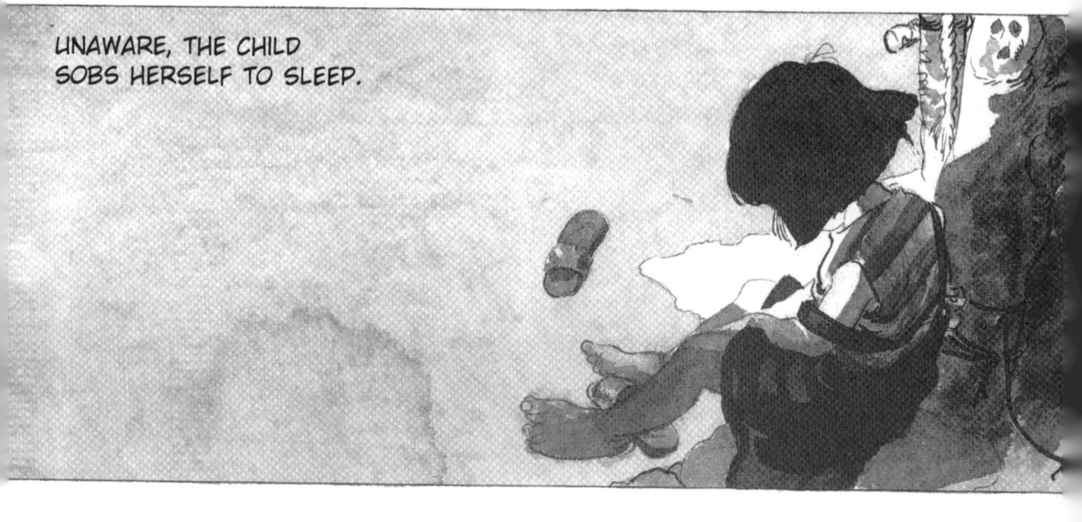
UNAWARE, THE CHILD SOBS HERSELF TO SLEEP.

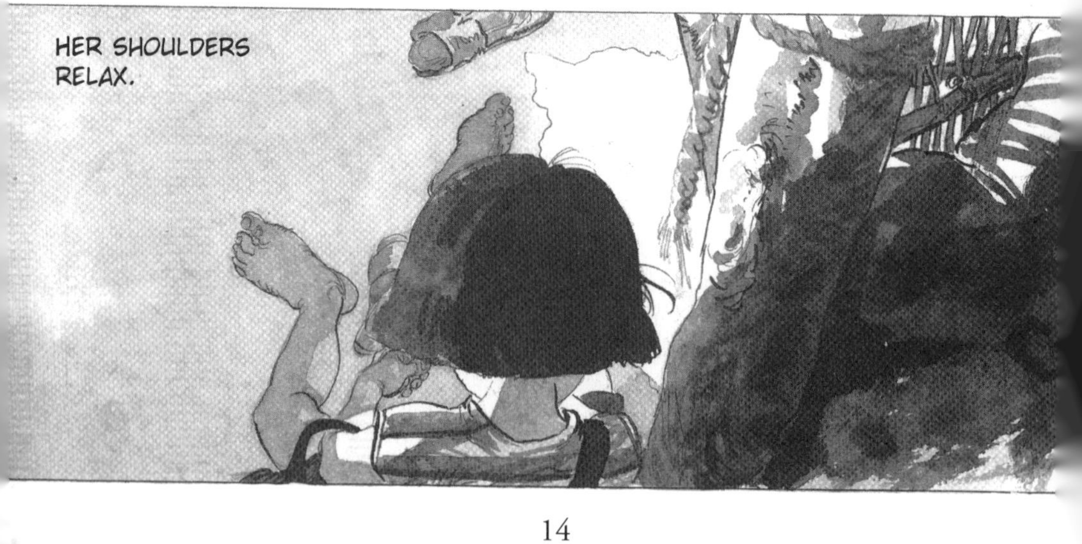
HER SHOULDERS RELAX.

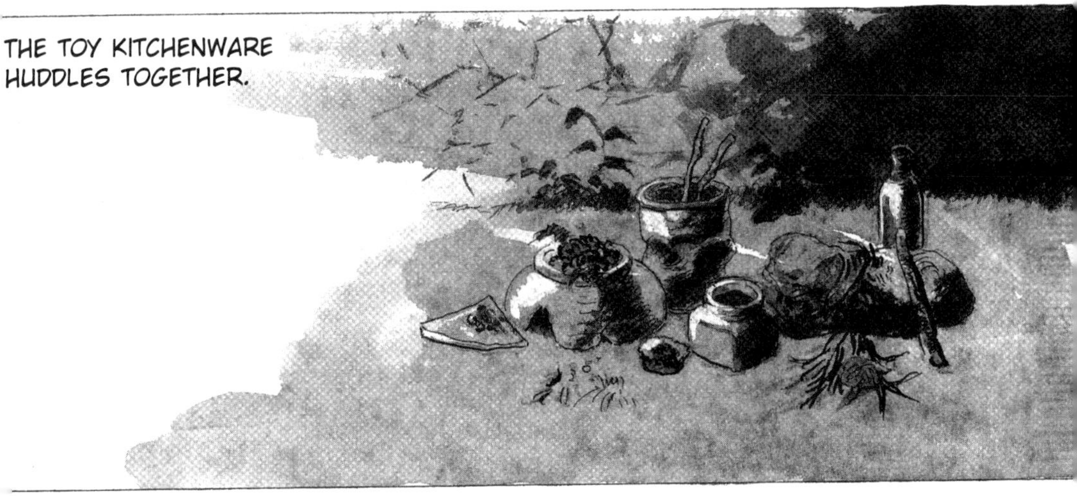
THE TOY KITCHENWARE HUDDLES TOGETHER.

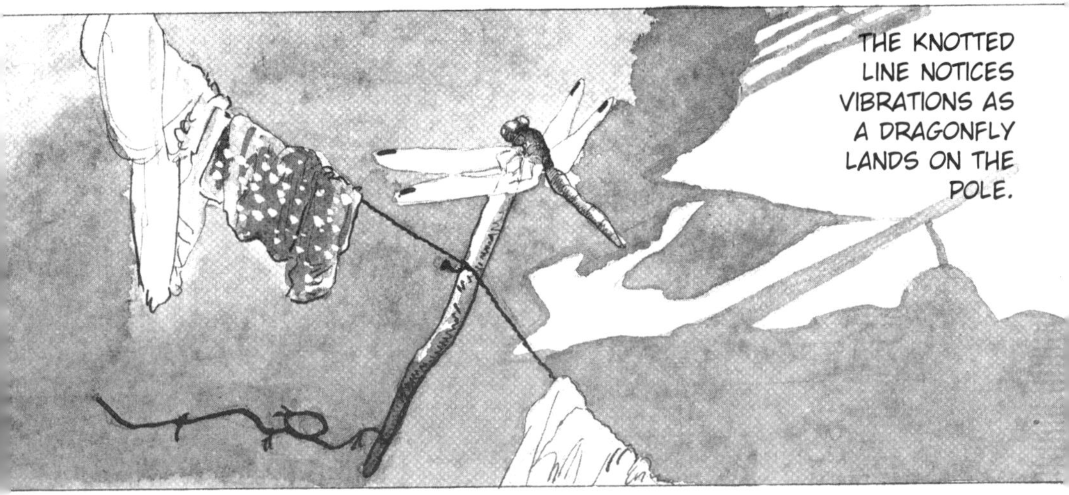
THE KNOTTED LINE NOTICES VIBRATIONS AS A DRAGONFLY LANDS ON THE POLE.

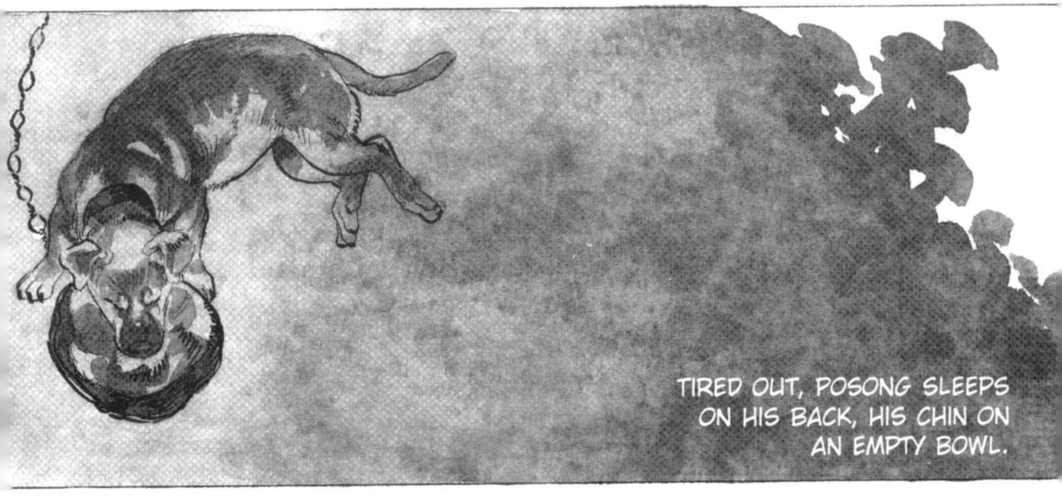
TIRED OUT, POSONG SLEEPS ON HIS BACK, HIS CHIN ON AN EMPTY BOWL.

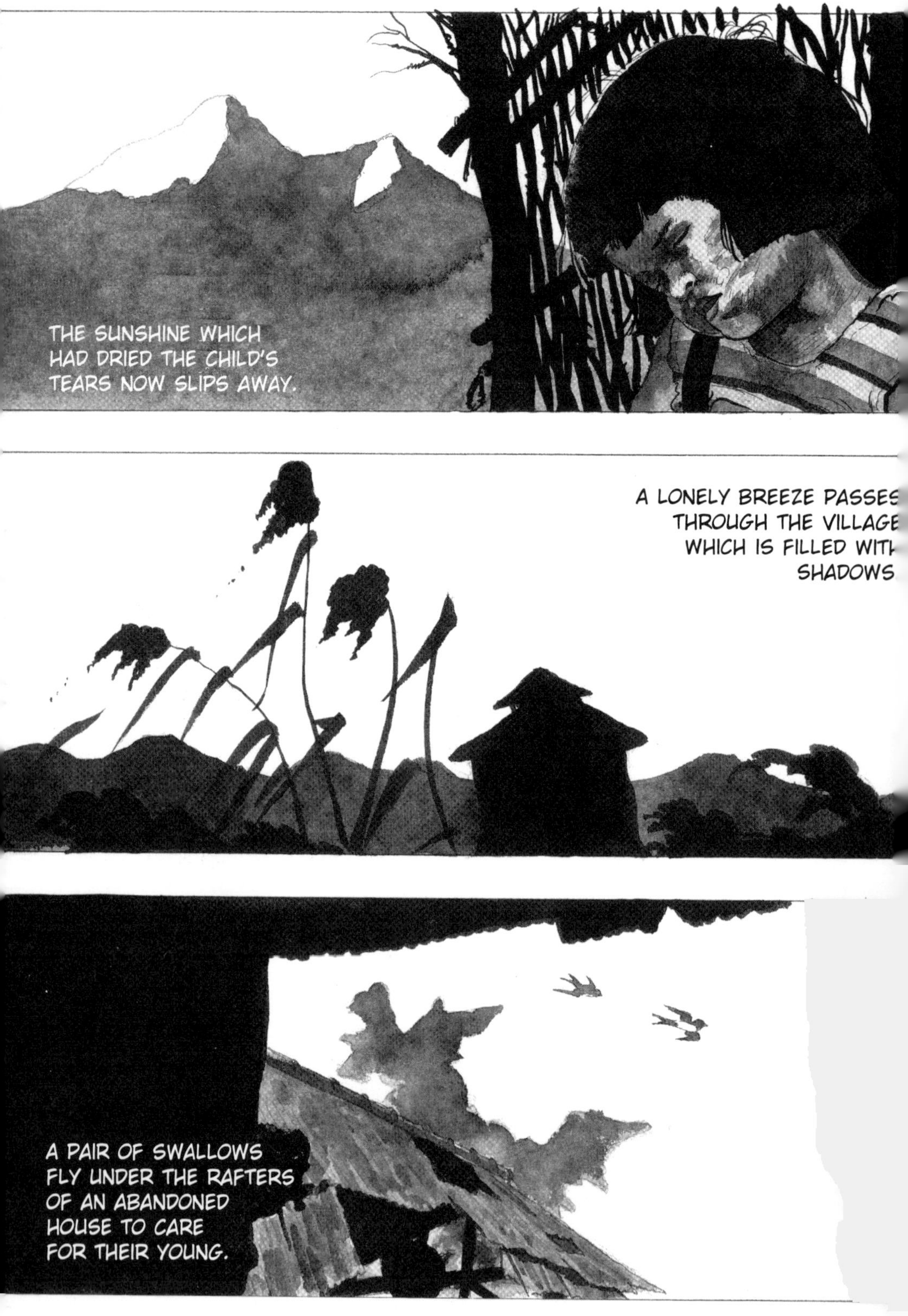
THE SUNSHINE WHICH HAD DRIED THE CHILD'S TEARS NOW SLIPS AWAY.
A LONELY BREEZE PASSES THROUGH THE VILLAGE WHICH IS FILLED WITH SHADOWS.
A PAIR OF SWALLOWS FLY UNDER THE RAFTERS OF AN ABANDONED HOUSE TO CARE FOR THEIR YOUNG.

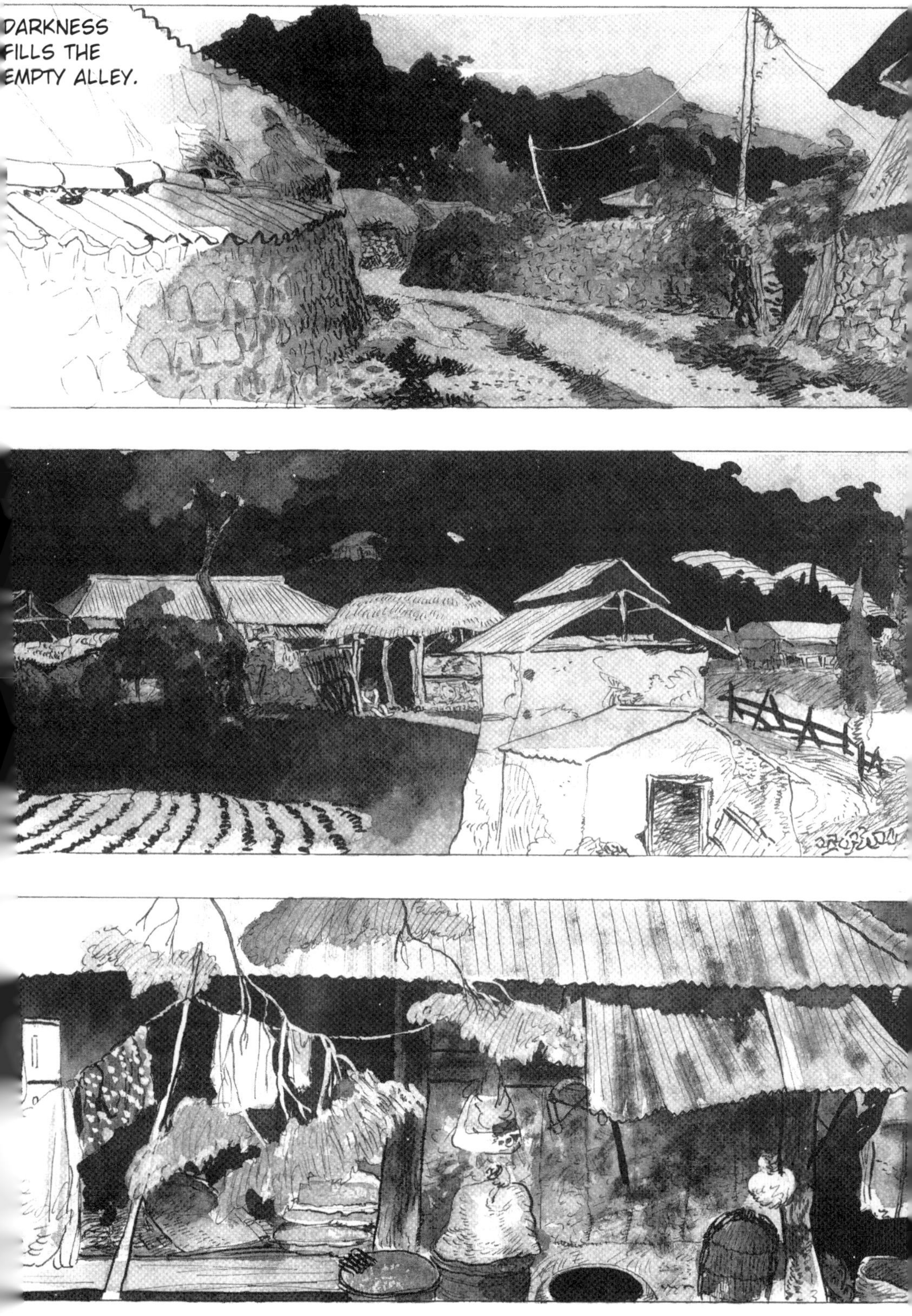
DARKNESS FILLS THE EMPTY ALLEY.

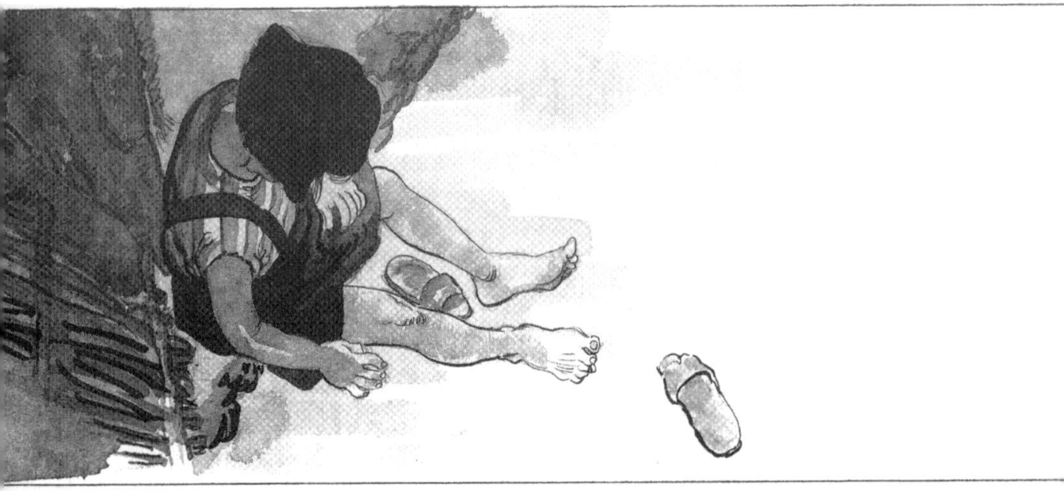
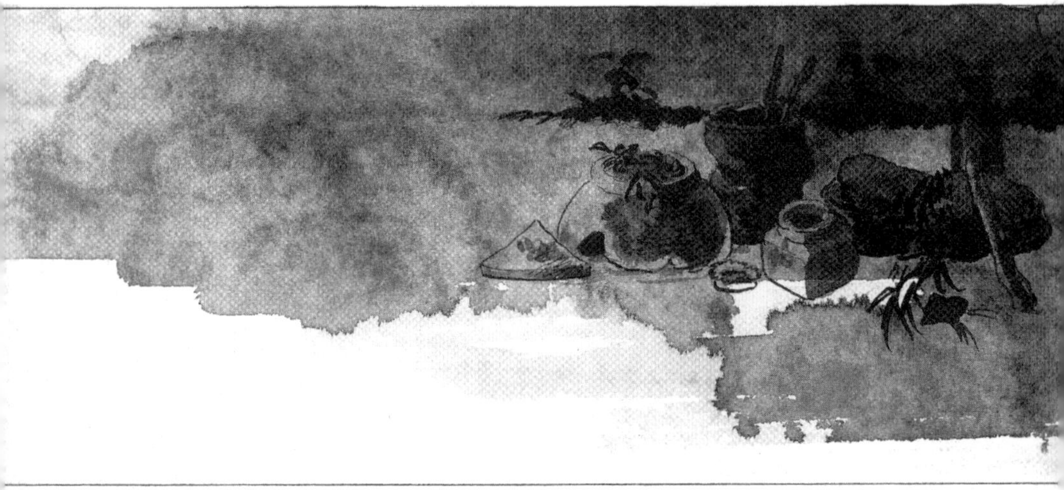
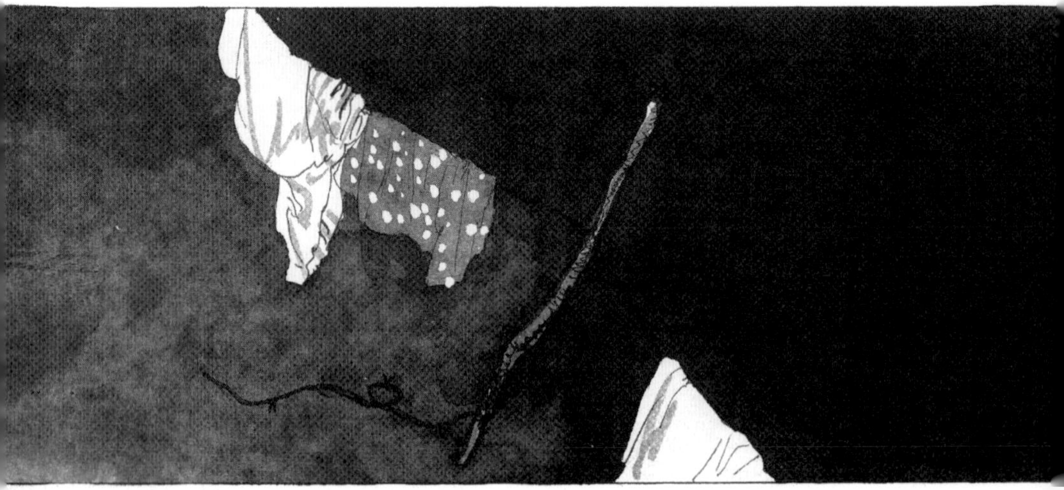

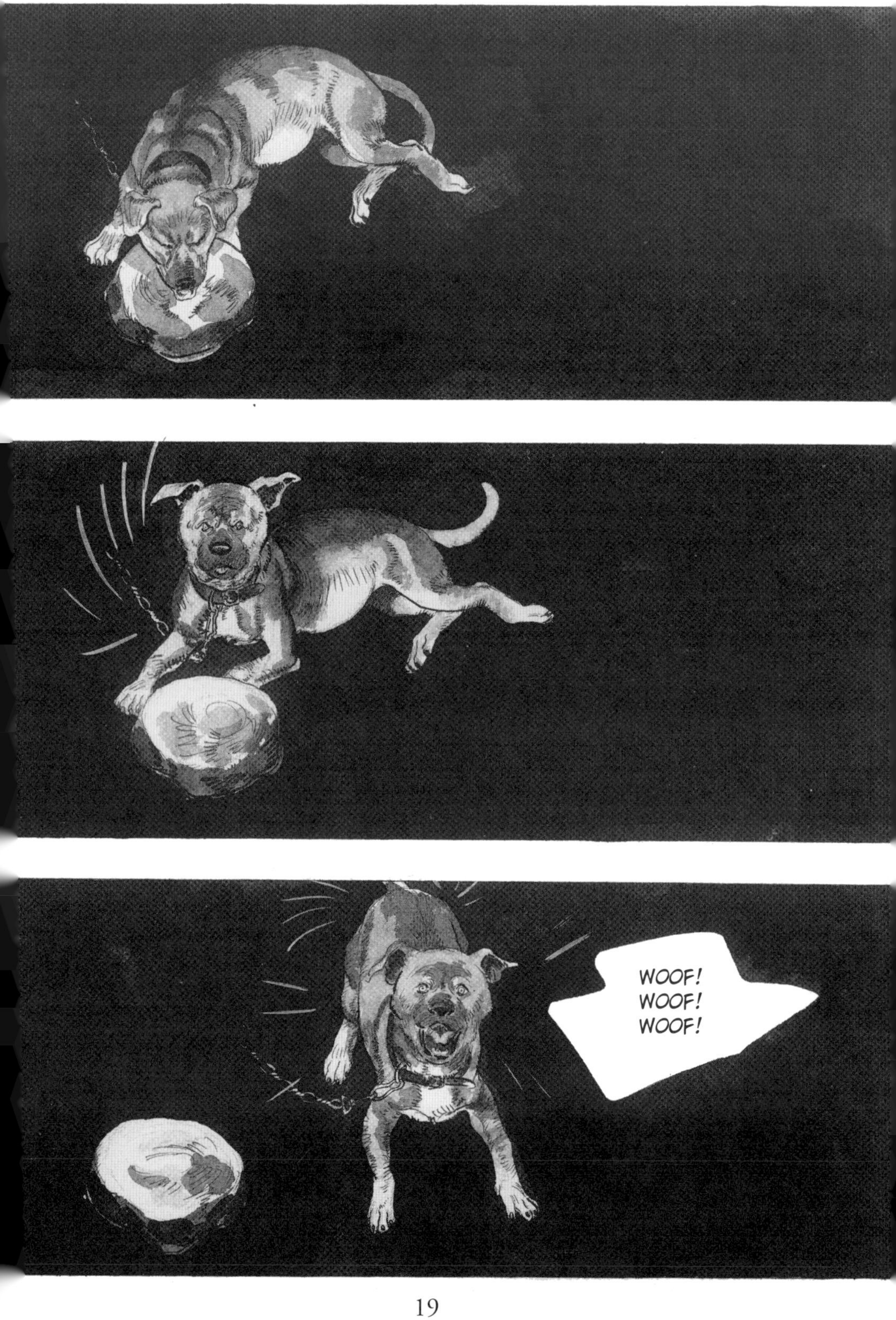
WOOF!
WOOF!
WOOF!

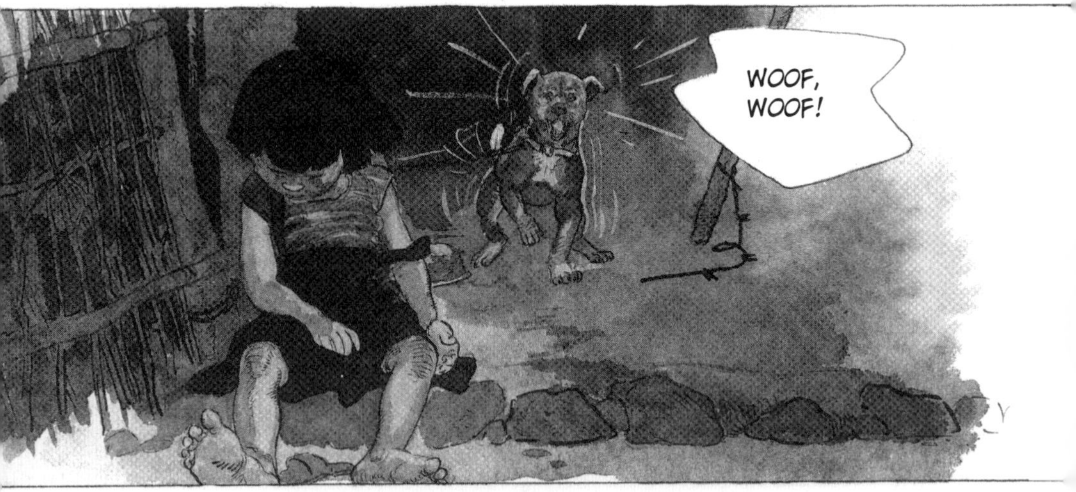
WOOF, WOOF!

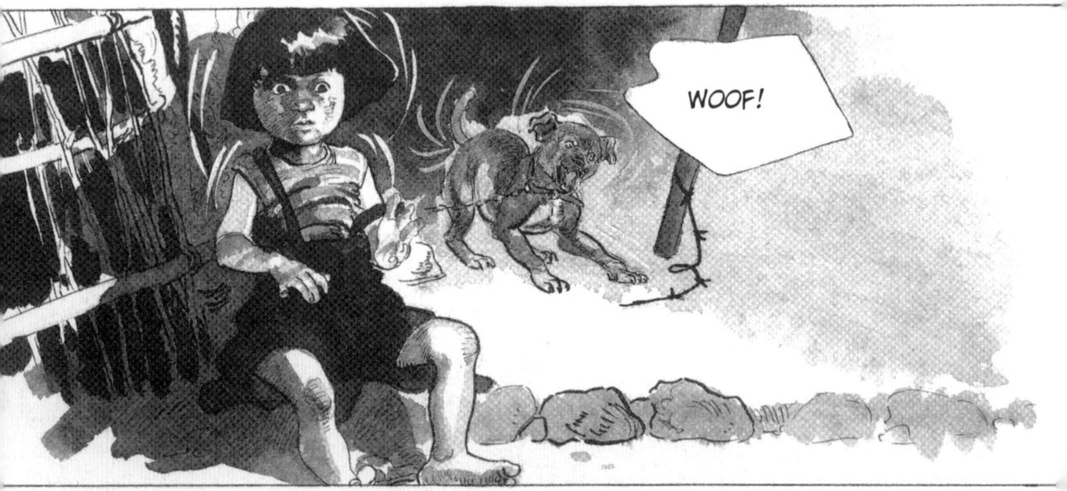
WOOF!

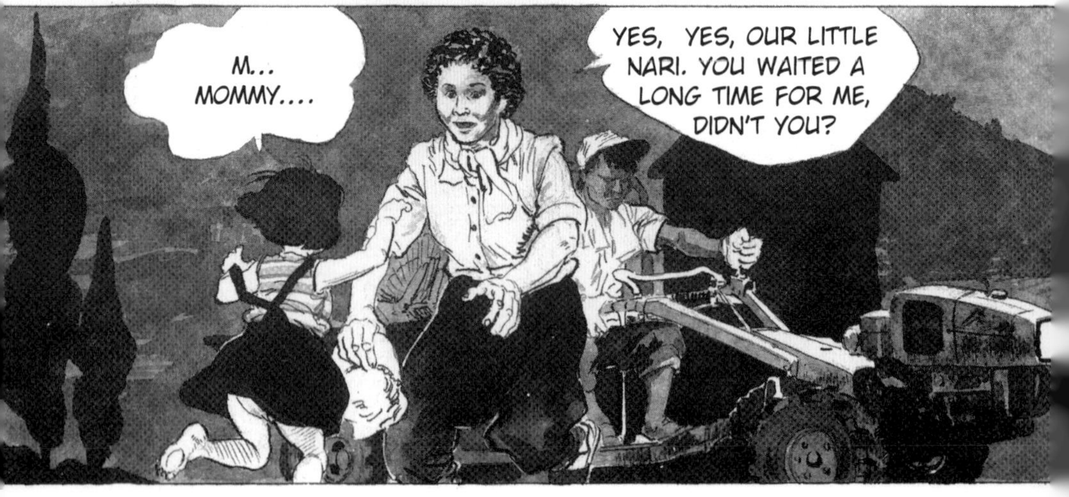
M... MOMMY....
YES, YES, OUR LITTLE NARI. YOU WAITED A LONG TIME FOR ME, DIDN'T YOU?

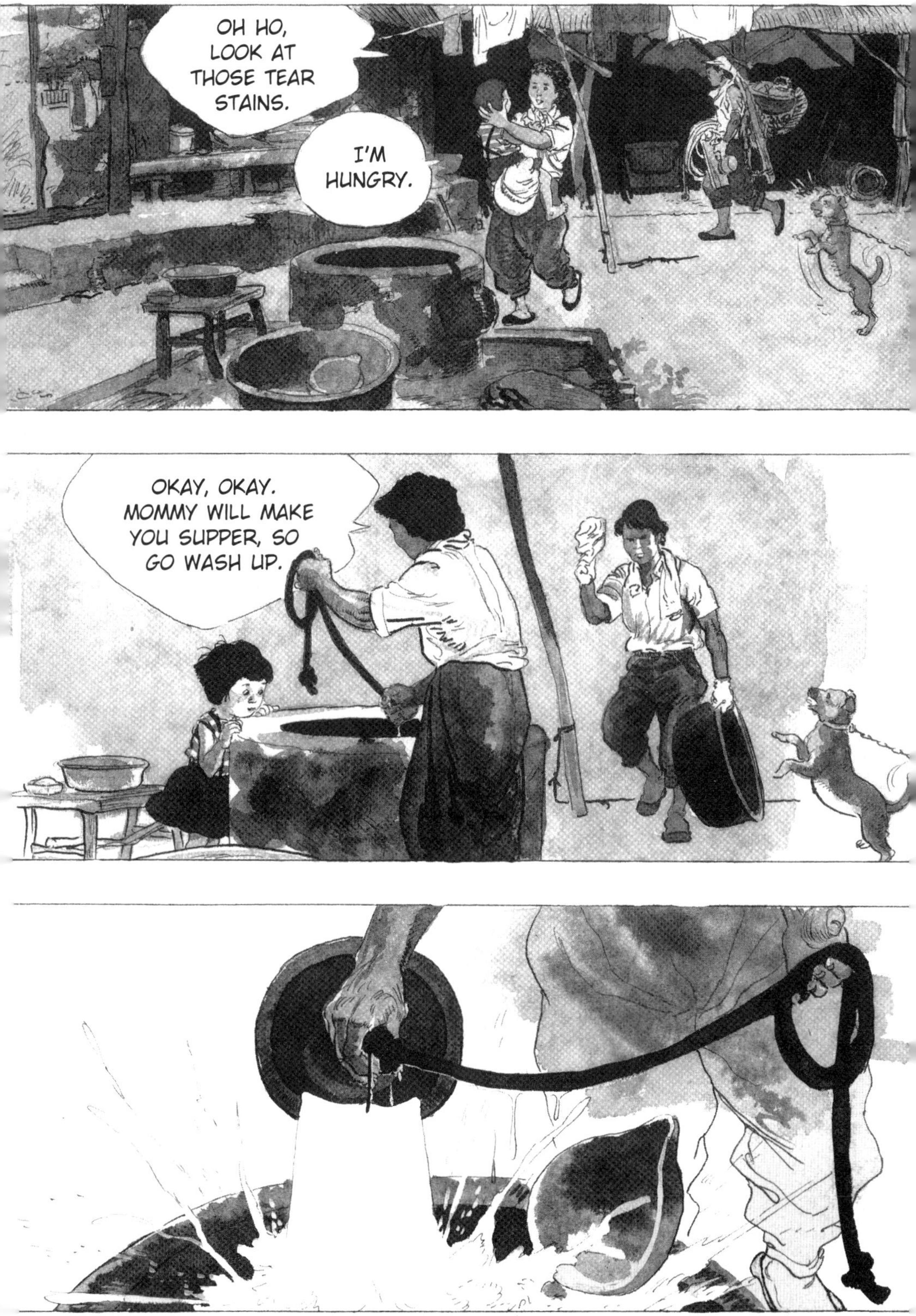
OH HO, LOOK AT THOSE TEAR STAINS.
I'M HUNGRY.
OKAY, OKAY. MOMMY WILL MAKE YOU SUPPER, SO GO WASH UP.

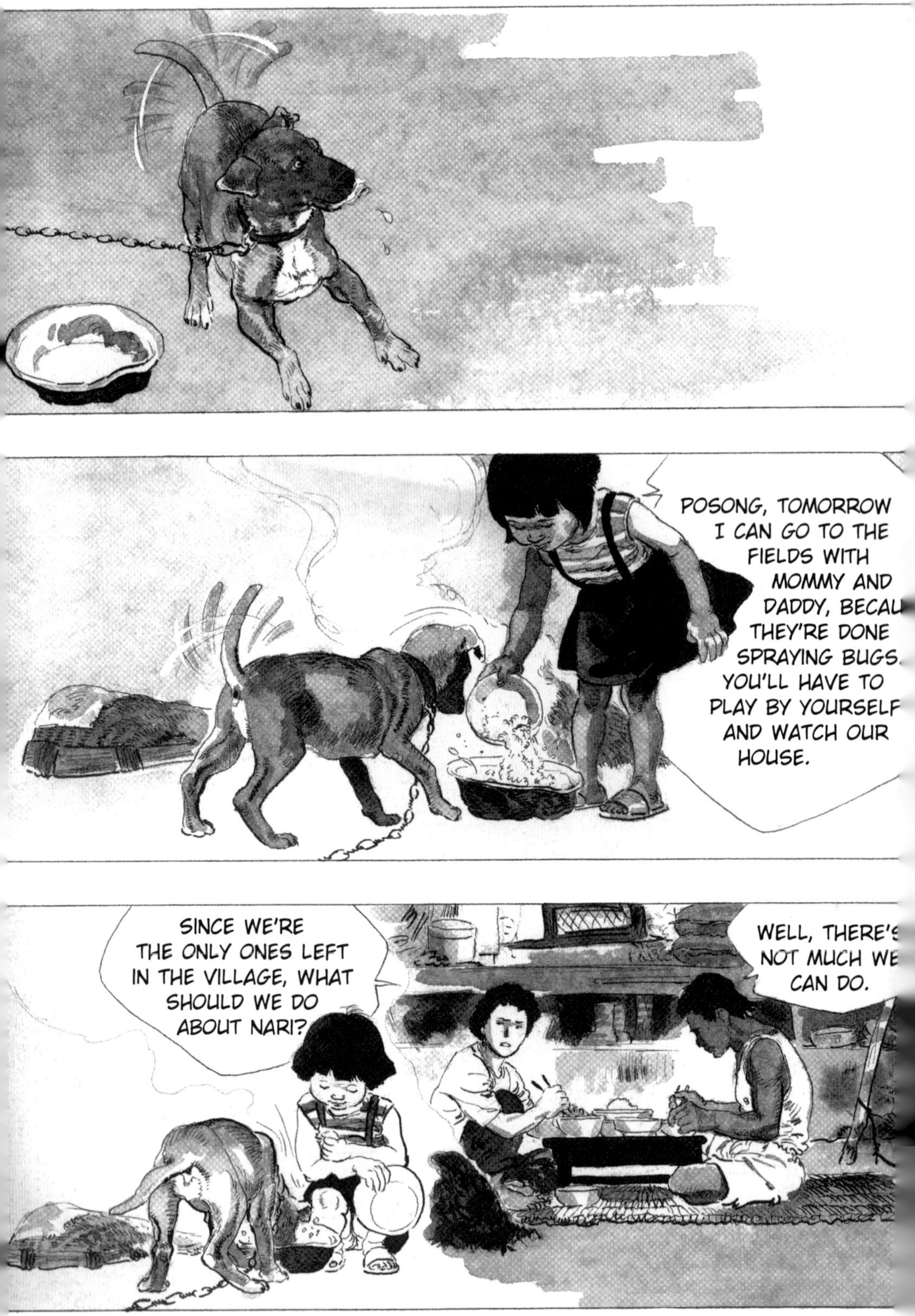
POSONG, TOMORROW I CAN GO TO THE FIELDS WITH MOMMY AND DADDY, BECAU THEY'RE DONE SPRAYING BUGS. YOU'LL HAVE TO PLAY BY YOURSELF AND WATCH OUR HOUSE.
SINCE WE'RE THE ONLY ONES LEFT IN THE VILLAGE, WHAT SHOULD WE DO ABOUT NARI?
WELL, THERE'S NOT MUCH WE CAN DO.

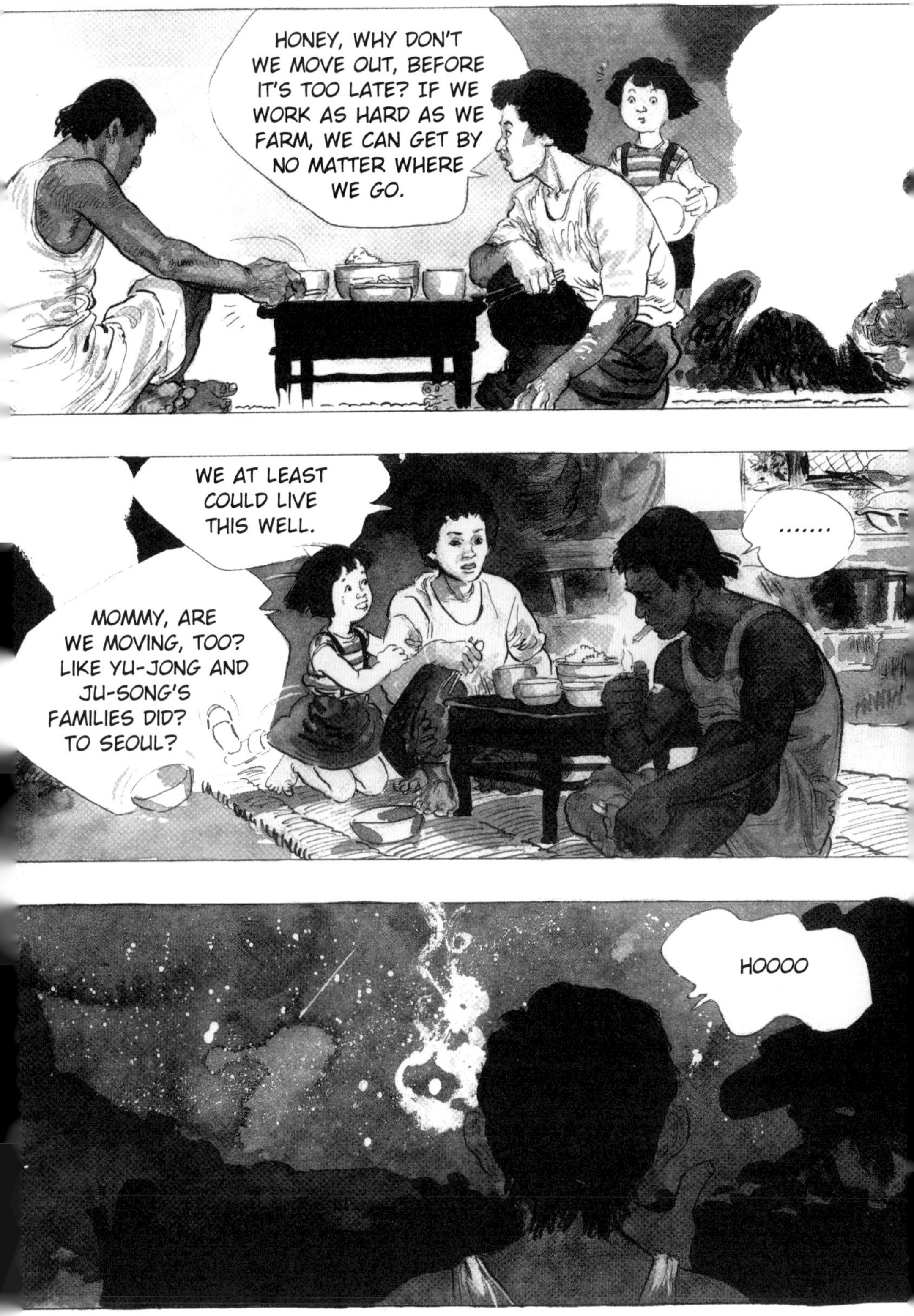
HONEY, WHY DON'T WE MOVE OUT, BEFORE IT'S TOO LATE? IF WE WORK AS HARD AS WE FARM, WE CAN GET BY NO MATTER WHERE WE GO.
WE AT LEAST COULD LIVE THIS WELL.
....
MOMMY, ARE WE MOVING, TOO? LIKE YU-JONG AND JU-SONG'S FAMILIES DID? TO SEOUL?
HOOOO

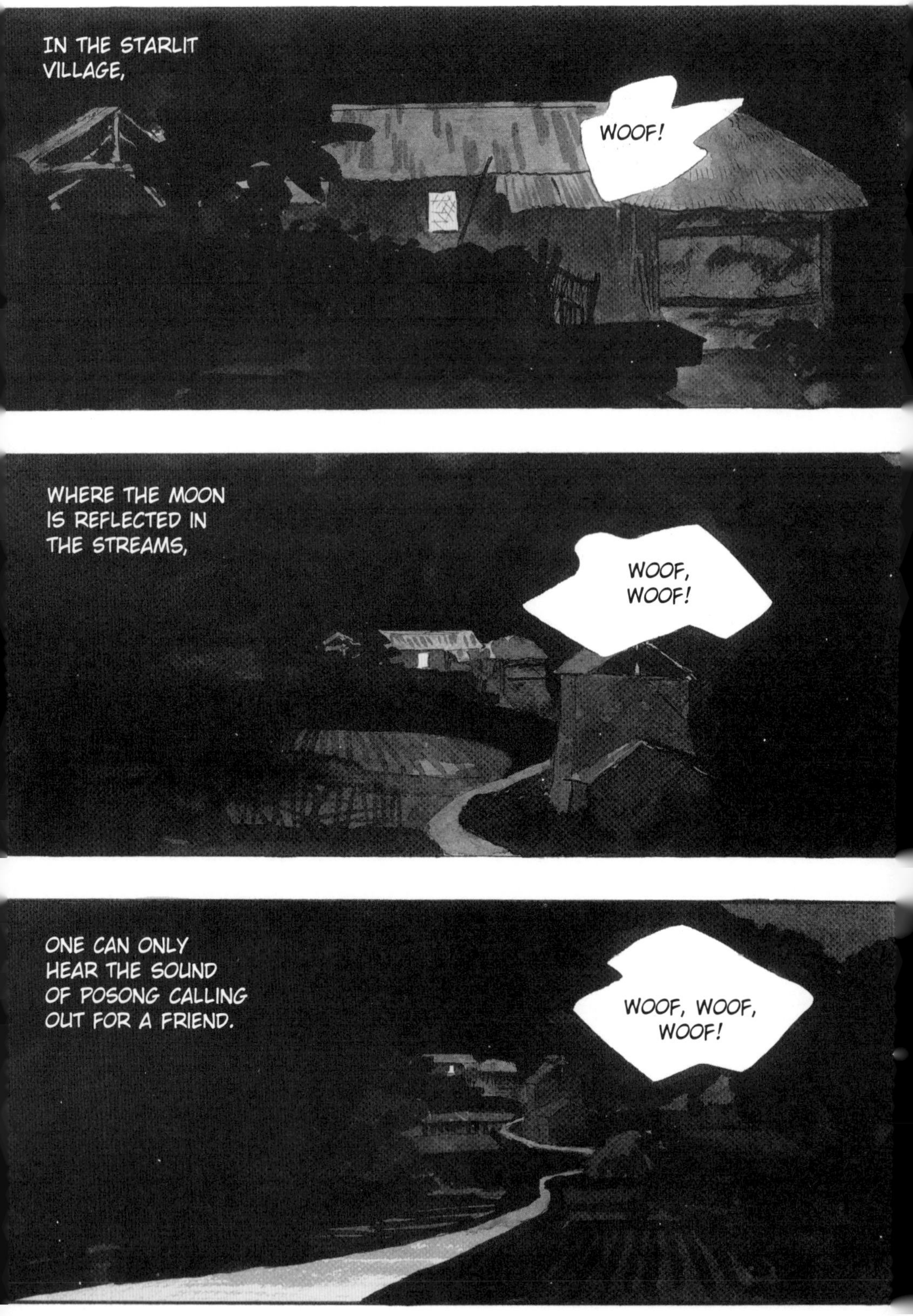
IN THE STARLIT VILLAGE,
WOOF!
WHERE THE MOON IS REFLECTED IN THE STREAMS,
WOOF, WOOF!
ONE CAN ONLY HEAR THE SOUND OF POSONG CALLING OUT FOR A FRIEND.
WOOF, WOOF, WOOF!

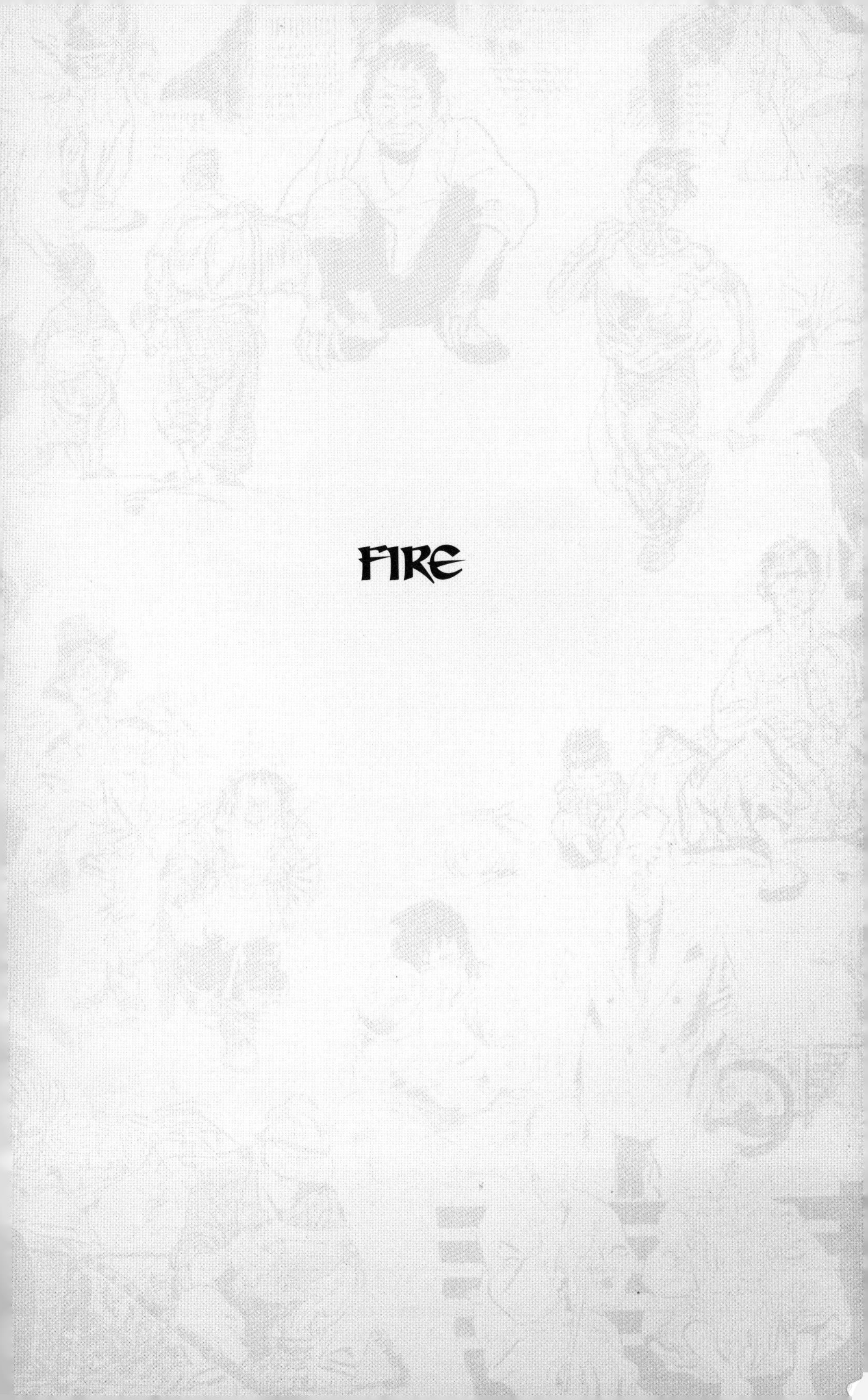

FIRE

SEYEONG O
SEPTEMBER 1988

-THE INSOLE OF THIS STUPID SHOE IS OKAY,
BUT THE OUTSIDE IS WORN OUT.

-JUST WEAR THEM A LITTLE LONGER. I'LL
BUY YOU A NEW PAIR.

-YOU CAN'T AFFORD TO BUY A NEW PAIR.
THEY'RE VERY EXPENSIVE.

-I WISH I HAD A SISTER LIKE OH-SIK'S. SHE
ALWAYS BUYS HIM PRESENTS ON CH'USOK*.

-A SISTER? STOP TALKING NONSENSE. GO
FEED THE PIGS THOSE ROTTEN APPLES I
BROUGHT FROM THE ORCHARD.

-ARE YOU THERE, KI-SU'S MOTHER? I CAME
TO BREED MY PIG WITH YOURS.

*CH'USOK IS KOREA'S THANKSGIVING DAY.

GROOEE

GROGRO

GROEEEE!

27

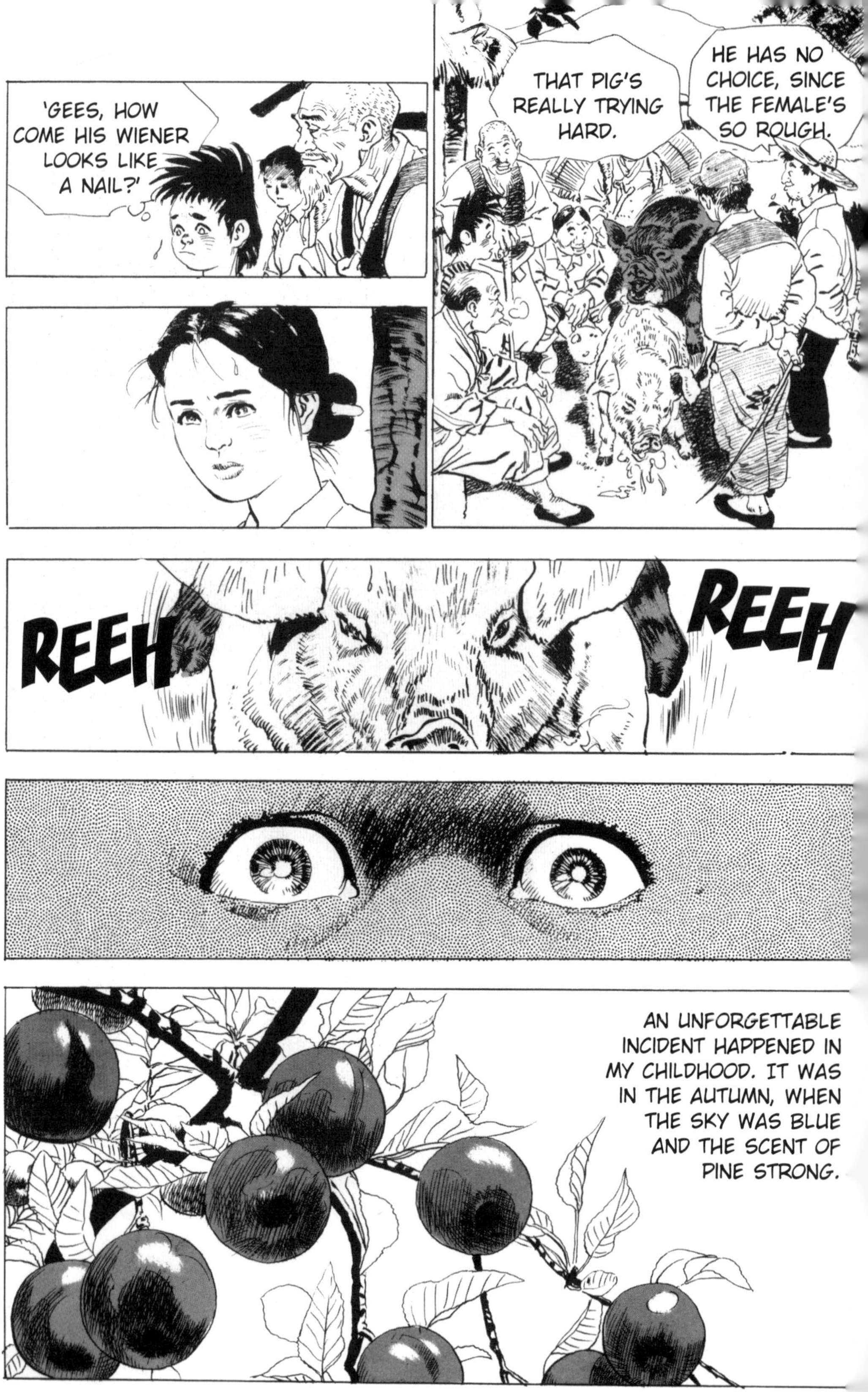
'GEES, HOW COME HIS WIENER LOOKS LIKE A NAIL?'
THAT PIG'S REALLY TRYING HARD.
HE HAS NO CHOICE, SINCE THE FEMALE'S SO ROUGH.
REEH
REEH
AN UNFORGETTABLE INCIDENT HAPPENED IN MY CHILDHOOD. IT WAS IN THE AUTUMN, WHEN THE SKY WAS BLUE AND THE SCENT OF PINE STRONG.

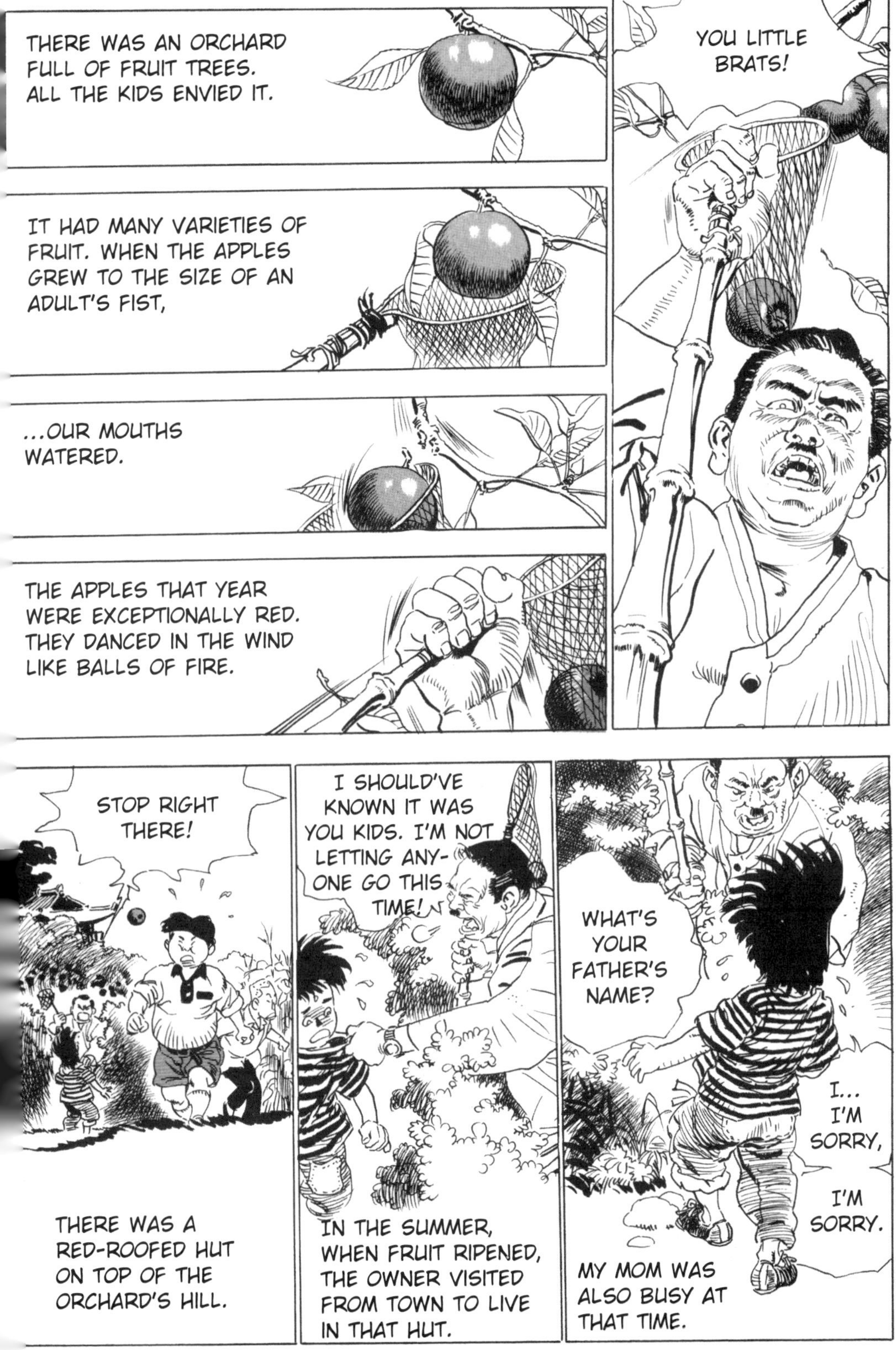
THERE WAS AN ORCHARD FULL OF FRUIT TREES. ALL THE KIDS ENVIED IT.
IT HAD MANY VARIETIES OF FRUIT. WHEN THE APPLES GREW TO THE SIZE OF AN ADULT'S FIST,
...OUR MOUTHS WATERED.
THE APPLES THAT YEAR WERE EXCEPTIONALLY RED. THEY DANCED IN THE WIND LIKE BALLS OF FIRE.
YOU LITTLE BRATS!
STOP RIGHT THERE!
THERE WAS A RED-ROOFED HUT ON TOP OF THE ORCHARD'S HILL.
I SHOULD'VE KNOWN IT WAS YOU KIDS. I'M NOT LETTING ANY-ONE GO THIS TIME!
IN THE SUMMER, WHEN FRUIT RIPENED, THE OWNER VISITED FROM TOWN TO LIVE IN THAT HUT.
WHAT'S YOUR FATHER'S NAME?
I... I'M SORRY,
I'M SORRY.
MY MOM WAS ALSO BUSY AT THAT TIME.

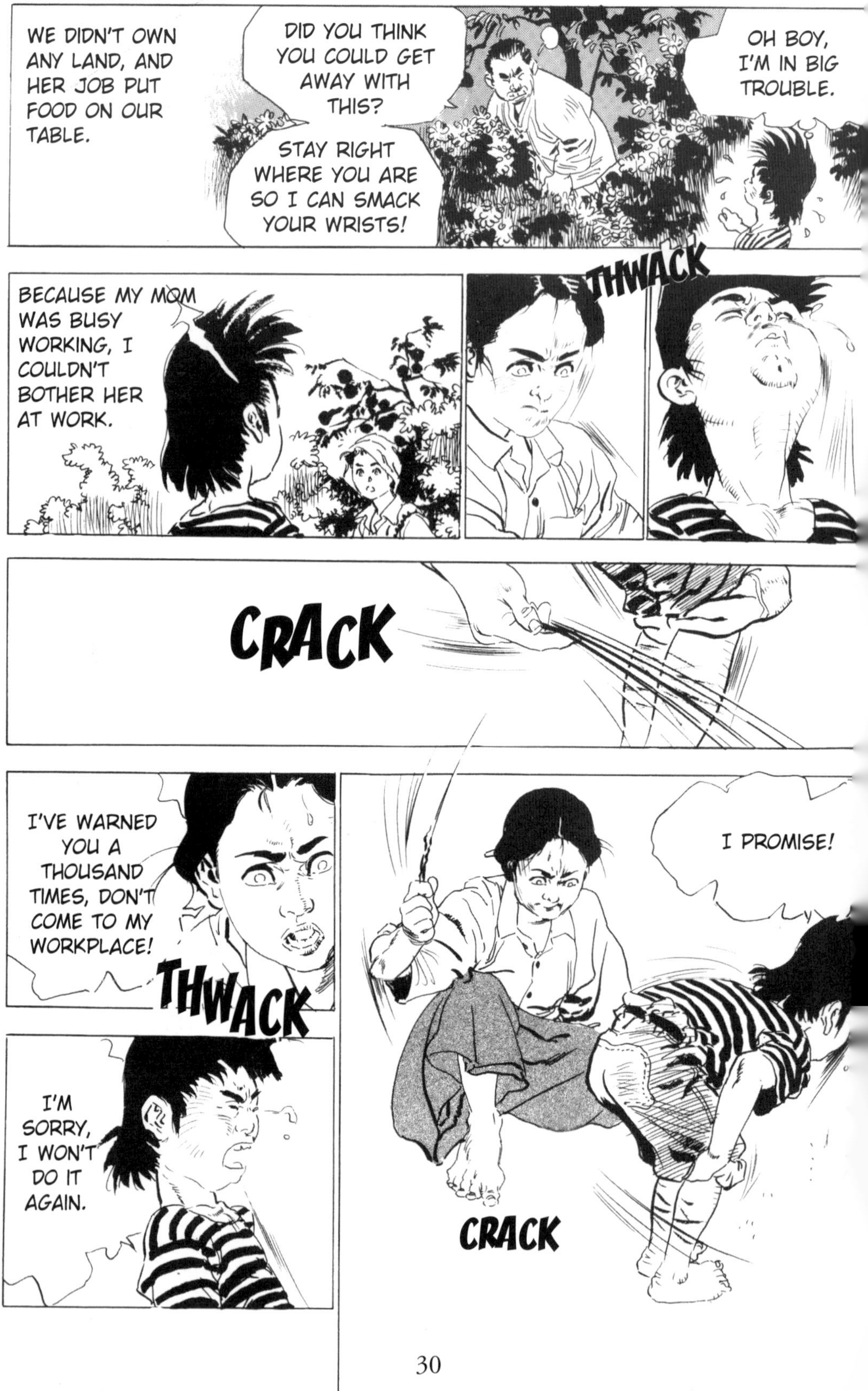
WE DIDN'T OWN ANY LAND, AND HER JOB PUT FOOD ON OUR TABLE.
DID YOU THINK YOU COULD GET AWAY WITH THIS?
STAY RIGHT WHERE YOU ARE SO I CAN SMACK YOUR WRISTS!
OH BOY, I'M IN BIG TROUBLE.
BECAUSE MY MOM WAS BUSY WORKING, I COULDN'T BOTHER HER AT WORK.
THWACK
CRACK
I'VE WARNED YOU A THOUSAND TIMES, DON'T COME TO MY WORKPLACE!
THWACK
I'M SORRY, I WON'T DO IT AGAIN.
I PROMISE!
CRACK

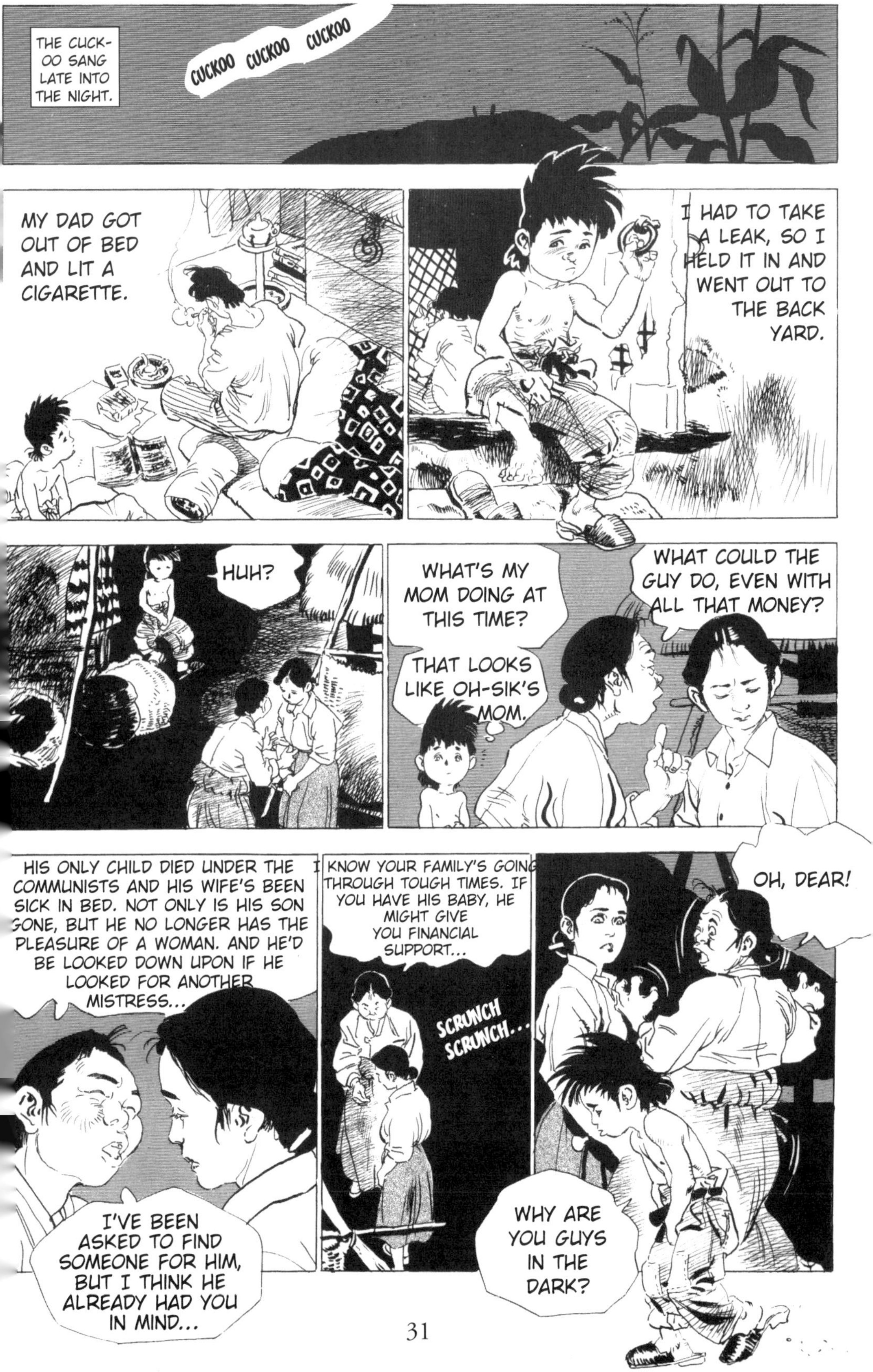
THE CUCK-OO SANG LATE INTO THE NIGHT.
CUCKOO CUCKOO CUCKOO
MY DAD GOT OUT OF BED AND LIT A CIGARETTE.
I HAD TO TAKE A LEAK, SO I HELD IT IN AND WENT OUT TO THE BACK YARD.
HUH?
WHAT'S MY MOM DOING AT THIS TIME?
THAT LOOKS LIKE OH-SIK'S MOM.
WHAT COULD THE GUY DO, EVEN WITH ALL THAT MONEY?
HIS ONLY CHILD DIED UNDER THE COMMUNISTS AND HIS WIFE'S BEEN SICK IN BED. NOT ONLY IS HIS SON GONE, BUT HE NO LONGER HAS THE PLEASURE OF A WOMAN. AND HE'D BE LOOKED DOWN UPON IF HE LOOKED FOR ANOTHER MISTRESS...
I'VE BEEN ASKED TO FIND SOMEONE FOR HIM, BUT I THINK HE ALREADY HAD YOU IN MIND...
I KNOW YOUR FAMILY'S GOING THROUGH TOUGH TIMES. IF YOU HAVE HIS BABY, HE MIGHT GIVE YOU FINANCIAL SUPPORT...
SCRUNCH SCRUNCH...
OH, DEAR!
WHY ARE YOU GUYS IN THE DARK?

WHAT ARE YOU DOING OUT THIS LATE AT NIGHT?

MY MOM WAS VERY PRETTY.

ON MARKET DAYS, SHE ALWAYS SAT IN FRONT OF HER OLD MIRROR.

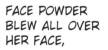

PSSSSSSSSSS

FACE POWDER BLEW ALL OVER HER FACE,

AND WHEN SHE RAISED HER LONG HAIR, THE BACK OF HER NECK WAS SO BRIGHT!

IT MADE ME FEEL DIZZY.

WHEN SHE DID THAT, MY DAD WOULD JUST LIE DOWN AND STARE AT BOOKS.

MY MOM WALKED AROUND THE MARKETPLACE AIMLESSLY.

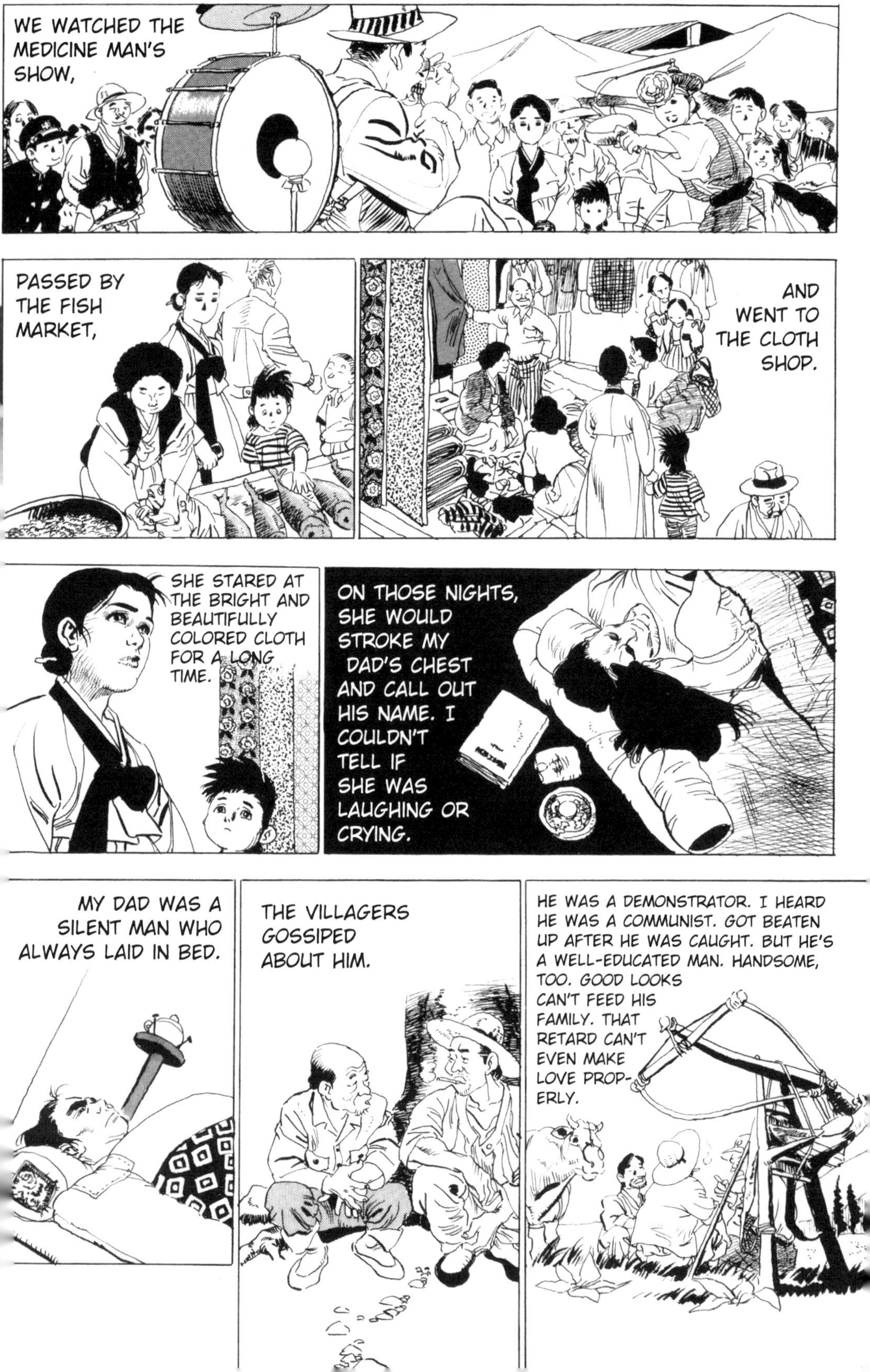
WE WATCHED THE MEDICINE MAN'S SHOW,
PASSED BY THE FISH MARKET,
AND WENT TO THE CLOTH SHOP.
SHE STARED AT THE BRIGHT AND BEAUTIFULLY COLORED CLOTH FOR A LONG TIME.
ON THOSE NIGHTS, SHE WOULD STROKE MY DAD'S CHEST AND CALL OUT HIS NAME. I COULDN'T TELL IF SHE WAS LAUGHING OR CRYING.
MY DAD WAS A SILENT MAN WHO ALWAYS LAID IN BED.
THE VILLAGERS GOSSIPED ABOUT HIM.
HE WAS A DEMONSTRATOR. I HEARD HE WAS A COMMUNIST. GOT BEATEN UP AFTER HE WAS CAUGHT. BUT HE'S A WELL-EDUCATED MAN. HANDSOME, TOO. GOOD LOOKS CAN'T FEED HIS FAMILY. THAT RETARD CAN'T EVEN MAKE LOVE PROP-ERLY.

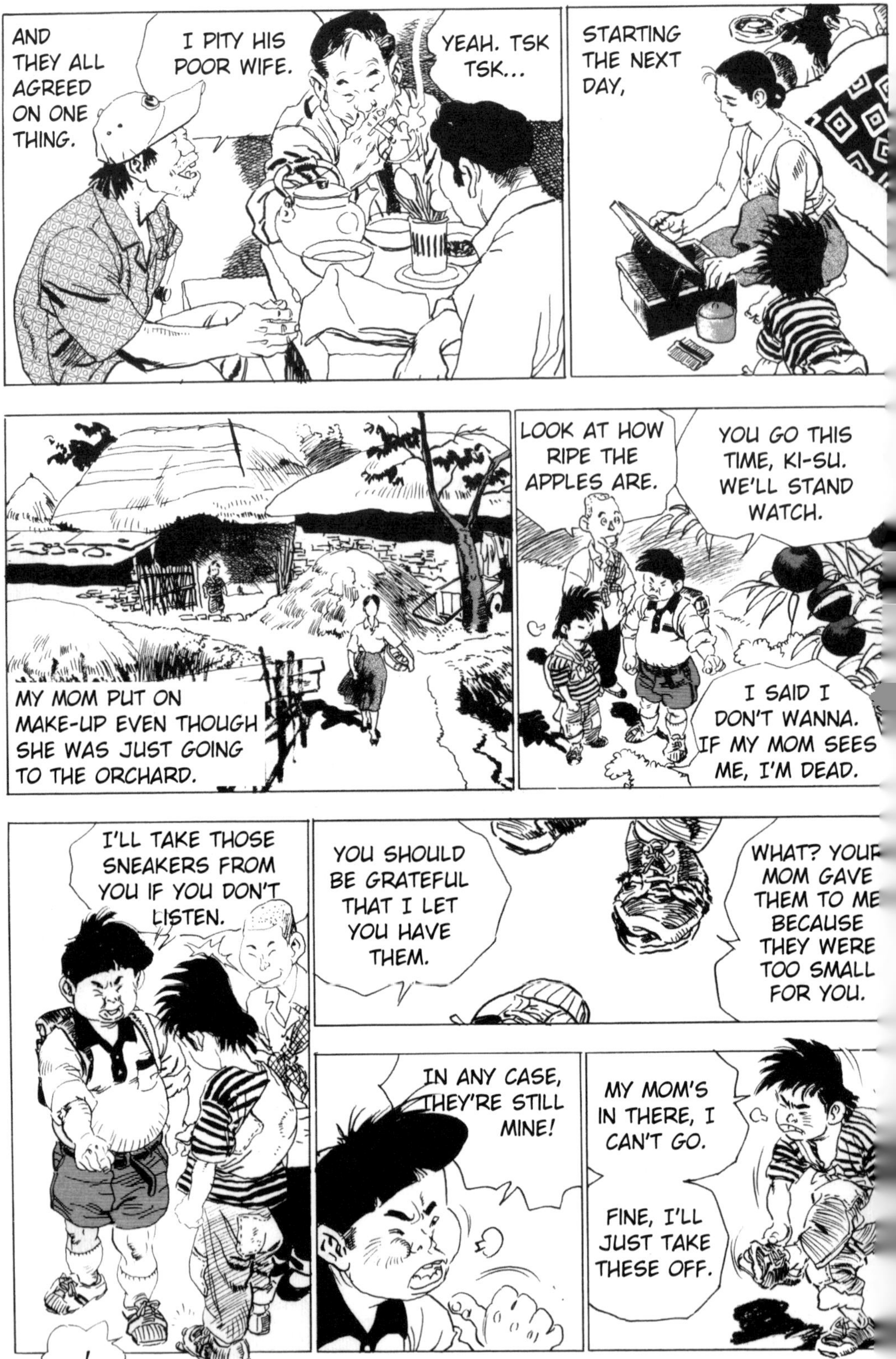
AND THEY ALL AGREED ON ONE THING.
I PITY HIS POOR WIFE.
YEAH. TSK TSK...
STARTING THE NEXT DAY,
MY MOM PUT ON MAKE-UP EVEN THOUGH SHE WAS JUST GOING TO THE ORCHARD.
LOOK AT HOW RIPE THE APPLES ARE.
YOU GO THIS TIME, KI-SU. WE'LL STAND WATCH.
I SAID I DON'T WANNA. IF MY MOM SEES ME, I'M DEAD.
I'LL TAKE THOSE SNEAKERS FROM YOU IF YOU DON'T LISTEN.
...!
YOU SHOULD BE GRATEFUL THAT I LET YOU HAVE THEM.
WHAT? YOUR MOM GAVE THEM TO ME BECAUSE THEY WERE TOO SMALL FOR YOU.
IN ANY CASE, THEY'RE STILL MINE!
MY MOM'S IN THERE, I CAN'T GO.
FINE, I'LL JUST TAKE THESE OFF.

YOU IDIOT, NO ONE'S GONNA TAKE THOSE OLD THINGS.

I WANT A NEW PAIR.

......

TOSS THE APPLES OVER HERE.

OH-SIK'S OLD SNEAKERS ENSLAVED ME TO HIM. HE ALWAYS TREATED ME LIKE A SERVANT.

I GRABBED AN APPLE AND TWISTED IT OFF.

THERE WAS ANOTHER APPLE HANGING IN THE SAME SPOT.

WHAT THE...?!

OH MY GOSH!

IT WAS MY MOM'S BUTT. I SAW IT ONCE WHEN SHE WAS BATHING IN THE KITCHEN.

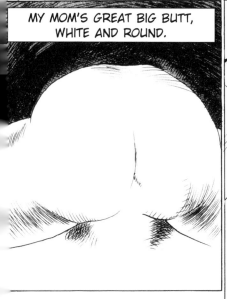

MY MOM'S GREAT BIG BUTT, WHITE AND ROUND.

IT BOUNCED MERCILESSLY. UNDERNEATH HER, I COULD SEE THE ORCHARD OWNER'S BURNING EYES.

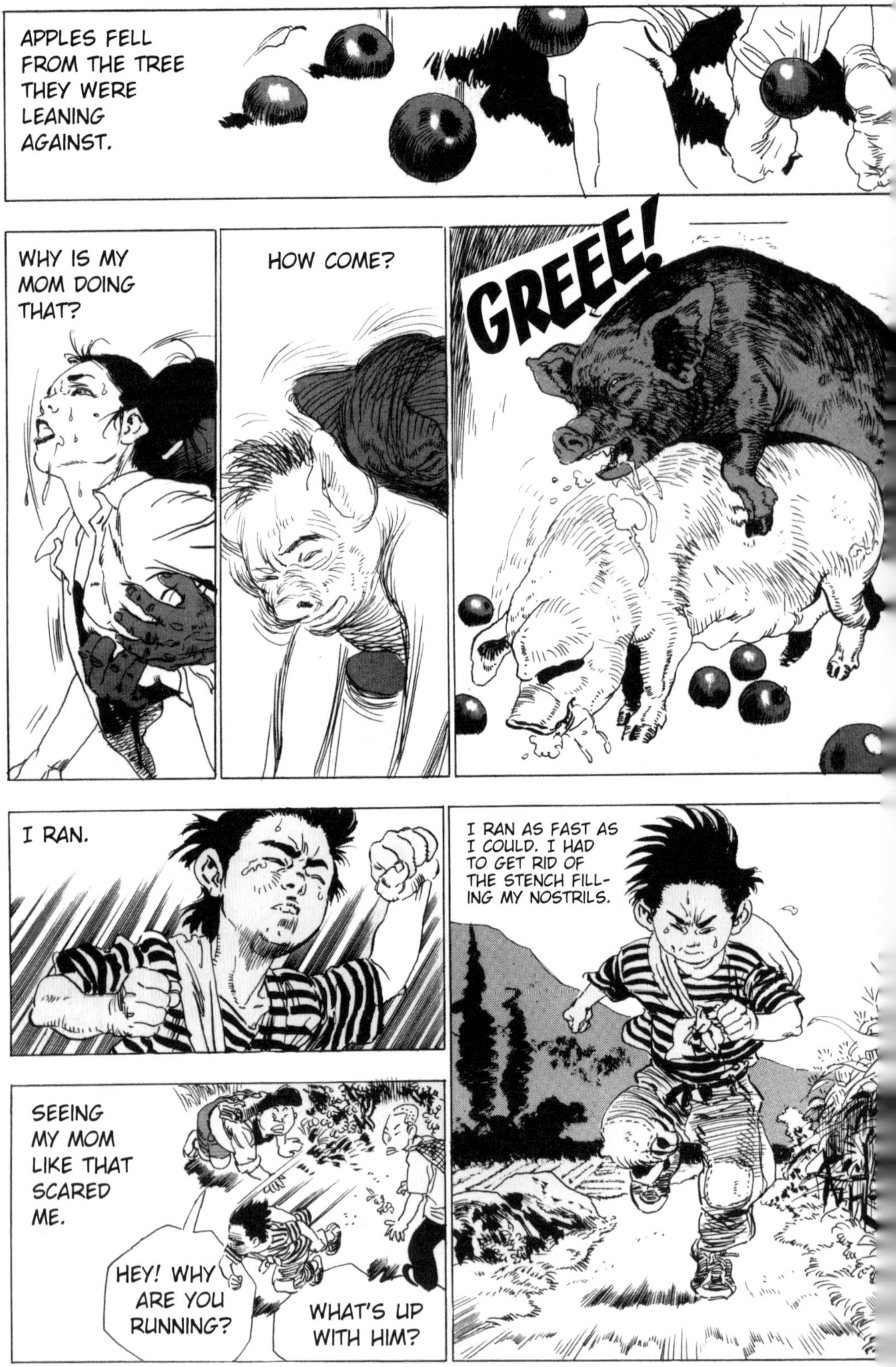
APPLES FELL FROM THE TREE THEY WERE LEANING AGAINST.
WHY IS MY MOM DOING THAT?
HOW COME?
GREEE!
I RAN.
I RAN AS FAST AS I COULD. I HAD TO GET RID OF THE STENCH FILLING MY NOSTRILS.
SEEING MY MOM LIKE THAT SCARED ME.
HEY! WHY ARE YOU RUNNING?
WHAT'S UP WITH HIM?

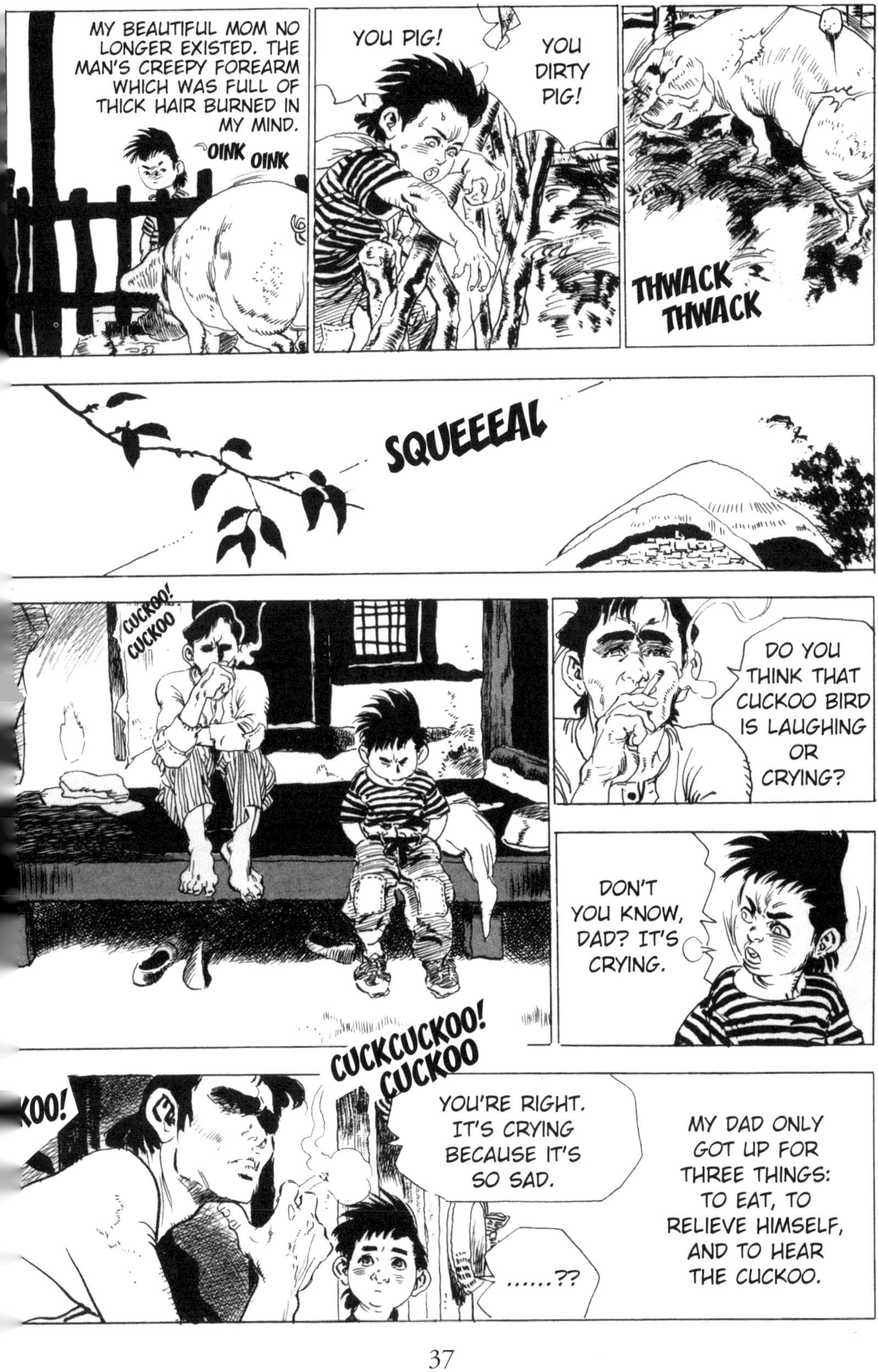
MY BEAUTIFUL MOM NO LONGER EXISTED. THE MAN'S CREEPY FOREARM WHICH WAS FULL OF THICK HAIR BURNED IN MY MIND.
OINK OINK
YOU PIG!
YOU DIRTY PIG!
THWACK THWACK
SQUEEEAL
CUCKOO! CUCKOO
DO YOU THINK THAT CUCKOO BIRD IS LAUGHING OR CRYING?
DON'T YOU KNOW, DAD? IT'S CRYING.
CUCKCUCKOO! CUCKOO
KOO!
YOU'RE RIGHT. IT'S CRYING BECAUSE IT'S SO SAD.
......??
MY DAD ONLY GOT UP FOR THREE THINGS: TO EAT, TO RELIEVE HIMSELF, AND TO HEAR THE CUCKOO.

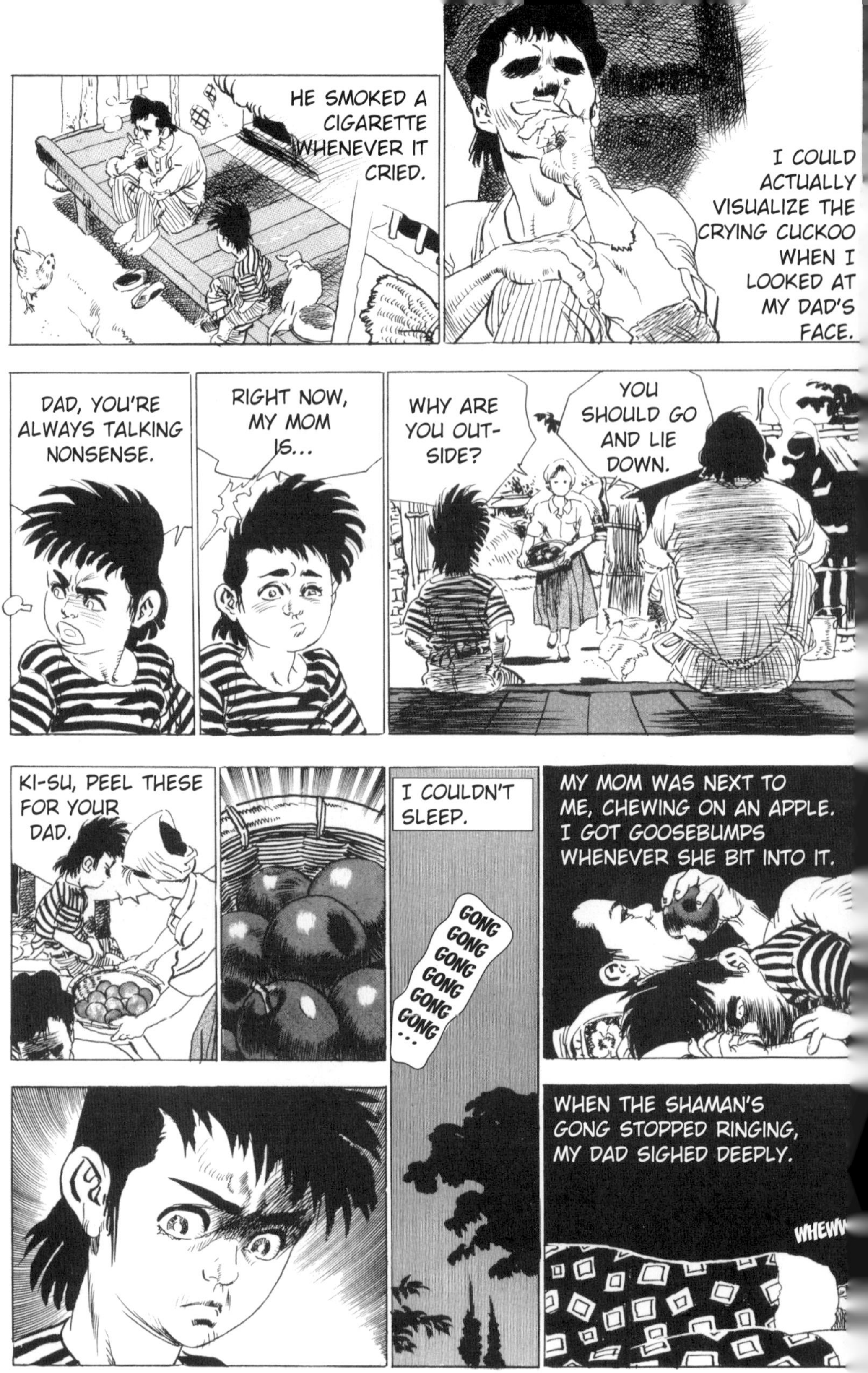
HE SMOKED A CIGARETTE WHENEVER IT CRIED.
I COULD ACTUALLY VISUALIZE THE CRYING CUCKOO WHEN I LOOKED AT MY DAD'S FACE.
DAD, YOU'RE ALWAYS TALKING NONSENSE.
RIGHT NOW, MY MOM IS...
WHY ARE YOU OUT-SIDE?
YOU SHOULD GO AND LIE DOWN.
KI-SU, PEEL THESE FOR YOUR DAD.
I COULDN'T SLEEP.
GONG GONG GONG GONG GONG GONG GONG...
MY MOM WAS NEXT TO ME, CHEWING ON AN APPLE. I GOT GOOSEBUMPS WHENEVER SHE BIT INTO IT.
WHEN THE SHAMAN'S GONG STOPPED RINGING, MY DAD SIGHED DEEPLY.
WHEWW

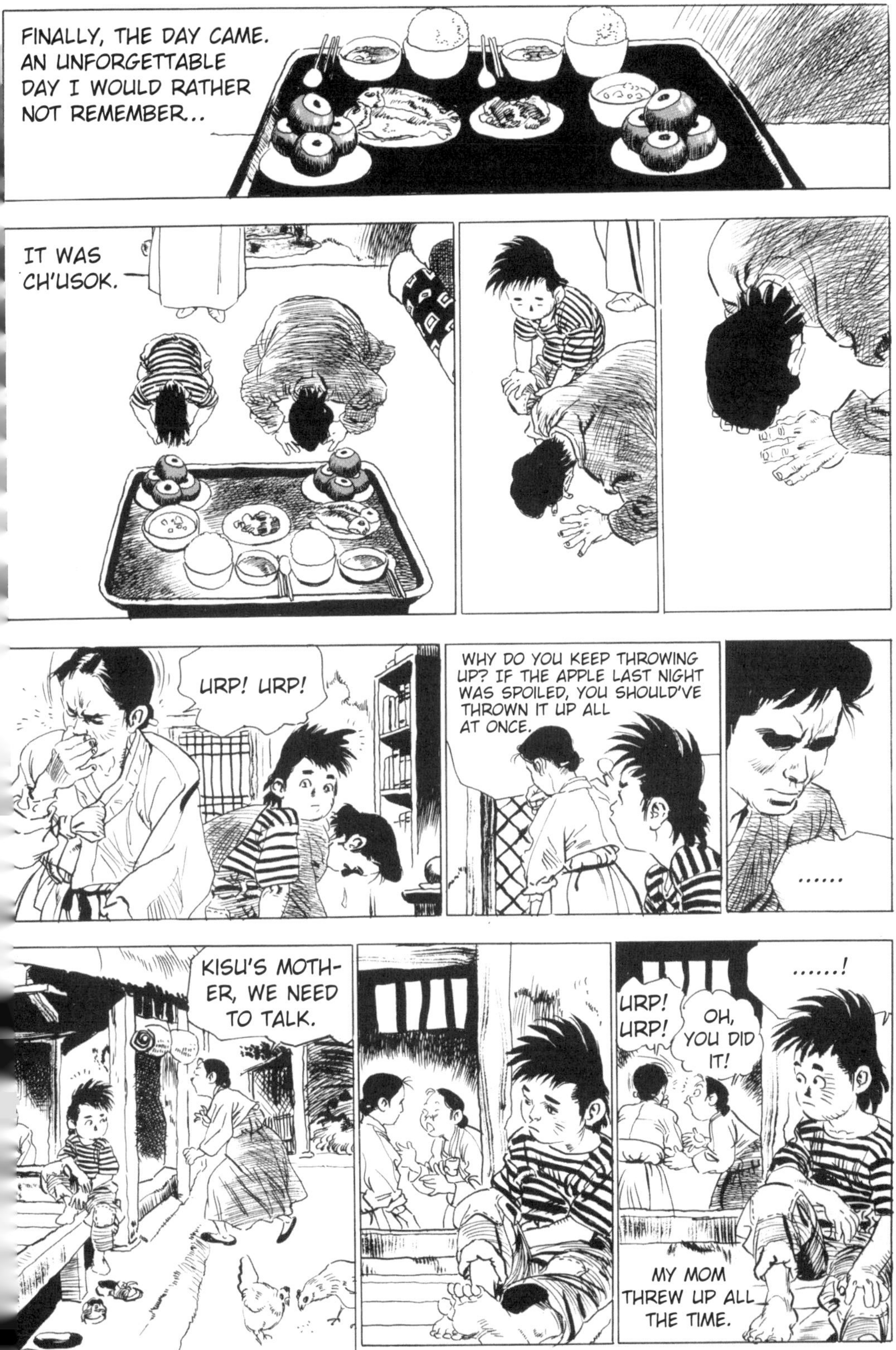
FINALLY, THE DAY CAME. AN UNFORGETTABLE DAY I WOULD RATHER NOT REMEMBER...
IT WAS CH'USOK.
URP! URP!
WHY DO YOU KEEP THROWING UP? IF THE APPLE LAST NIGHT WAS SPOILED, YOU SHOULD'VE THROWN IT UP ALL AT ONCE.
......
KISU'S MOTHER, WE NEED TO TALK.
......!
URP! URP!
OH, YOU DID IT!
MY MOM THREW UP ALL THE TIME.

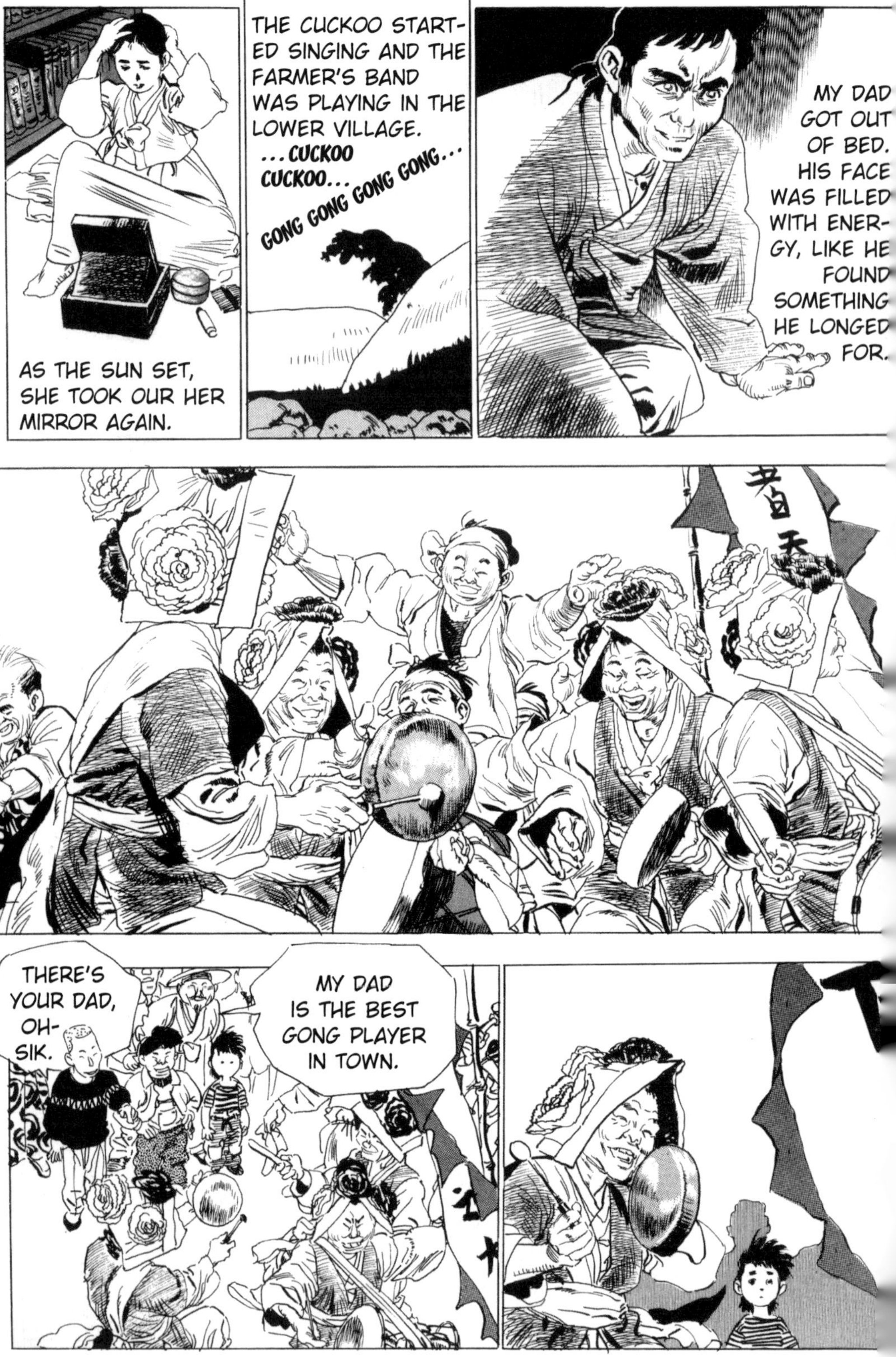
AS THE SUN SET, SHE TOOK OUR HER MIRROR AGAIN.
THE CUCKOO STARTED SINGING AND THE FARMER'S BAND WAS PLAYING IN THE LOWER VILLAGE.
...CUCKOO CUCKOO...
GONG GONG GONG GONG...
MY DAD GOT OUT OF BED. HIS FACE WAS FILLED WITH ENERGY, LIKE HE FOUND SOMETHING HE LONGED FOR.
THERE'S YOUR DAD, OH-SIK.
MY DAD IS THE BEST GONG PLAYER IN TOWN.

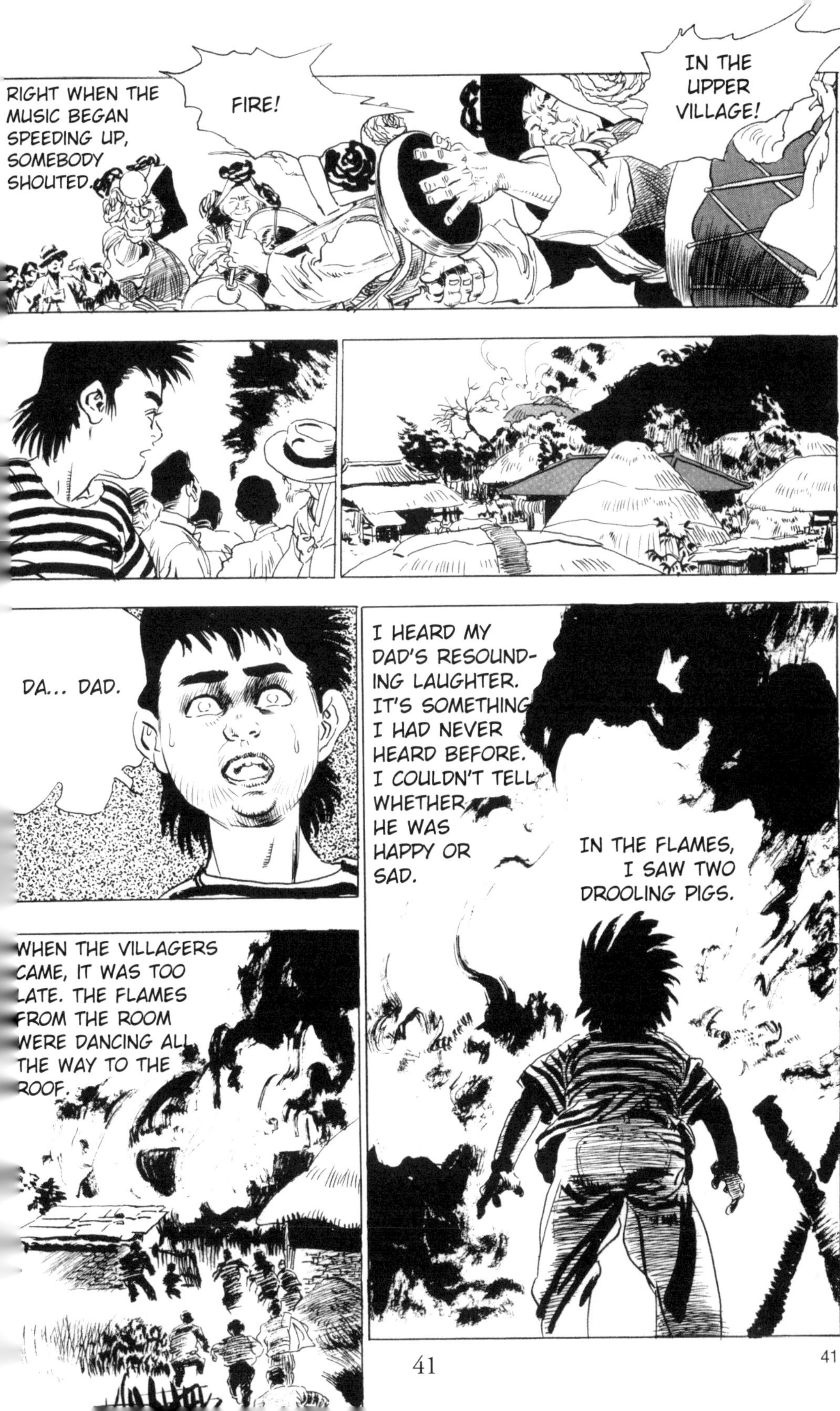
RIGHT WHEN THE MUSIC BEGAN SPEEDING UP, SOMEBODY SHOUTED.
FIRE!
IN THE UPPER VILLAGE!
DA... DAD.
WHEN THE VILLAGERS CAME, IT WAS TOO LATE. THE FLAMES FROM THE ROOM WERE DANCING ALL THE WAY TO THE ROOF.
I HEARD MY DAD'S RESOUNDING LAUGHTER. IT'S SOMETHING I HAD NEVER HEARD BEFORE. I COULDN'T TELL WHETHER HE WAS HAPPY OR SAD.
IN THE FLAMES, I SAW TWO DROOLING PIGS.

41

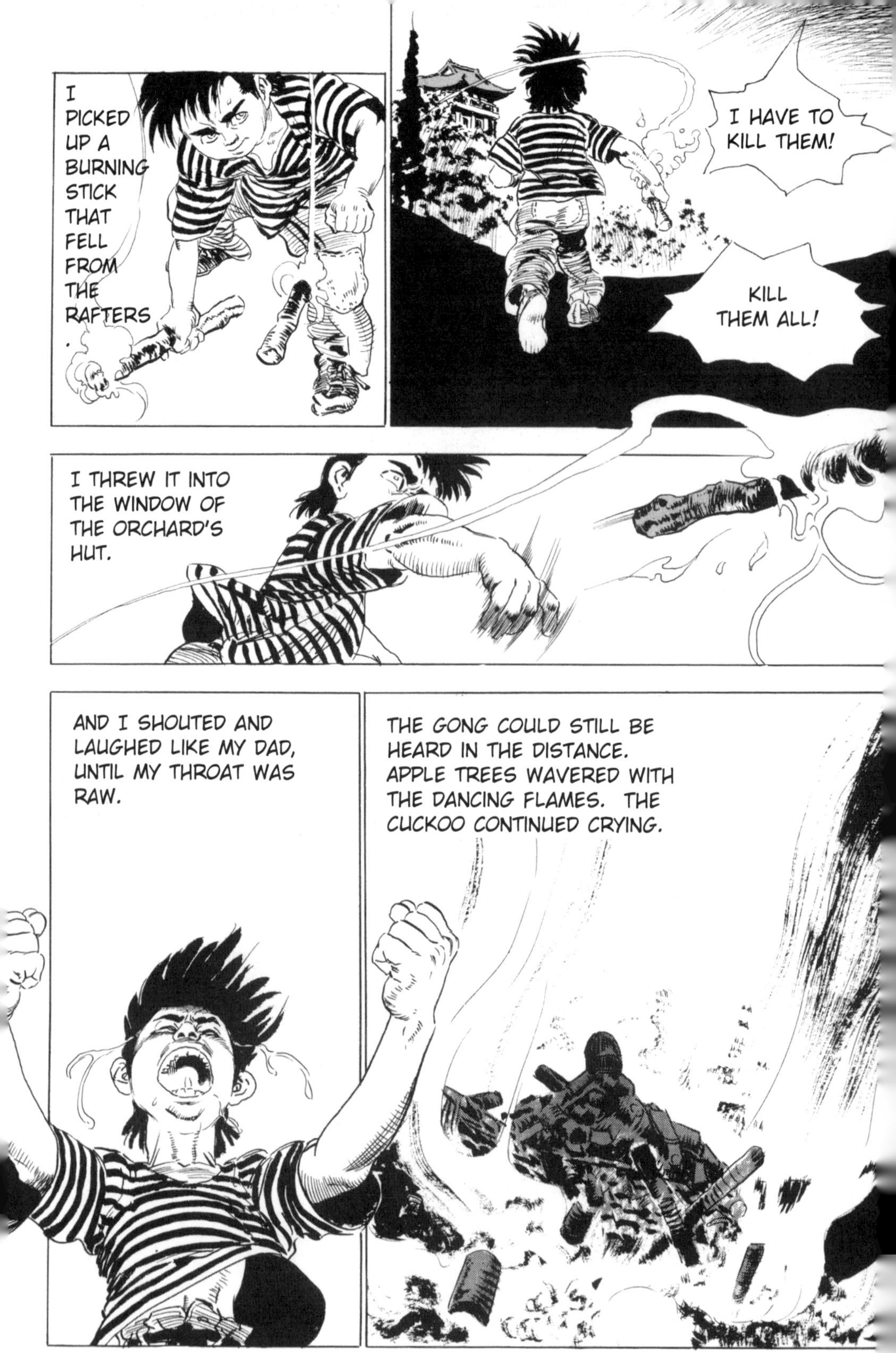
I PICKED UP A BURNING STICK THAT FELL FROM THE RAFTERS.
I HAVE TO KILL THEM!
KILL THEM ALL!
I THREW IT INTO THE WINDOW OF THE ORCHARD'S HUT.
AND I SHOUTED AND LAUGHED LIKE MY DAD, UNTIL MY THROAT WAS RAW.
THE GONG COULD STILL BE HEARD IN THE DISTANCE. APPLE TREES WAVERED WITH THE DANCING FLAMES. THE CUCKOO CONTINUED CRYING.

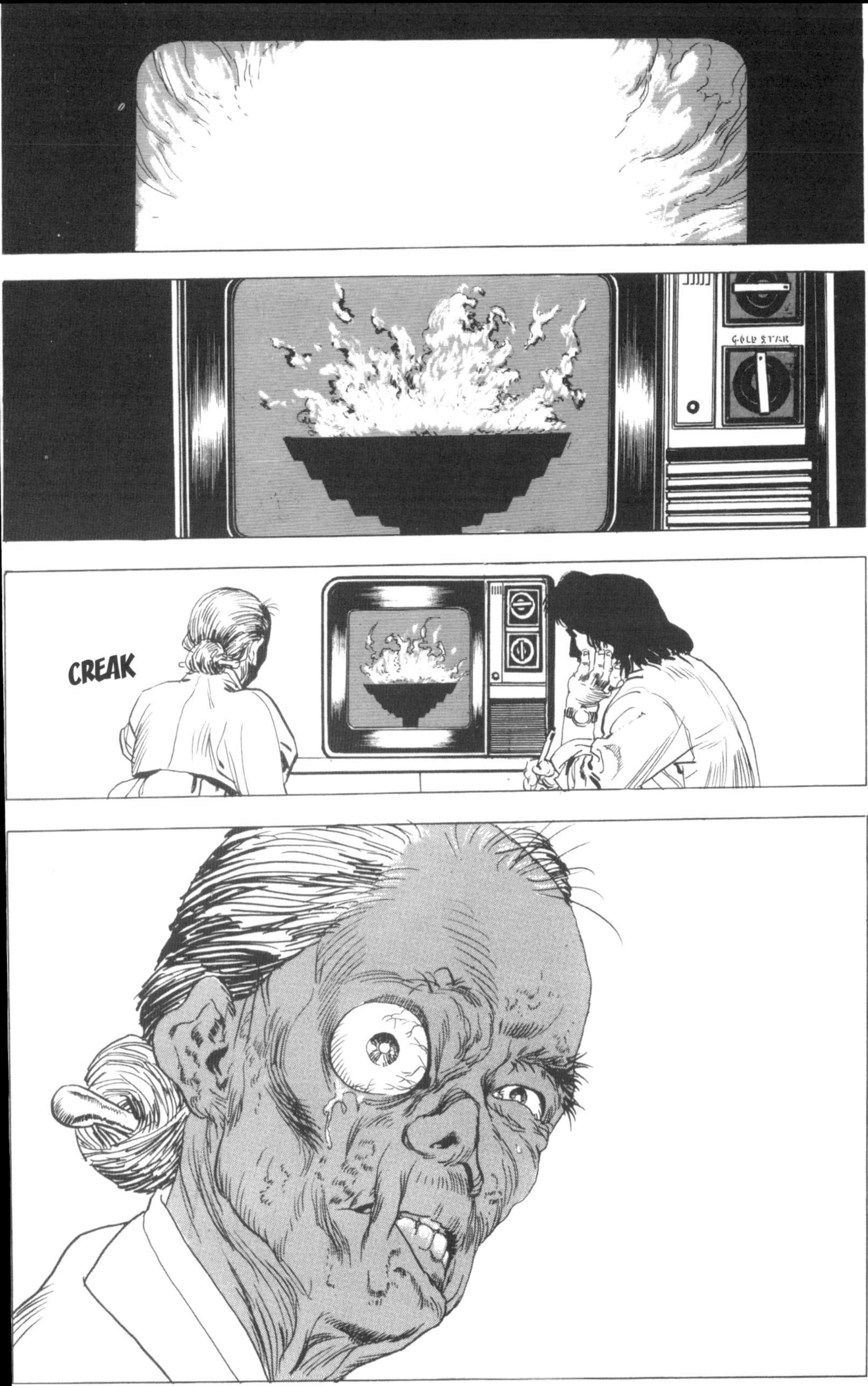
GOLD STAR
CREAK

ESCAPE

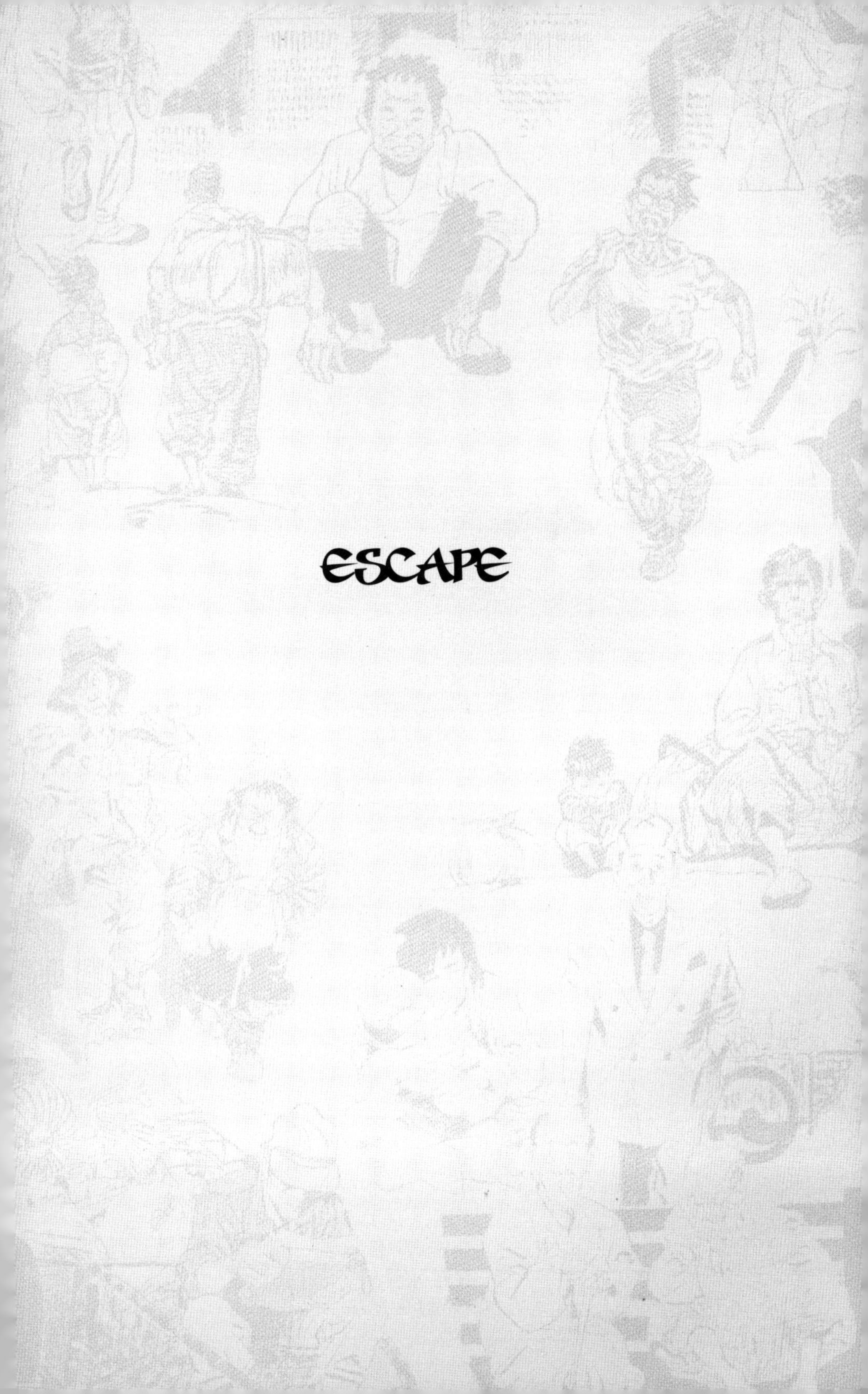

SEYEONG O
NOVEMBER 1990

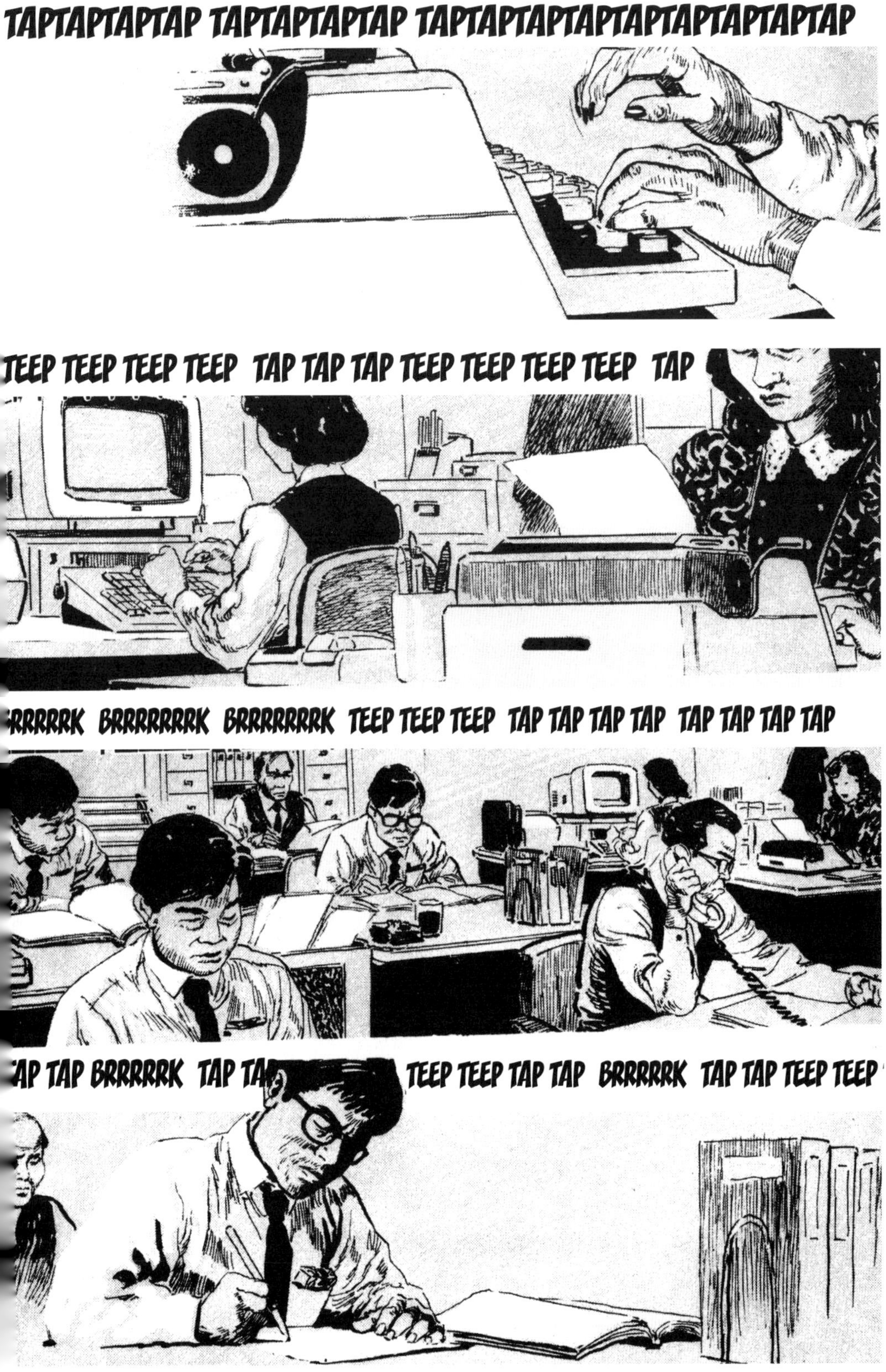
TAPTAPTAPTAP TAPTAPTAPTAP TAPTAPTAPTAPTAPTAPTAPTAPTAP
TEEP TEEP TEEP TEEP TAP TAP TAP TEEP TEEP TEEP TEEP TAP
RRRRRK BRRRRRRRK BRRRRRRRK TEEP TEEP TEEP TAP TAP TAP TAP TAP TAP TAP TAP
AP TAP BRRRRRK TAP TA
TEEP TEEP TAP TAP BRRRRRK TAP TAP TEEP TEEP

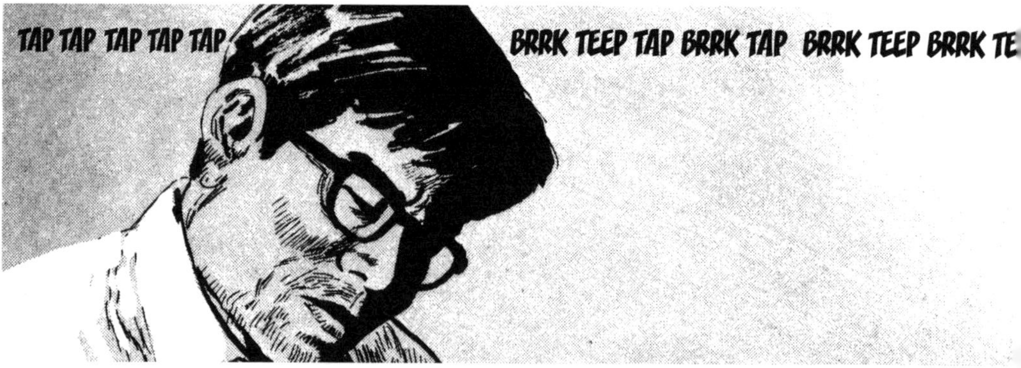
TAP TAP TAP TAP TAP
BRRK TEEP TAP BRRK TAP
BRRK TEEP BRRK TE

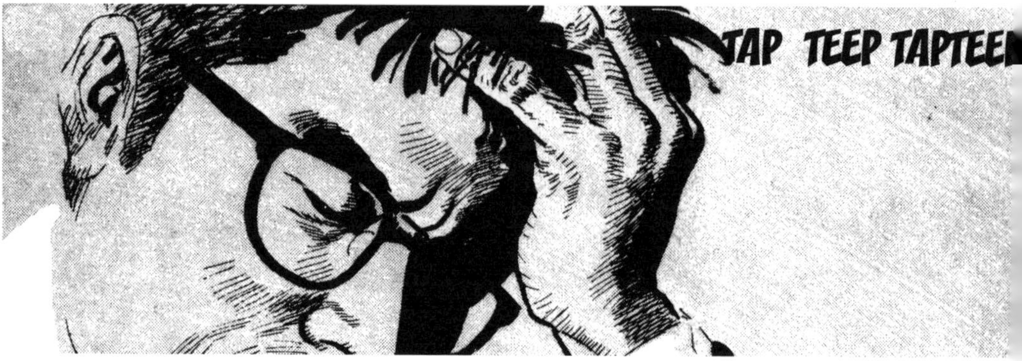
TAP TEEP TAPTEE

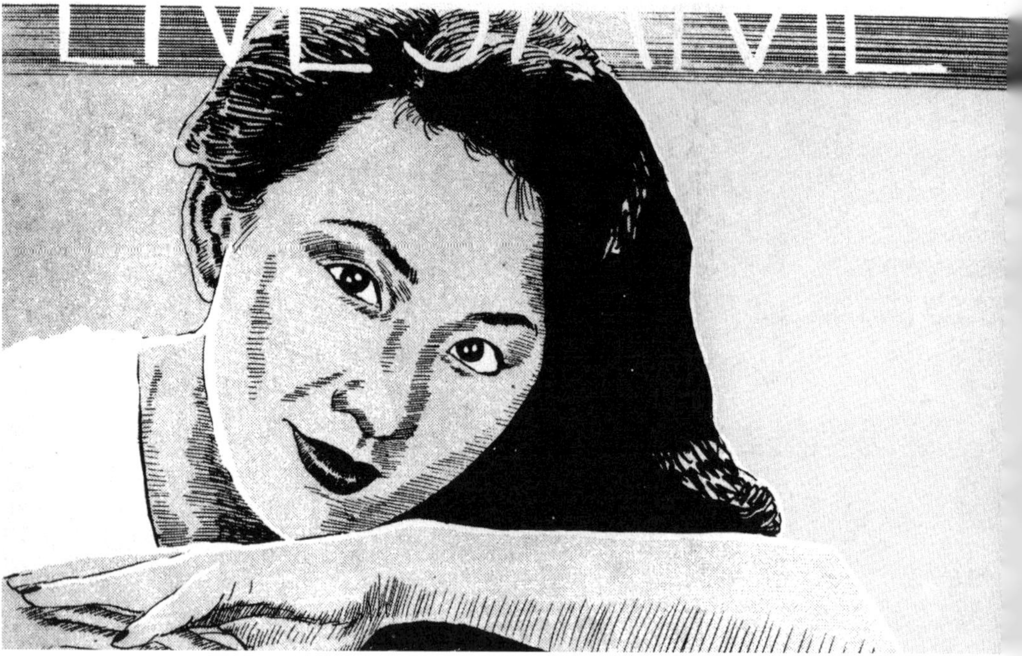

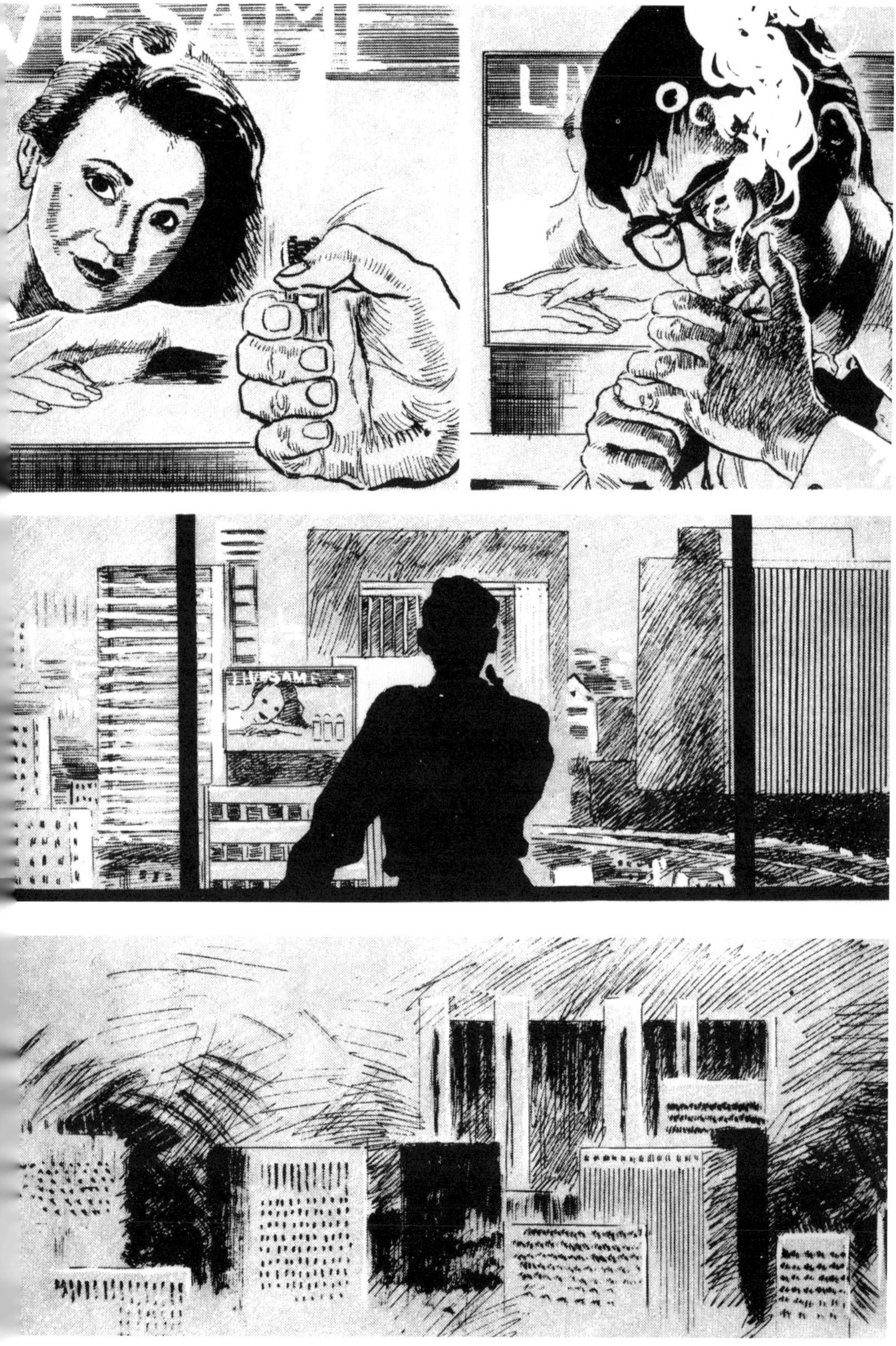

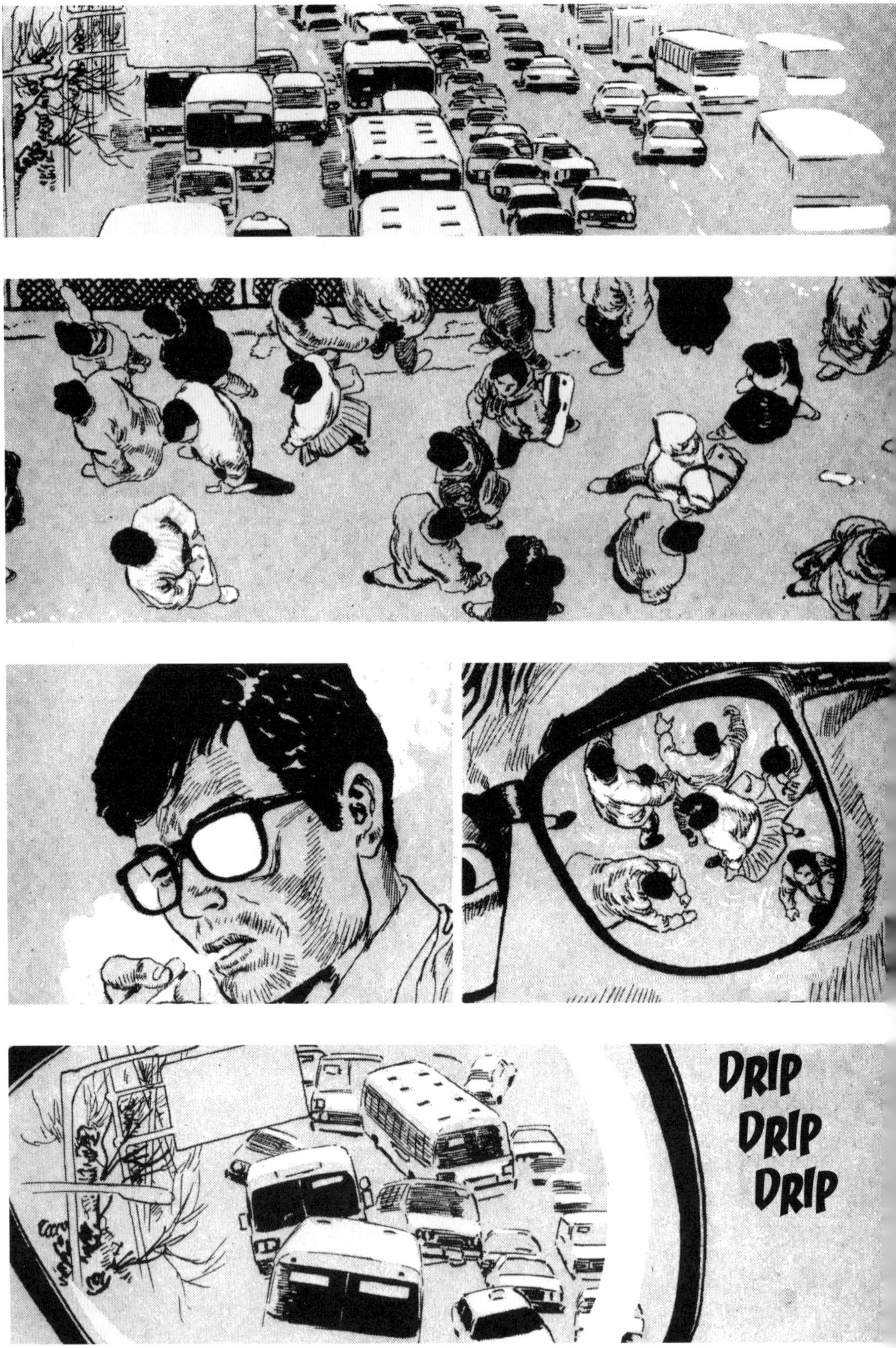
DRIP
DRIP
DRIP

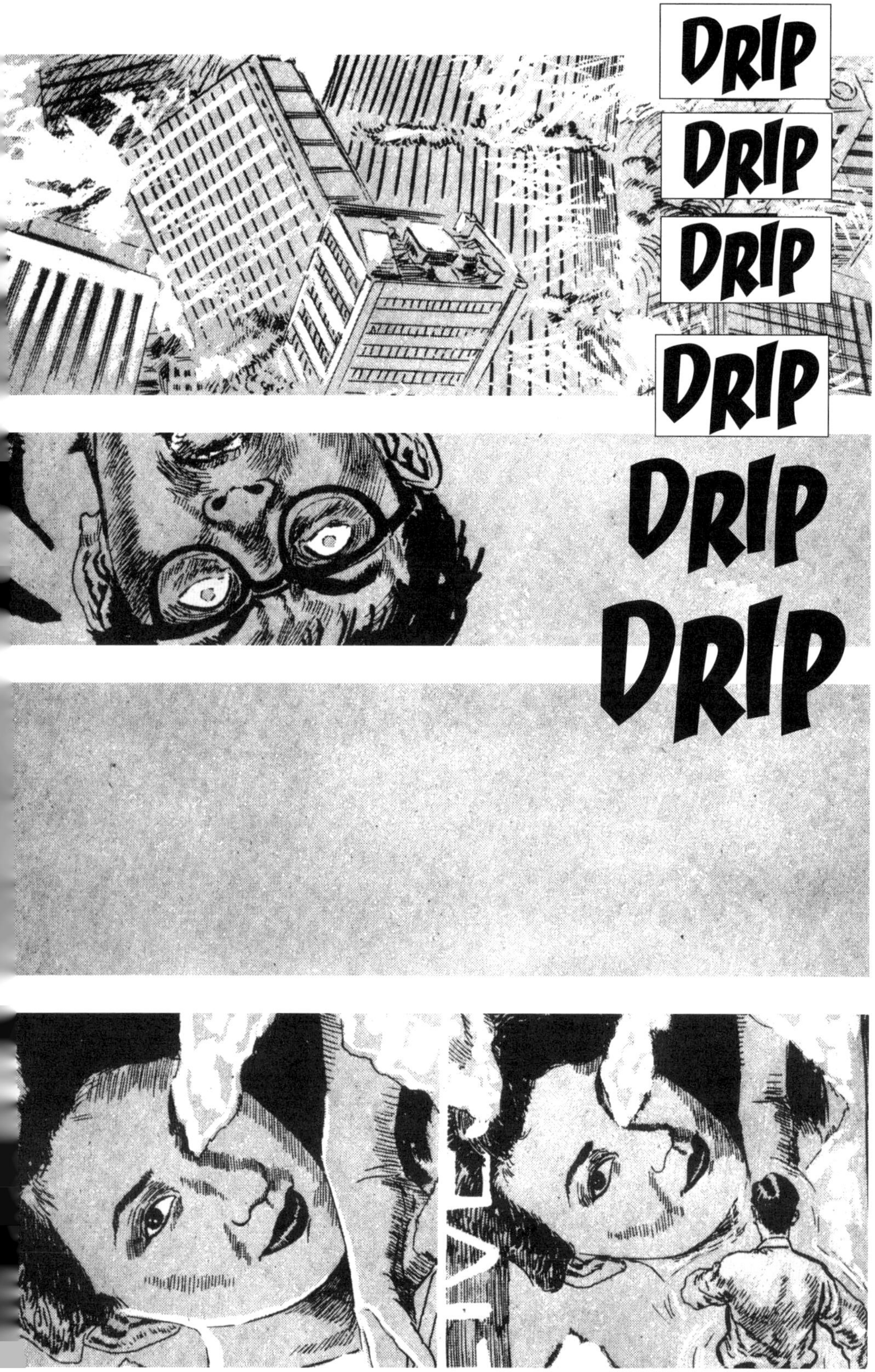
DRIP
DRIP
DRIP
DRIP
DRIP
DRIP

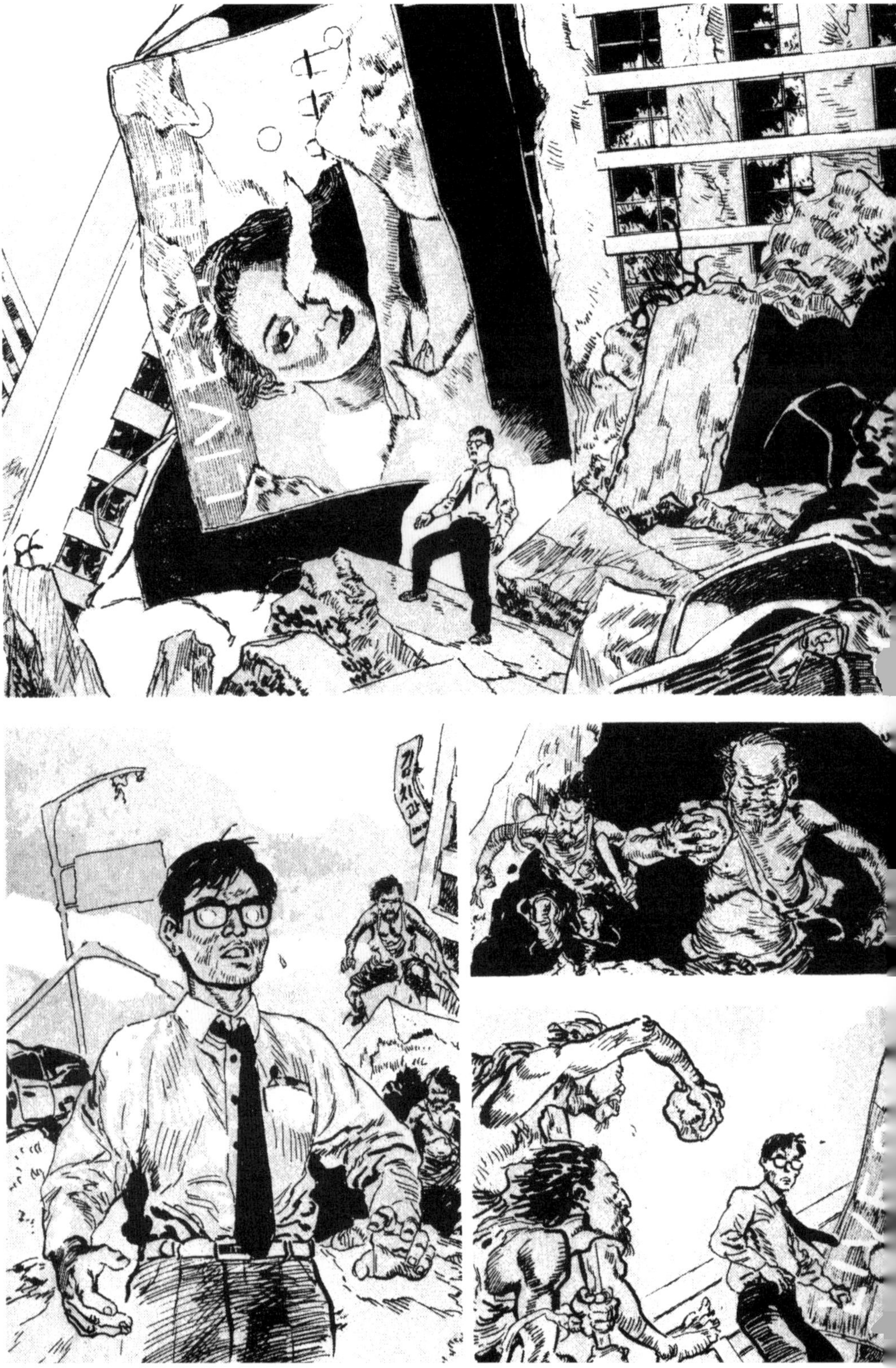

김치과

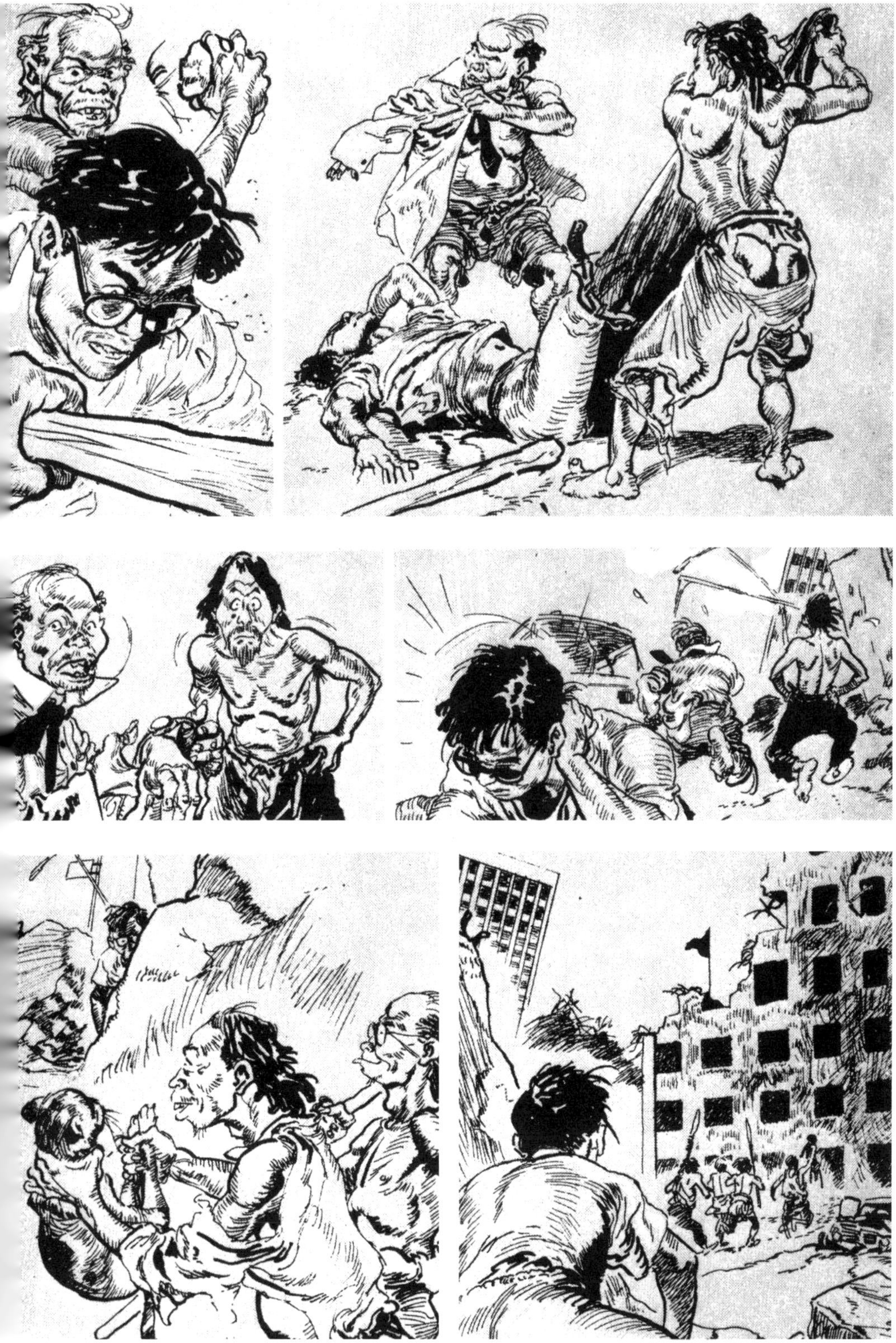

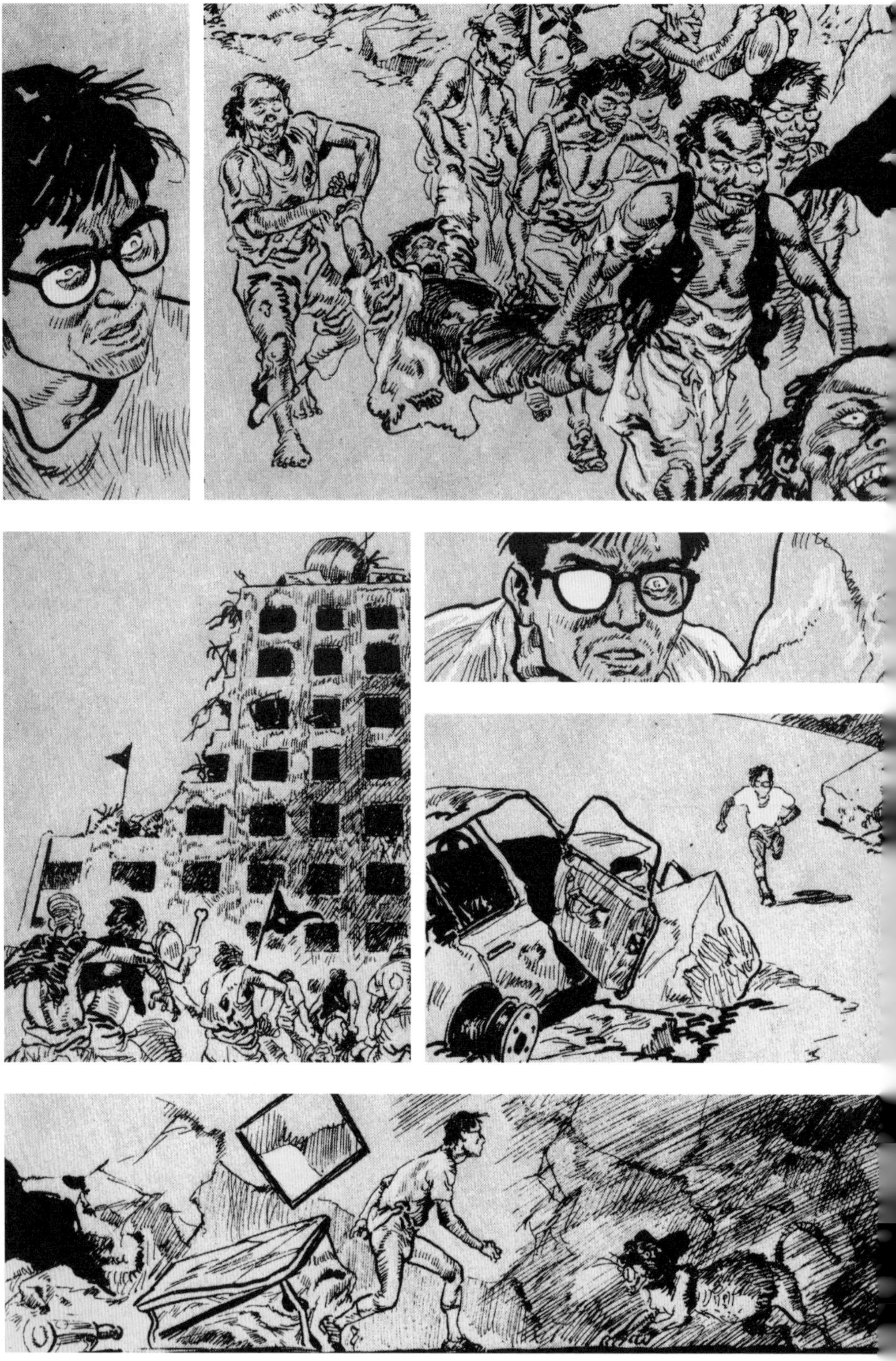

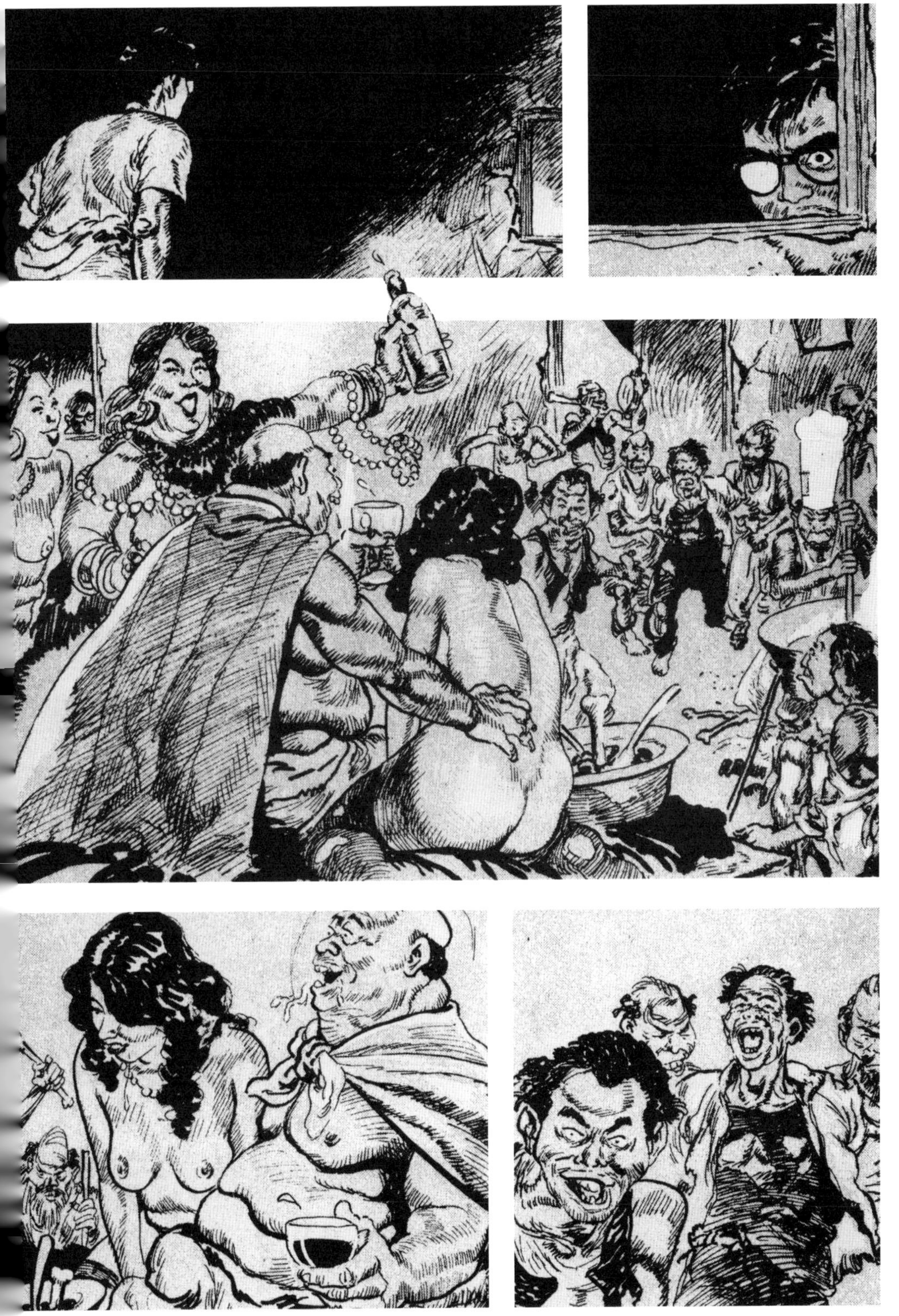

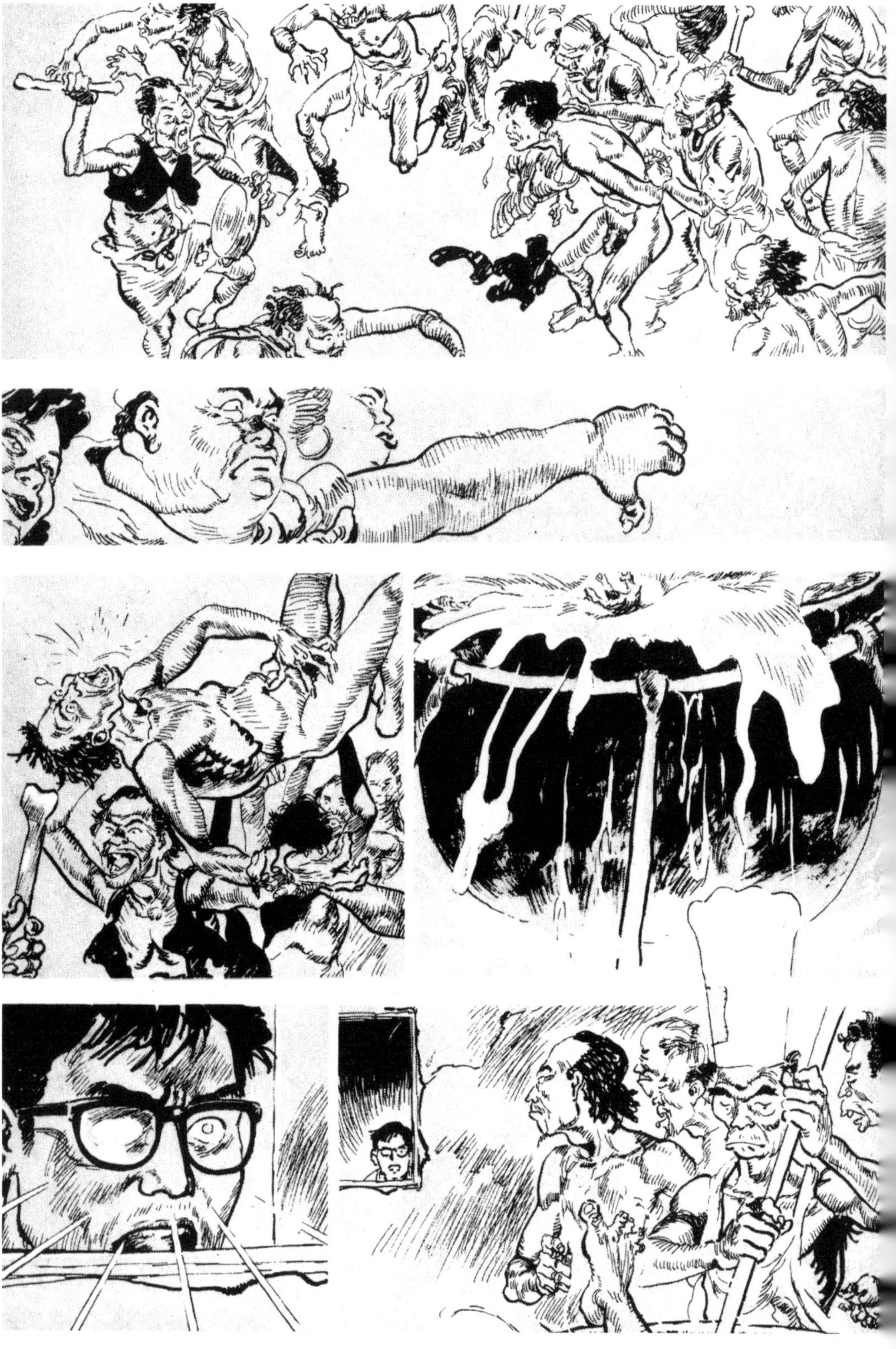

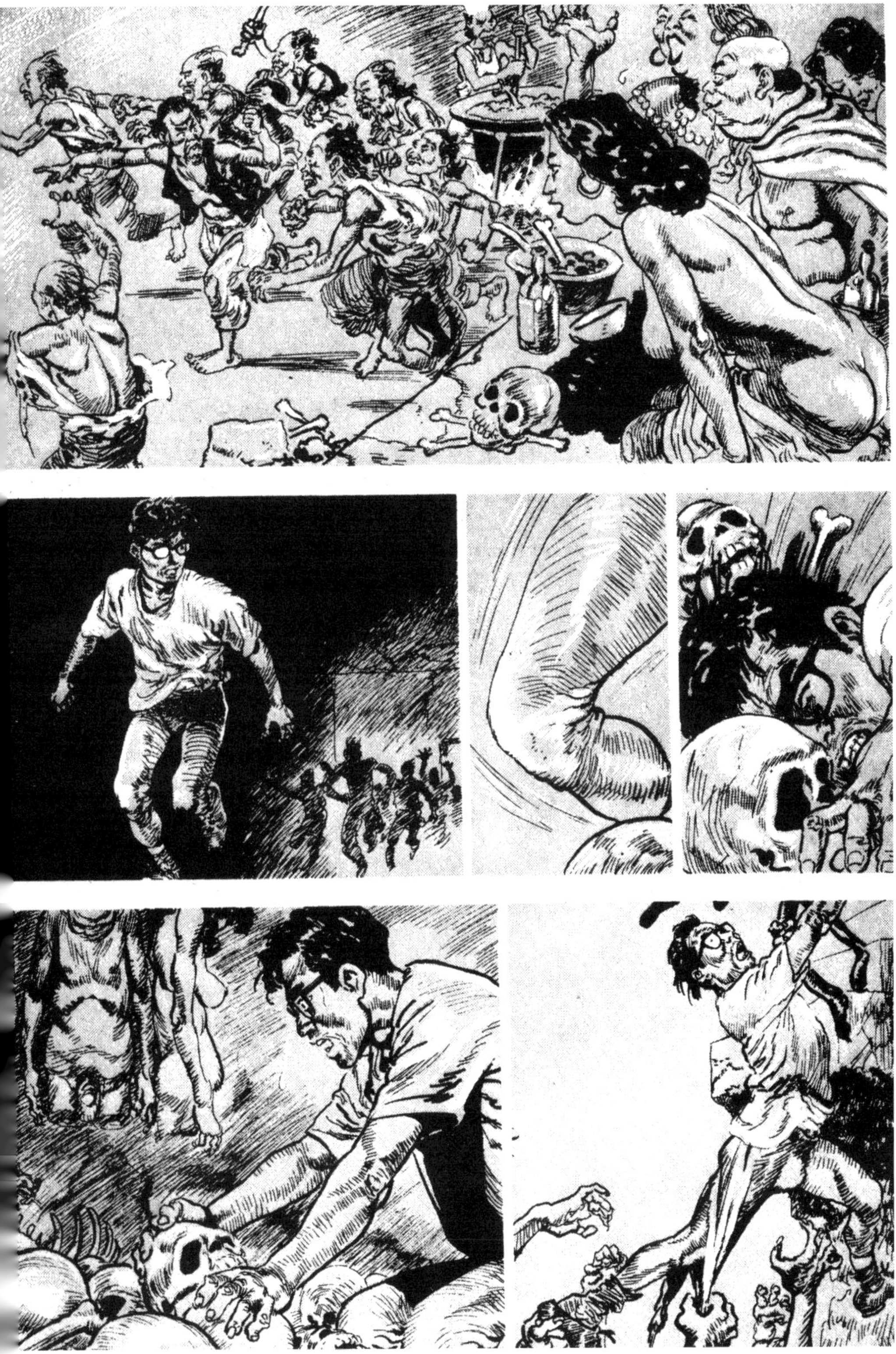

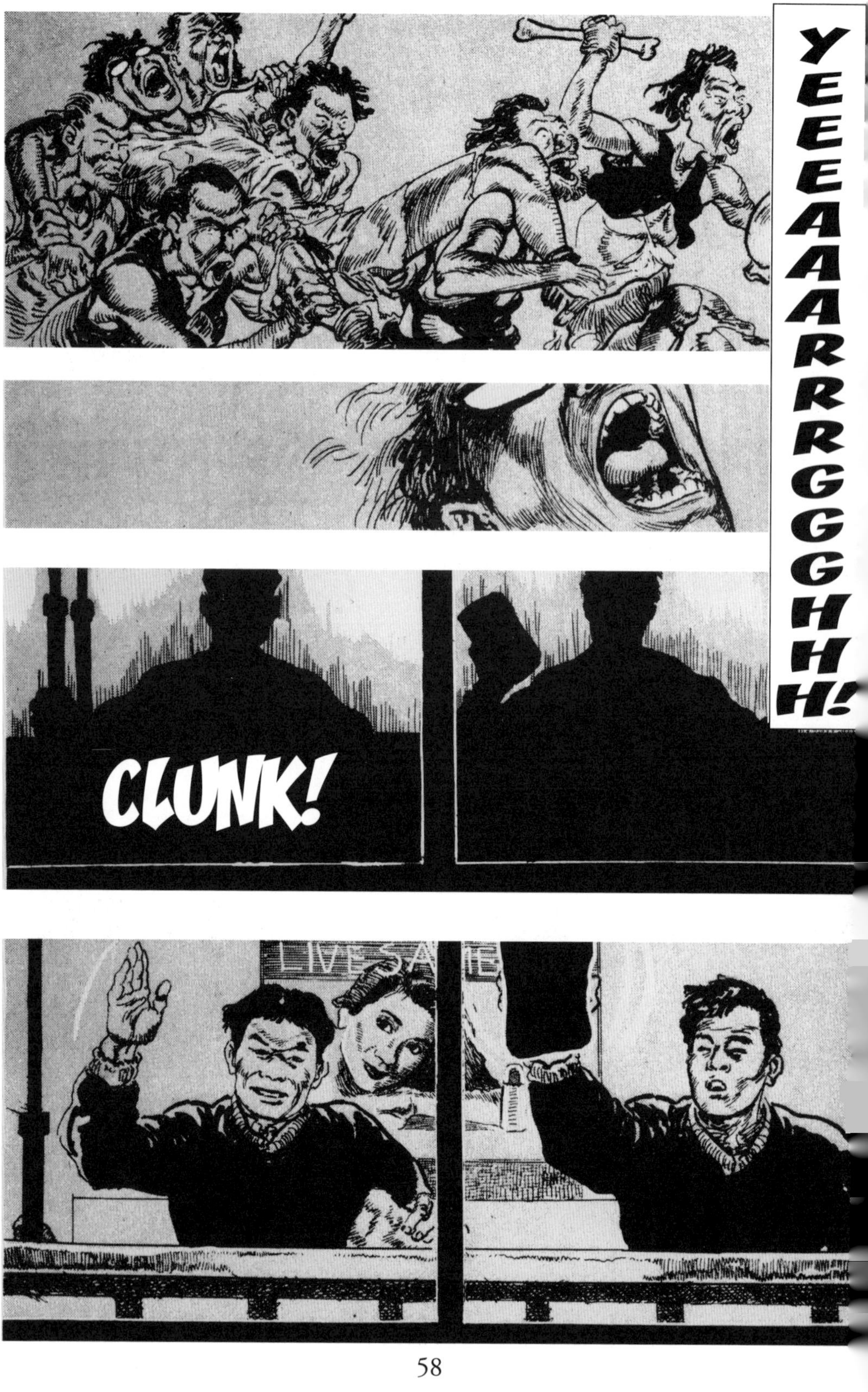
YEEEAAARRRGGGHHH!
CLUNK!

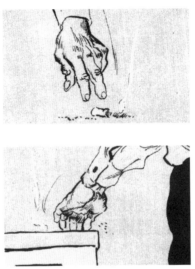

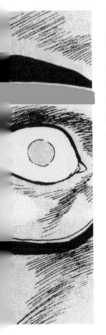

59

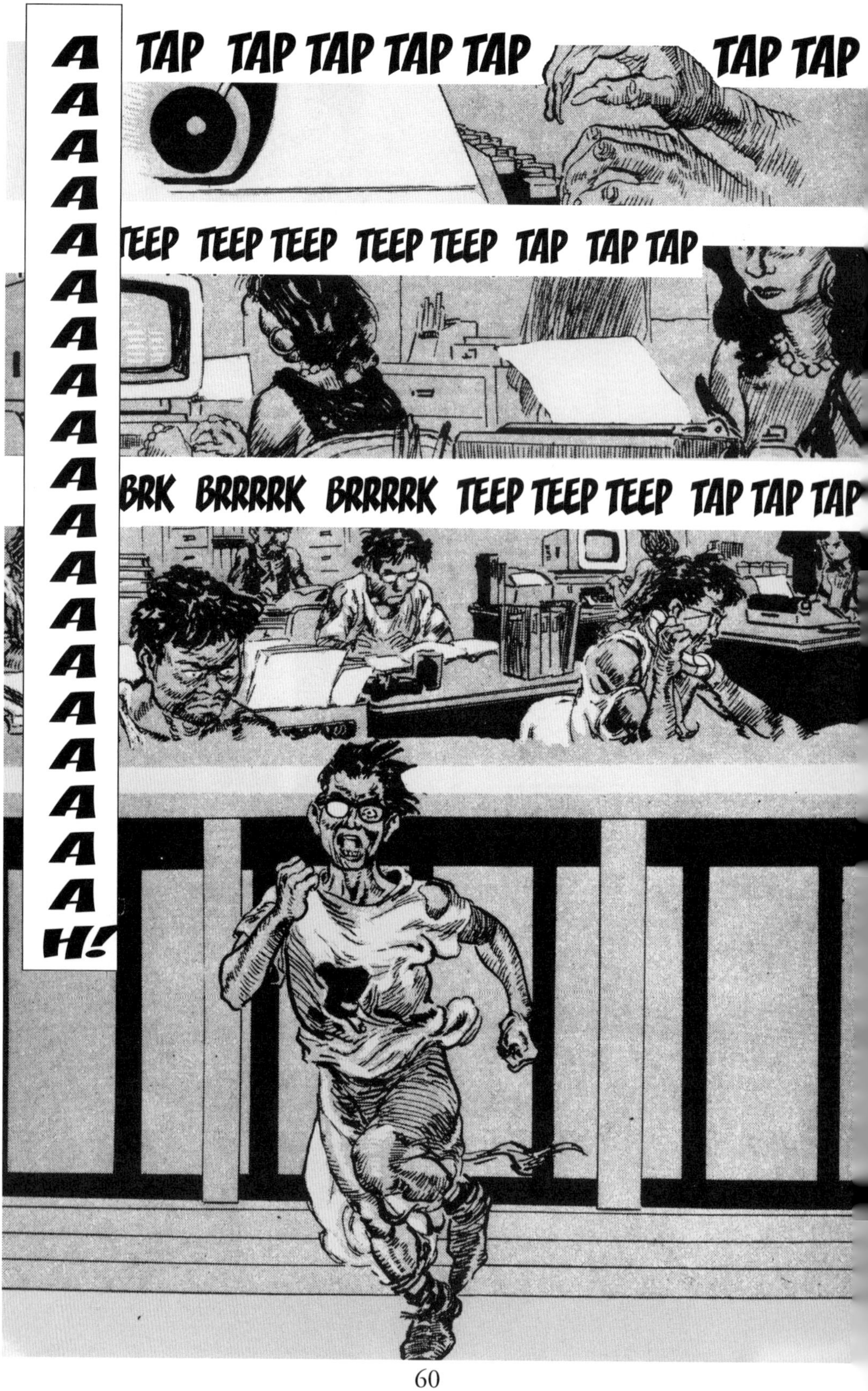
AAAAAAAAAAAAAAAAAAAH!
TAP TAP TAP TAP TAP TAP TAP
TEEP TEEP TEEP TEEP TEEP TAP TAP TAP
BRK BRRRRK BRRRRK TEEP TEEP TEEP TAP TAP TAP

TEAR GAS

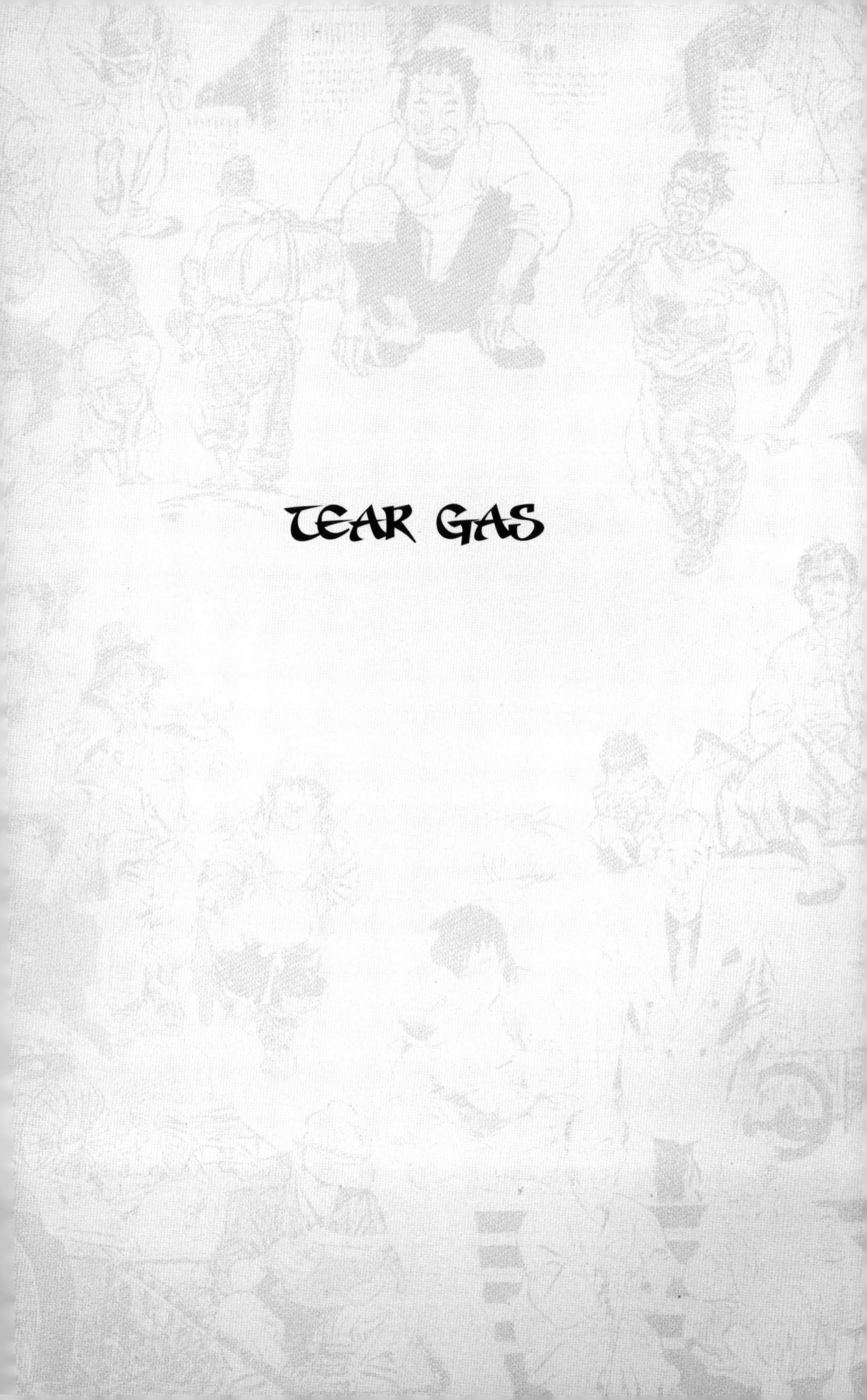

SEYEONG O
JUNE 1990

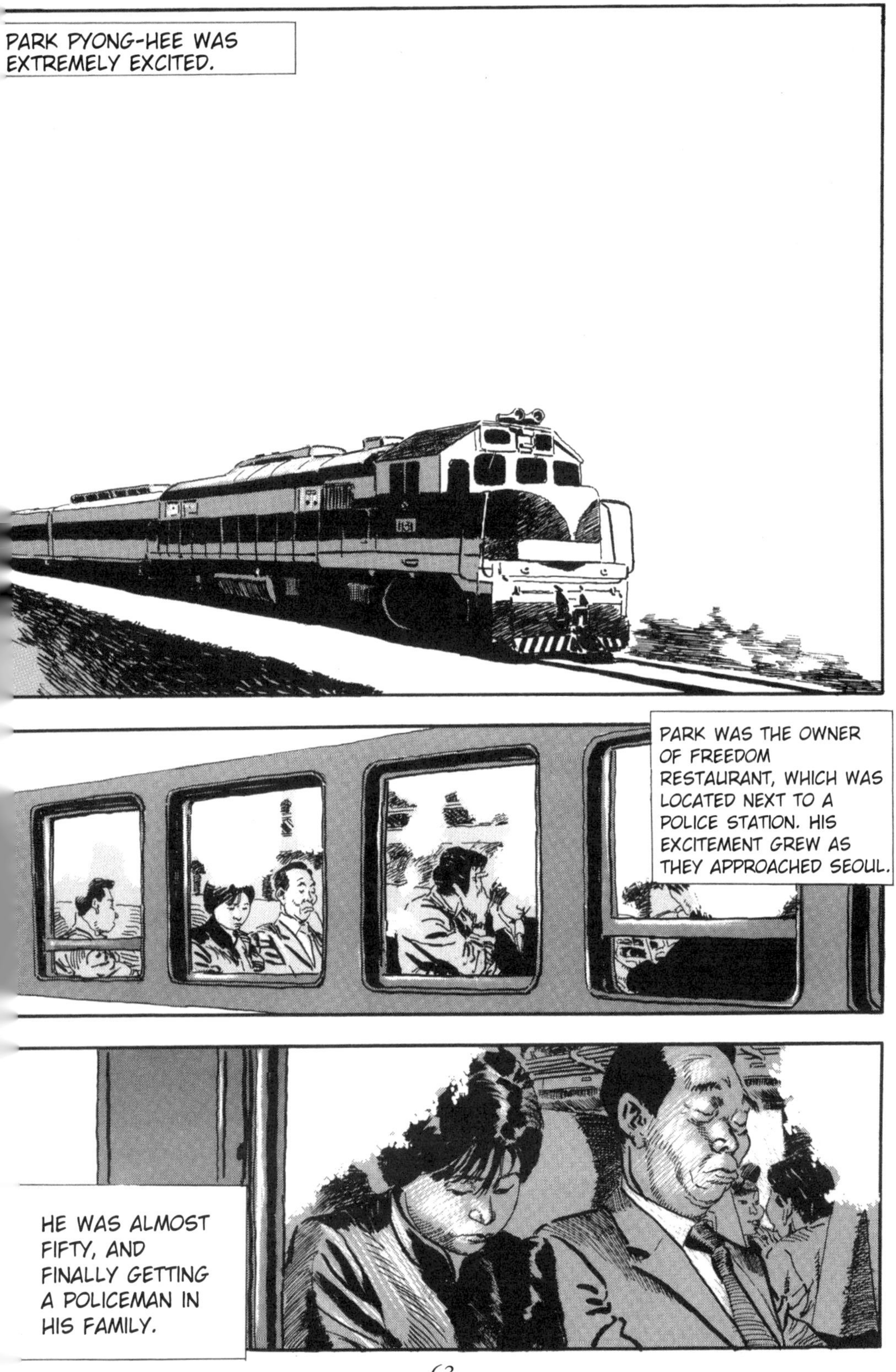
PARK PYONG-HEE WAS EXTREMELY EXCITED.
PARK WAS THE OWNER OF FREEDOM RESTAURANT, WHICH WAS LOCATED NEXT TO A POLICE STATION. HIS EXCITEMENT GREW AS THEY APPROACHED SEOUL.
HE WAS ALMOST FIFTY, AND FINALLY GETTING A POLICEMAN IN HIS FAMILY.

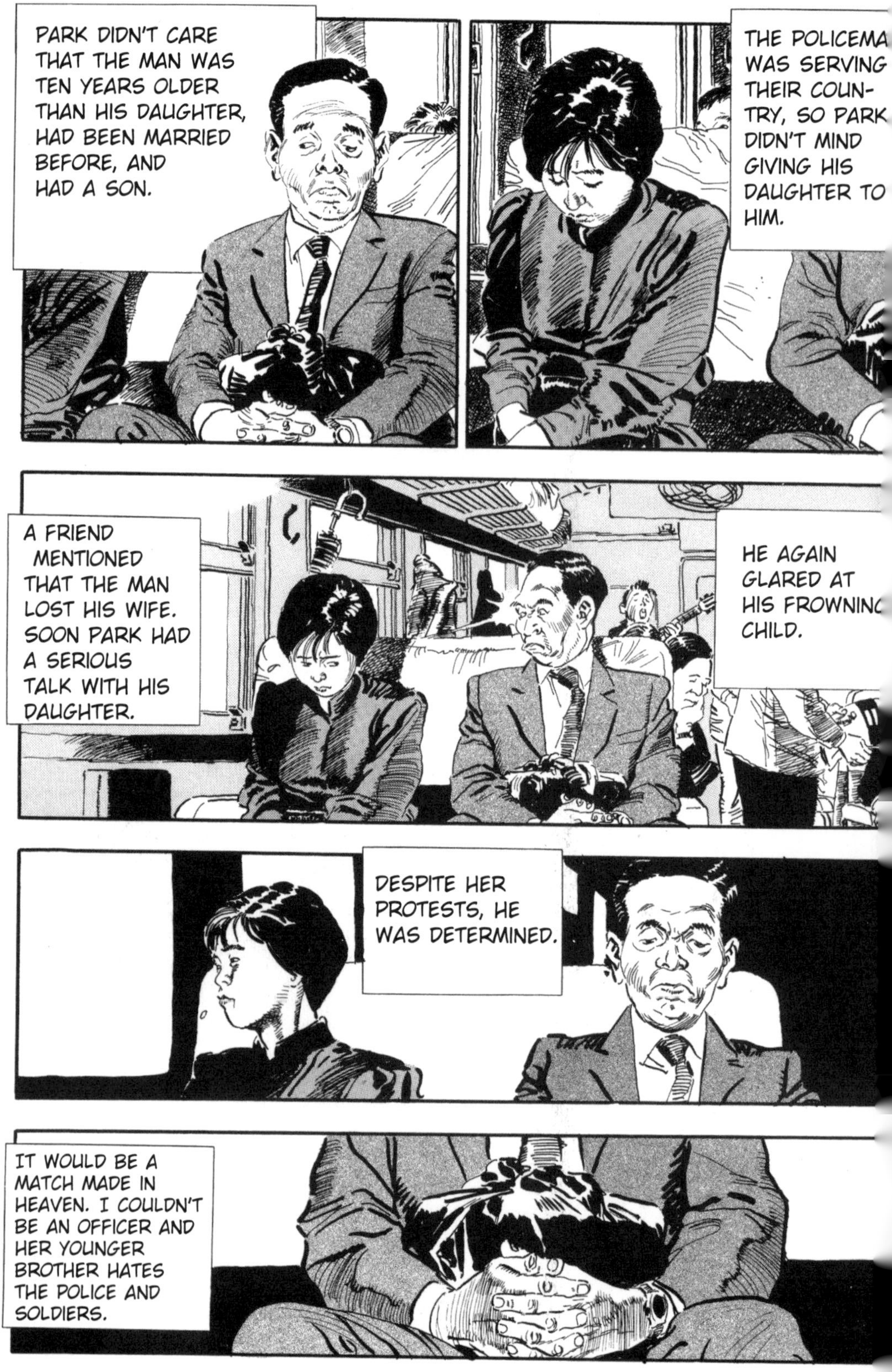
PARK DIDN'T CARE THAT THE MAN WAS TEN YEARS OLDER THAN HIS DAUGHTER, HAD BEEN MARRIED BEFORE, AND HAD A SON.
THE POLICEMA WAS SERVING THEIR COUN-TRY, SO PARK DIDN'T MIND GIVING HIS DAUGHTER TO HIM.
A FRIEND MENTIONED THAT THE MAN LOST HIS WIFE. SOON PARK HAD A SERIOUS TALK WITH HIS DAUGHTER.
HE AGAIN GLARED AT HIS FROWNIN CHILD.
DESPITE HER PROTESTS, HE WAS DETERMINED.
IT WOULD BE A MATCH MADE IN HEAVEN. I COULDN'T BE AN OFFICER AND HER YOUNGER BROTHER HATES THE POLICE AND SOLDIERS.

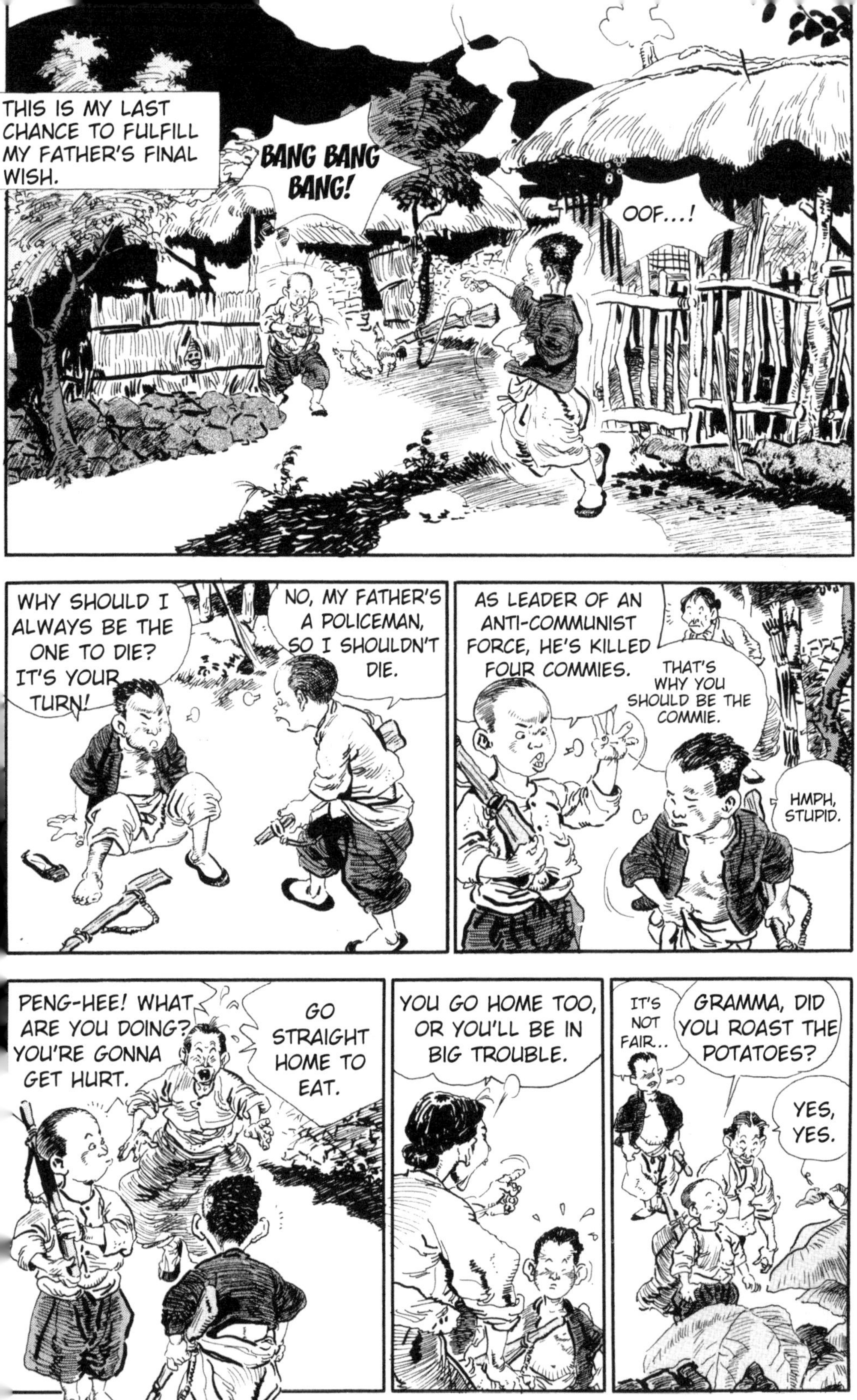

THIS IS MY LAST CHANCE TO FULFILL MY FATHER'S FINAL WISH.
BANG BANG BANG!
OOF...!
WHY SHOULD I ALWAYS BE THE ONE TO DIE? IT'S YOUR TURN!
NO, MY FATHER'S A POLICEMAN, SO I SHOULDN'T DIE.
AS LEADER OF AN ANTI-COMMUNIST FORCE, HE'S KILLED FOUR COMMIES.
THAT'S WHY YOU SHOULD BE THE COMMIE.
HMPH, STUPID.
PENG-HEE! WHAT ARE YOU DOING? YOU'RE GONNA GET HURT.
GO STRAIGHT HOME TO EAT.
YOU GO HOME TOO, OR YOU'LL BE IN BIG TROUBLE.
IT'S NOT FAIR...
GRAMMA, DID YOU ROAST THE POTATOES?
YES, YES.

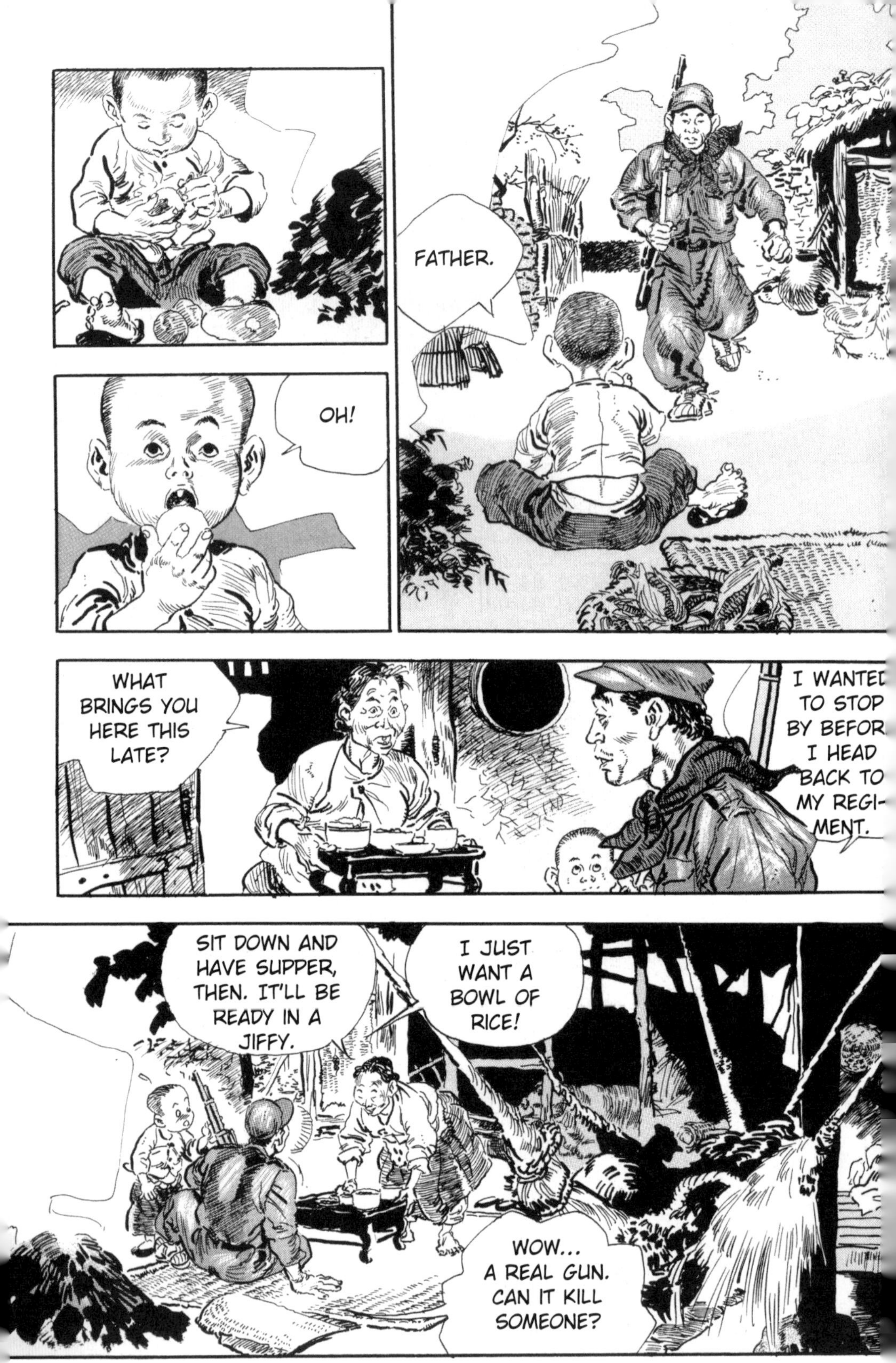
OH!
FATHER.
WHAT BRINGS YOU HERE THIS LATE?
I WANTED TO STOP BY BEFOR I HEAD BACK TO MY REGI-MENT.
SIT DOWN AND HAVE SUPPER, THEN. IT'LL BE READY IN A JIFFY.
I JUST WANT A BOWL OF RICE!
WOW... A REAL GUN. CAN IT KILL SOMEONE?

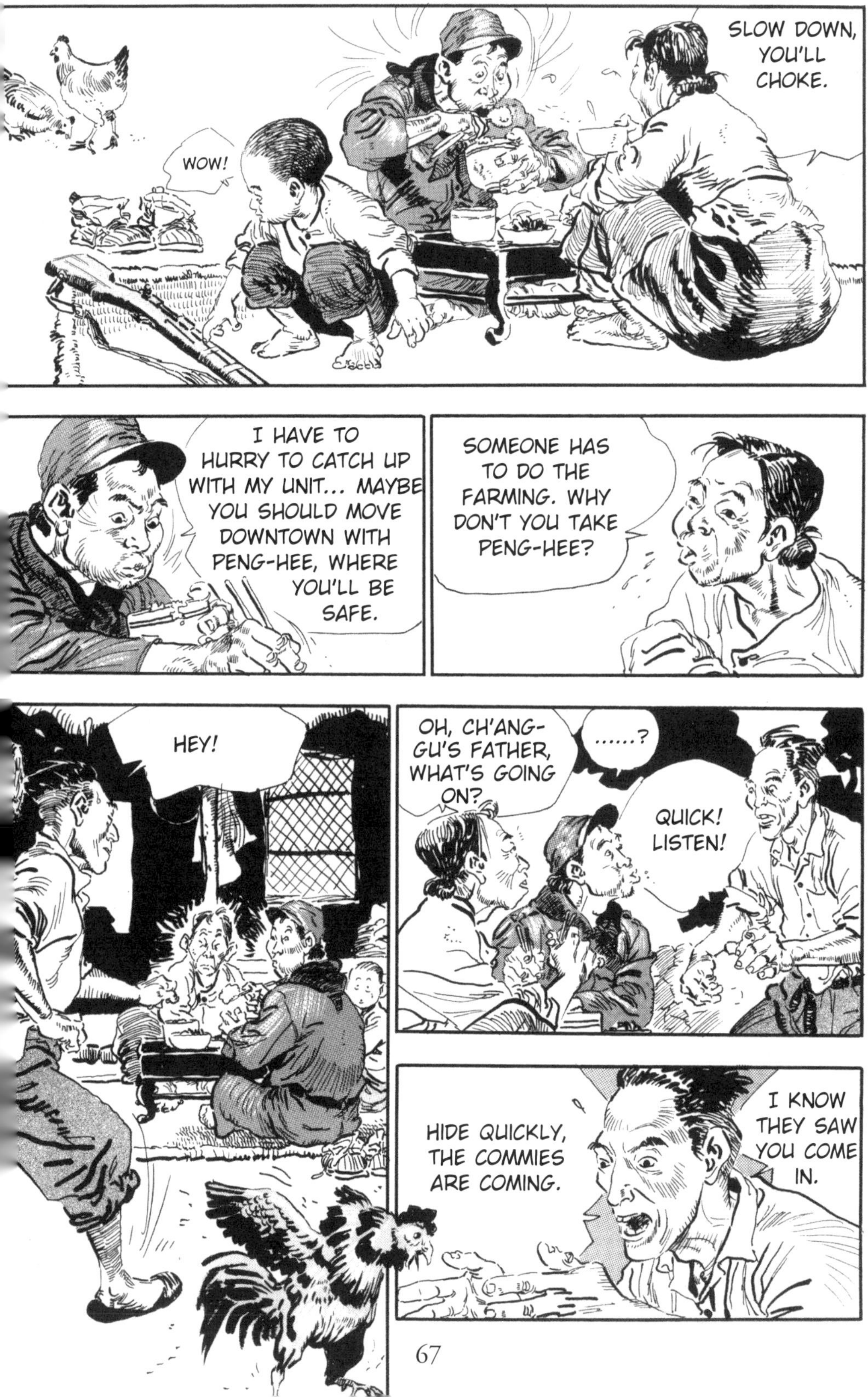

SLOW DOWN, YOU'LL CHOKE.
WOW!
I HAVE TO HURRY TO CATCH UP WITH MY UNIT... MAYBE YOU SHOULD MOVE DOWNTOWN WITH PENG-HEE, WHERE YOU'LL BE SAFE.
SOMEONE HAS TO DO THE FARMING. WHY DON'T YOU TAKE PENG-HEE?
HEY!
OH, CH'ANG-GU'S FATHER, WHAT'S GOING ON?
......?
QUICK! LISTEN!
I KNOW THEY SAW YOU COME IN.
HIDE QUICKLY, THE COMMIES ARE COMING.

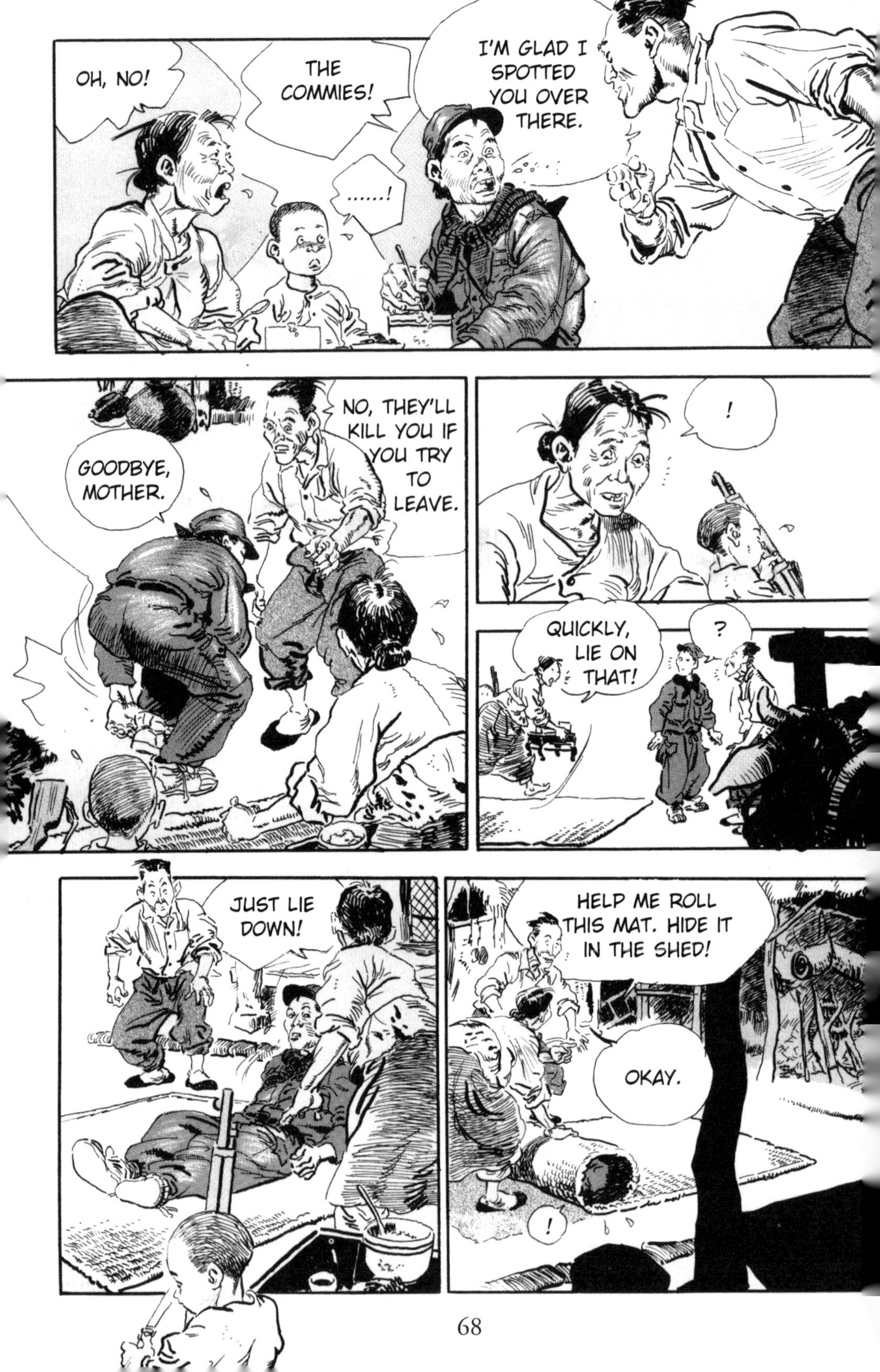
OH, NO!
THE COMMIES!
......!
I'M GLAD I SPOTTED YOU OVER THERE.
GOODBYE, MOTHER.
NO, THEY'LL KILL YOU IF YOU TRY TO LEAVE.
!
QUICKLY, LIE ON THAT!
?
JUST LIE DOWN!
HELP ME ROLL THIS MAT. HIDE IT IN THE SHED!
OKAY.
!

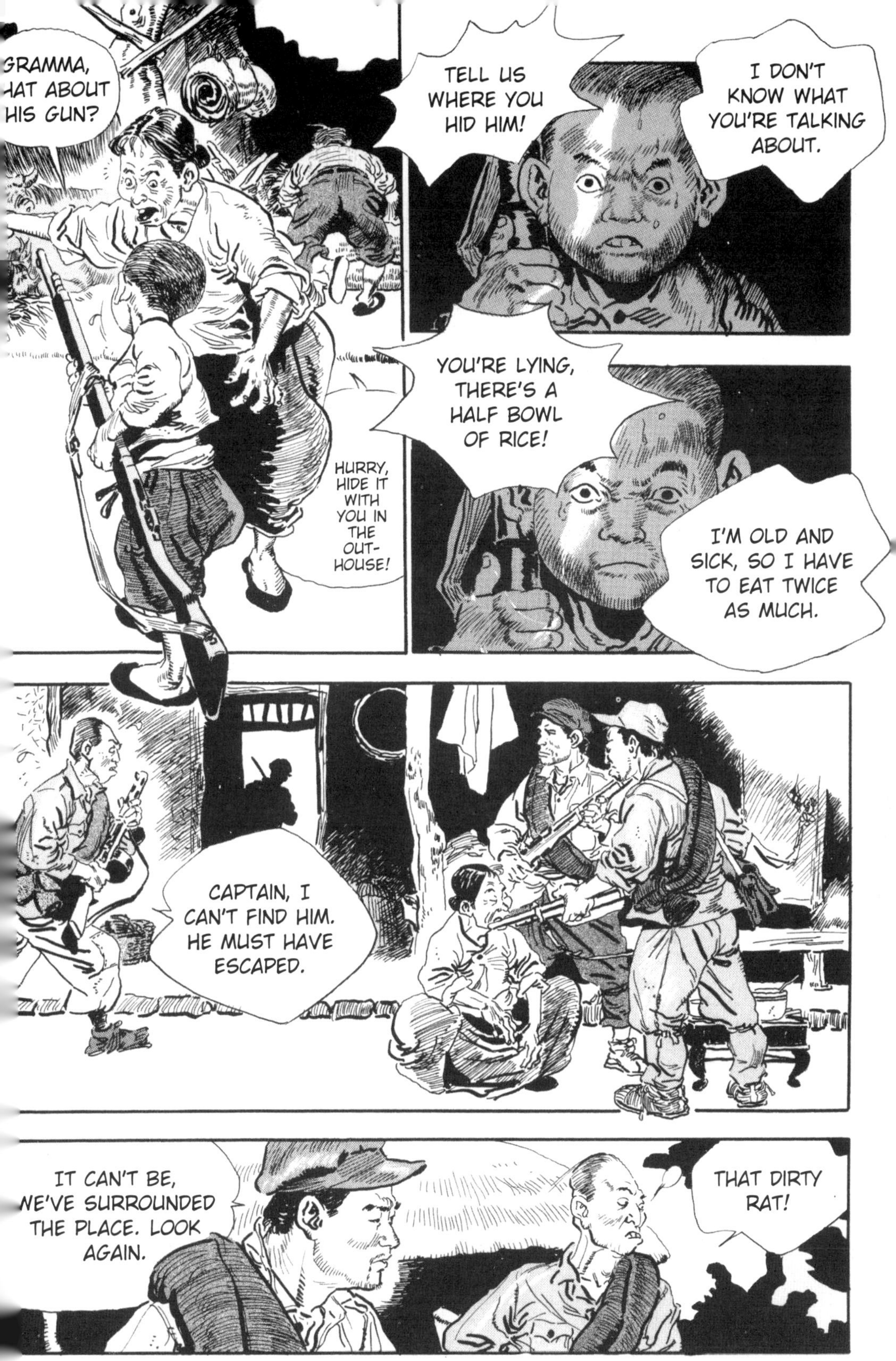
GRAMMA, HAT ABOUT HIS GUN?
HURRY, HIDE IT WITH YOU IN THE OUT-HOUSE!
TELL US WHERE YOU HID HIM!
I DON'T KNOW WHAT YOU'RE TALKING ABOUT.
YOU'RE LYING, THERE'S A HALF BOWL OF RICE!
I'M OLD AND SICK, SO I HAVE TO EAT TWICE AS MUCH.
CAPTAIN, I CAN'T FIND HIM. HE MUST HAVE ESCAPED.
IT CAN'T BE, NE'VE SURROUNDED THE PLACE. LOOK AGAIN.
THAT DIRTY RAT!

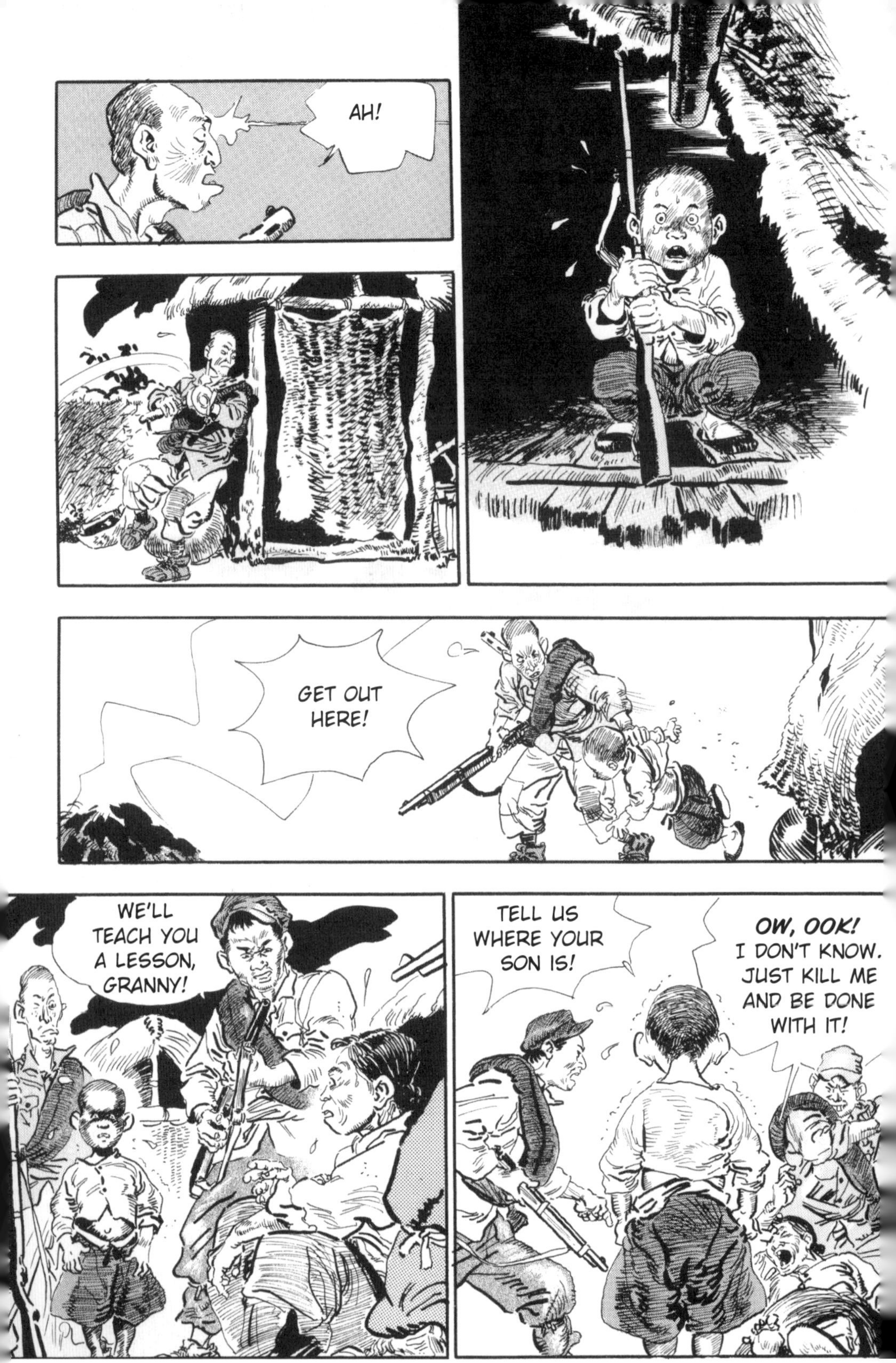
AH!
GET OUT HERE!
WE'LL TEACH YOU A LESSON, GRANNY!
TELL US WHERE YOUR SON IS!
OW, OOK! I DON'T KNOW. JUST KILL ME AND BE DONE WITH IT!

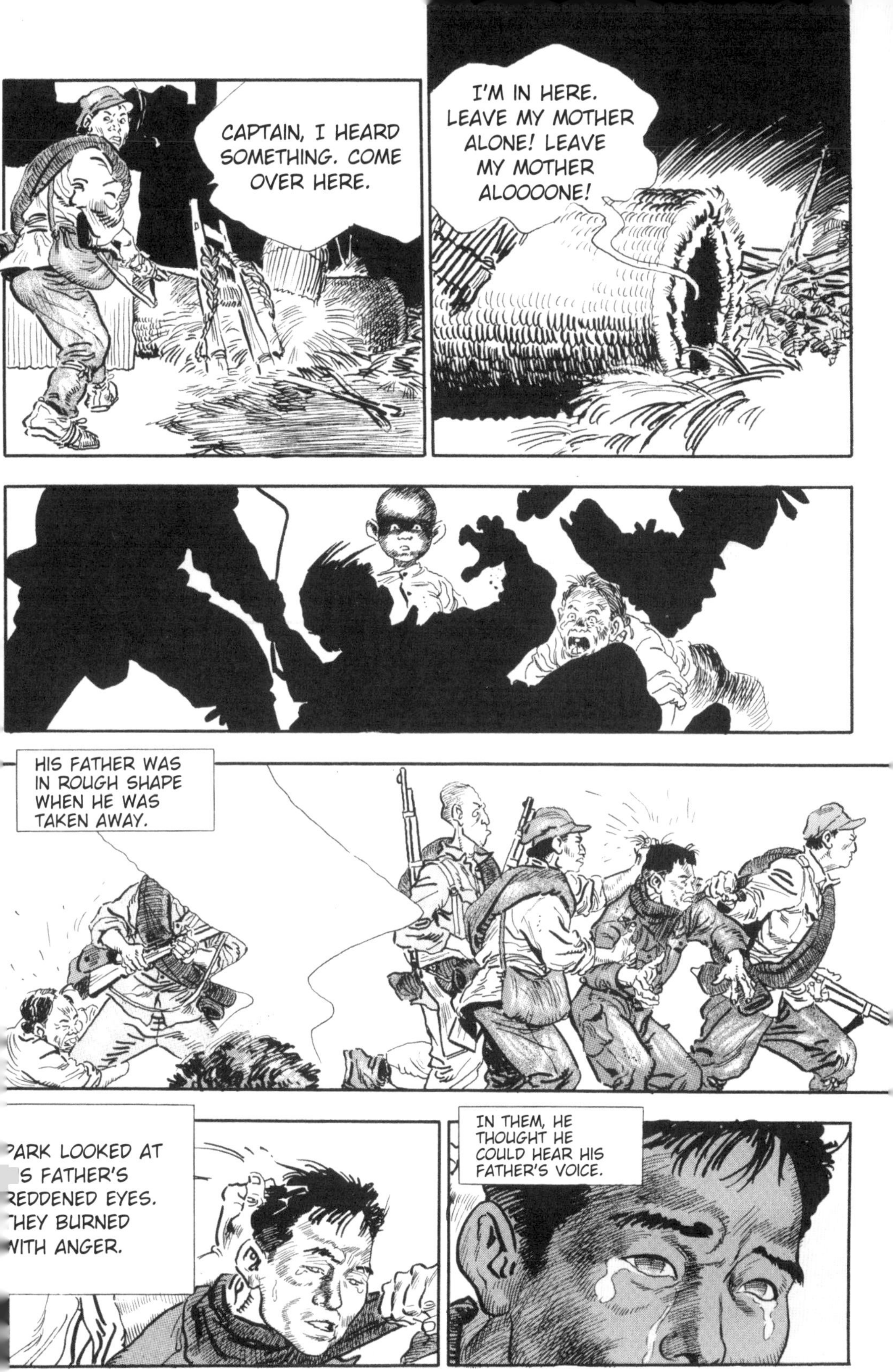
CAPTAIN, I HEARD SOMETHING. COME OVER HERE.
I'M IN HERE. LEAVE MY MOTHER ALONE! LEAVE MY MOTHER ALOOOONE!
HIS FATHER WAS IN ROUGH SHAPE WHEN HE WAS TAKEN AWAY.
PARK LOOKED AT S FATHER'S REDDENED EYES. HEY BURNED WITH ANGER.
IN THEM, HE THOUGHT HE COULD HEAR HIS FATHER'S VOICE.

THE VOICE YELLED, "BE A POLICEMAN AND WIPE OUT COMMUNISM!"

HIS FATHER'S BURNING EYES ORDERED HIM TO DO THAT.

PARK STARTED VOMITING AS HIS FATHER DISAPPEARED THROUGH THE SMOKE OF THE SMUDGE POT.

BARF YOARGH

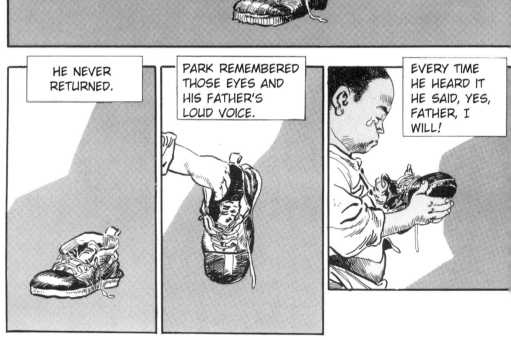

HE NEVER RETURNED.

PARK REMEMBERED THOSE EYES AND HIS FATHER'S LOUD VOICE.

EVERY TIME HE HEARD IT HE SAID, YES, FATHER, I WILL!

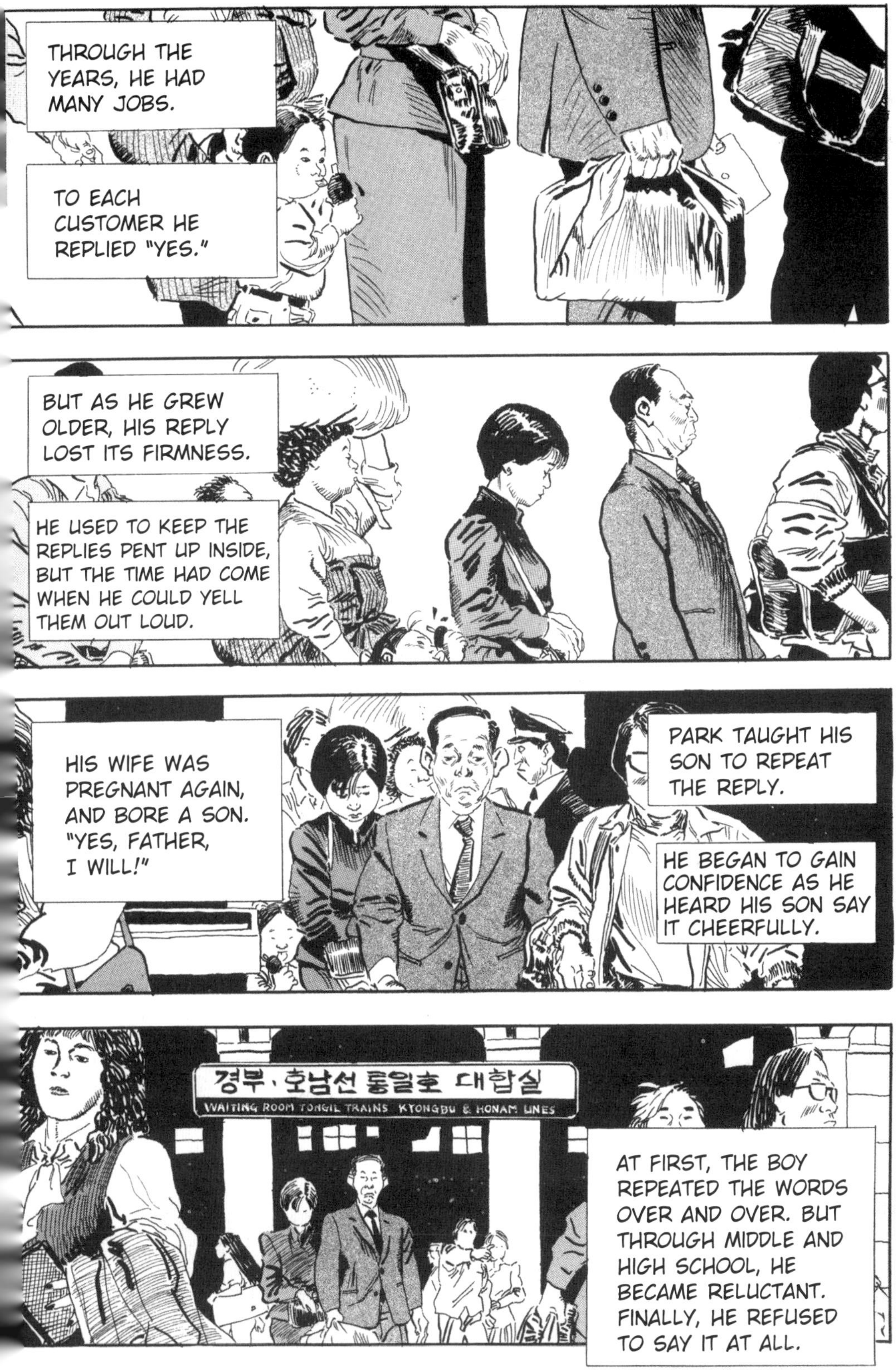
THROUGH THE YEARS, HE HAD MANY JOBS.
TO EACH CUSTOMER HE REPLIED "YES."
BUT AS HE GREW OLDER, HIS REPLY LOST ITS FIRMNESS.
HE USED TO KEEP THE REPLIES PENT UP INSIDE, BUT THE TIME HAD COME WHEN HE COULD YELL THEM OUT LOUD.
HIS WIFE WAS PREGNANT AGAIN, AND BORE A SON. "YES, FATHER, I WILL!"
PARK TAUGHT HIS SON TO REPEAT THE REPLY.
HE BEGAN TO GAIN CONFIDENCE AS HE HEARD HIS SON SAY IT CHEERFULLY.
경부, 호남선 통일호 대합실
WAITING ROOM TONGIL TRAINS KYONGBU & HONAM LINES
AT FIRST, THE BOY REPEATED THE WORDS OVER AND OVER. BUT THROUGH MIDDLE AND HIGH SCHOOL, HE BECAME RELUCTANT. FINALLY, HE REFUSED TO SAY IT AT ALL.

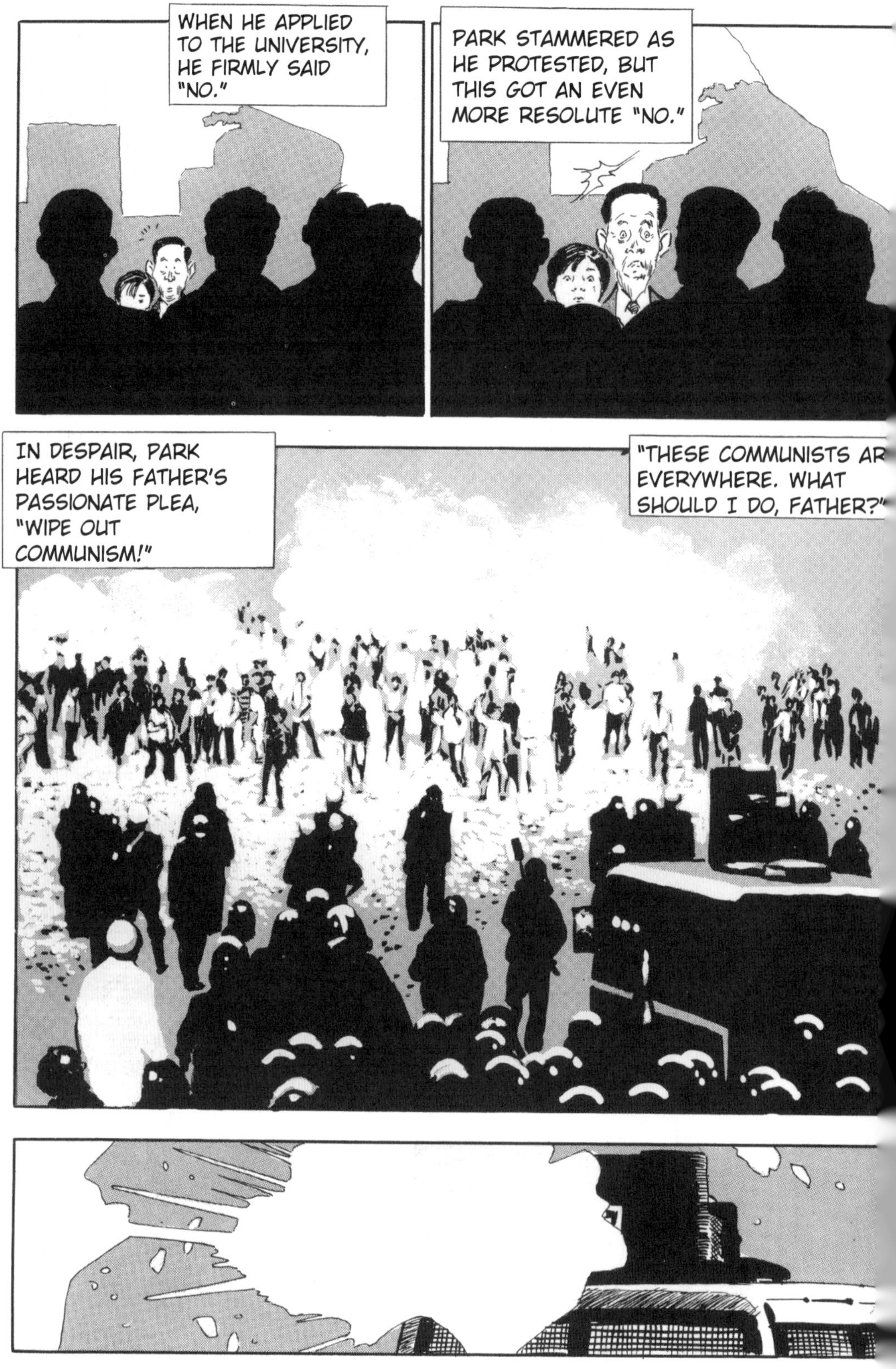
WHEN HE APPLIED TO THE UNIVERSITY, HE FIRMLY SAID "NO."
PARK STAMMERED AS HE PROTESTED, BUT THIS GOT AN EVEN MORE RESOLUTE "NO."
IN DESPAIR, PARK HEARD HIS FATHER'S PASSIONATE PLEA, "WIPE OUT COMMUNISM!"
"THESE COMMUNISTS AR EVERYWHERE. WHAT SHOULD I DO, FATHER?"

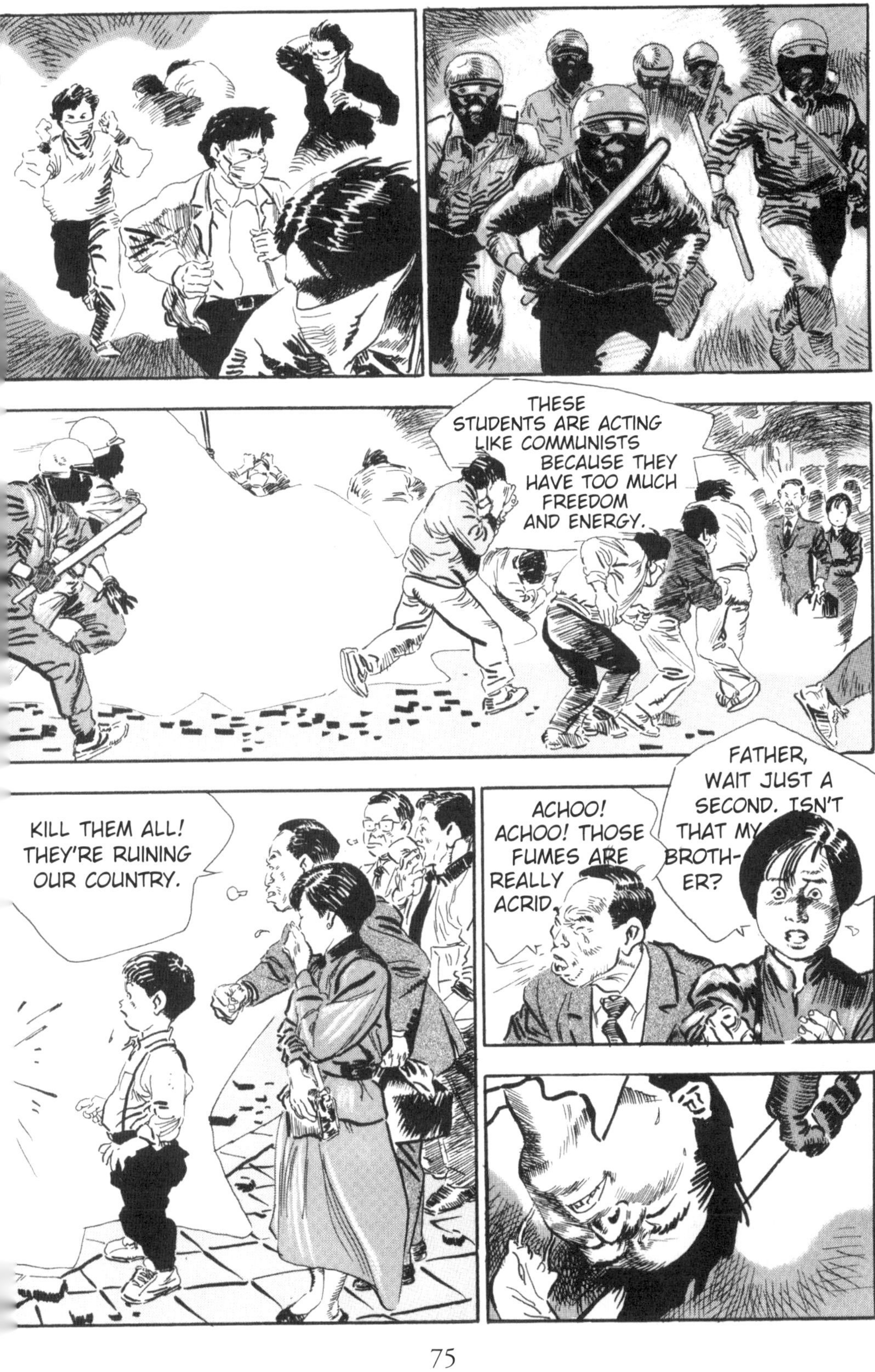
THESE STUDENTS ARE ACTING LIKE COMMUNISTS BECAUSE THEY HAVE TOO MUCH FREEDOM AND ENERGY.
KILL THEM ALL! THEY'RE RUINING OUR COUNTRY.
FATHER, WAIT JUST A SECOND. ISN'T THAT MY BROTH-ER?
ACHOO! ACHOO! THOSE FUMES ARE REALLY ACRID.

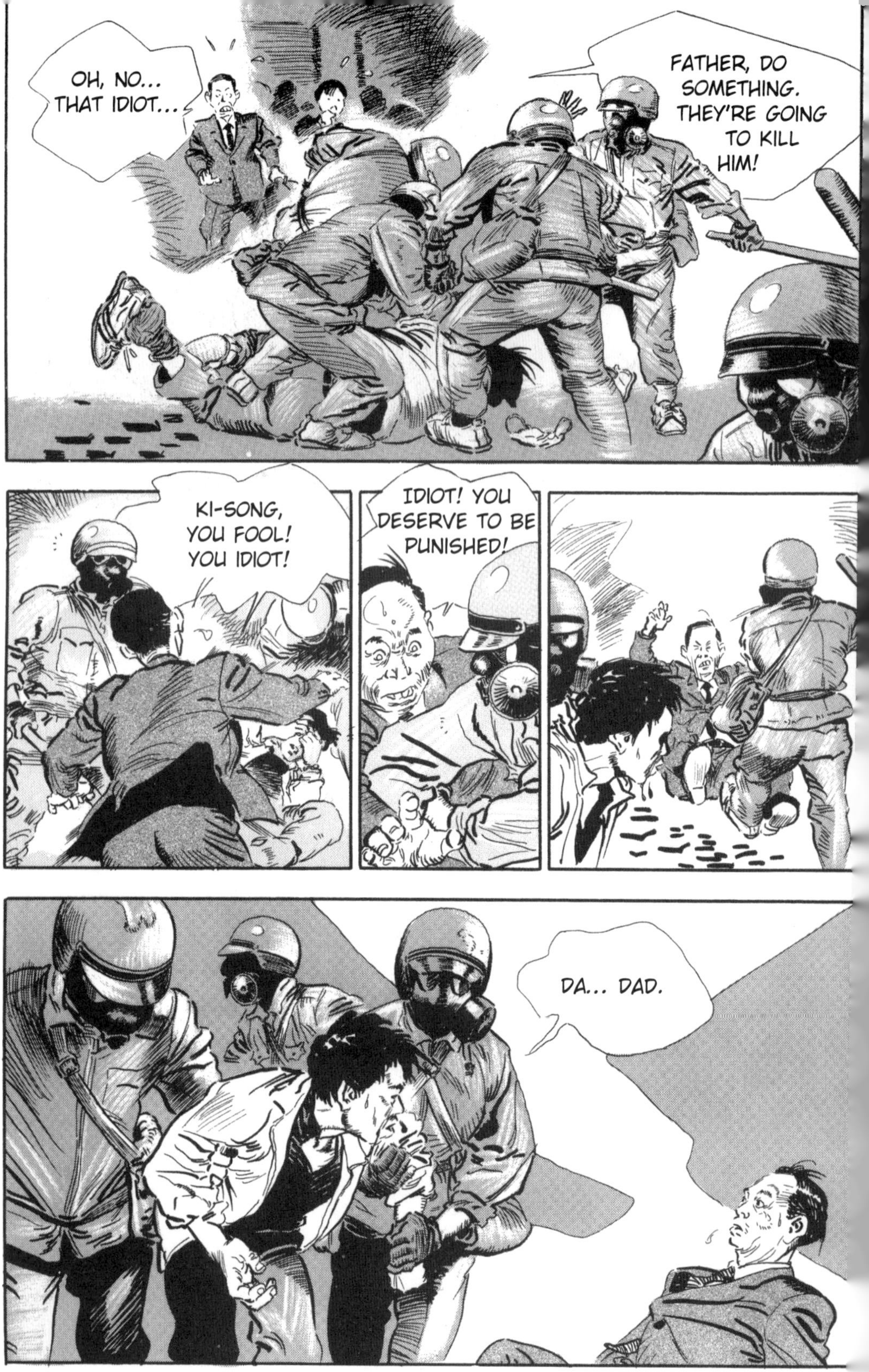
OH, NO... THAT IDIOT...
FATHER, DO SOMETHING. THEY'RE GOING TO KILL HIM!
KI-SONG, YOU FOOL! YOU IDIOT!
IDIOT! YOU DESERVE TO BE PUNISHED!
DA... DAD.

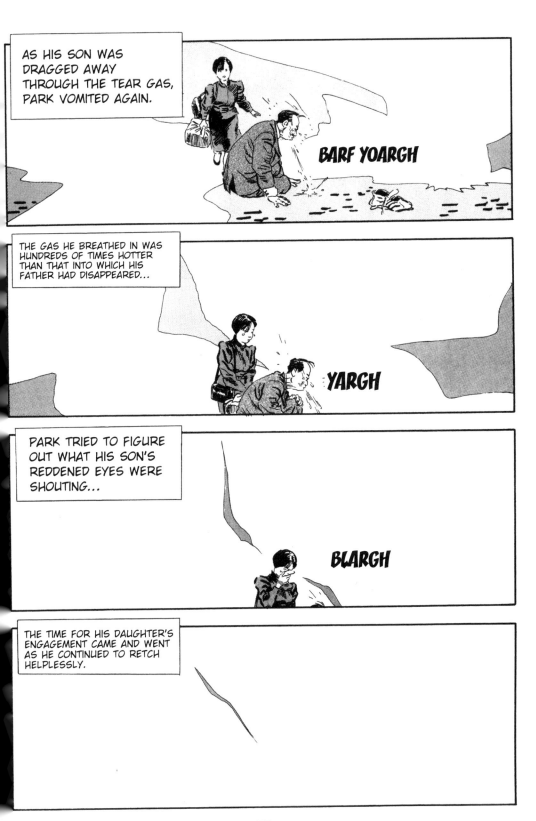

AS HIS SON WAS
DRAGGED AWAY
THROUGH THE TEAR GAS,
PARK VOMITED AGAIN.

BARF YOARGH

THE GAS HE BREATHED IN WAS
HUNDREDS OF TIMES HOTTER
THAN THAT INTO WHICH HIS
FATHER HAD DISAPPEARED...

YARGH

PARK TRIED TO FIGURE
OUT WHAT HIS SON'S
REDDENED EYES WERE
SHOUTING...

BLARGH

THE TIME FOR HIS DAUGHTER'S
ENGAGEMENT CAME AND WENT
AS HE CONTINUED TO RETCH
HELPLESSLY.

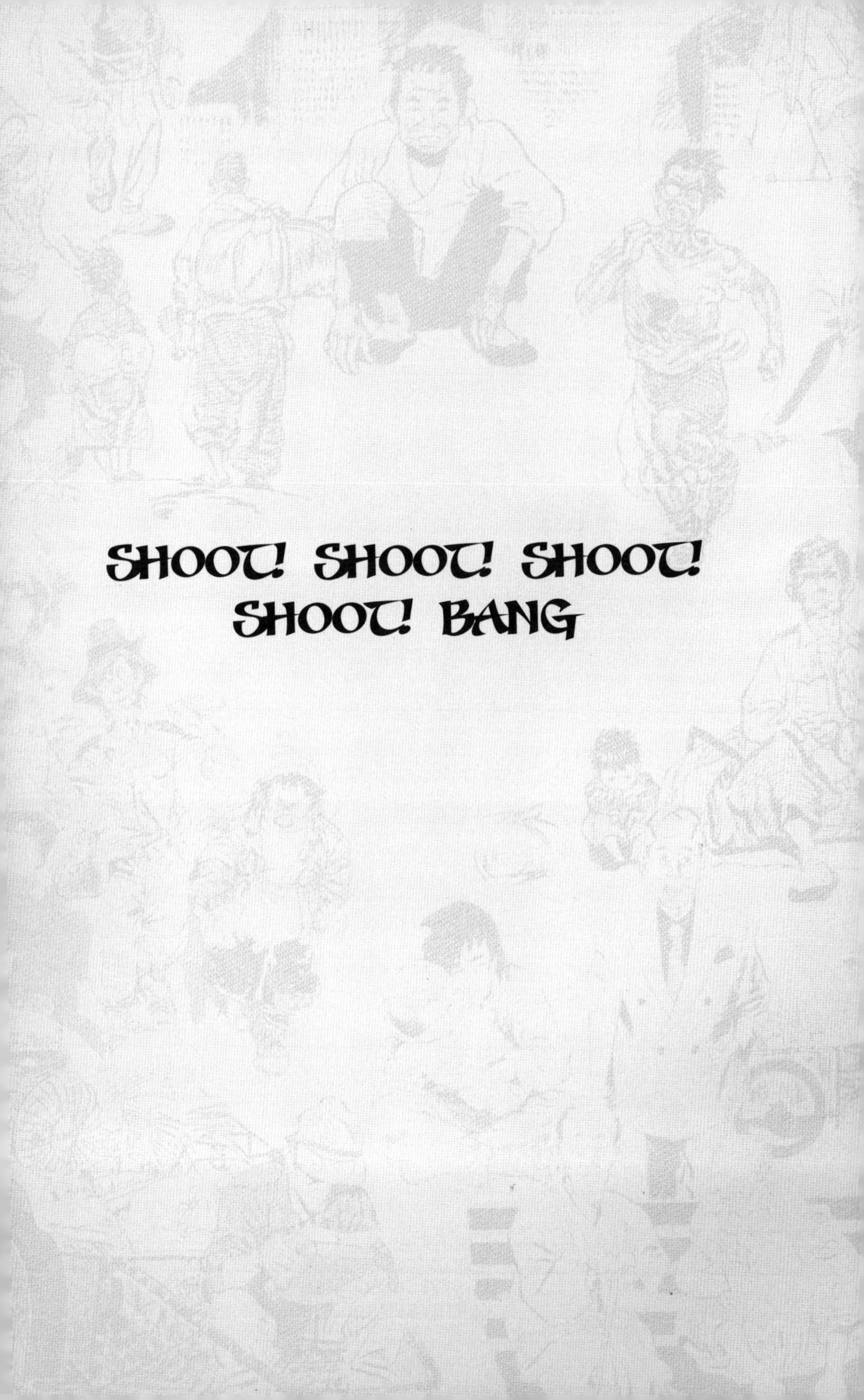

SHOOT! SHOOT! SHOOT! SHOOT! BANG

SEYEONG O
SEPTEMBER 1988

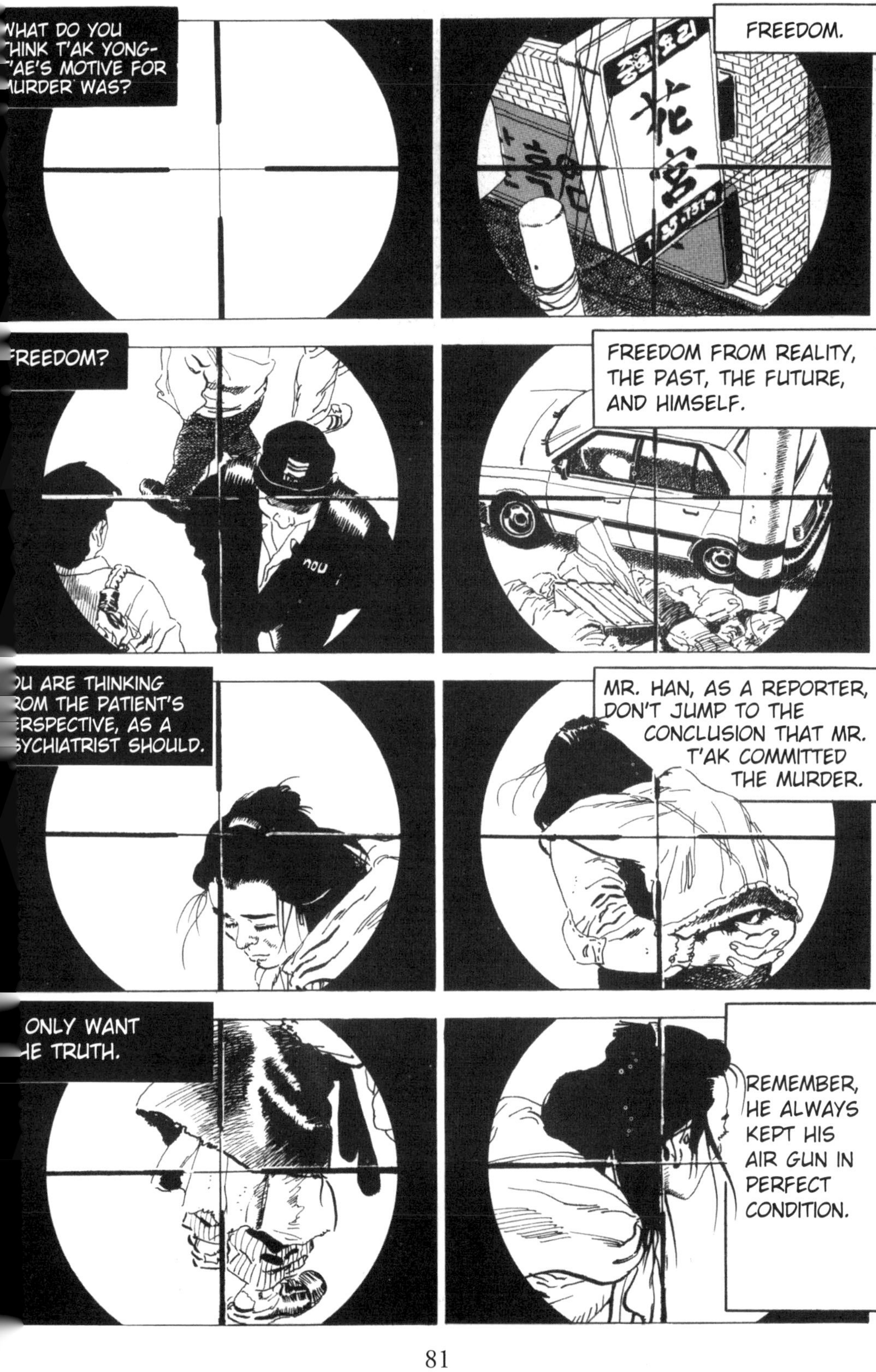

WHAT DO YOU THINK T'AK YONG-T'AE'S MOTIVE FOR MURDER WAS?
FREEDOM.
花宮
FREEDOM?
FREEDOM FROM REALITY, THE PAST, THE FUTURE, AND HIMSELF.
YOU ARE THINKING FROM THE PATIENT'S PERSPECTIVE, AS A PSYCHIATRIST SHOULD.
MR. HAN, AS A REPORTER, DON'T JUMP TO THE CONCLUSION THAT MR. T'AK COMMITTED THE MURDER.
I ONLY WANT THE TRUTH.
REMEMBER, HE ALWAYS KEPT HIS AIR GUN IN PERFECT CONDITION.

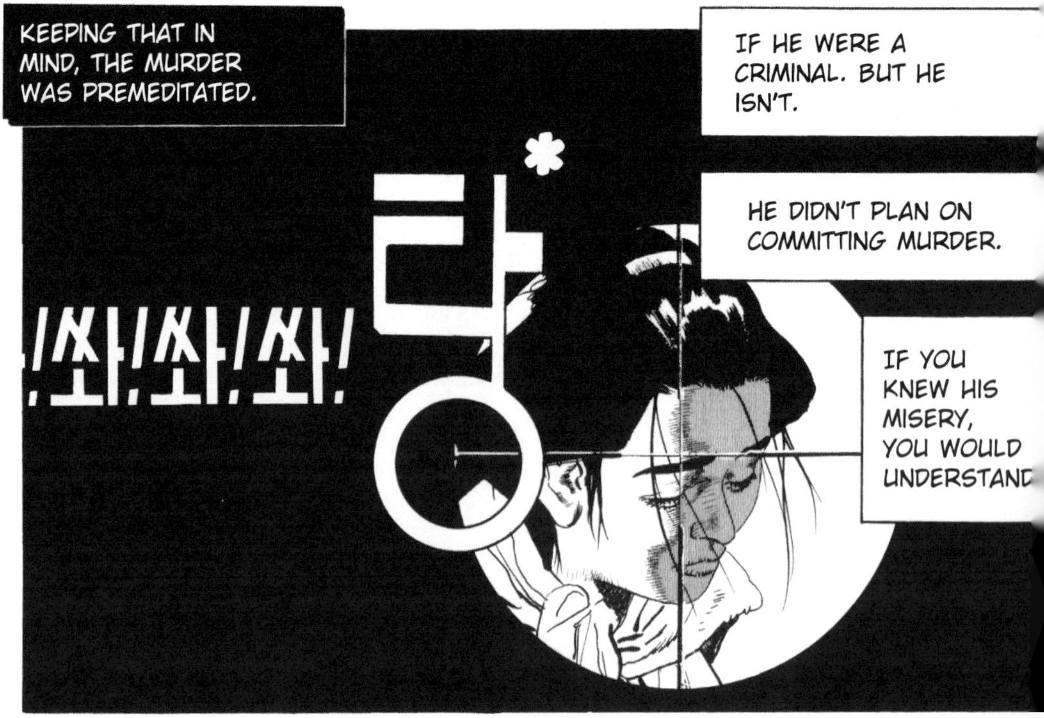
KEEPING THAT IN MIND, THE MURDER WAS PREMEDITATED.
IF HE WERE A CRIMINAL. BUT HE ISN'T.
HE DIDN'T PLAN ON COMMITTING MURDER.
쏴!쏴!쏴!
탕*
IF YOU KNEW HIS MISERY, YOU WOULD UNDERSTAND

*SHOOT! SHOOT! SHOOT! SHOOT! BANG!

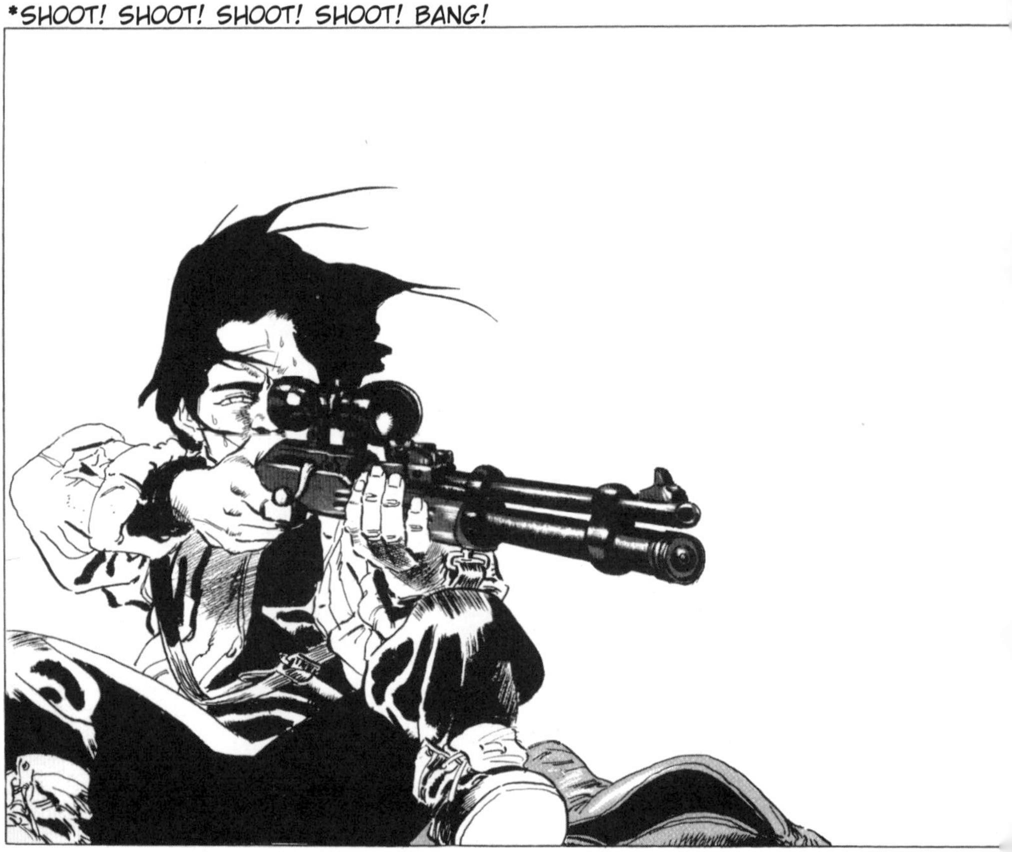

MR. HAN! DID YOU LOOK AT HIS MILITARY RECORD?*

IN THE 80'S, HE WAS IN THE AIRBORNE AT KWANGJU1.

AFTERWARDS, HE WAS PUT IN A PSYCHIATRIC UNIT.

HE HAD A MORBID FEAR.

WHAT DOES THAT HAVE TO DO WITH THIS CASE?

WITH HIS POOR MOTHER'S HELP, HE ENTERED UNIVERSITY.

*ON MAY 18TH OF 1980, THE RESIDENTS OF KWANGJU, MANY OF WHOM WERE STUDENTS, RIOTED TO OVERTHROW THE KOREAN MILITARY DICTATORSHIP. AS THE RIOT POLICE WERE ALSO STUDENTS, IT WAS OFTEN STUDENT AGAINST STUDENT.

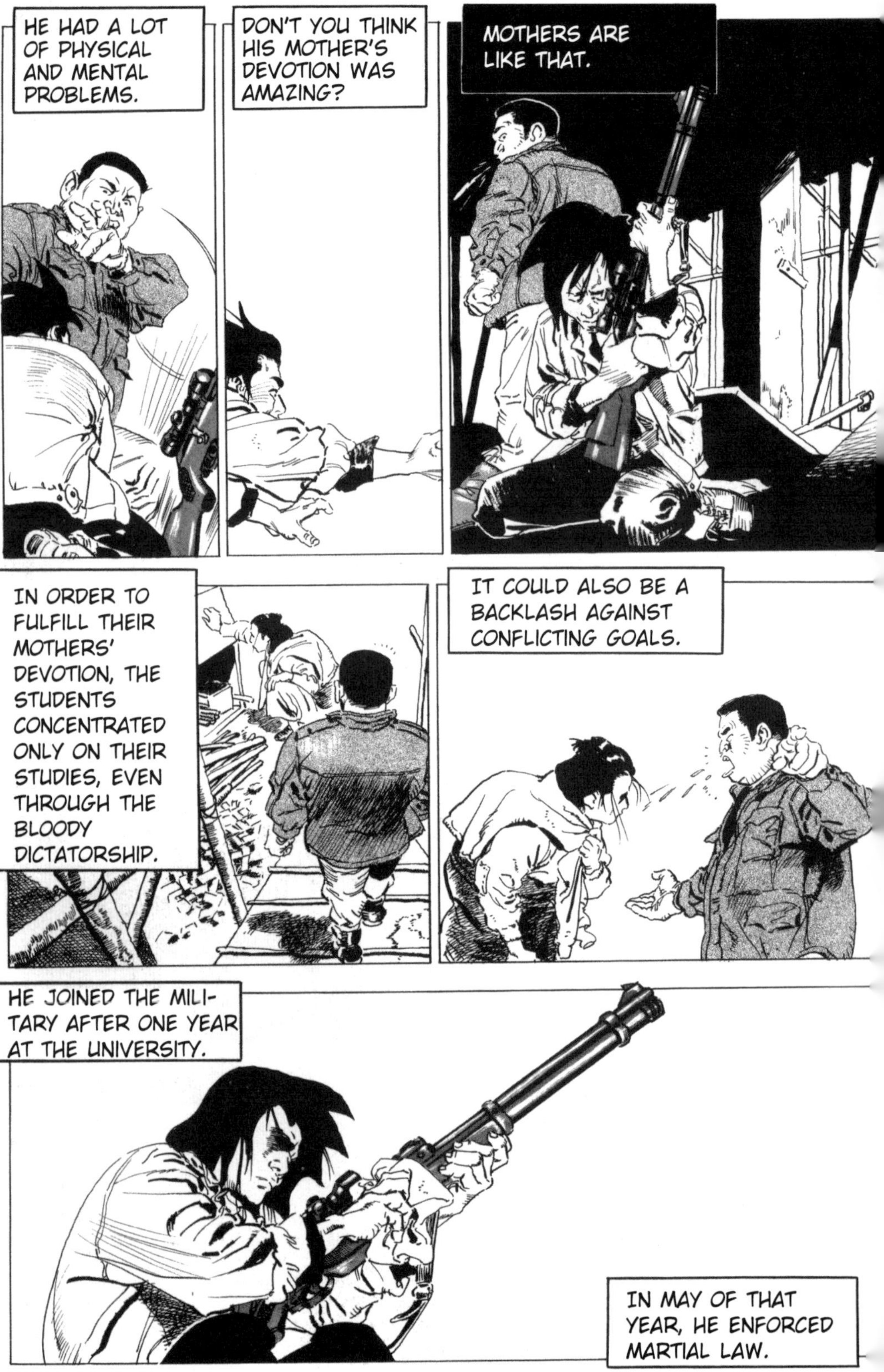
HE HAD A LOT OF PHYSICAL AND MENTAL PROBLEMS.
DON'T YOU THINK HIS MOTHER'S DEVOTION WAS AMAZING?
MOTHERS ARE LIKE THAT.
IN ORDER TO FULFILL THEIR MOTHERS' DEVOTION, THE STUDENTS CONCENTRATED ONLY ON THEIR STUDIES, EVEN THROUGH THE BLOODY DICTATORSHIP.
IT COULD ALSO BE A BACKLASH AGAINST CONFLICTING GOALS.
HE JOINED THE MILITARY AFTER ONE YEAR AT THE UNIVERSITY.
IN MAY OF THAT YEAR, HE ENFORCED MARTIAL LAW.

I ASSUME HE HAD HIS FIRST SHOCK AT THE SCENE OF THE CRIME.

HE WAS JUST RECRUITED, AND COULD STILL MAKE RATIONAL DECISIONS.

THEN HE FACED TERRIBLE FEAR,

BECAUSE OF AN INTOLERABLE CRIMINAL ACT.

AT THAT MOMENT... SOMETHING IMPORTANT HAPPENED.

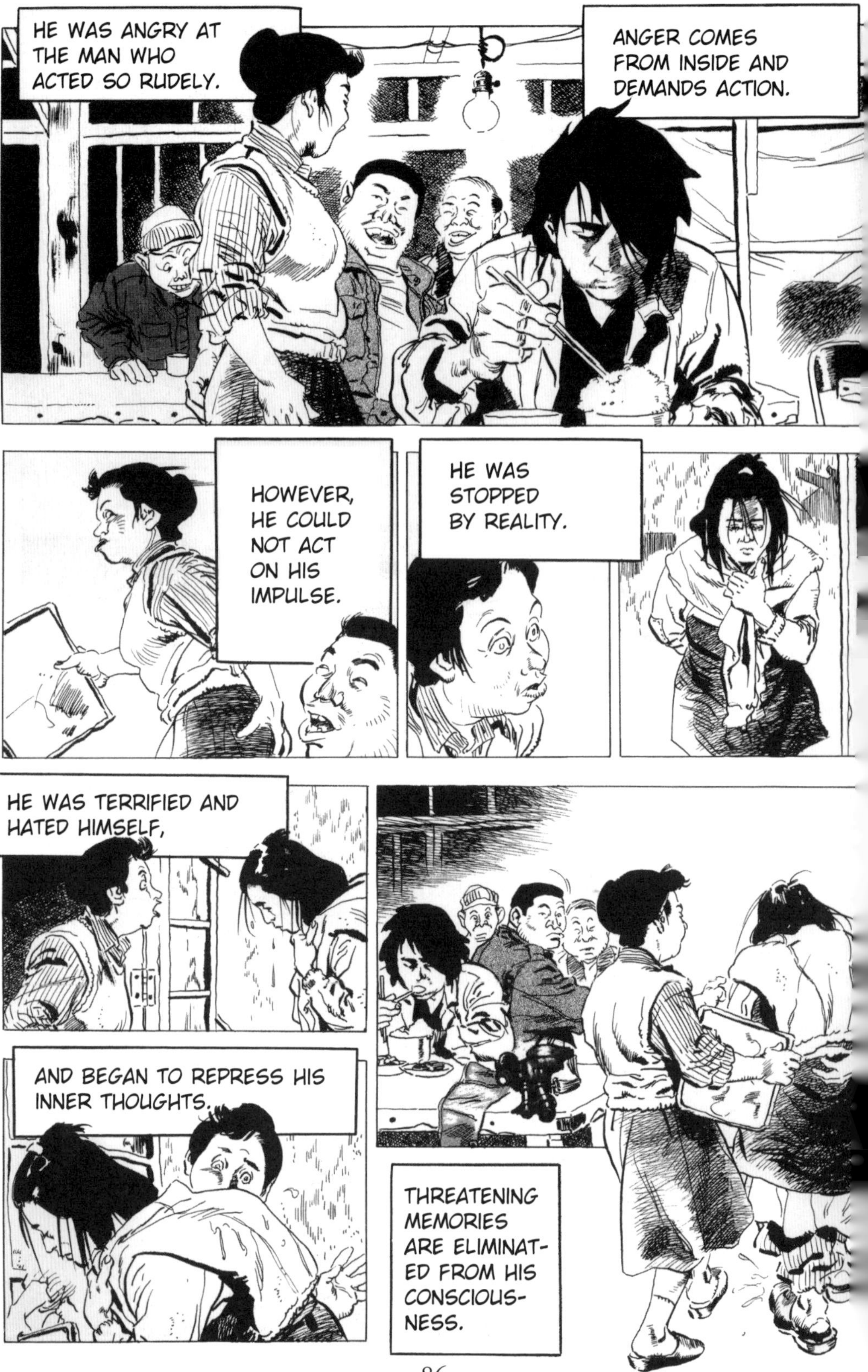
HE WAS ANGRY AT THE MAN WHO ACTED SO RUDELY.
ANGER COMES FROM INSIDE AND DEMANDS ACTION.
HOWEVER, HE COULD NOT ACT ON HIS IMPULSE.
HE WAS STOPPED BY REALITY.
HE WAS TERRIFIED AND HATED HIMSELF,
AND BEGAN TO REPRESS HIS INNER THOUGHTS.
THREATENING MEMORIES ARE ELIMINATED FROM HIS CONSCIOUSNESS.

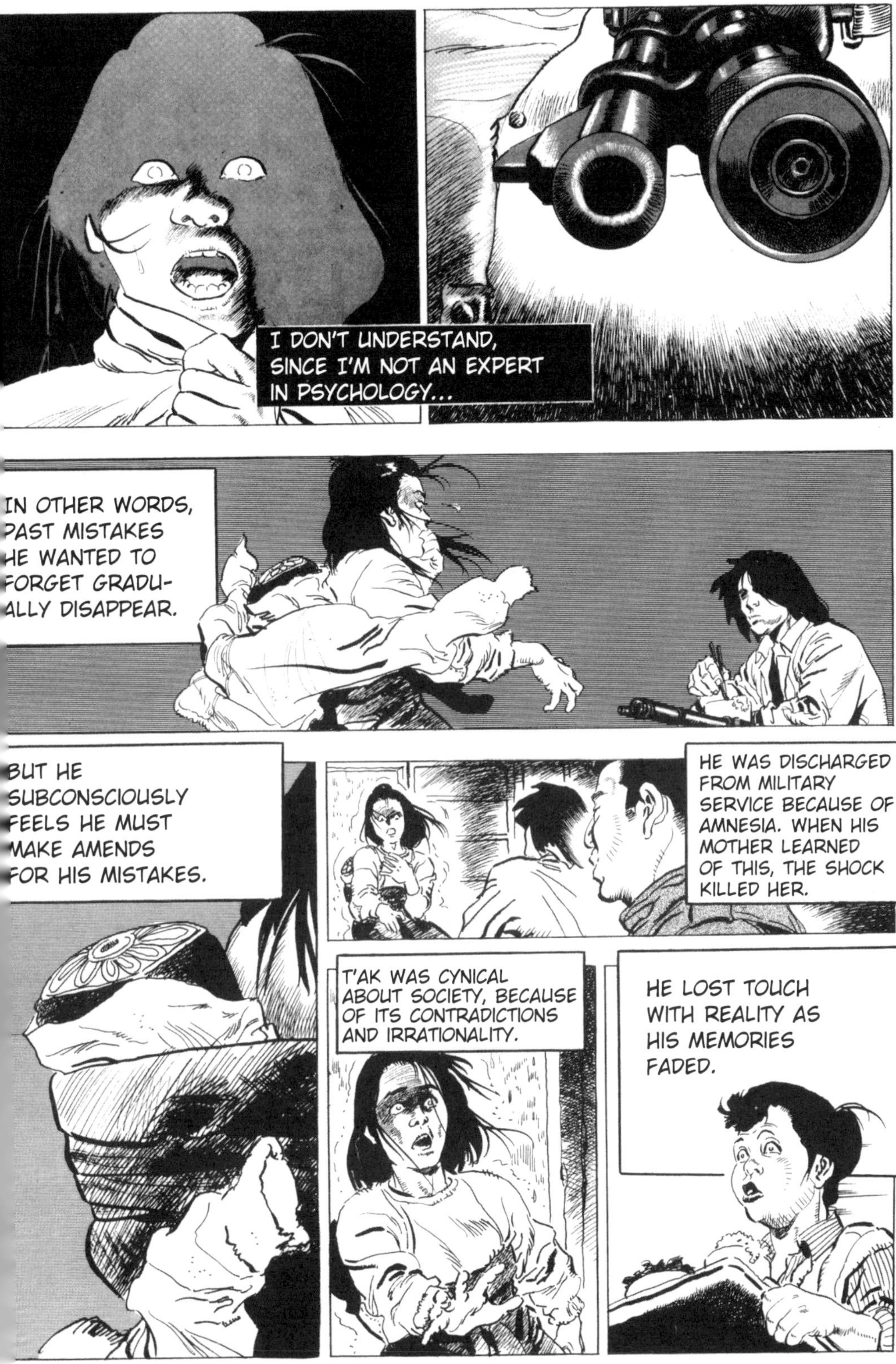
I DON'T UNDERSTAND, SINCE I'M NOT AN EXPERT IN PSYCHOLOGY...
IN OTHER WORDS, PAST MISTAKES HE WANTED TO FORGET GRADU-ALLY DISAPPEAR.
BUT HE SUBCONSCIOUSLY FEELS HE MUST MAKE AMENDS FOR HIS MISTAKES.
HE WAS DISCHARGED FROM MILITARY SERVICE BECAUSE OF AMNESIA. WHEN HIS MOTHER LEARNED OF THIS, THE SHOCK KILLED HER.
T'AK WAS CYNICAL ABOUT SOCIETY, BECAUSE OF ITS CONTRADICTIONS AND IRRATIONALITY.
HE LOST TOUCH WITH REALITY AS HIS MEMORIES FADED.

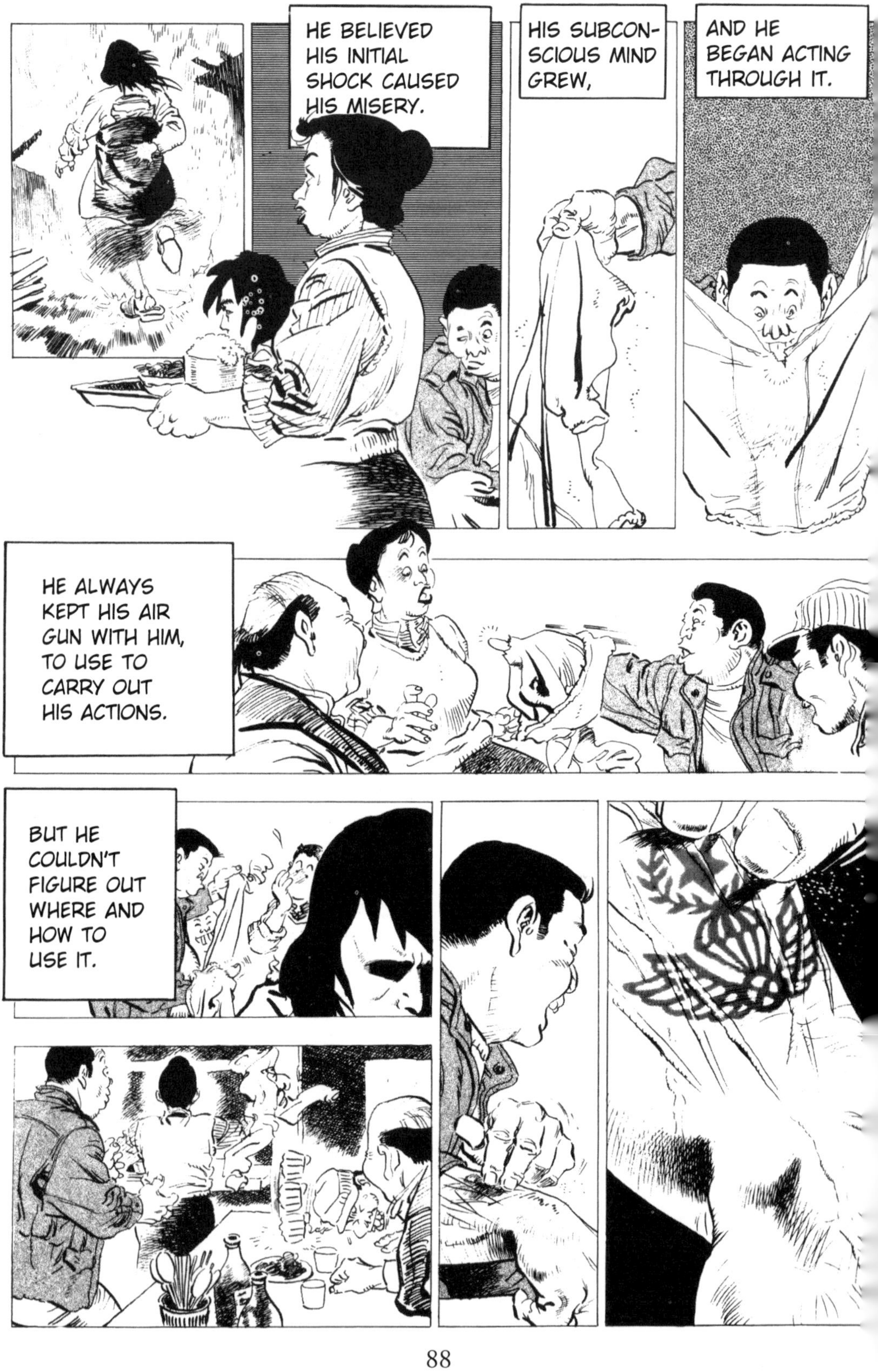
HE BELIEVED HIS INITIAL SHOCK CAUSED HIS MISERY.
HIS SUBCONSCIOUS MIND GREW,
AND HE BEGAN ACTING THROUGH IT.
HE ALWAYS KEPT HIS AIR GUN WITH HIM, TO USE TO CARRY OUT HIS ACTIONS.
BUT HE COULDN'T FIGURE OUT WHERE AND HOW TO USE IT.

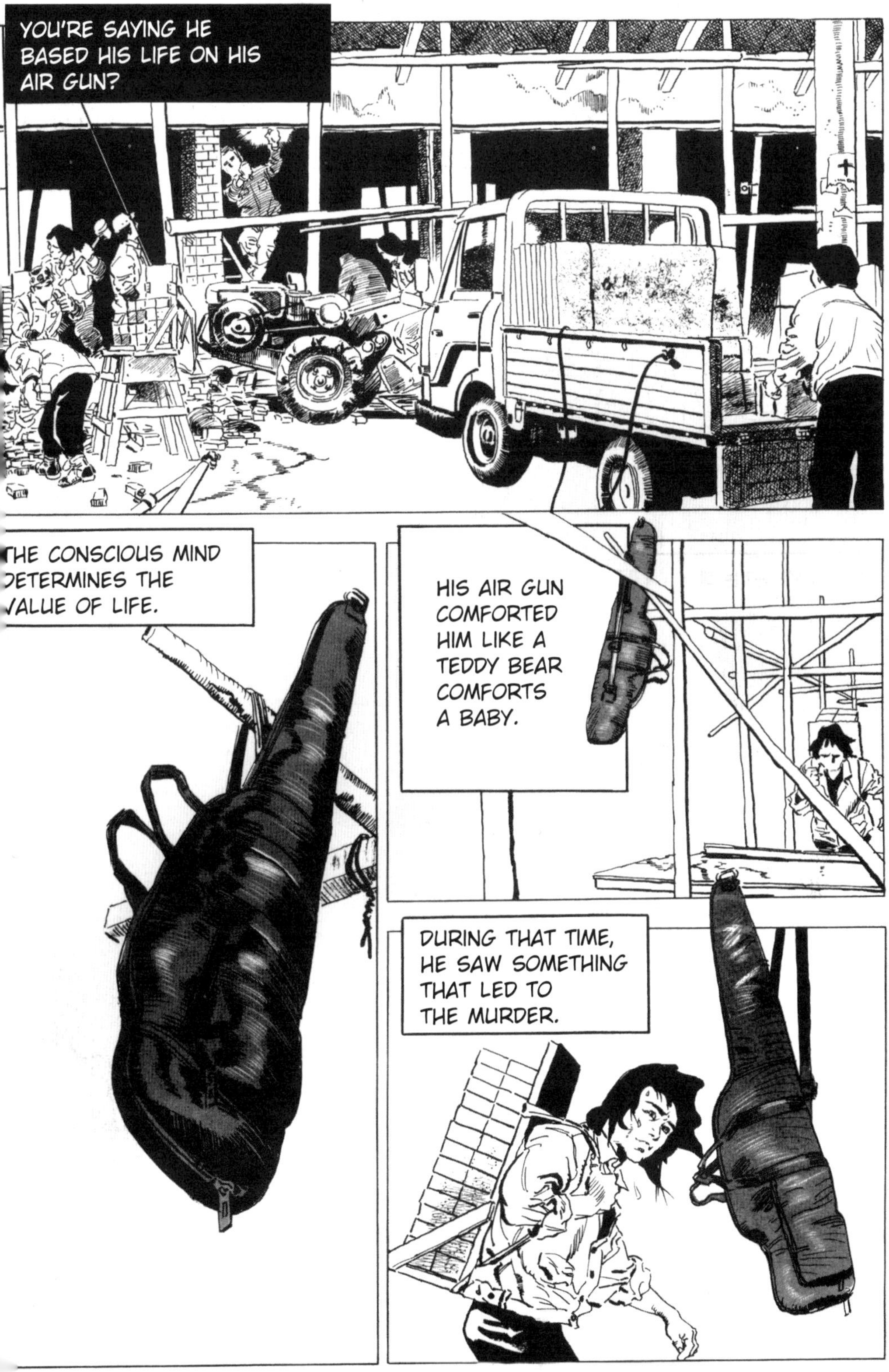
YOU'RE SAYING HE BASED HIS LIFE ON HIS AIR GUN?
THE CONSCIOUS MIND DETERMINES THE VALUE OF LIFE.
HIS AIR GUN COMFORTED HIM LIKE A TEDDY BEAR COMFORTS A BABY.
DURING THAT TIME, HE SAW SOMETHING THAT LED TO THE MURDER.

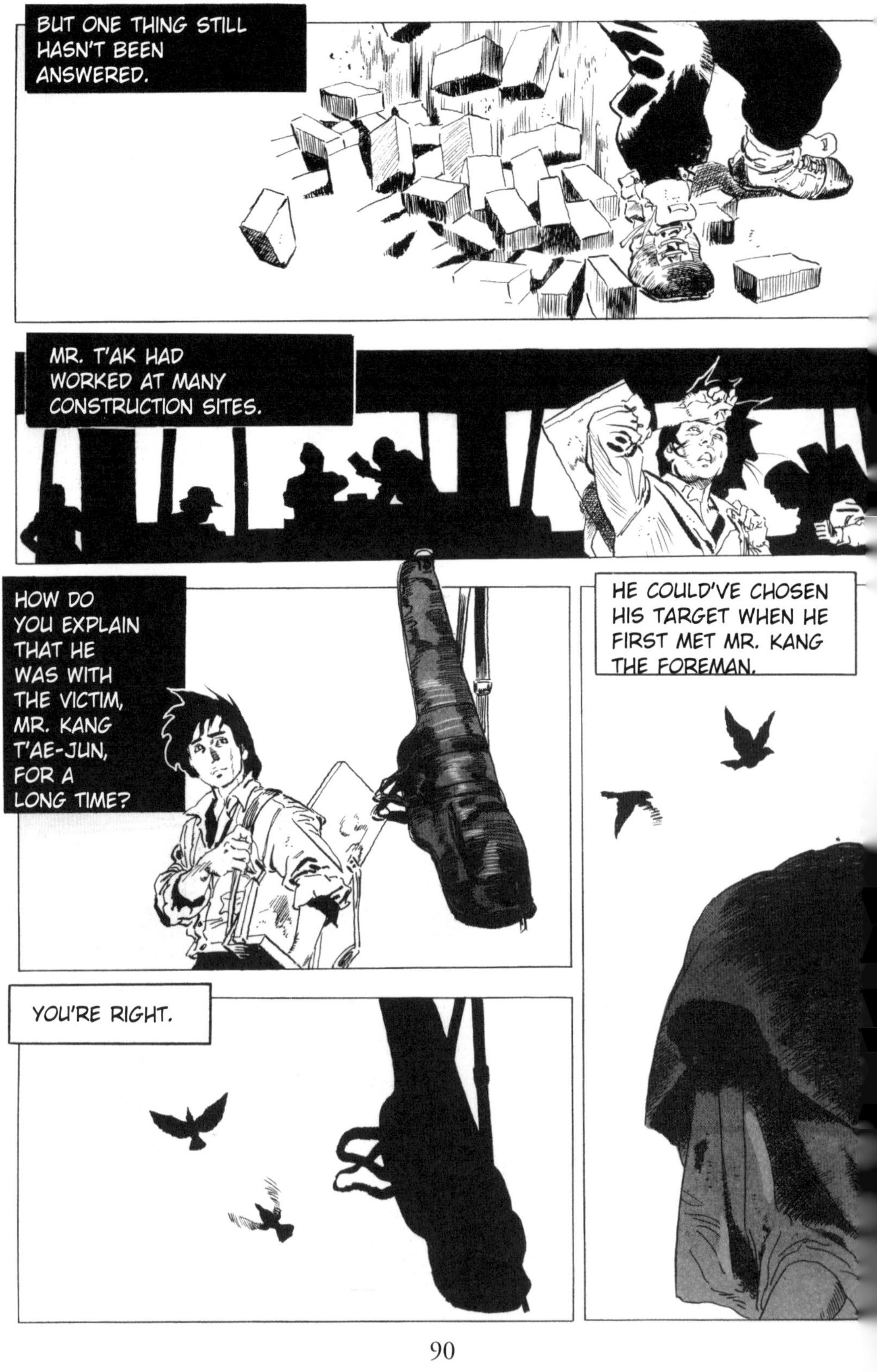
BUT ONE THING STILL HASN'T BEEN ANSWERED.
MR. T'AK HAD WORKED AT MANY CONSTRUCTION SITES.
HOW DO YOU EXPLAIN THAT HE WAS WITH THE VICTIM, MR. KANG T'AE-JUN, FOR A LONG TIME?
HE COULD'VE CHOSEN HIS TARGET WHEN HE FIRST MET MR. KANG THE FOREMAN.
YOU'RE RIGHT.

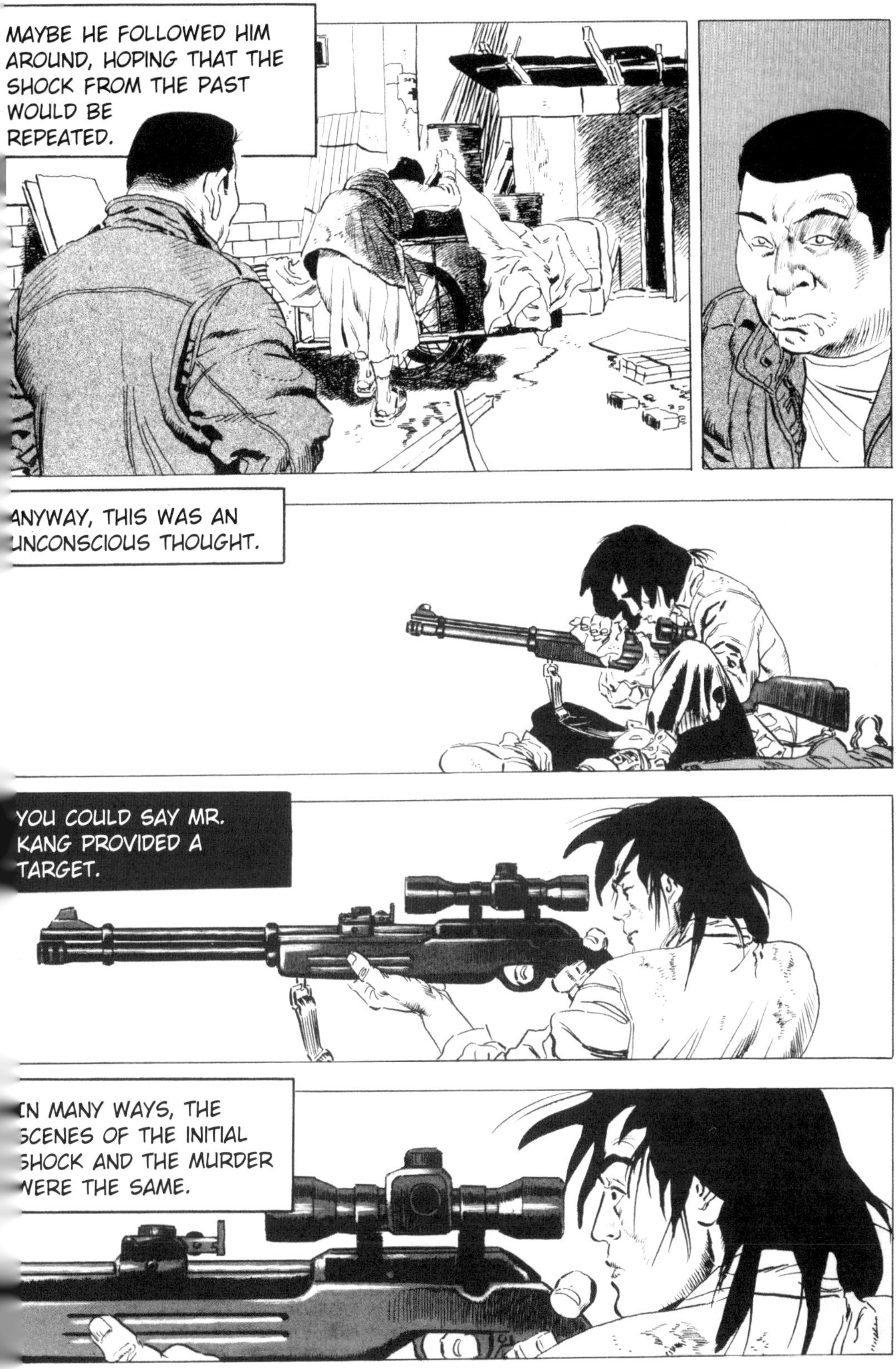
MAYBE HE FOLLOWED HIM AROUND, HOPING THAT THE SHOCK FROM THE PAST WOULD BE REPEATED.
ANYWAY, THIS WAS AN UNCONSCIOUS THOUGHT.
YOU COULD SAY MR. KANG PROVIDED A TARGET.
IN MANY WAYS, THE SCENES OF THE INITIAL SHOCK AND THE MURDER WERE THE SAME.

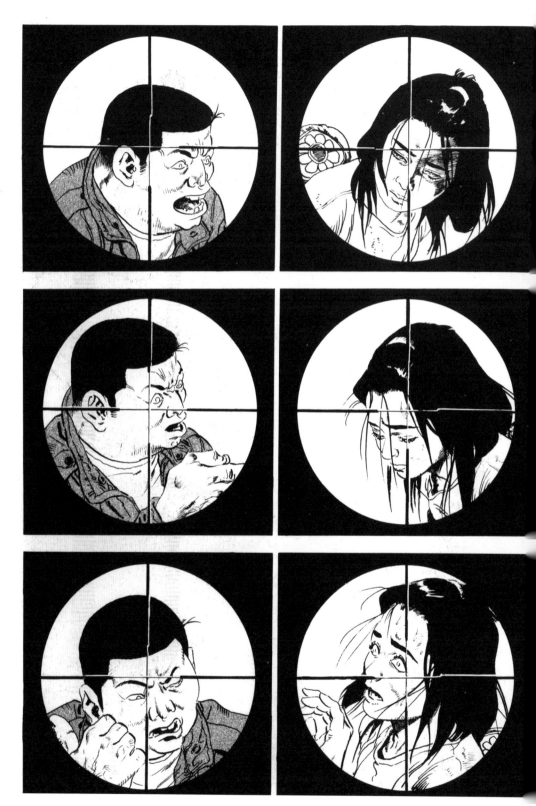

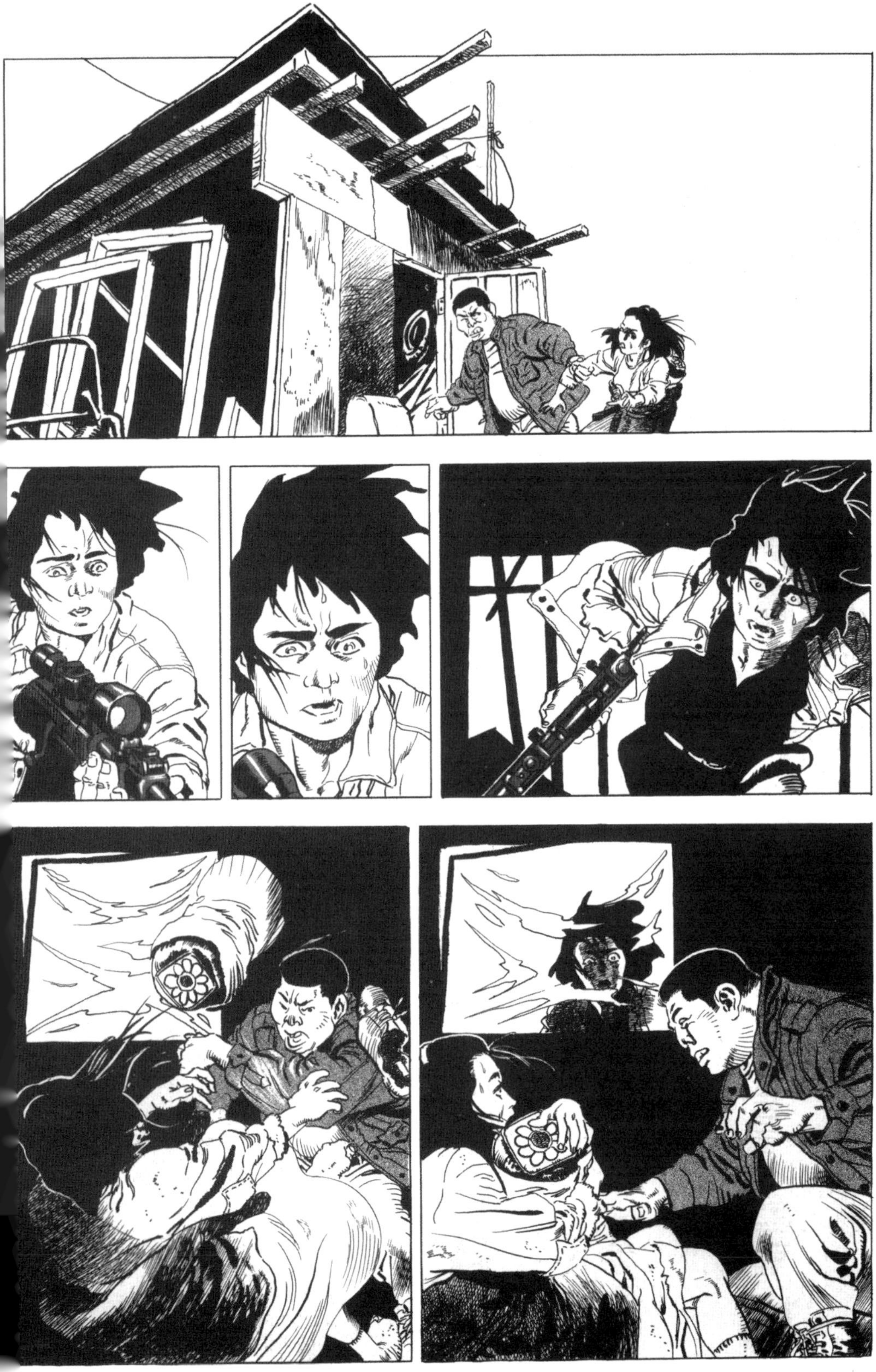

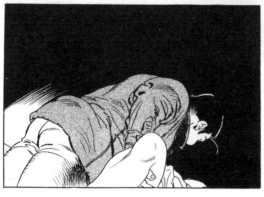 

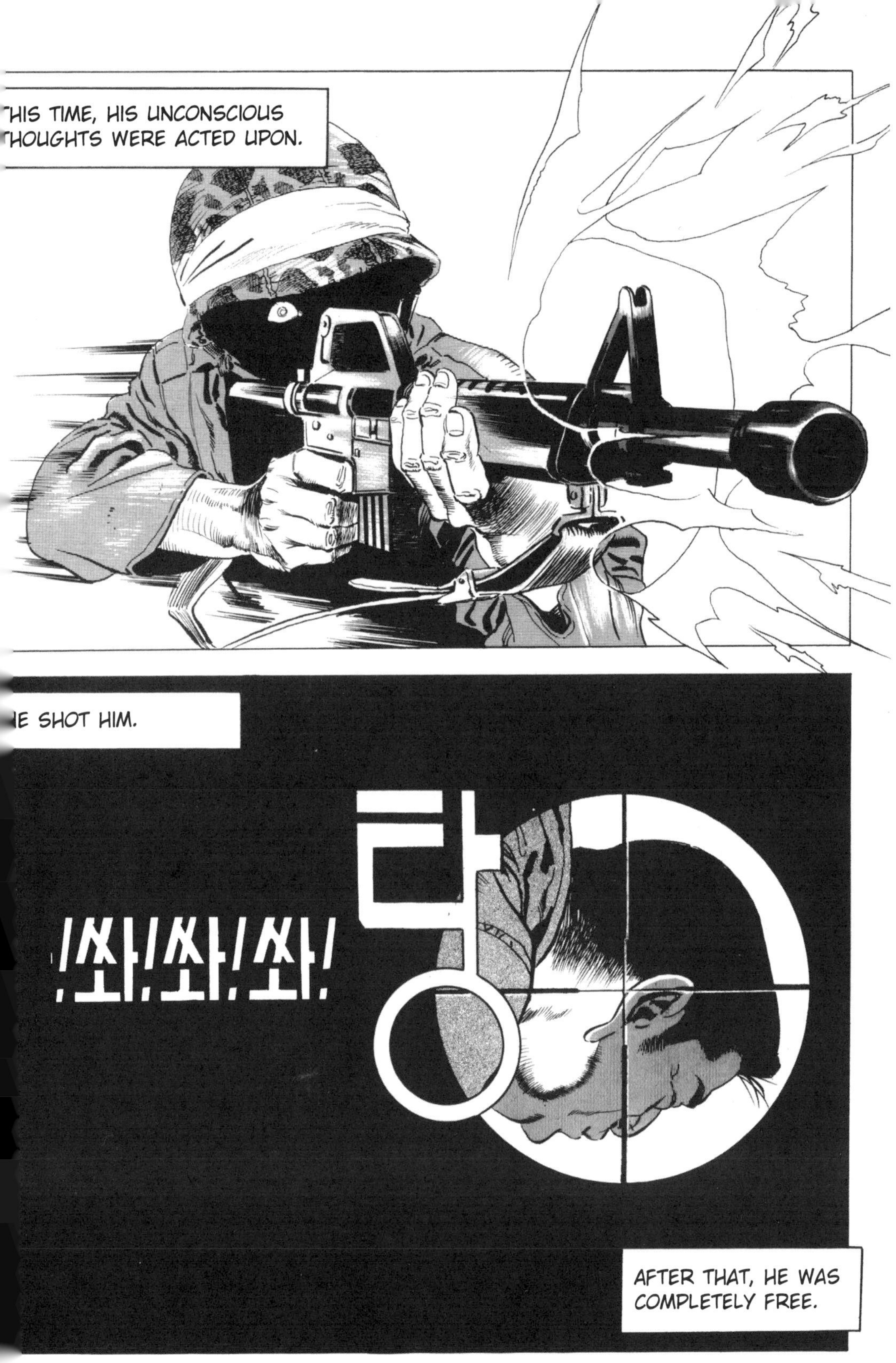
THIS TIME, HIS UNCONSCIOUS THOUGHTS WERE ACTED UPON.
HE SHOT HIM.
!쏴!쏴!쏴!
탕
AFTER THAT, HE WAS COMPLETELY FREE.

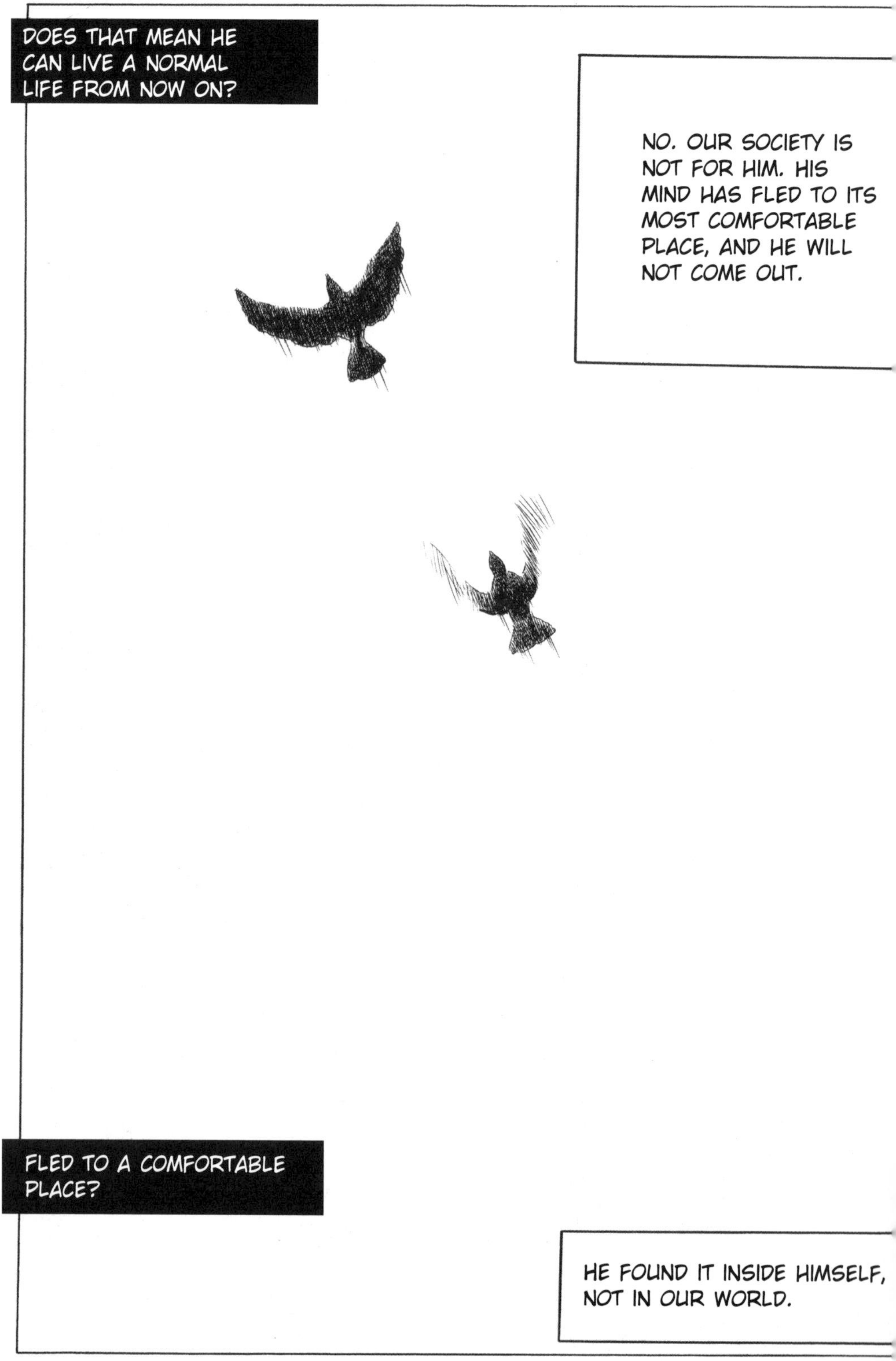
DOES THAT MEAN HE CAN LIVE A NORMAL LIFE FROM NOW ON?
NO. OUR SOCIETY IS NOT FOR HIM. HIS MIND HAS FLED TO ITS MOST COMFORTABLE PLACE, AND HE WILL NOT COME OUT.
FLED TO A COMFORTABLE PLACE?
HE FOUND IT INSIDE HIMSELF, NOT IN OUR WORLD.

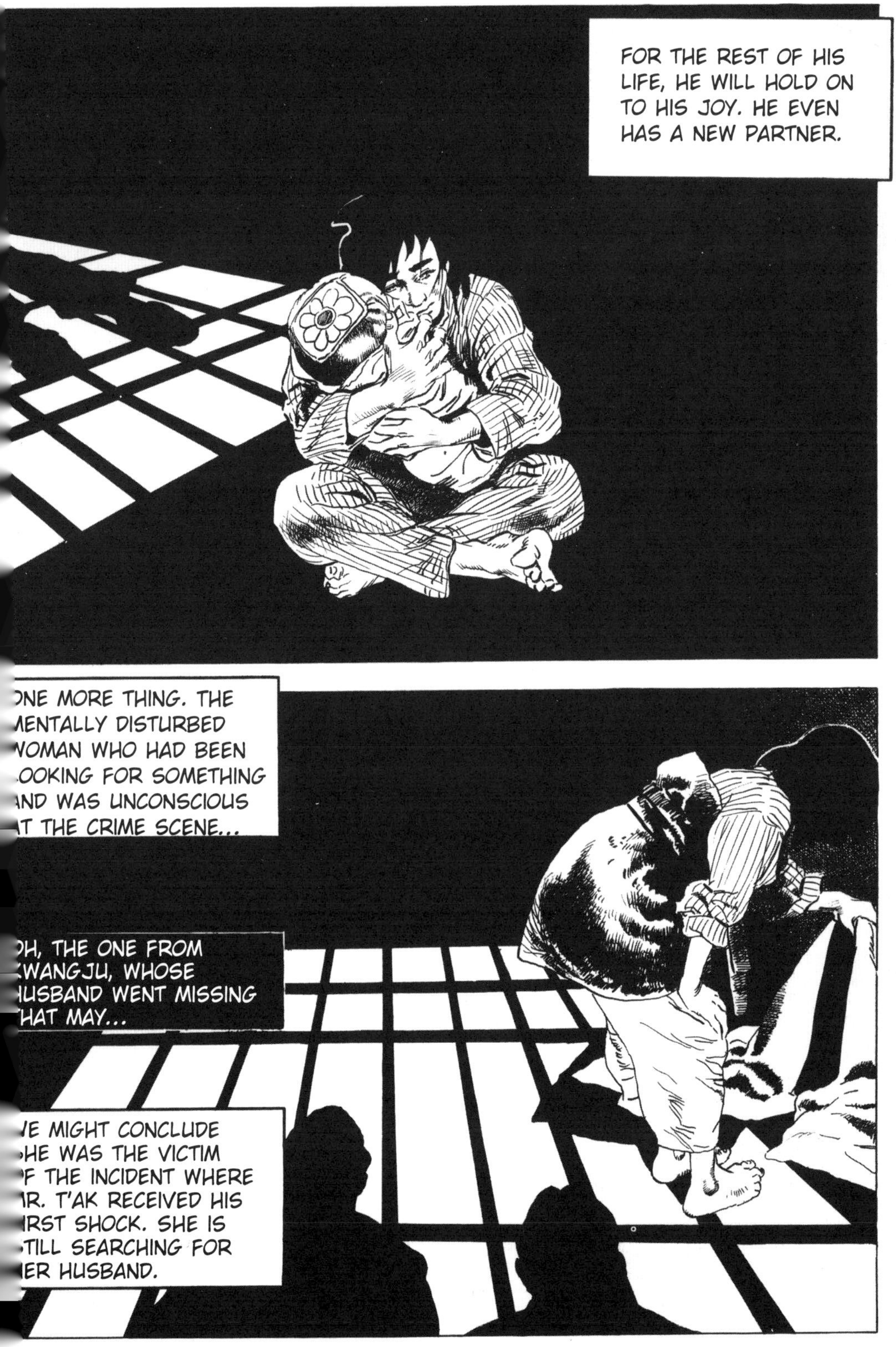
FOR THE REST OF HIS LIFE, HE WILL HOLD ON TO HIS JOY. HE EVEN HAS A NEW PARTNER.
ONE MORE THING. THE MENTALLY DISTURBED WOMAN WHO HAD BEEN LOOKING FOR SOMETHING AND WAS UNCONSCIOUS AT THE CRIME SCENE...
OH, THE ONE FROM KWANGJU, WHOSE HUSBAND WENT MISSING THAT MAY...
WE MIGHT CONCLUDE SHE WAS THE VICTIM OF THE INCIDENT WHERE MR. T'AK RECEIVED HIS FIRST SHOCK. SHE IS STILL SEARCHING FOR HER HUSBAND.

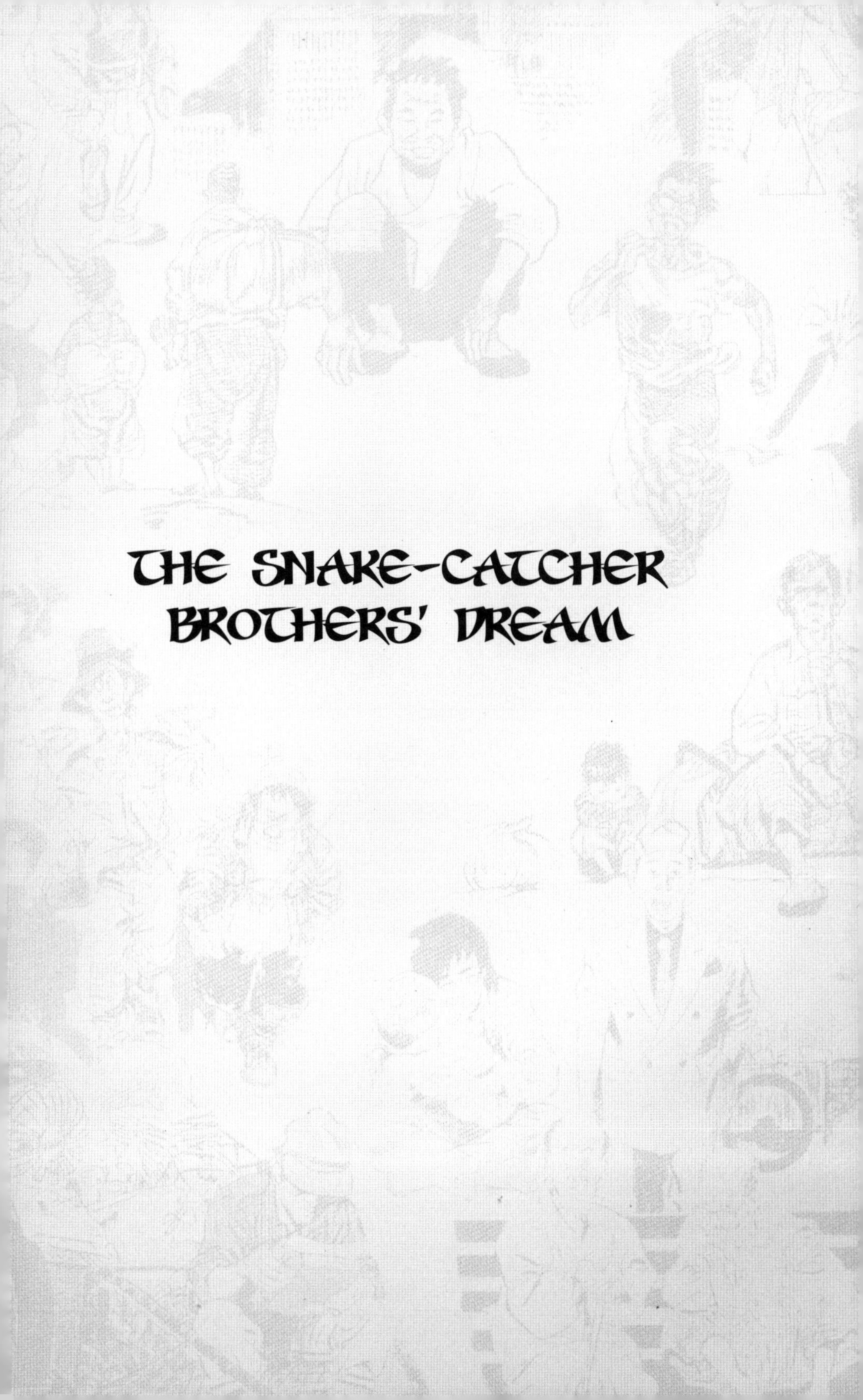

THE SNAKE-CATCHER BROTHERS' DREAM

SEYEONG O
OCTOBER 1989

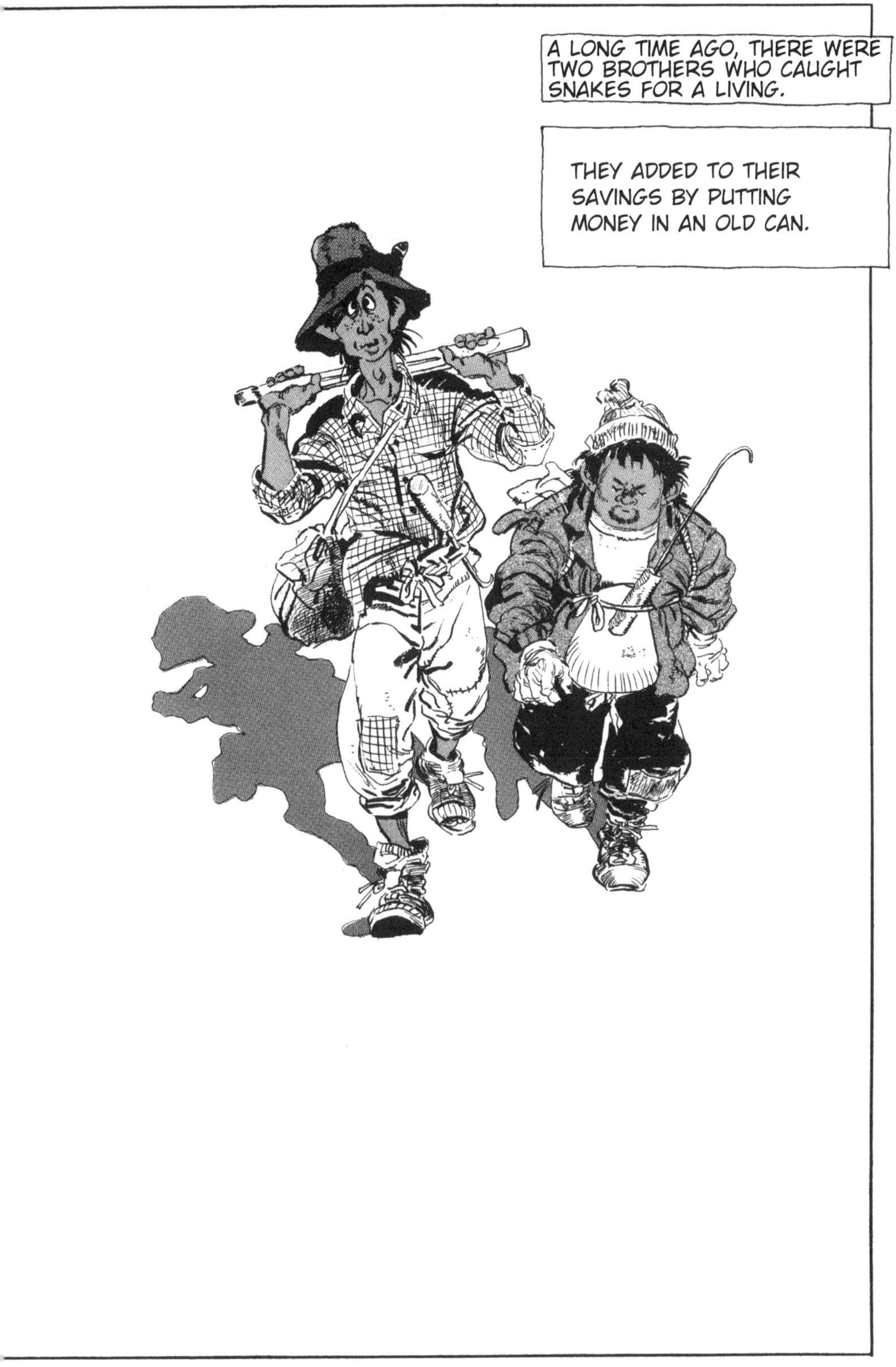
A LONG TIME AGO, THERE WERE TWO BROTHERS WHO CAUGHT SNAKES FOR A LIVING.
THEY ADDED TO THEIR SAVINGS BY PUTTING MONEY IN AN OLD CAN.

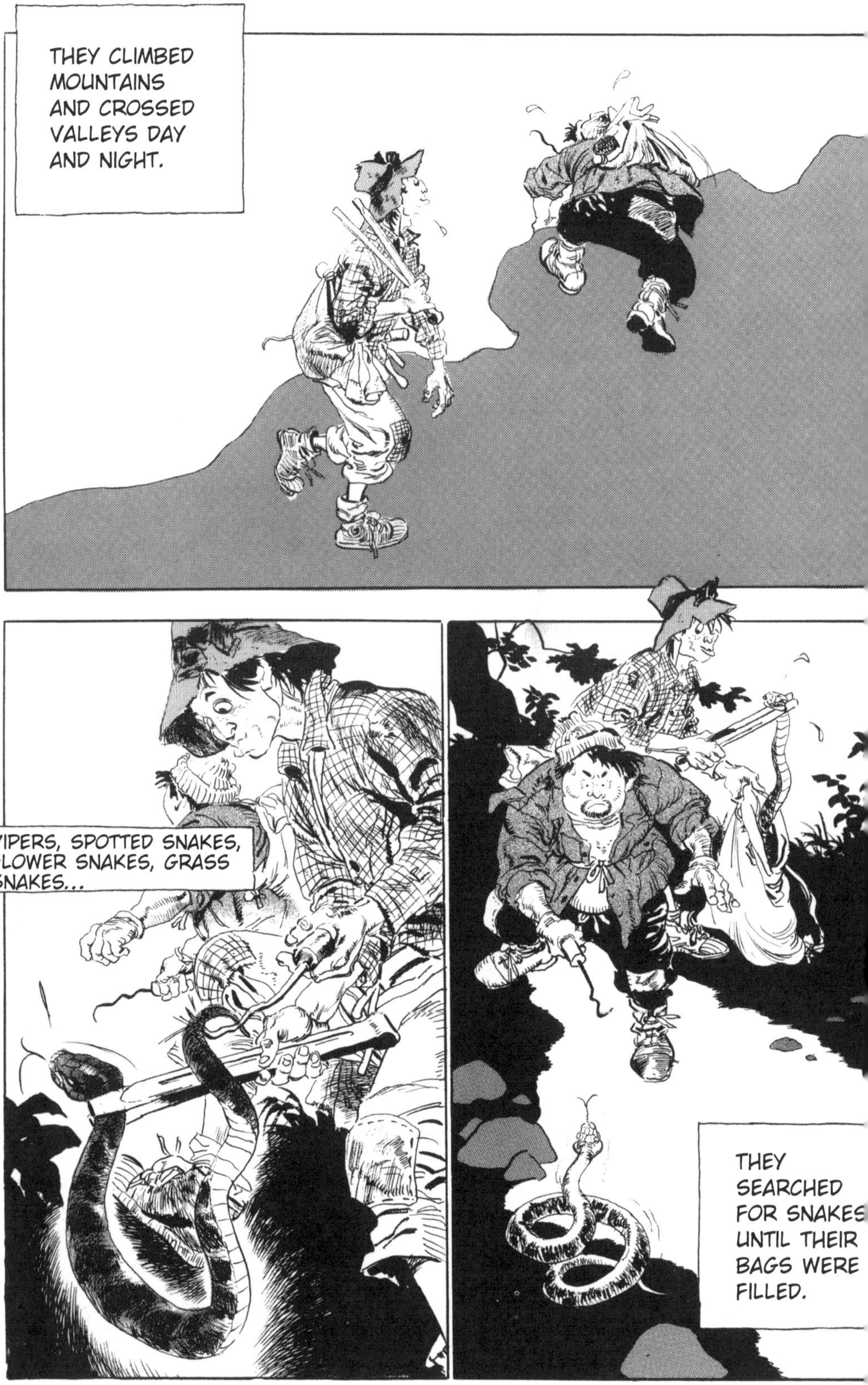
THEY CLIMBED MOUNTAINS AND CROSSED VALLEYS DAY AND NIGHT.
VIPERS, SPOTTED SNAKES, FLOWER SNAKES, GRASS SNAKES...
THEY SEARCHED FOR SNAKES UNTIL THEIR BAGS WERE FILLED.

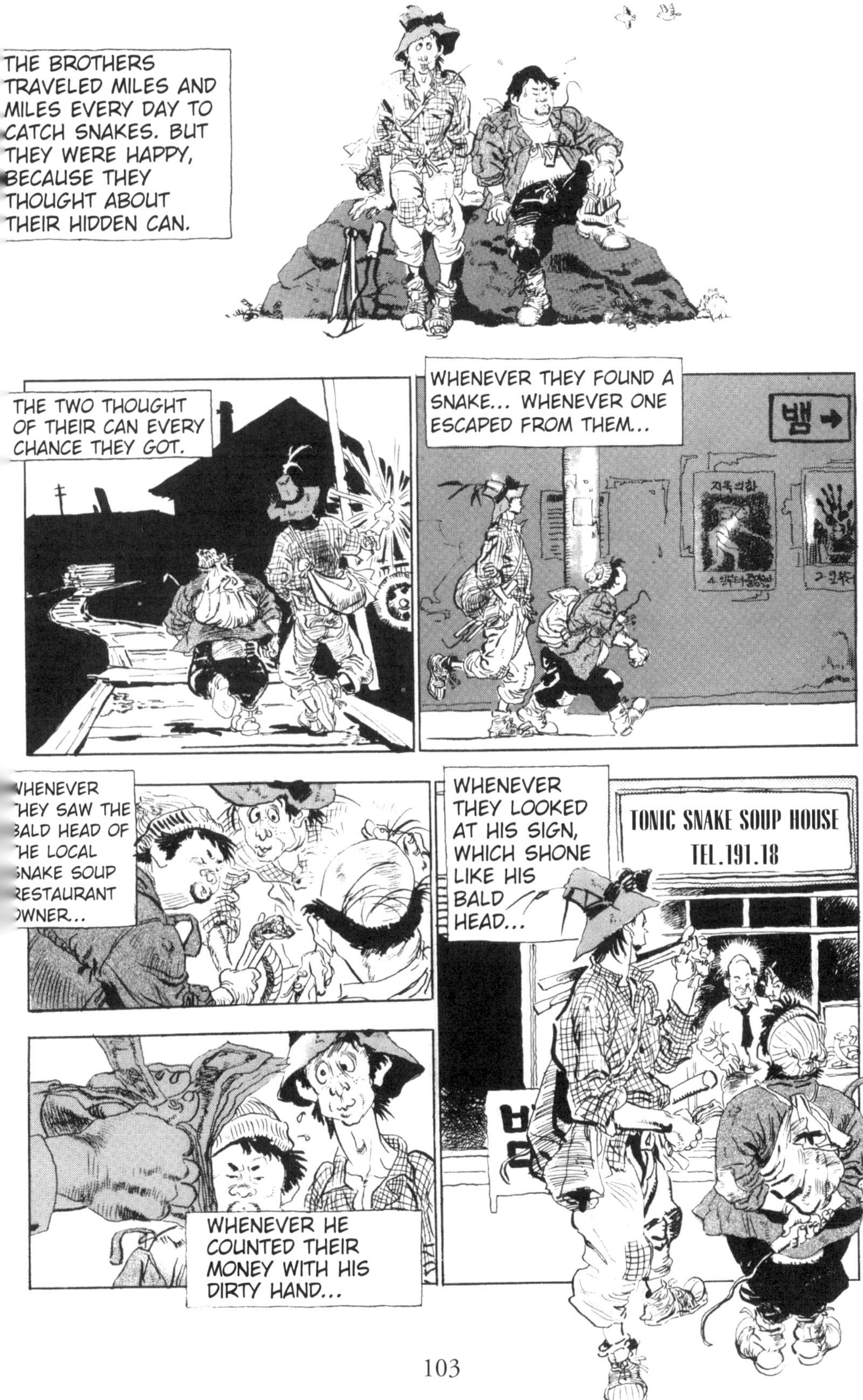
THE BROTHERS TRAVELED MILES AND MILES EVERY DAY TO CATCH SNAKES. BUT THEY WERE HAPPY, BECAUSE THEY THOUGHT ABOUT THEIR HIDDEN CAN.
THE TWO THOUGHT OF THEIR CAN EVERY CHANCE THEY GOT.
WHENEVER THEY FOUND A SNAKE... WHENEVER ONE ESCAPED FROM THEM...
뱀 →
WHENEVER THEY SAW THE BALD HEAD OF THE LOCAL SNAKE SOUP RESTAURANT OWNER...
WHENEVER THEY LOOKED AT HIS SIGN, WHICH SHONE LIKE HIS BALD HEAD...
TONIC SNAKE SOUP HOUSE
TEL.191.18
WHENEVER HE COUNTED THEIR MONEY WITH HIS DIRTY HAND...

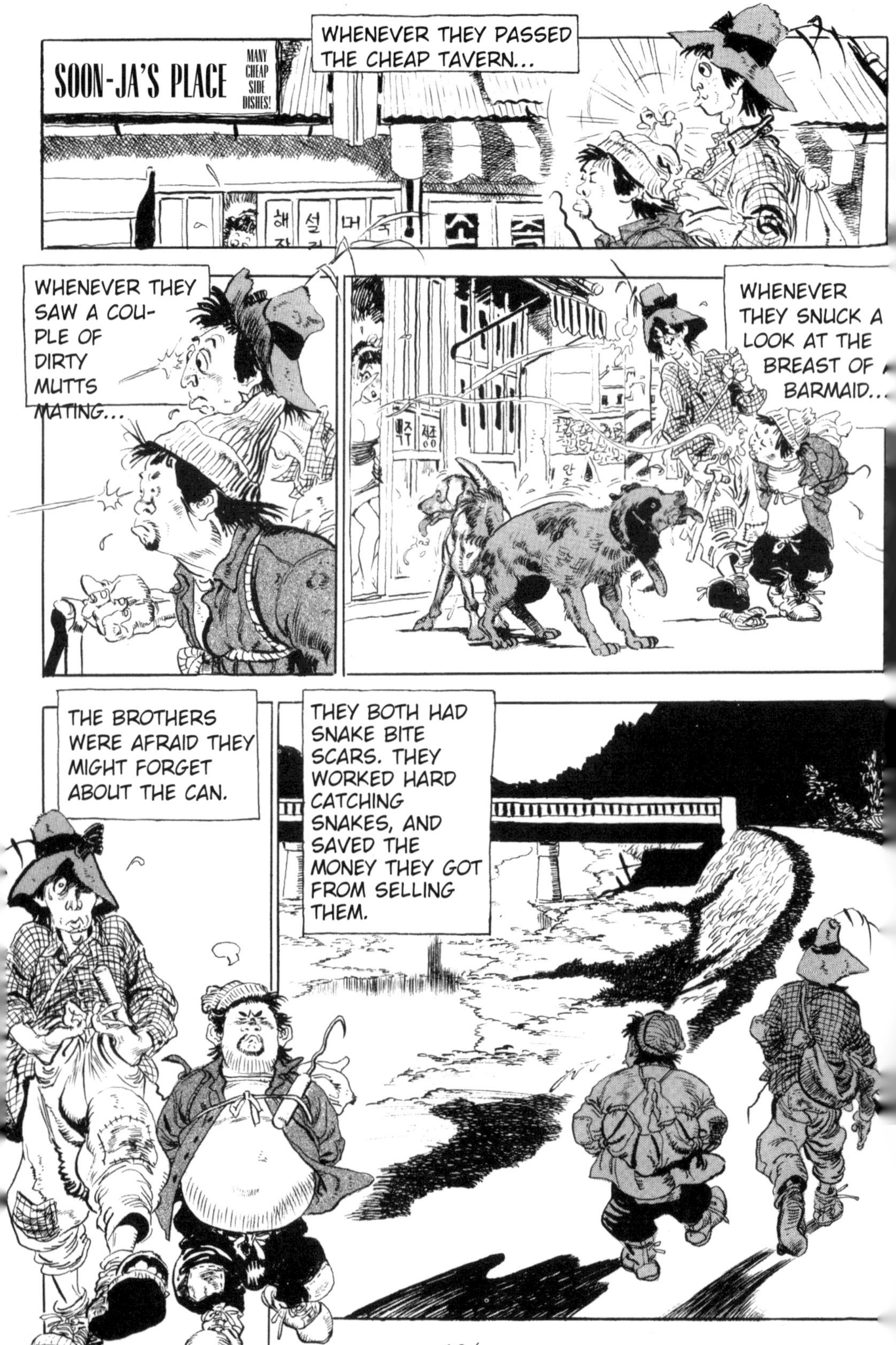
SOON-JA'S PLACE
MANY CHEAP SIDE DISHES!
WHENEVER THEY PASSED THE CHEAP TAVERN...
WHENEVER THEY SAW A COUPLE OF DIRTY MUTTS MATING...
WHENEVER THEY SNUCK A LOOK AT THE BREAST OF A BARMAID...
THE BROTHERS WERE AFRAID THEY MIGHT FORGET ABOUT THE CAN.
THEY BOTH HAD SNAKE BITE SCARS. THEY WORKED HARD CATCHING SNAKES, AND SAVED THE MONEY THEY GOT FROM SELLING THEM.

ALL OF THAT MONEY...

WAS FED TO THE OLD, BLACKENED CAN.

THE BROTHERS ALWAYS THOUGHT OF THAT CAN.

THEY BROUGHT IT OUT EVERY DAY TO COUNT THEIR SAVINGS AND EXAMINE IT FOR DENTS.

AFTER EVERYTHING CHECKED OUT, THEY WOULD IMAGINE A SHOP SIGN OF THEIR OWN.

ON THE SIGN WOULD BE WRITTEN TWO BROTHERS SNAKE SOUP RESTAURANT.

THAT OLD CAN WAS THE ONE AND ONLY HOPE THEY HAD TO ACHIEVE THOSE DREAMS.

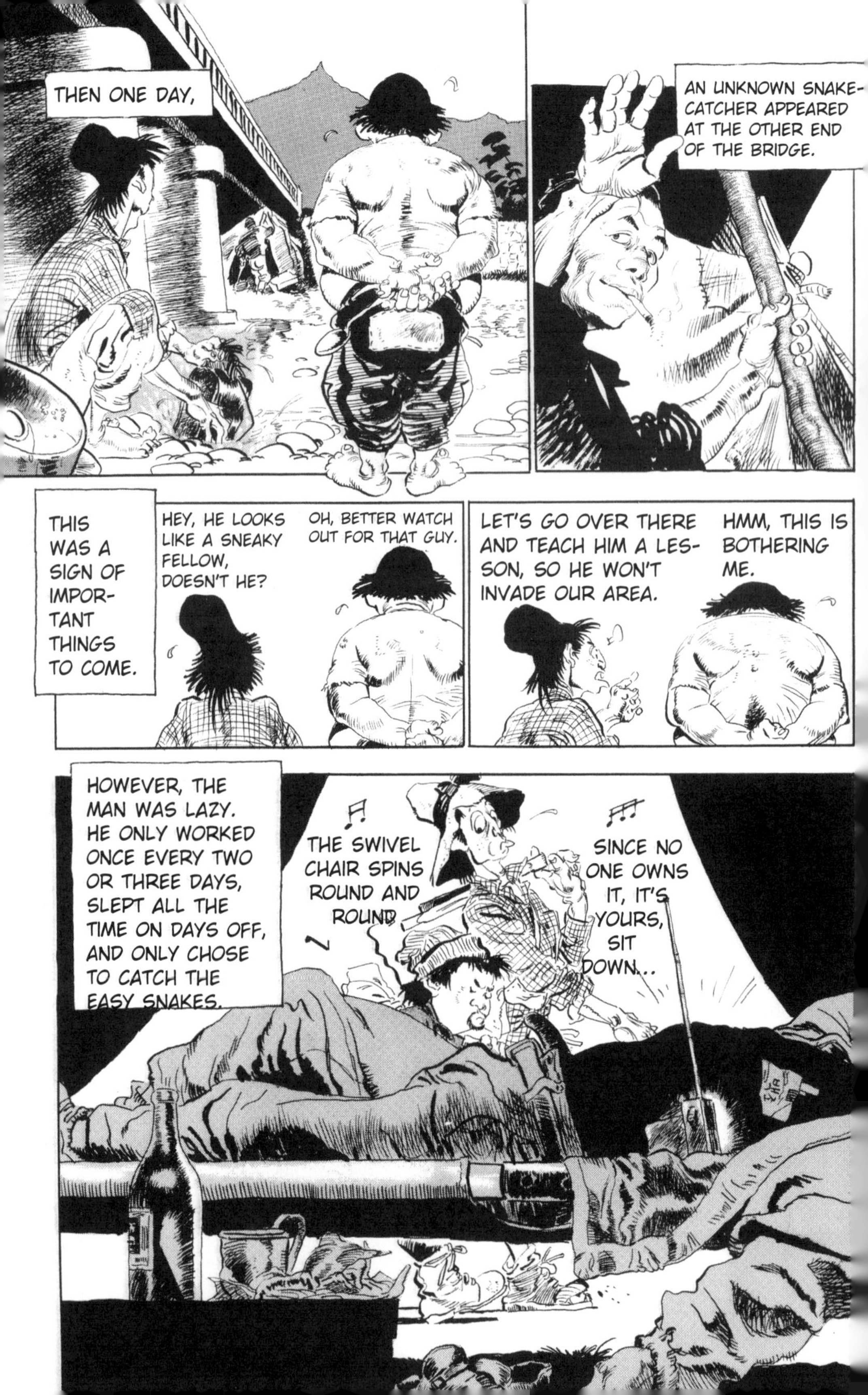
THEN ONE DAY,
AN UNKNOWN SNAKE-CATCHER APPEARED AT THE OTHER END OF THE BRIDGE.
THIS WAS A SIGN OF IMPORTANT THINGS TO COME.
HEY, HE LOOKS LIKE A SNEAKY FELLOW, DOESN'T HE?
OH, BETTER WATCH OUT FOR THAT GUY.
LET'S GO OVER THERE AND TEACH HIM A LESSON, SO HE WON'T INVADE OUR AREA.
HMM, THIS IS BOTHERING ME.
HOWEVER, THE MAN WAS LAZY. HE ONLY WORKED ONCE EVERY TWO OR THREE DAYS, SLEPT ALL THE TIME ON DAYS OFF, AND ONLY CHOSE TO CATCH THE EASY SNAKES.
THE SWIVEL CHAIR SPINS ROUND AND ROUND
SINCE NO ONE OWNS IT, IT'S YOURS, SIT DOWN...

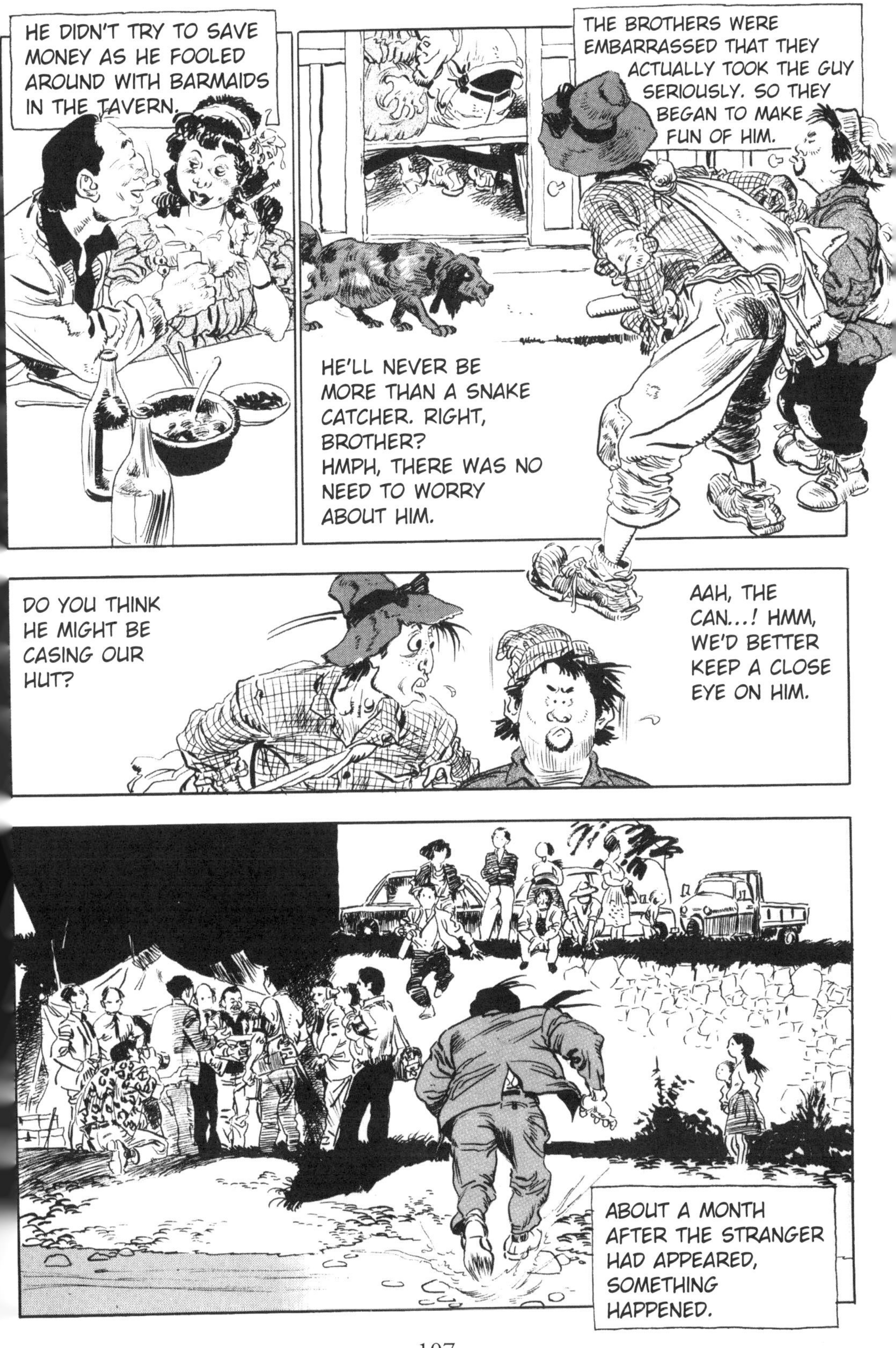
HE DIDN'T TRY TO SAVE MONEY AS HE FOOLED AROUND WITH BARMAIDS IN THE TAVERN.
THE BROTHERS WERE EMBARRASSED THAT THEY ACTUALLY TOOK THE GUY SERIOUSLY. SO THEY BEGAN TO MAKE FUN OF HIM.
HE'LL NEVER BE MORE THAN A SNAKE CATCHER. RIGHT, BROTHER?
HMPH, THERE WAS NO NEED TO WORRY ABOUT HIM.
DO YOU THINK HE MIGHT BE CASING OUR HUT?
AAH, THE CAN...! HMM, WE'D BETTER KEEP A CLOSE EYE ON HIM.
ABOUT A MONTH AFTER THE STRANGER HAD APPEARED, SOMETHING HAPPENED.

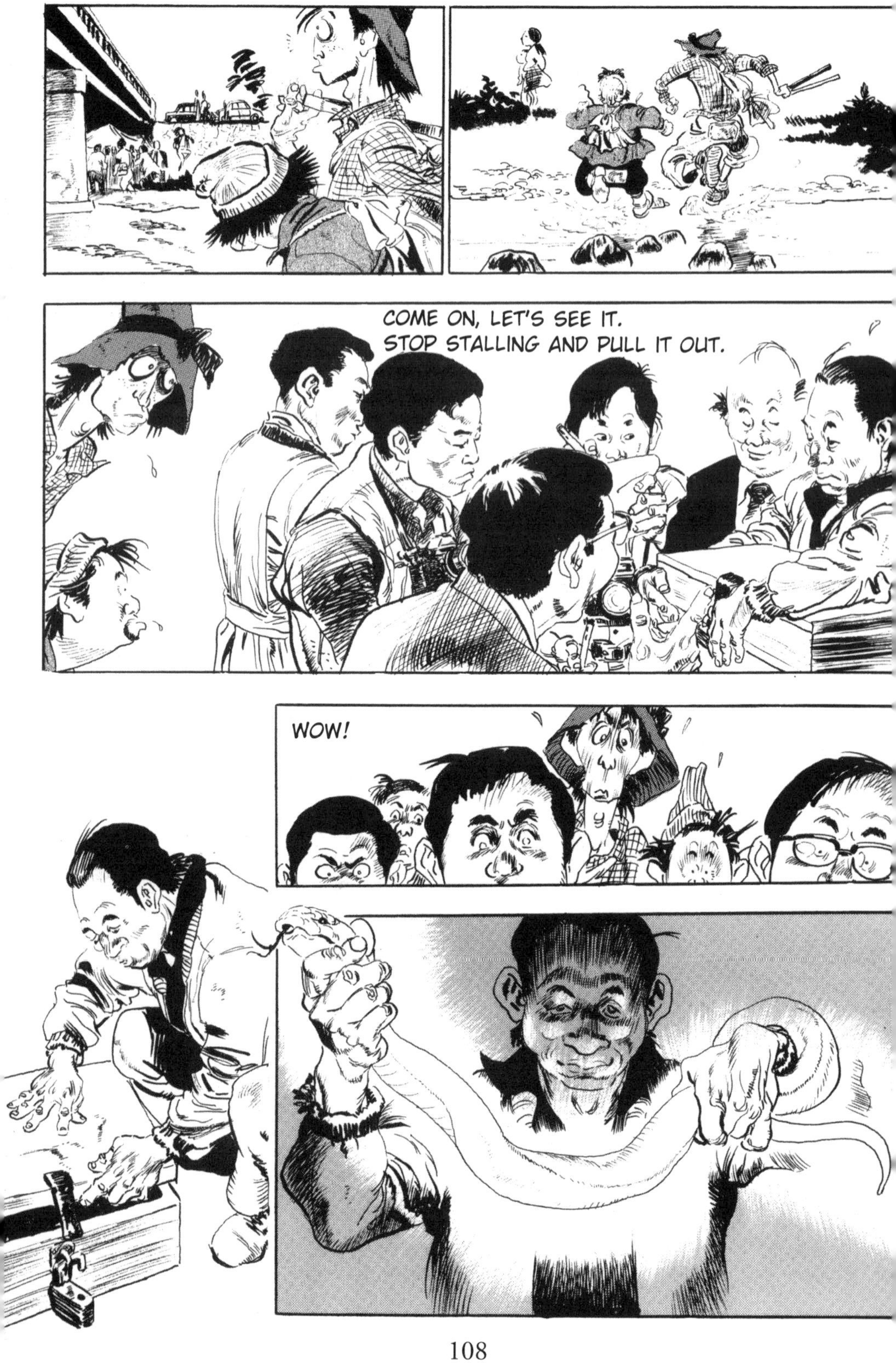

COME ON, LET'S SEE IT.
STOP STALLING AND PULL IT OUT.
WOW!

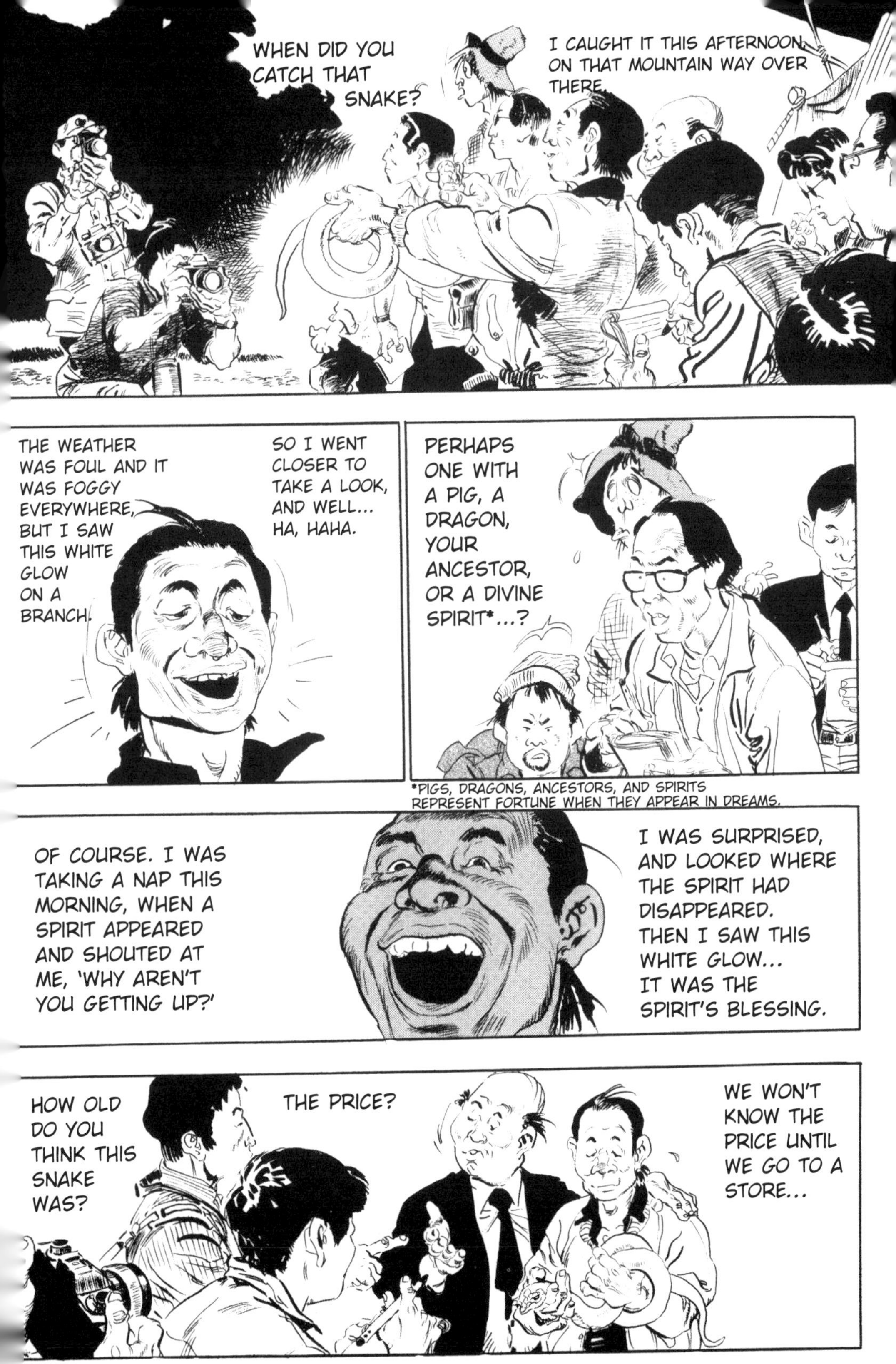
WHEN DID YOU CATCH THAT SNAKE?
I CAUGHT IT THIS AFTERNOON ON THAT MOUNTAIN WAY OVER THERE.
THE WEATHER WAS FOUL AND IT WAS FOGGY EVERYWHERE, BUT I SAW THIS WHITE GLOW ON A BRANCH.
SO I WENT CLOSER TO TAKE A LOOK, AND WELL... HA, HAHA.
PERHAPS ONE WITH A PIG, A DRAGON, YOUR ANCESTOR, OR A DIVINE SPIRIT*...?
*PIGS, DRAGONS, ANCESTORS, AND SPIRITS REPRESENT FORTUNE WHEN THEY APPEAR IN DREAMS.
OF COURSE. I WAS TAKING A NAP THIS MORNING, WHEN A SPIRIT APPEARED AND SHOUTED AT ME, 'WHY AREN'T YOU GETTING UP?'
I WAS SURPRISED, AND LOOKED WHERE THE SPIRIT HAD DISAPPEARED. THEN I SAW THIS WHITE GLOW... IT WAS THE SPIRIT'S BLESSING.
HOW OLD DO YOU THINK THIS SNAKE WAS?
THE PRICE?
WE WON'T KNOW THE PRICE UNTIL WE GO TO A STORE...

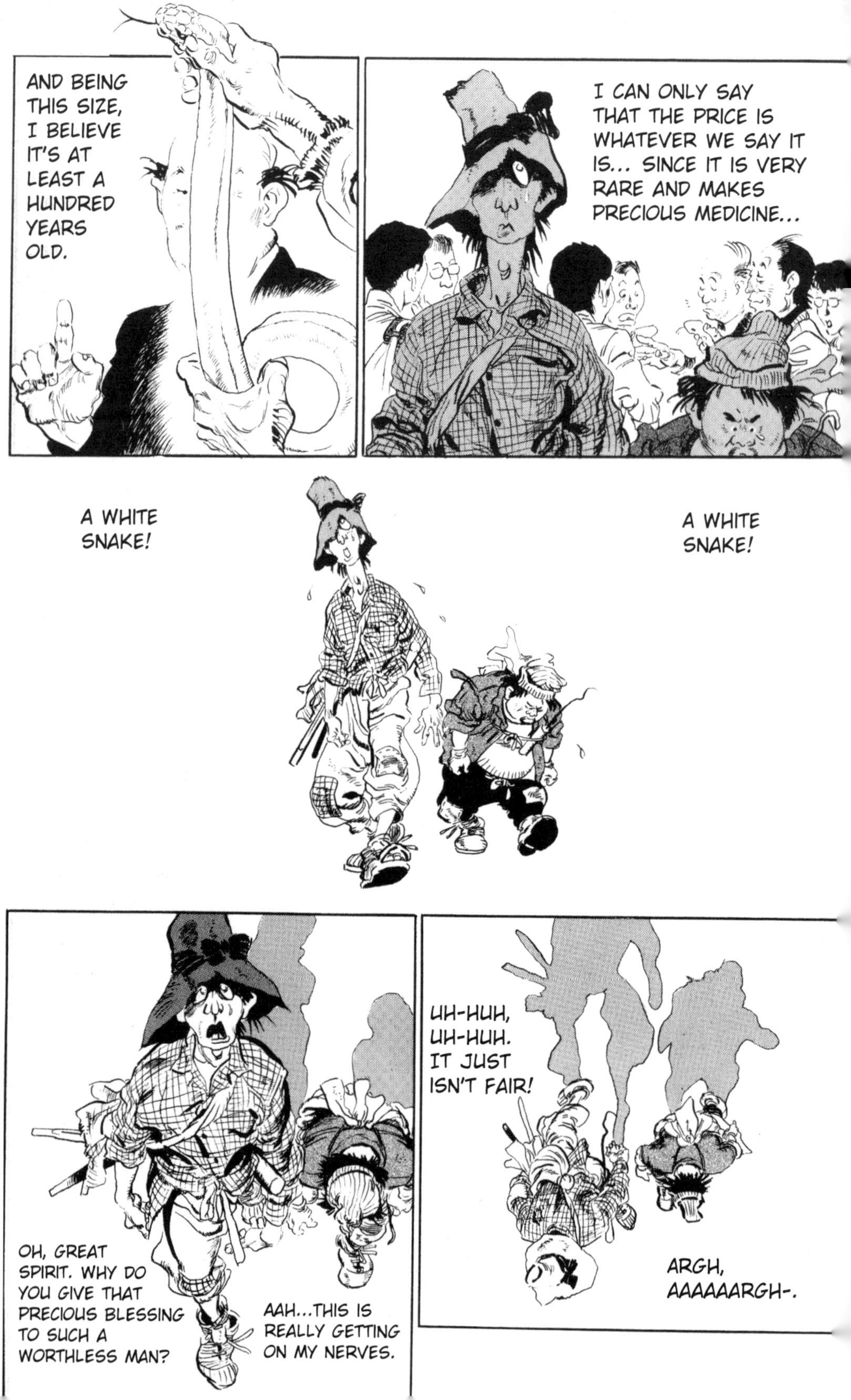
AND BEING THIS SIZE, I BELIEVE IT'S AT LEAST A HUNDRED YEARS OLD.
I CAN ONLY SAY THAT THE PRICE IS WHATEVER WE SAY IT IS... SINCE IT IS VERY RARE AND MAKES PRECIOUS MEDICINE...
A WHITE SNAKE!
A WHITE SNAKE!
OH, GREAT SPIRIT. WHY DO YOU GIVE THAT PRECIOUS BLESSING TO SUCH A WORTHLESS MAN?
AAH...THIS IS REALLY GETTING ON MY NERVES.
UH-HUH, UH-HUH. IT JUST ISN'T FAIR!
ARGH, AAAAAARGH-.

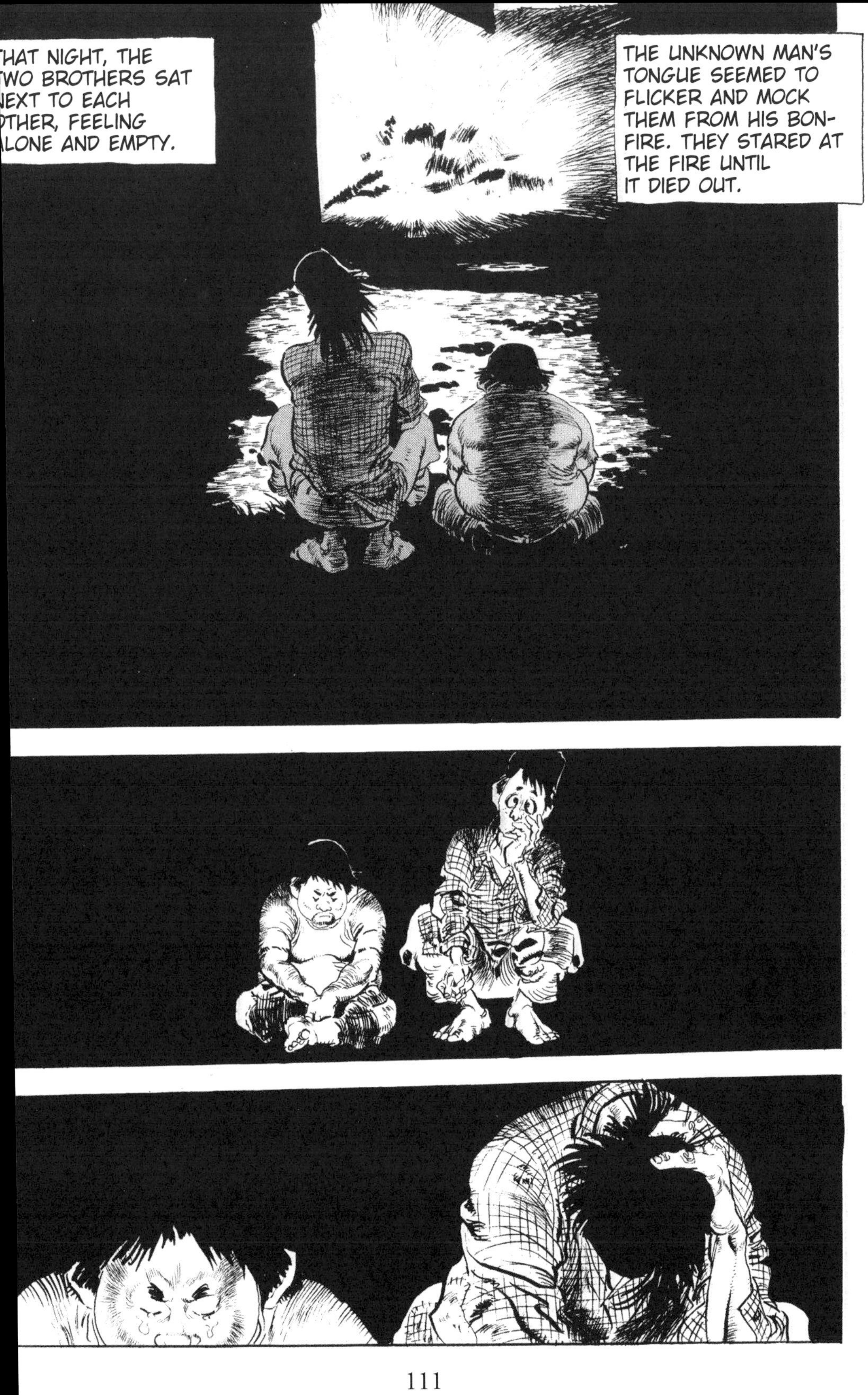
THAT NIGHT, THE TWO BROTHERS SAT NEXT TO EACH OTHER, FEELING ALONE AND EMPTY.
THE UNKNOWN MAN'S TONGUE SEEMED TO FLICKER AND MOCK THEM FROM HIS BON-FIRE. THEY STARED AT THE FIRE UNTIL IT DIED OUT.

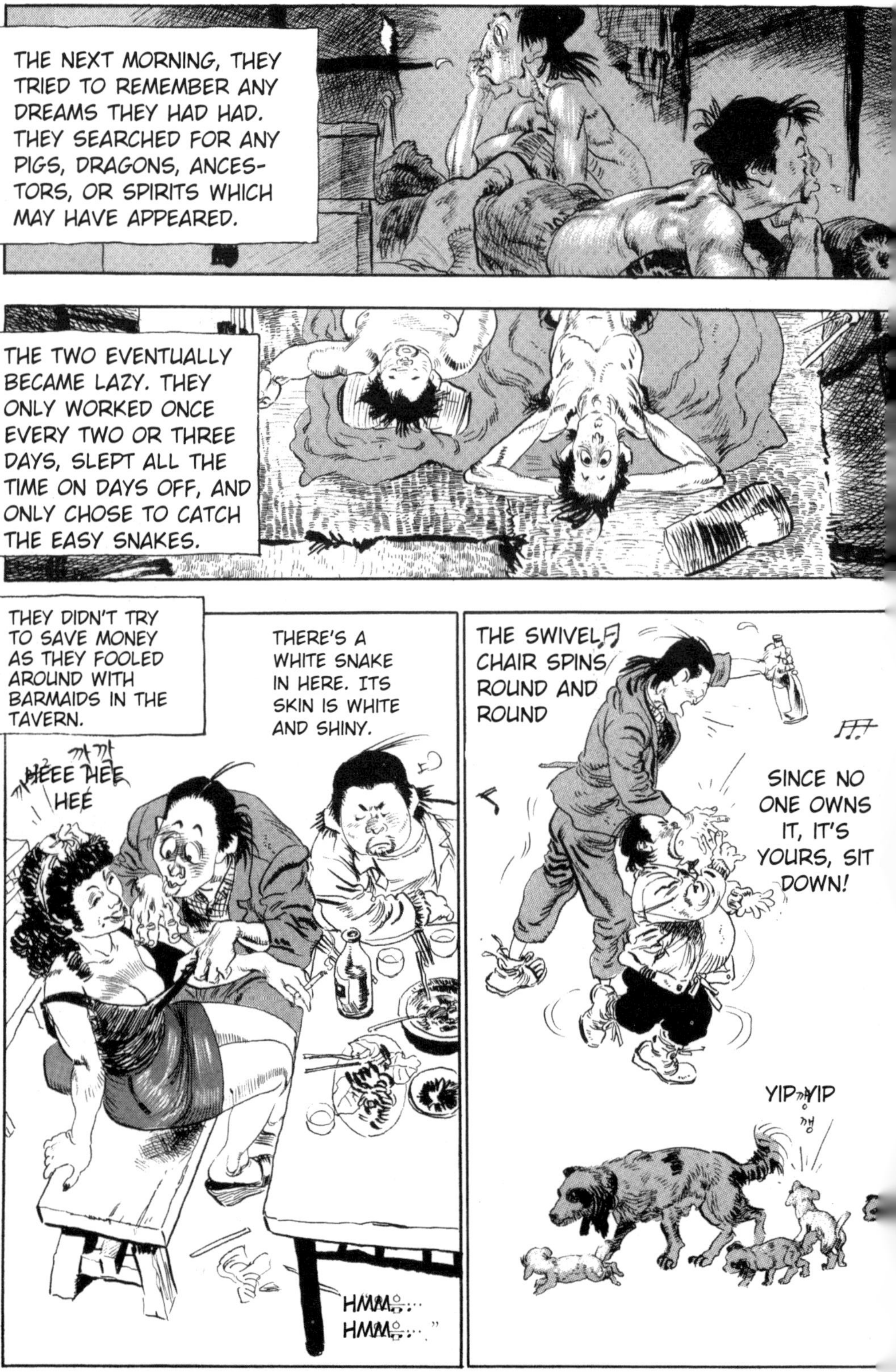
THE NEXT MORNING, THEY TRIED TO REMEMBER ANY DREAMS THEY HAD HAD. THEY SEARCHED FOR ANY PIGS, DRAGONS, ANCESTORS, OR SPIRITS WHICH MAY HAVE APPEARED.
THE TWO EVENTUALLY BECAME LAZY. THEY ONLY WORKED ONCE EVERY TWO OR THREE DAYS, SLEPT ALL THE TIME ON DAYS OFF, AND ONLY CHOSE TO CATCH THE EASY SNAKES.
THEY DIDN'T TRY TO SAVE MONEY AS THEY FOOLED AROUND WITH BARMAIDS IN THE TAVERN.
HEEE HEE HEE
까까
THERE'S A WHITE SNAKE IN HERE. ITS SKIN IS WHITE AND SHINY.
"HMM음... HMM음..."
THE SWIVEL CHAIR SPINS ROUND AND ROUND
SINCE NO ONE OWNS IT, IT'S YOURS, SIT DOWN!
YIP깽YIP
깽

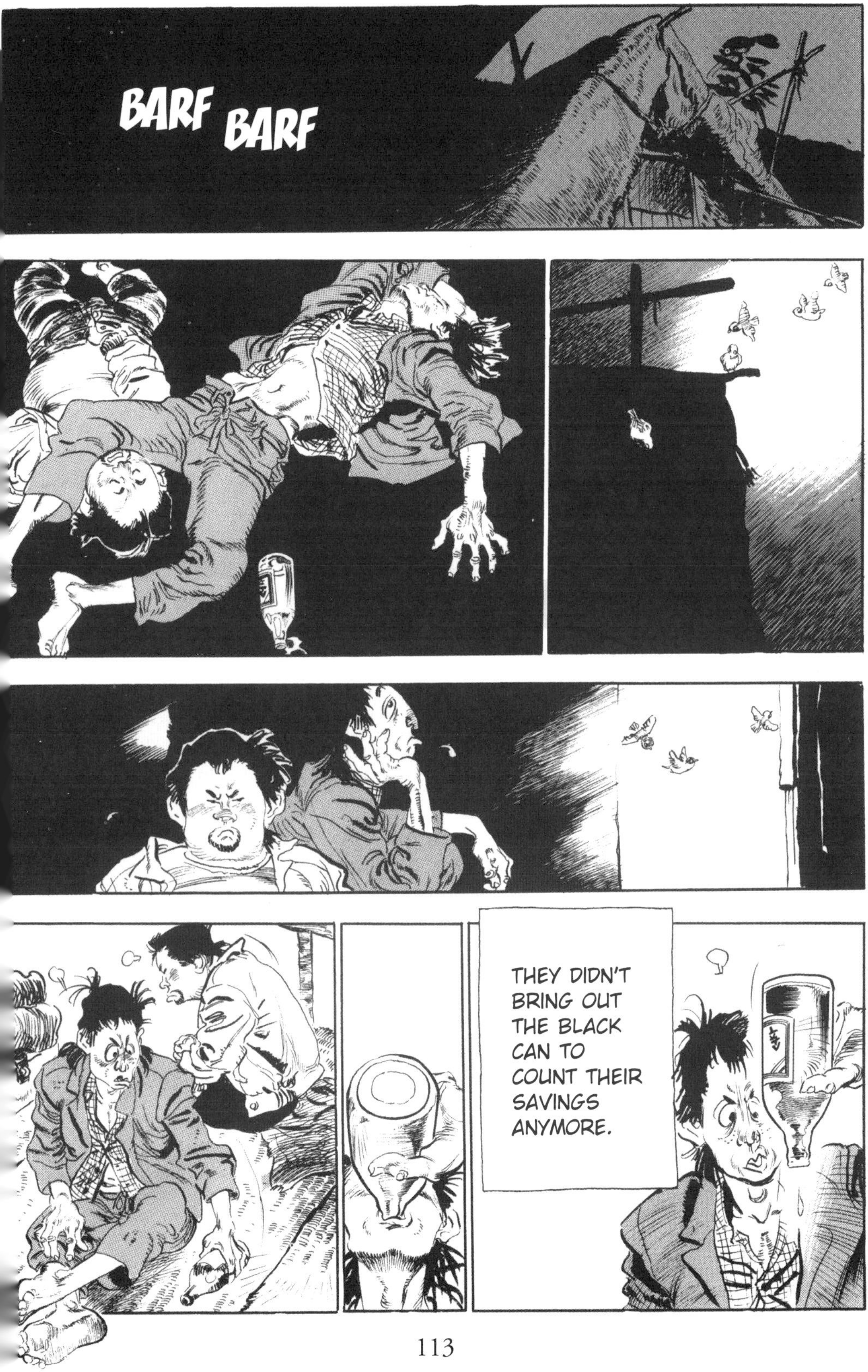
BARF BARF
THEY DIDN'T BRING OUT THE BLACK CAN TO COUNT THEIR SAVINGS ANYMORE.

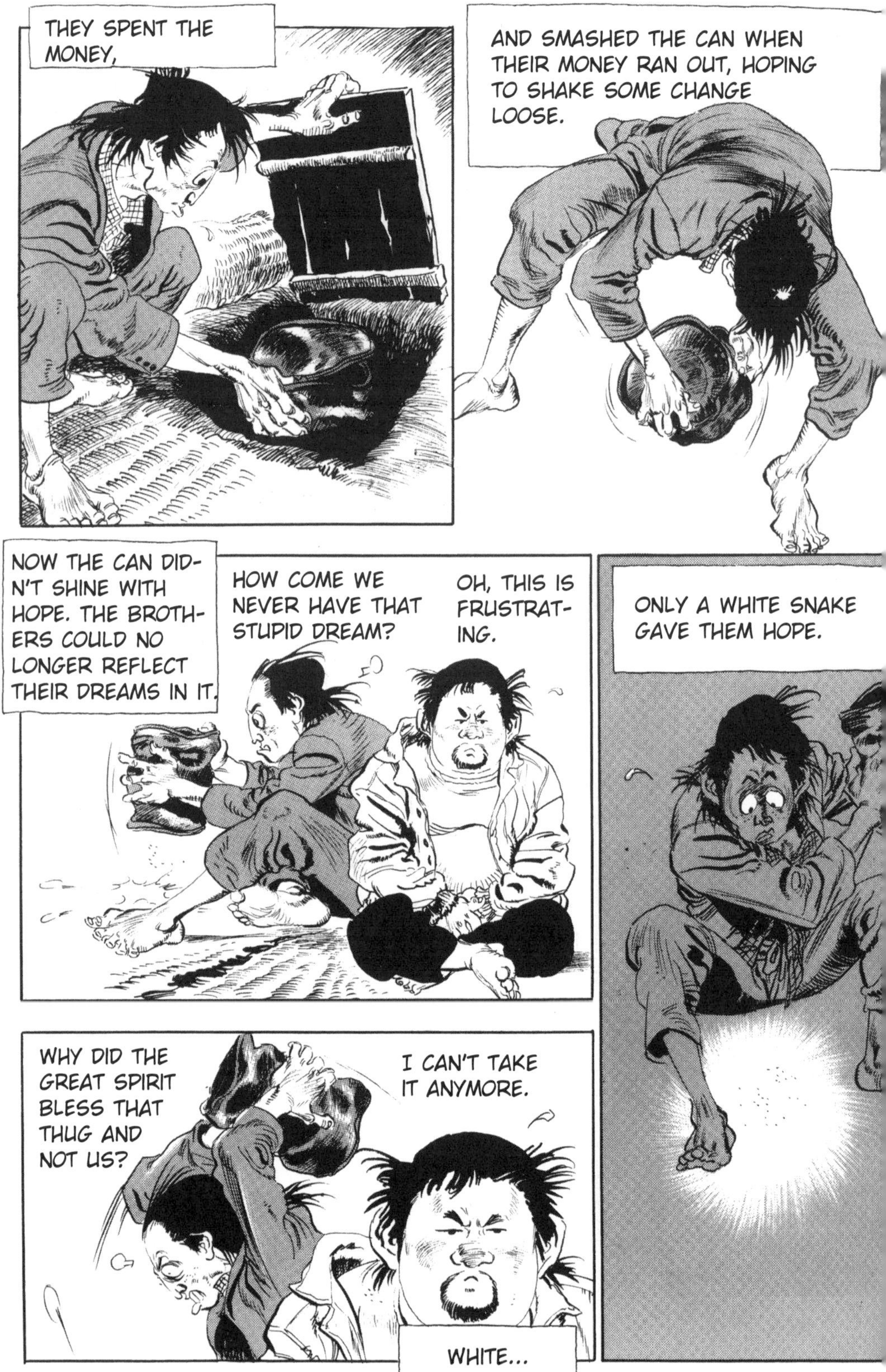
THEY SPENT THE MONEY,
AND SMASHED THE CAN WHEN THEIR MONEY RAN OUT, HOPING TO SHAKE SOME CHANGE LOOSE.
NOW THE CAN DIDN'T SHINE WITH HOPE. THE BROTHERS COULD NO LONGER REFLECT THEIR DREAMS IN IT.
HOW COME WE NEVER HAVE THAT STUPID DREAM?
OH, THIS IS FRUSTRATING.
WHY DID THE GREAT SPIRIT BLESS THAT THUG AND NOT US?
I CAN'T TAKE IT ANYMORE.
WHITE...
ONLY A WHITE SNAKE GAVE THEM HOPE.

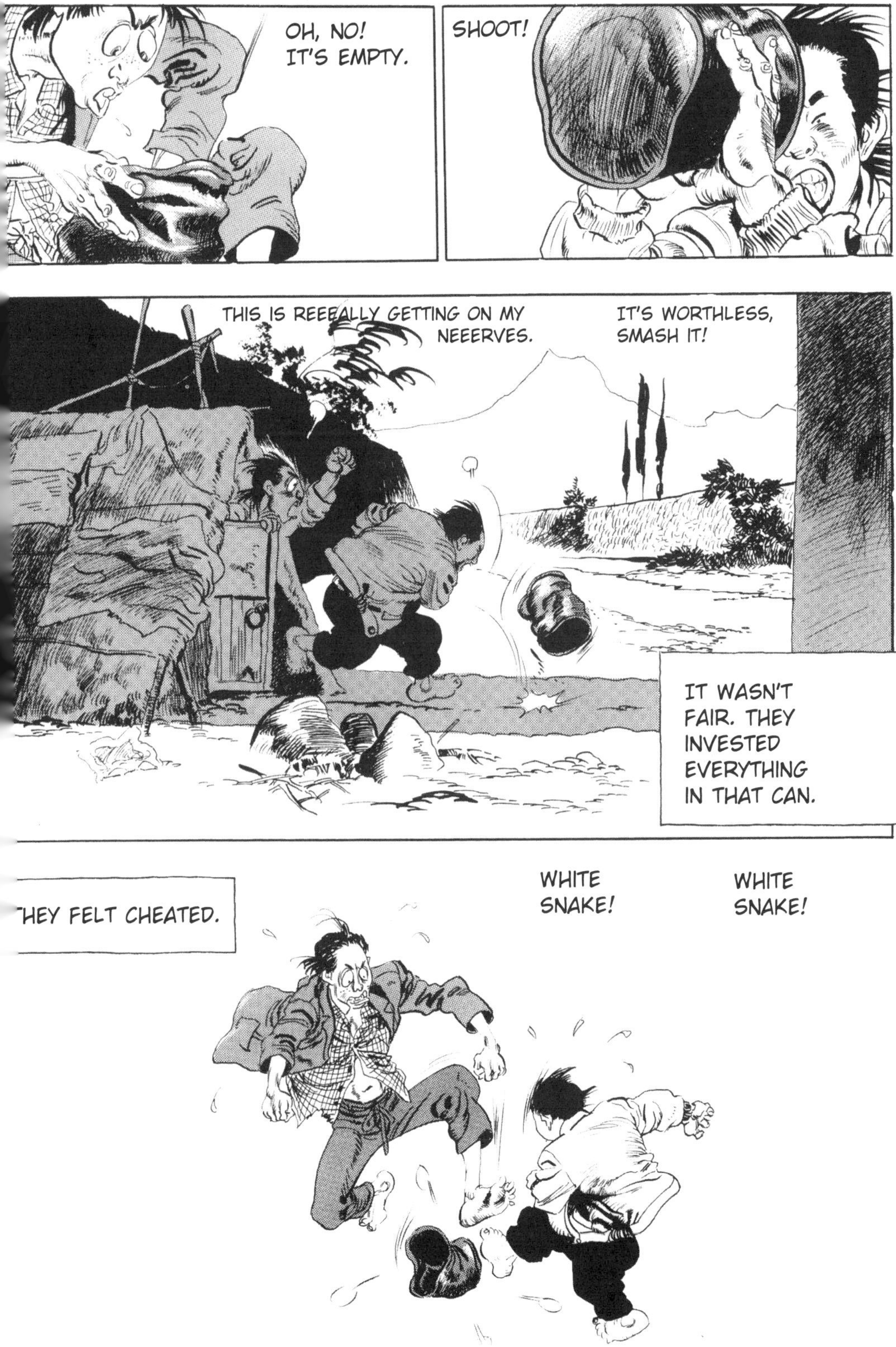
OH, NO! IT'S EMPTY.
SHOOT!
THIS IS REEEALLY GETTING ON MY NEEERVES.
IT'S WORTHLESS, SMASH IT!
IT WASN'T FAIR. THEY INVESTED EVERYTHING IN THAT CAN.
THEY FELT CHEATED.
WHITE SNAKE!
WHITE SNAKE!

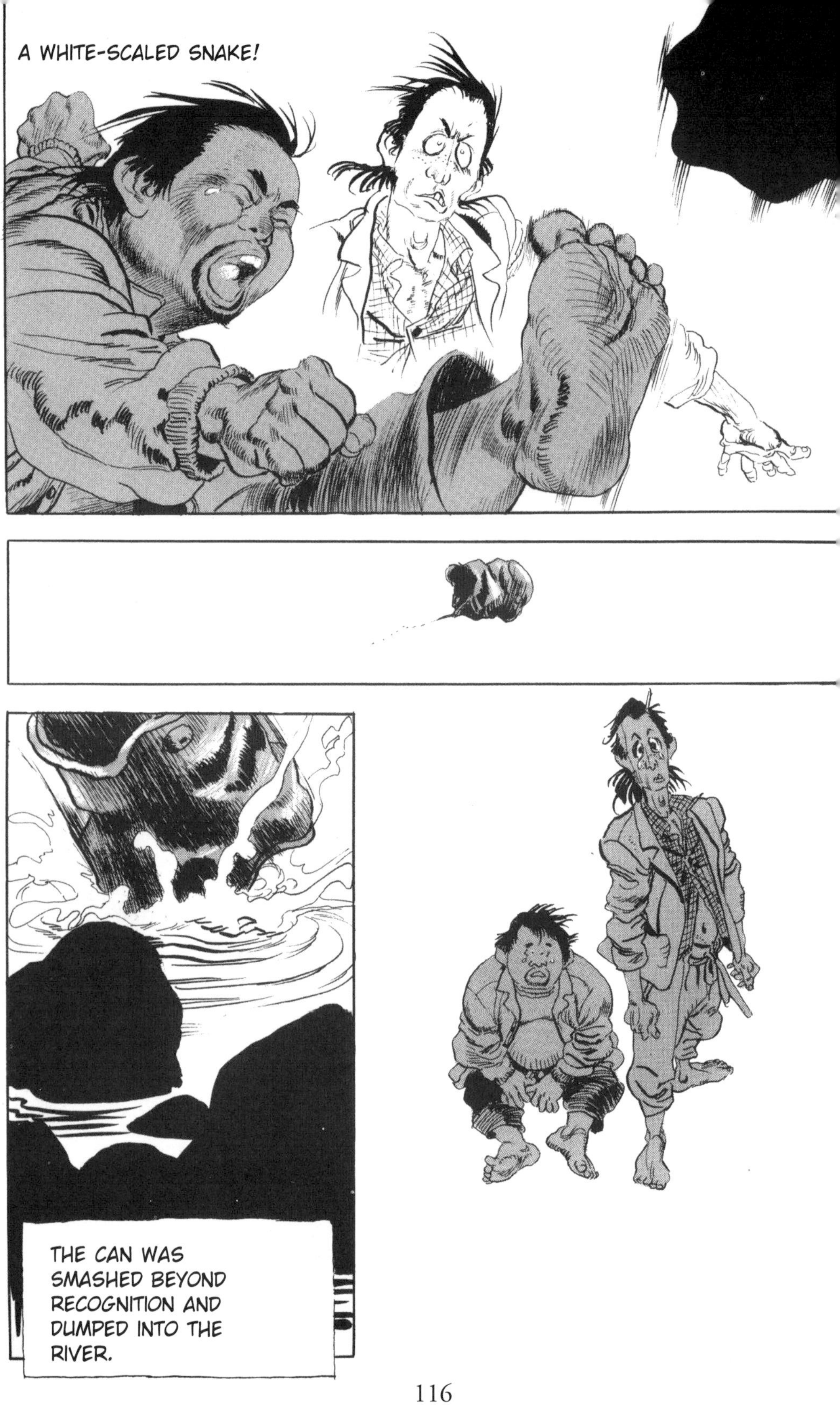
A WHITE-SCALED SNAKE!
THE CAN WAS SMASHED BEYOND RECOGNITION AND DUMPED INTO THE RIVER.

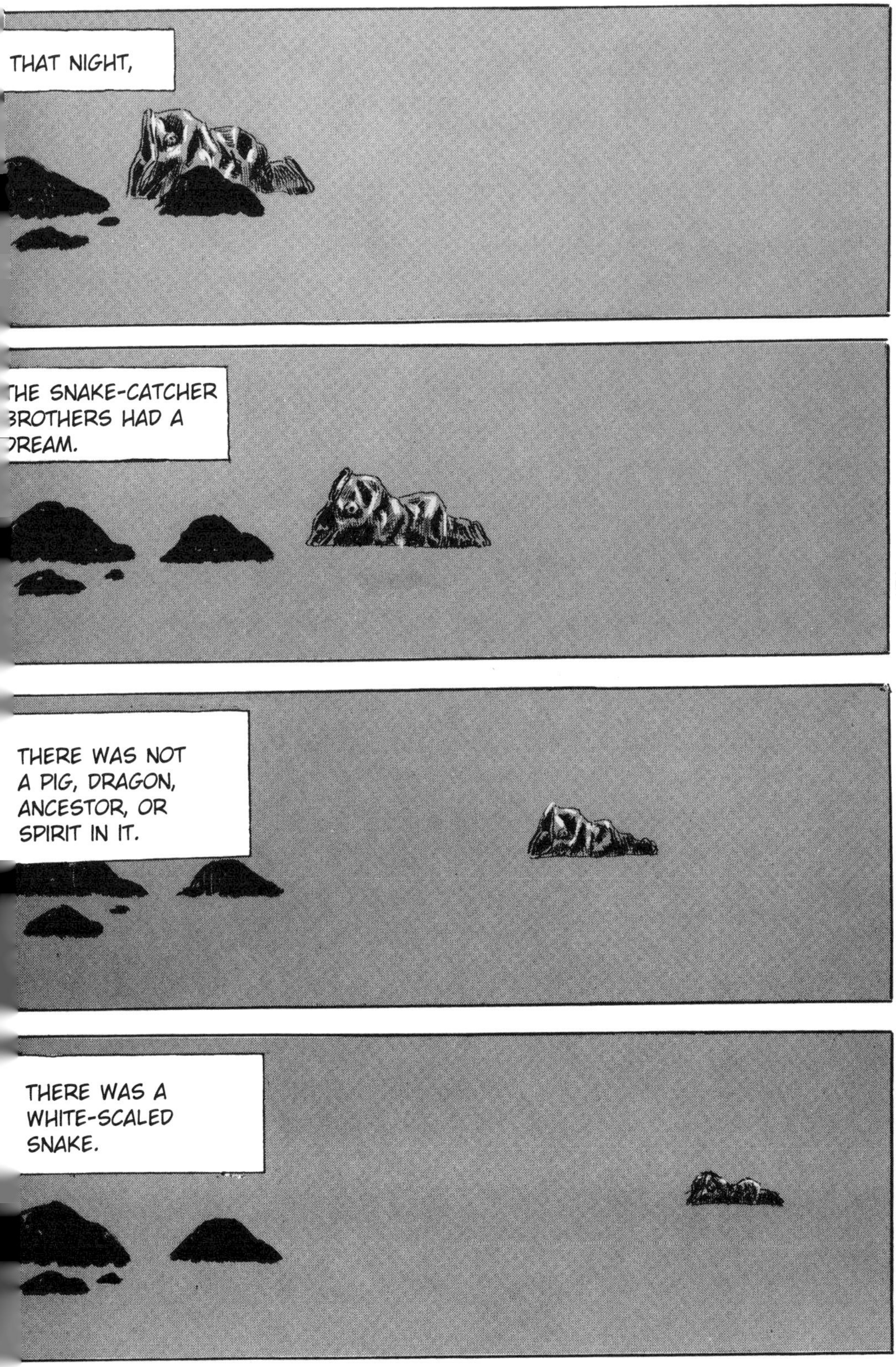
THAT NIGHT,
THE SNAKE-CATCHER BROTHERS HAD A DREAM.
THERE WAS NOT A PIG, DRAGON, ANCESTOR, OR SPIRIT IN IT.
THERE WAS A WHITE-SCALED SNAKE.

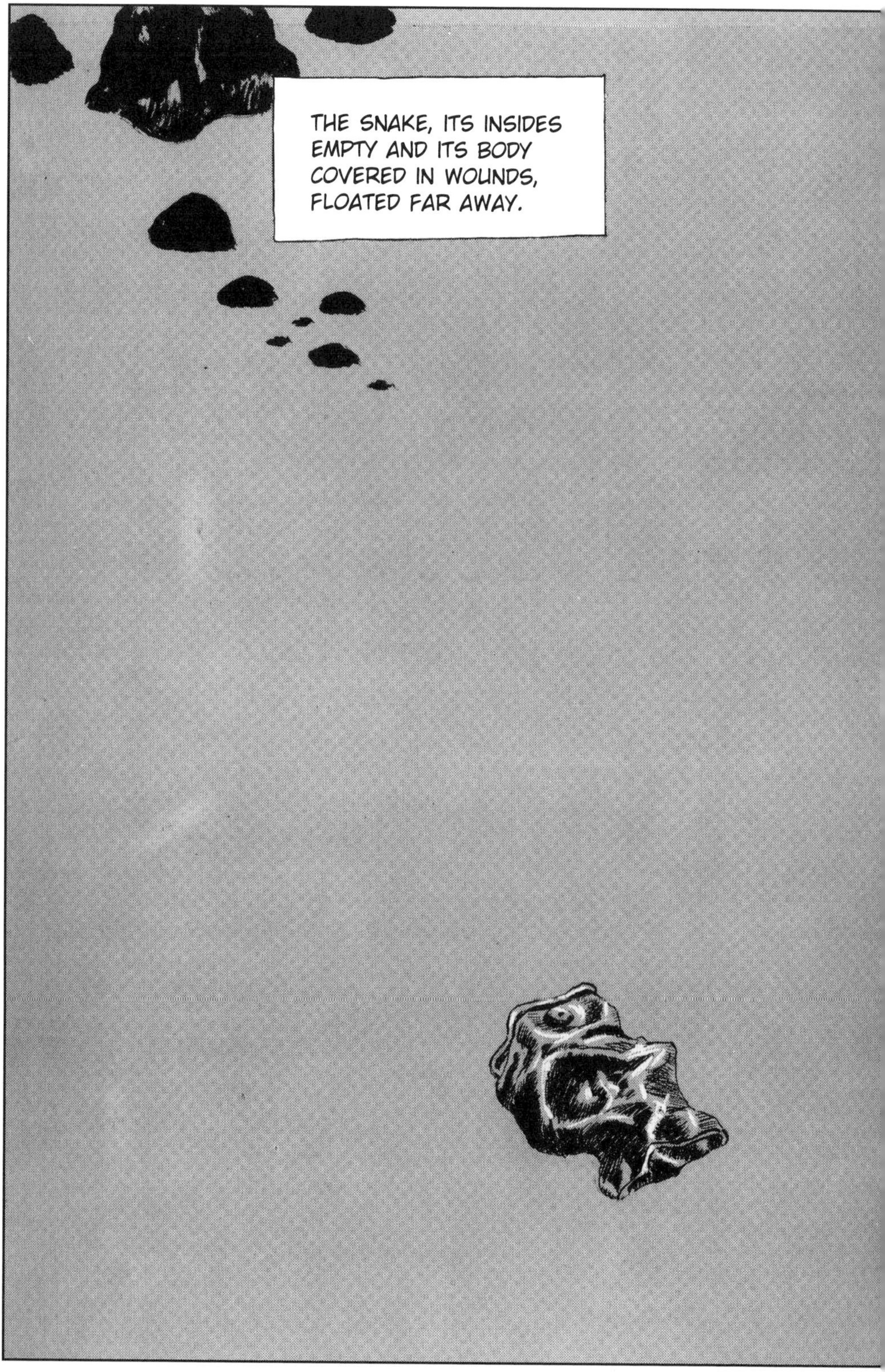
THE SNAKE, ITS INSIDES EMPTY AND ITS BODY COVERED IN WOUNDS, FLOATED FAR AWAY.

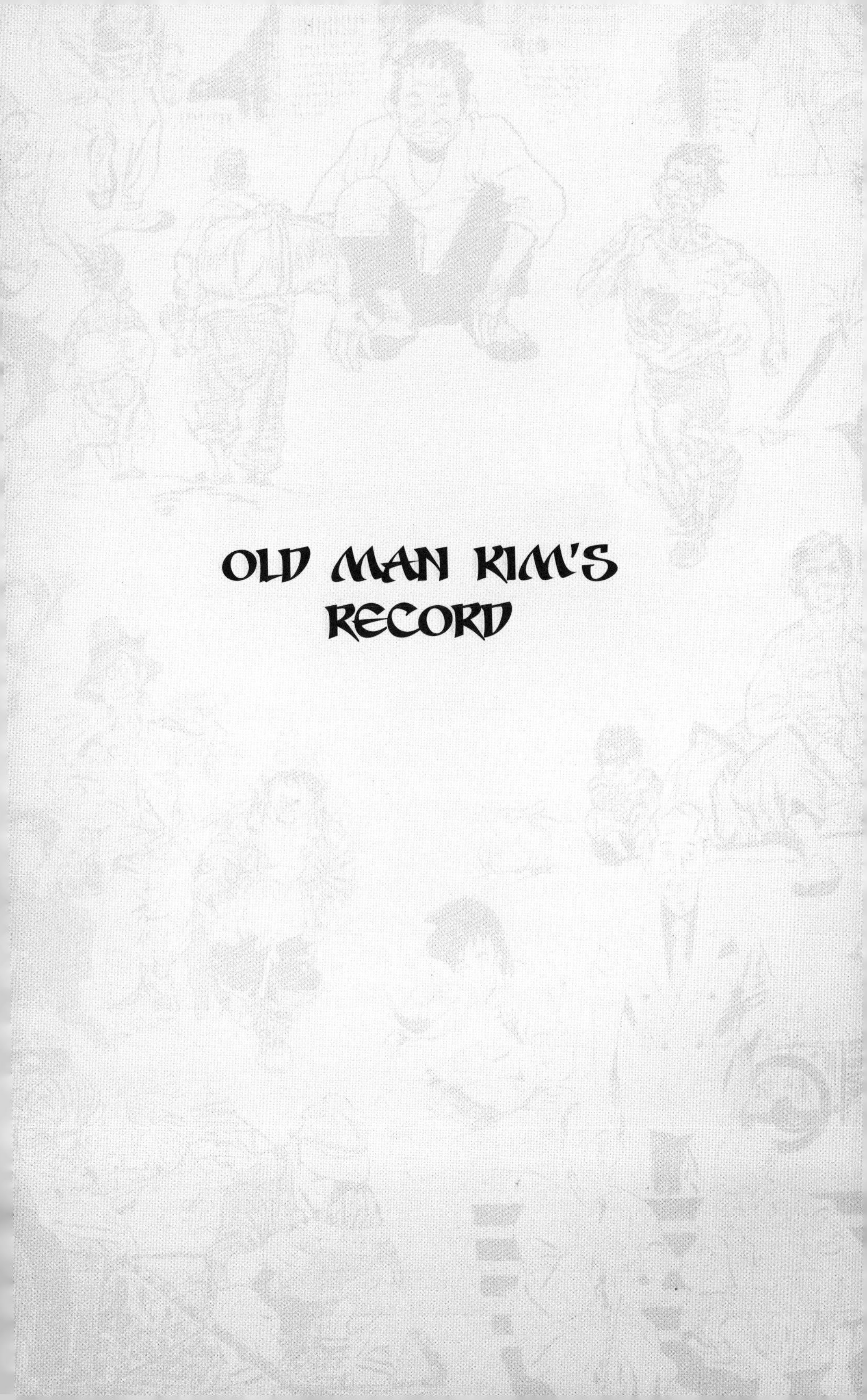

OLD MAN KIM'S RECORD

SEYEONG O
AUGUST 1989

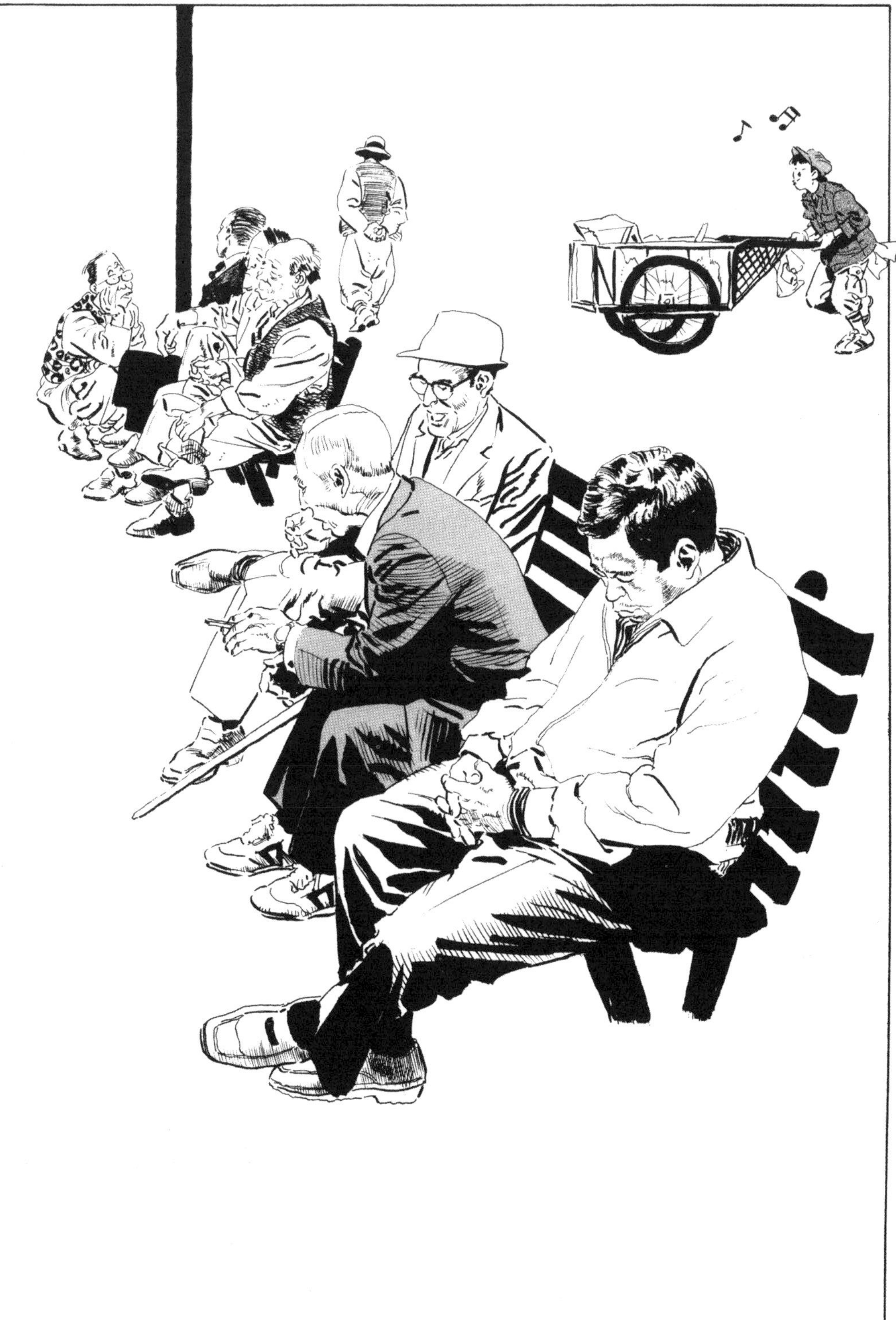

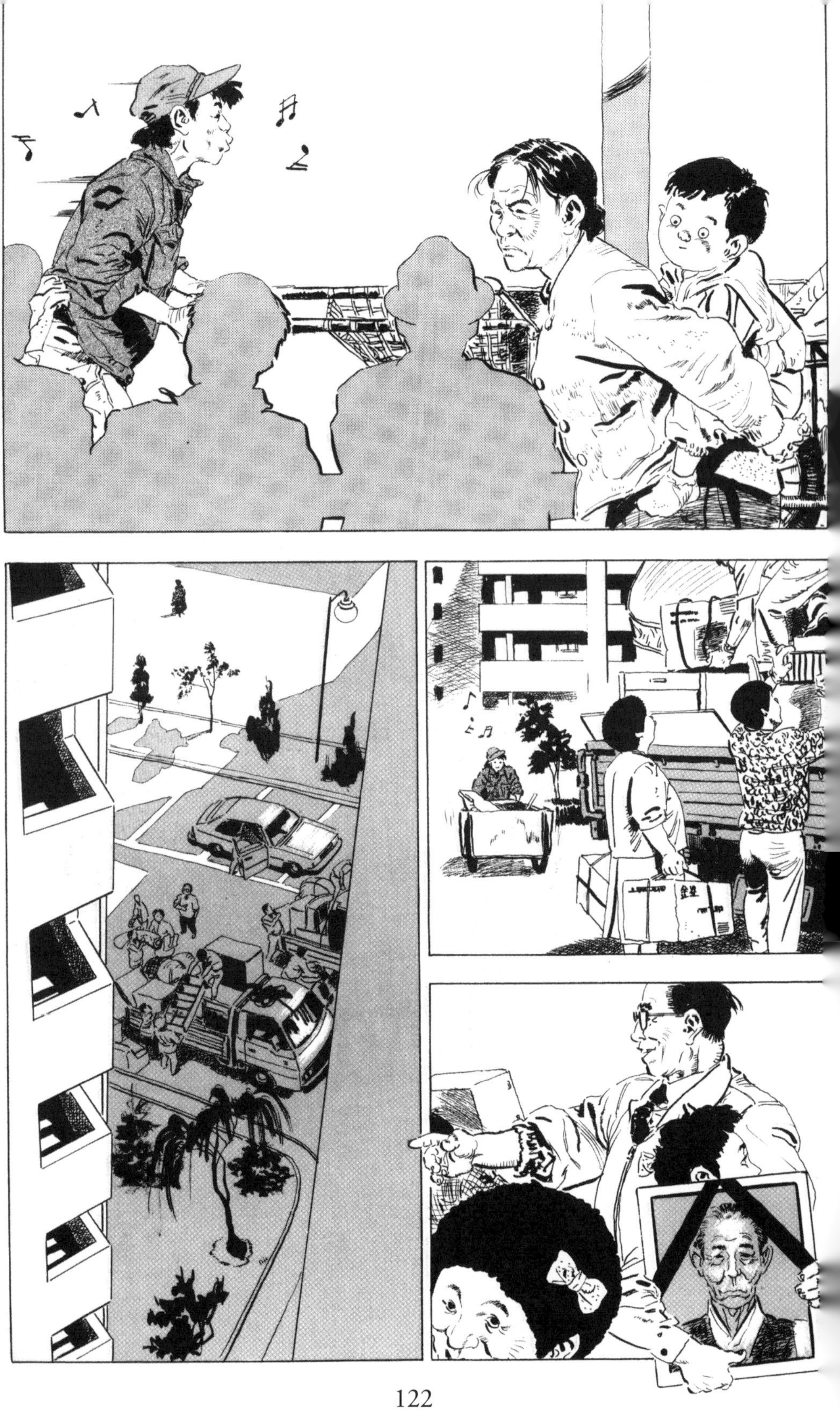

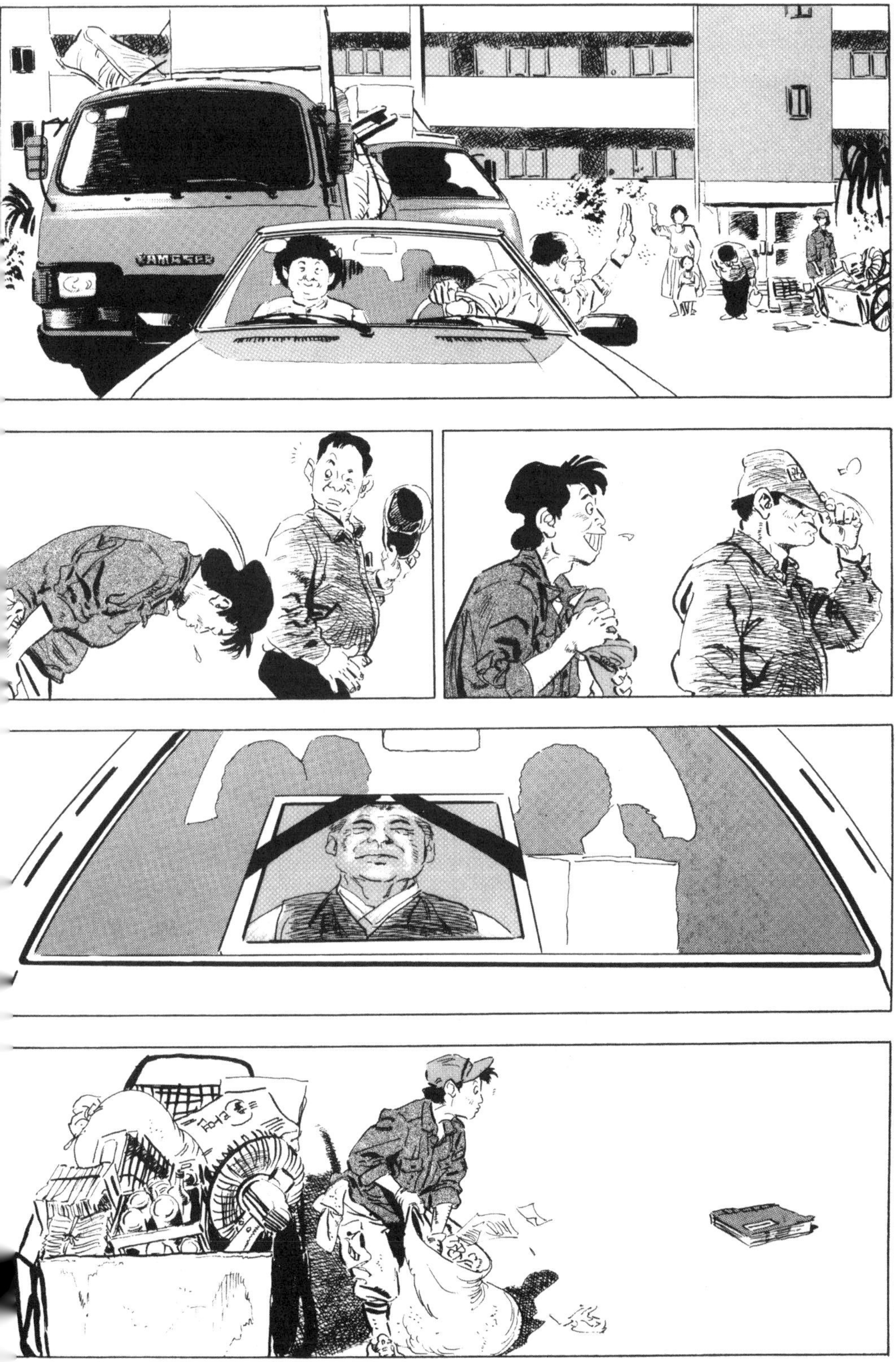

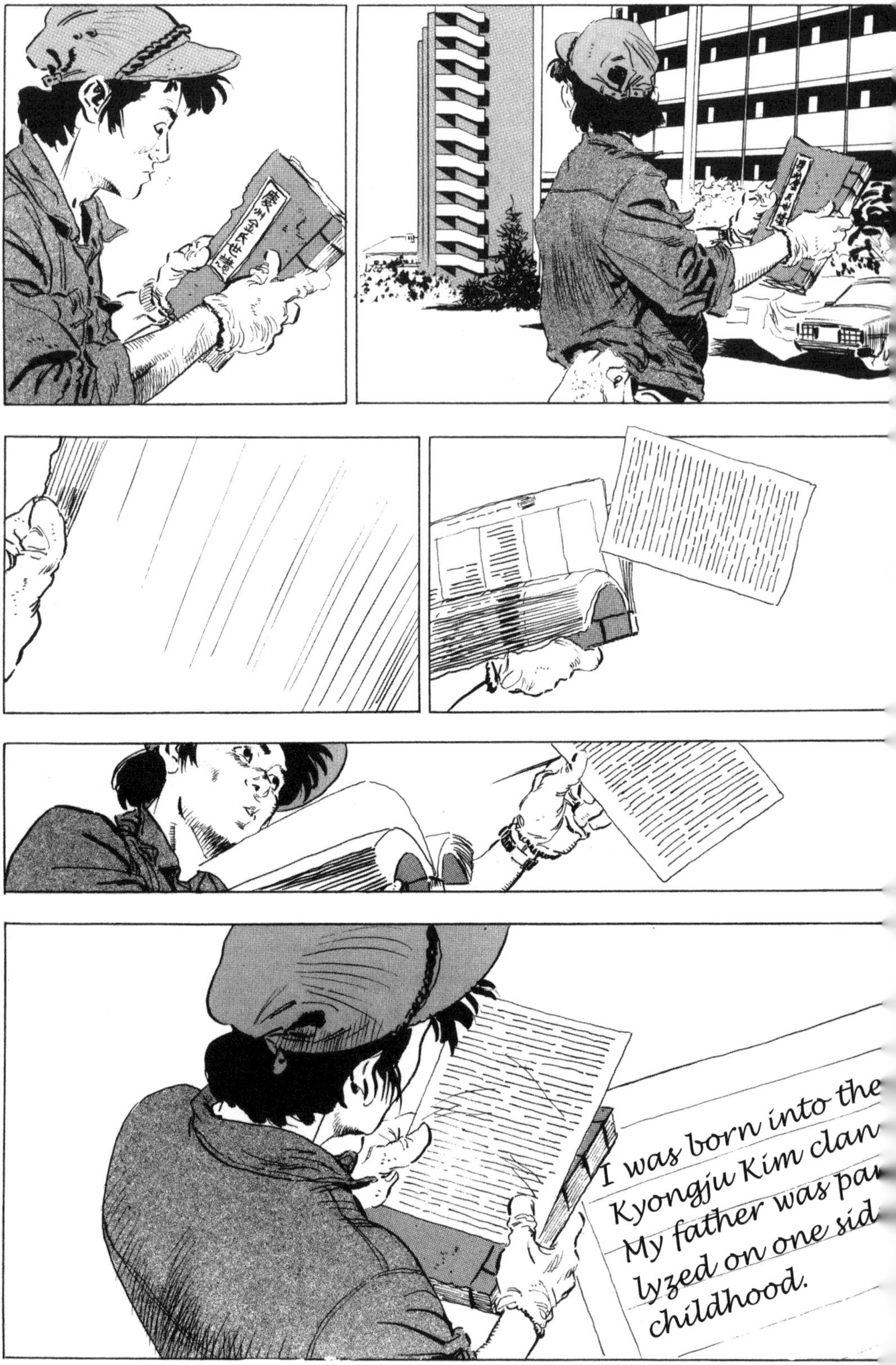
I was born into the
Kyongju Kim clan
My father was pa
lyzed on one sid
childhood.

MY MOTHER CAME FROM THE KIMHAE KIM CLAN. MY GRANDMOTHER DIED WHEN SHE WAS SEVEN DAYS OLD.

MY GRANDFATHER CARRIED MY MOTHER AND HIS GONG AS THEY TRAVELED AROUND THE COUNTRY.

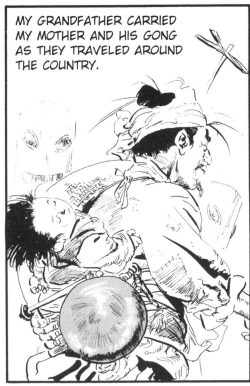

THEY SETTLED IN KOMJONG LI WHEN SHE WAS NINE. LATER, SHE MARRIED MY FATHER.

THAT'S HOW SHE BECAME A DAUGHTER -IN-LAW IN THAT KIM FAMILY.

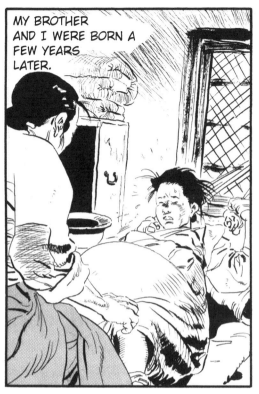

MY BROTHER AND I WERE BORN A FEW YEARS LATER.

IT SEEMED LIKE SHE COULD NOW LIVE PEACEFULLY.

BUT SHE BECAME VERY ILL AT AGE THIRTY FIVE, AND WAS BEDRIDDEN.

I WAS ELEVEN WHEN THE JAPANESE INVADED.

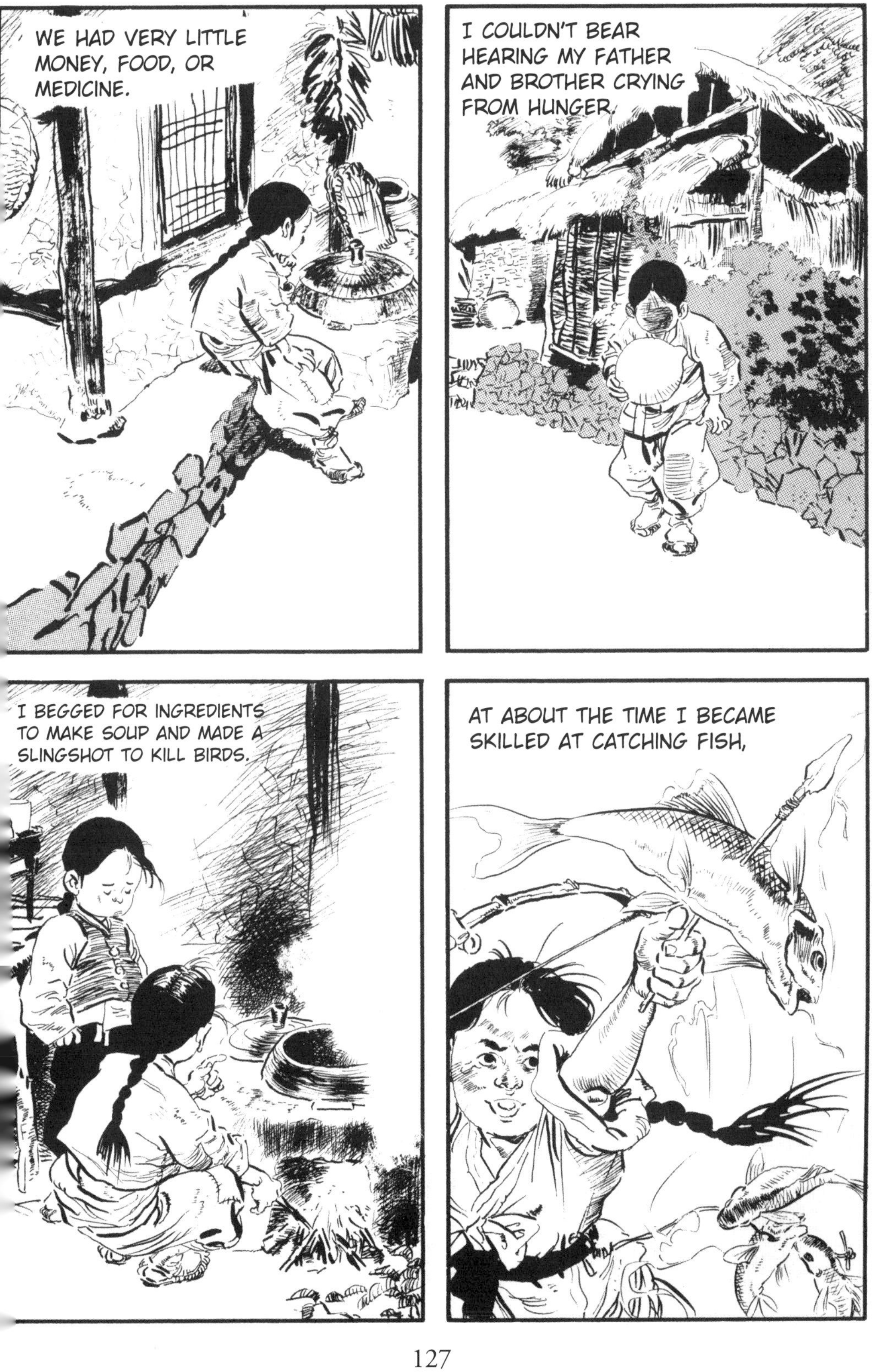
WE HAD VERY LITTLE MONEY, FOOD, OR MEDICINE.
I COULDN'T BEAR HEARING MY FATHER AND BROTHER CRYING FROM HUNGER.
I BEGGED FOR INGREDIENTS TO MAKE SOUP AND MADE A SLINGSHOT TO KILL BIRDS.
AT ABOUT THE TIME I BECAME SKILLED AT CATCHING FISH,

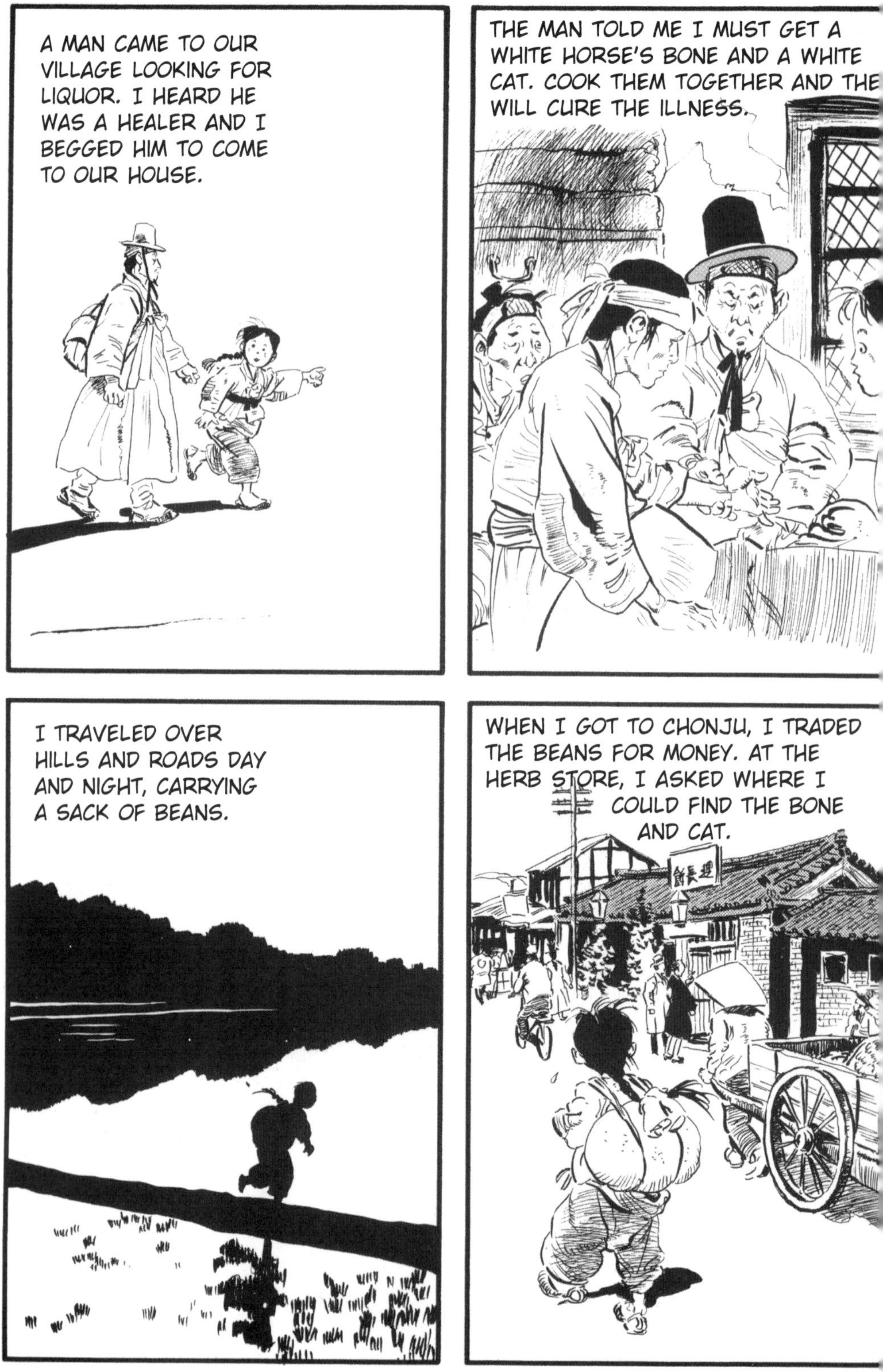
A MAN CAME TO OUR VILLAGE LOOKING FOR LIQUOR. I HEARD HE WAS A HEALER AND I BEGGED HIM TO COME TO OUR HOUSE.
THE MAN TOLD ME I MUST GET A WHITE HORSE'S BONE AND A WHITE CAT. COOK THEM TOGETHER AND THE WILL CURE THE ILLNESS.
I TRAVELED OVER HILLS AND ROADS DAY AND NIGHT, CARRYING A SACK OF BEANS.
WHEN I GOT TO CHONJU, I TRADED THE BEANS FOR MONEY. AT THE HERB STORE, I ASKED WHERE I COULD FIND THE BONE AND CAT.

THE OWNER OF THE STORE TOLD ME I'D NEVER FIND THEM. IF I ASKED THE WRONG PEOPLE FOR THEM, THEY'D CHEAT ME OUT OF MY MONEY.

I WAS AFRAID, SO I HURRIED BACK TO MY SHELTER IN THE ALLEY. THERE I SAW A GREY HORSE PULLING A CARRIAGE FULL OF ROCKS.

I THOUGHT EVEN A GRAY HORSE MIGHT BE GOOD ENOUGH.

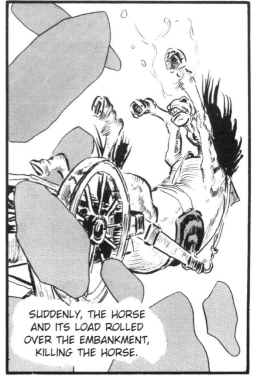

SUDDENLY, THE HORSE AND ITS LOAD ROLLED OVER THE EMBANKMENT, KILLING THE HORSE.

129

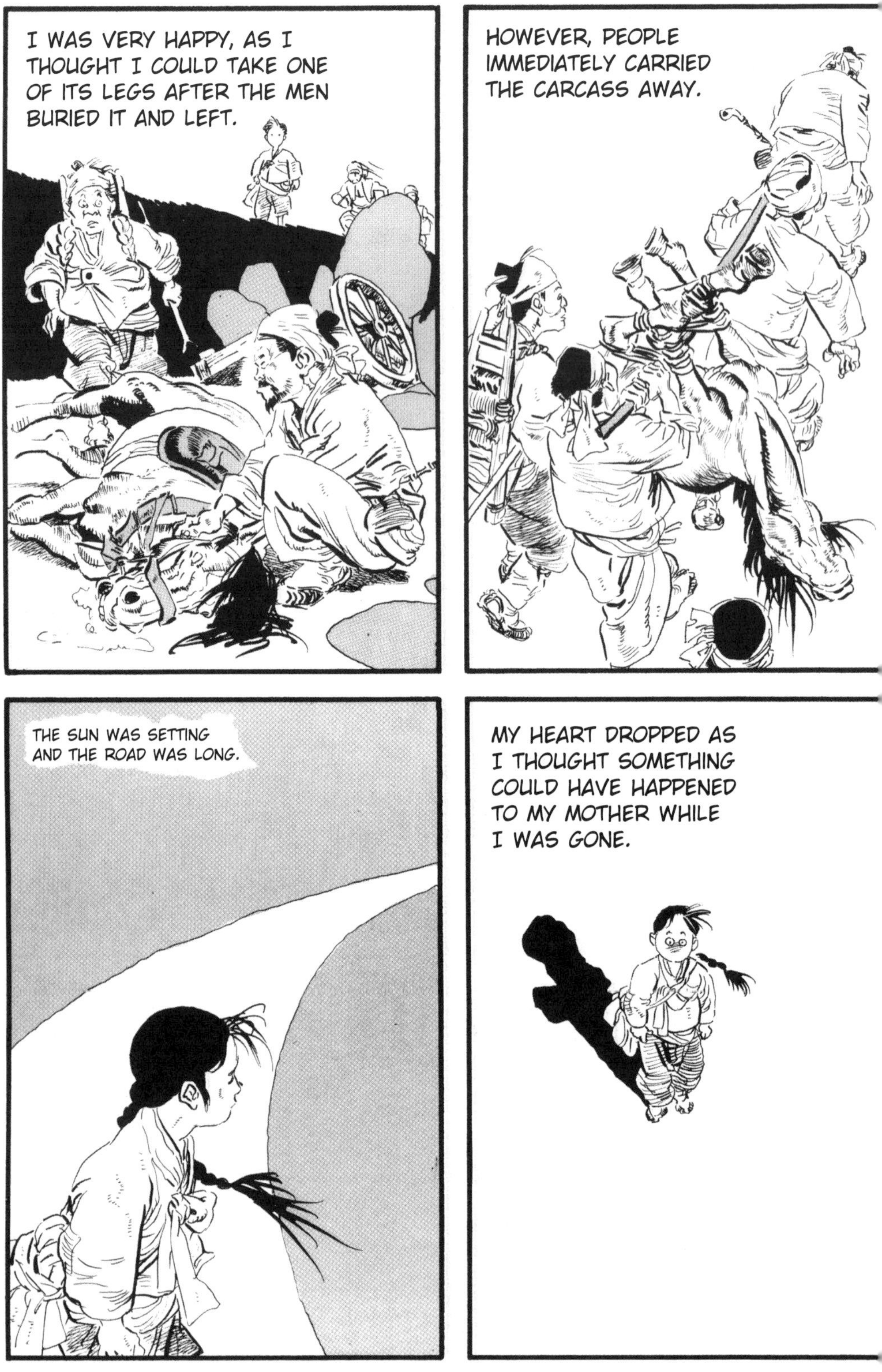
I WAS VERY HAPPY, AS I THOUGHT I COULD TAKE ONE OF ITS LEGS AFTER THE MEN BURIED IT AND LEFT.
HOWEVER, PEOPLE IMMEDIATELY CARRIED THE CARCASS AWAY.
THE SUN WAS SETTING AND THE ROAD WAS LONG.
MY HEART DROPPED AS I THOUGHT SOMETHING COULD HAVE HAPPENED TO MY MOTHER WHILE I WAS GONE.

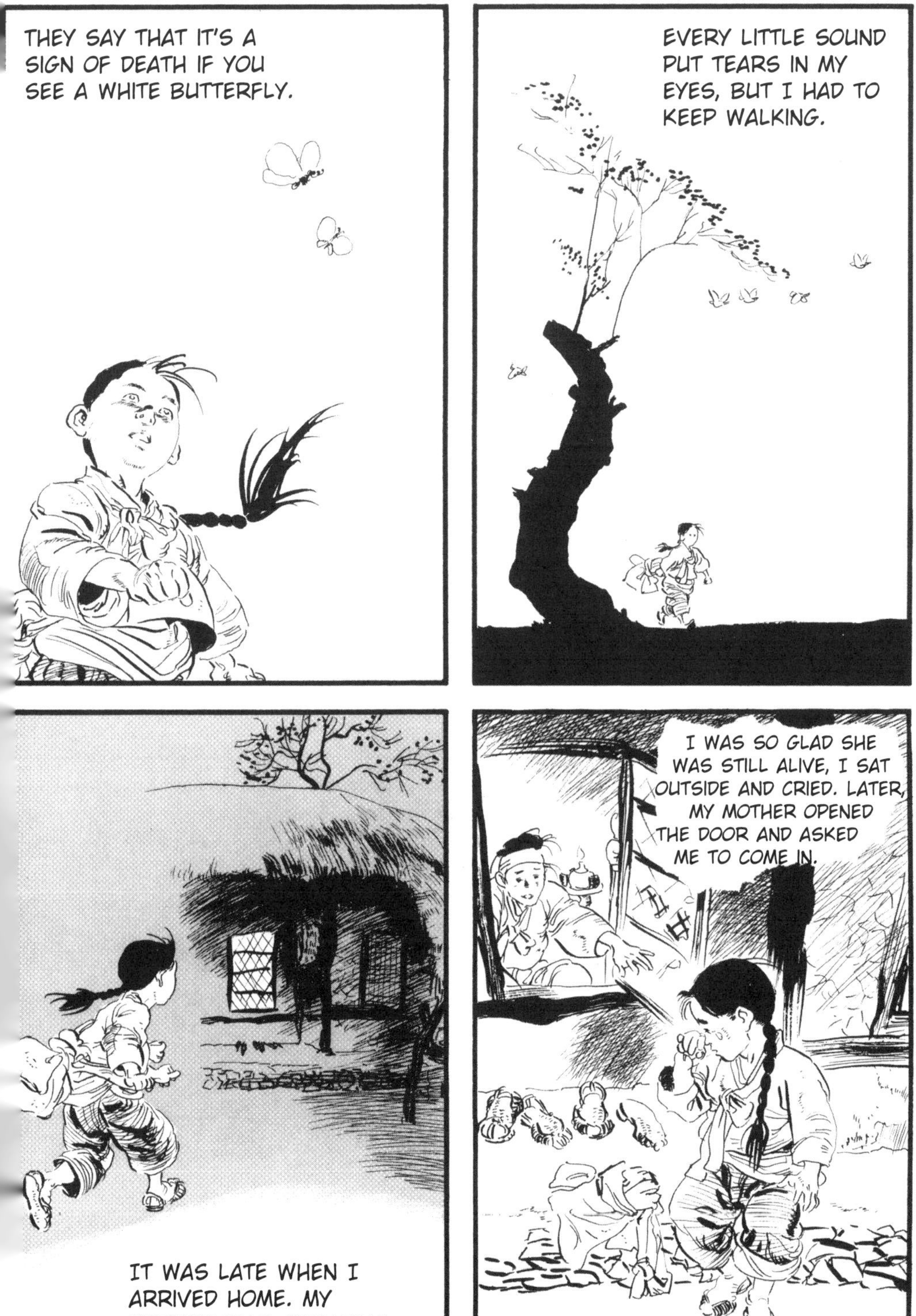
THEY SAY THAT IT'S A SIGN OF DEATH IF YOU SEE A WHITE BUTTERFLY.
EVERY LITTLE SOUND PUT TEARS IN MY EYES, BUT I HAD TO KEEP WALKING.
IT WAS LATE WHEN I ARRIVED HOME. MY MOTHER WAS GROANING WITH PAIN.
I WAS SO GLAD SHE WAS STILL ALIVE, I SAT OUTSIDE AND CRIED. LATER, MY MOTHER OPENED THE DOOR AND ASKED ME TO COME IN.

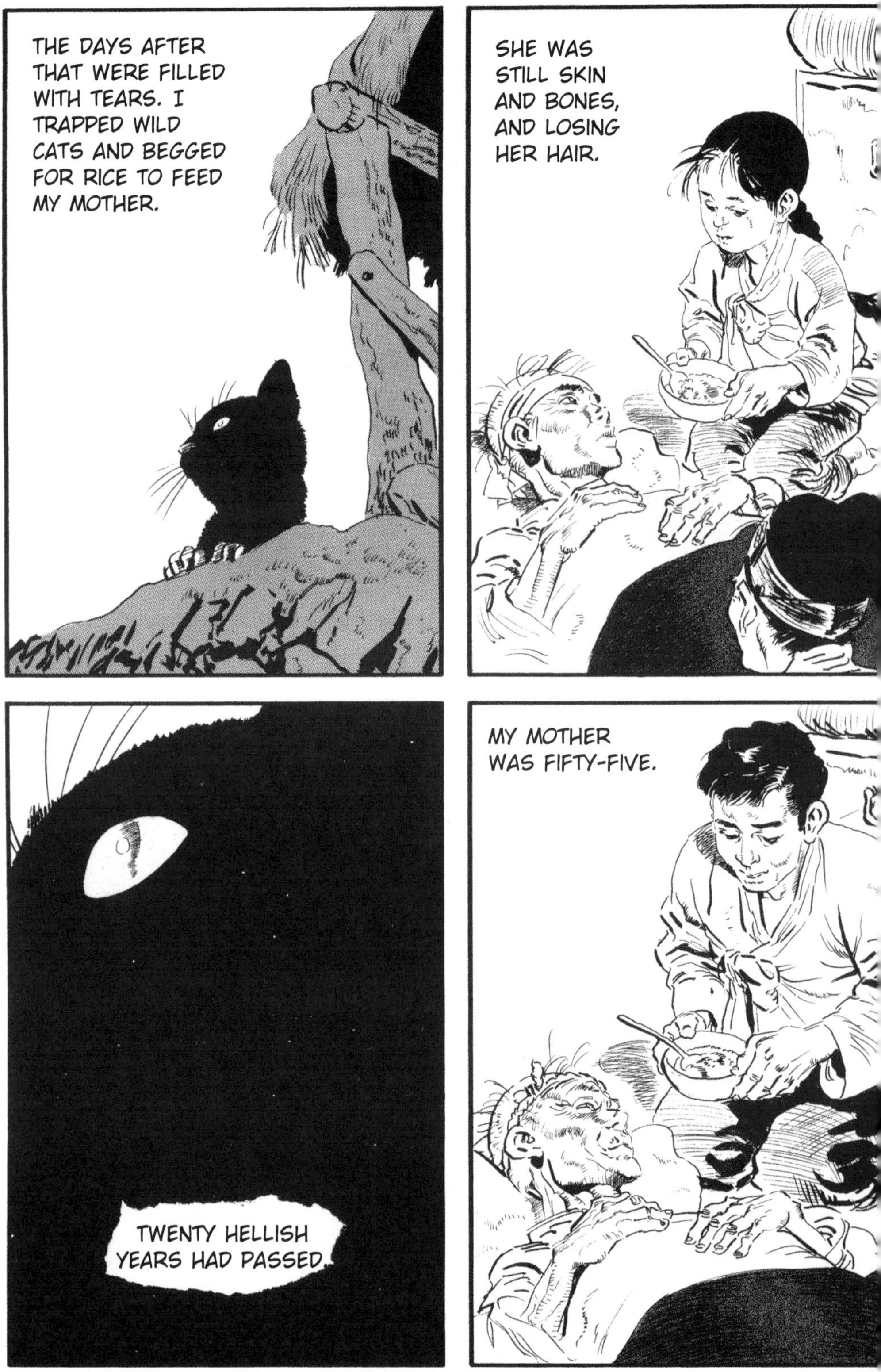
THE DAYS AFTER THAT WERE FILLED WITH TEARS. I TRAPPED WILD CATS AND BEGGED FOR RICE TO FEED MY MOTHER.
SHE WAS STILL SKIN AND BONES, AND LOSING HER HAIR.
TWENTY HELLISH YEARS HAD PASSED.
MY MOTHER WAS FIFTY-FIVE.

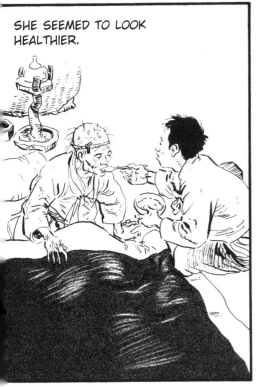

SHE SEEMED TO LOOK HEALTHIER.

HER HAIR STARTED GROWING AGAIN.

ONE DAY, WHILE STROLLING WITH HER, I SAW A DOG FIGHTING A ROE DEER.

I WAS PLEASED, AND I HELPED THE DOG KILL THE DEER.

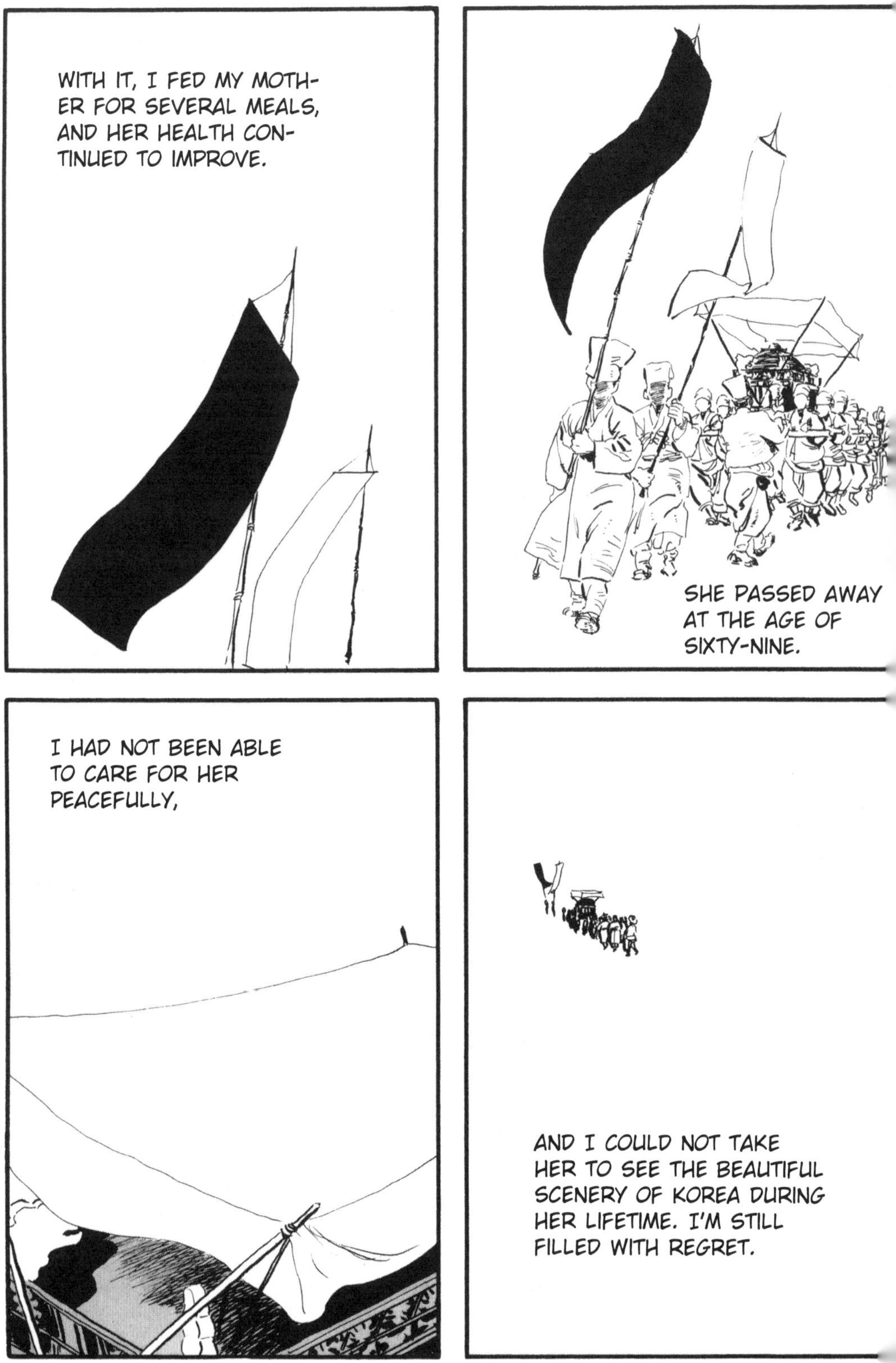

WITH IT, I FED MY MOTH-
ER FOR SEVERAL MEALS,
AND HER HEALTH CON-
TINUED TO IMPROVE.

SHE PASSED AWAY
AT THE AGE OF
SIXTY-NINE.

I HAD NOT BEEN ABLE
TO CARE FOR HER
PEACEFULLY,

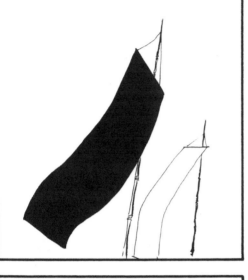

AND I COULD NOT TAKE
HER TO SEE THE BEAUTIFUL
SCENERY OF KOREA DURING
HER LIFETIME. I'M STILL
FILLED WITH REGRET.

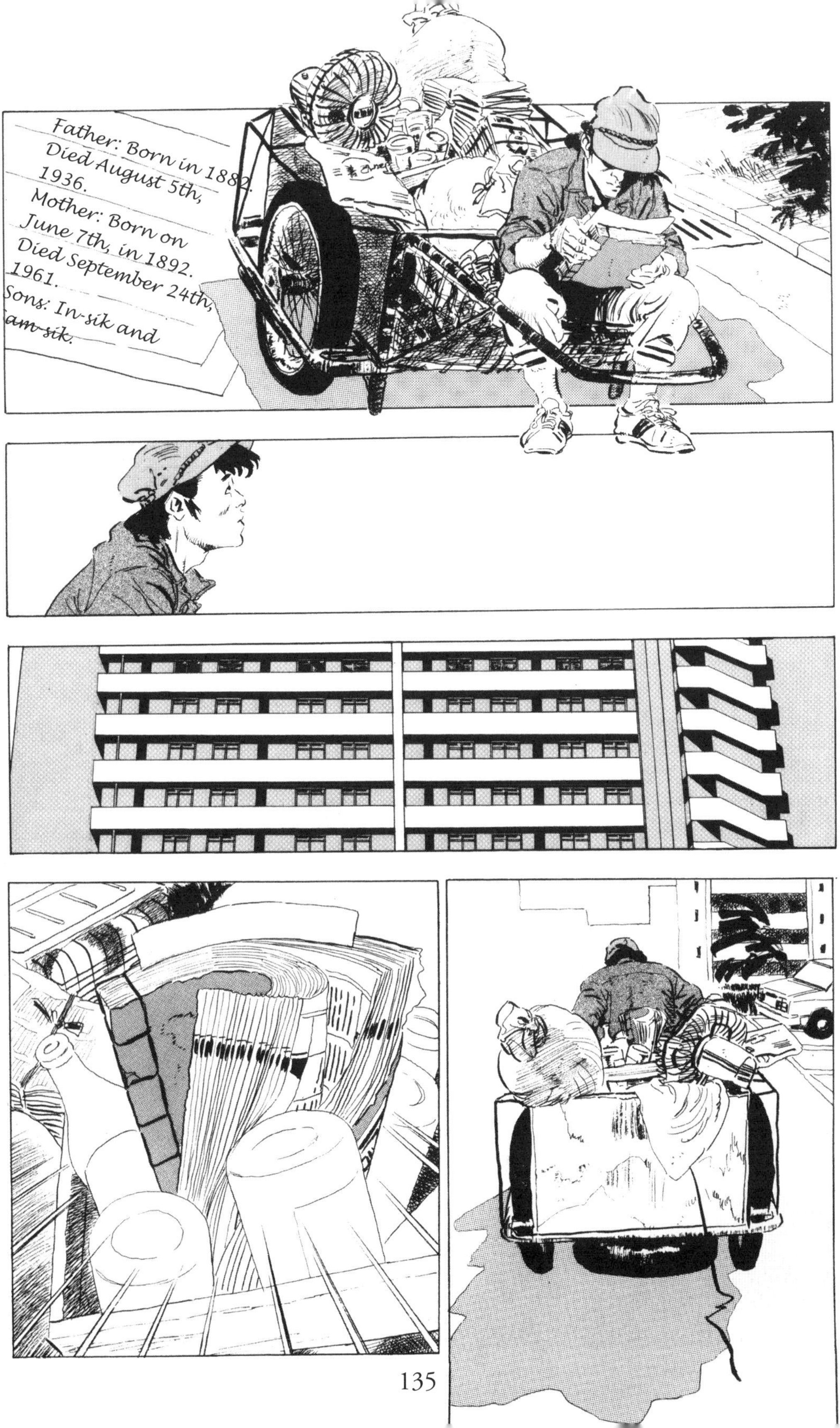
Father: Born in 1882.
Died August 5th,
1936.
Mother: Born on
June 7th, in 1892.
Died September 24th,
1961.
Sons: In-sik and
am-sik.

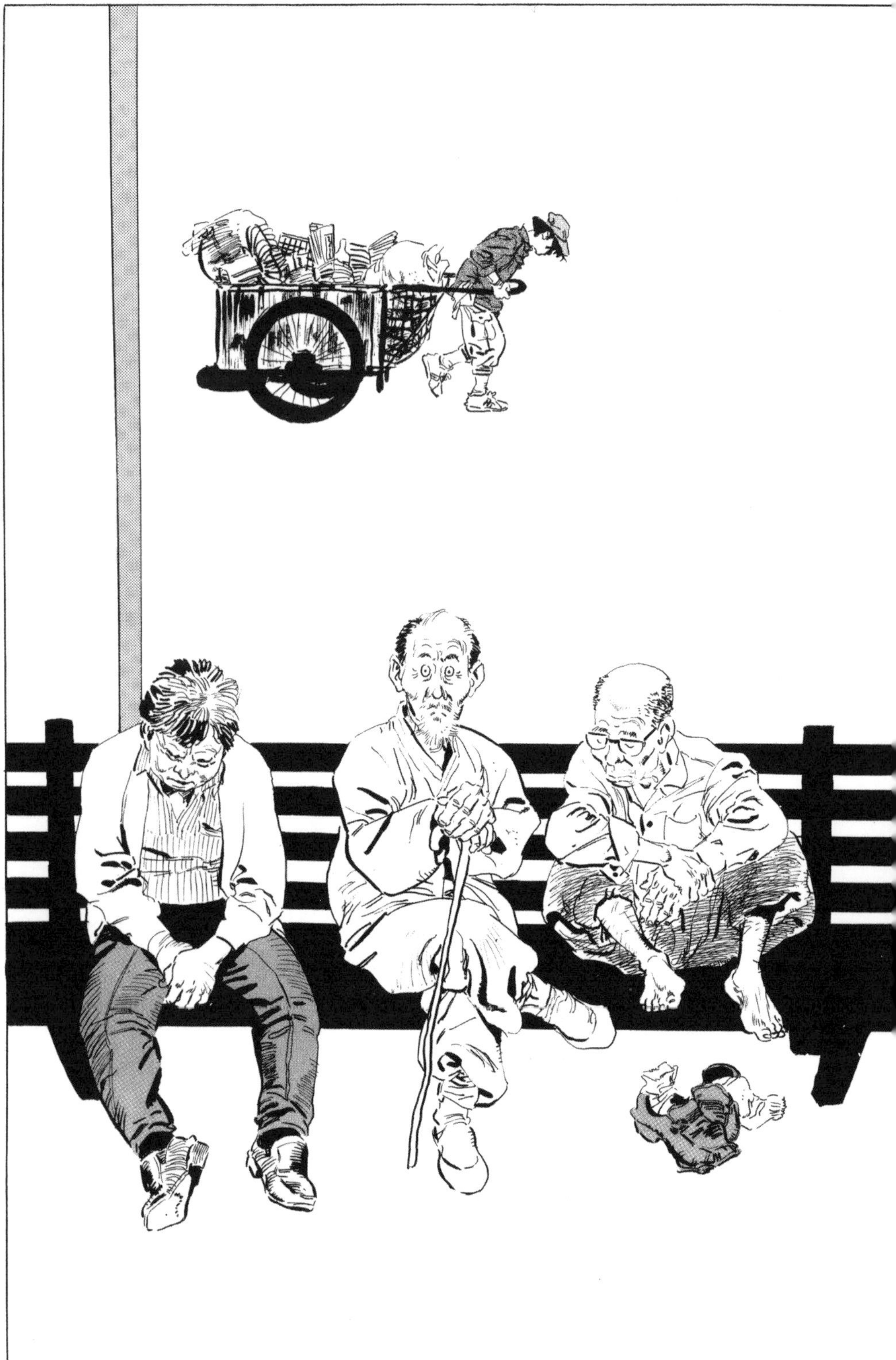

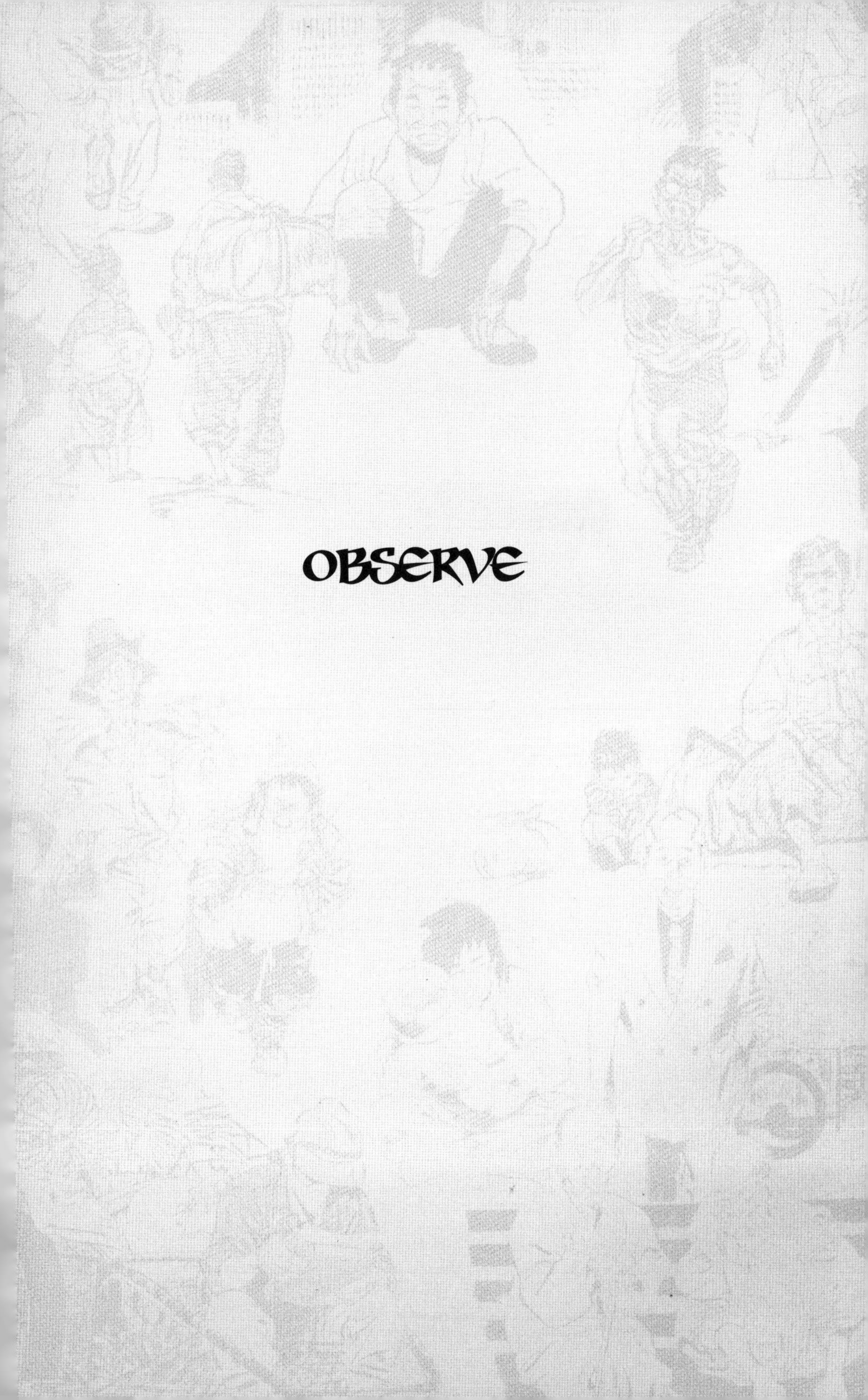

OBSERVE

SEYEONG O
NOVEMBER 1989

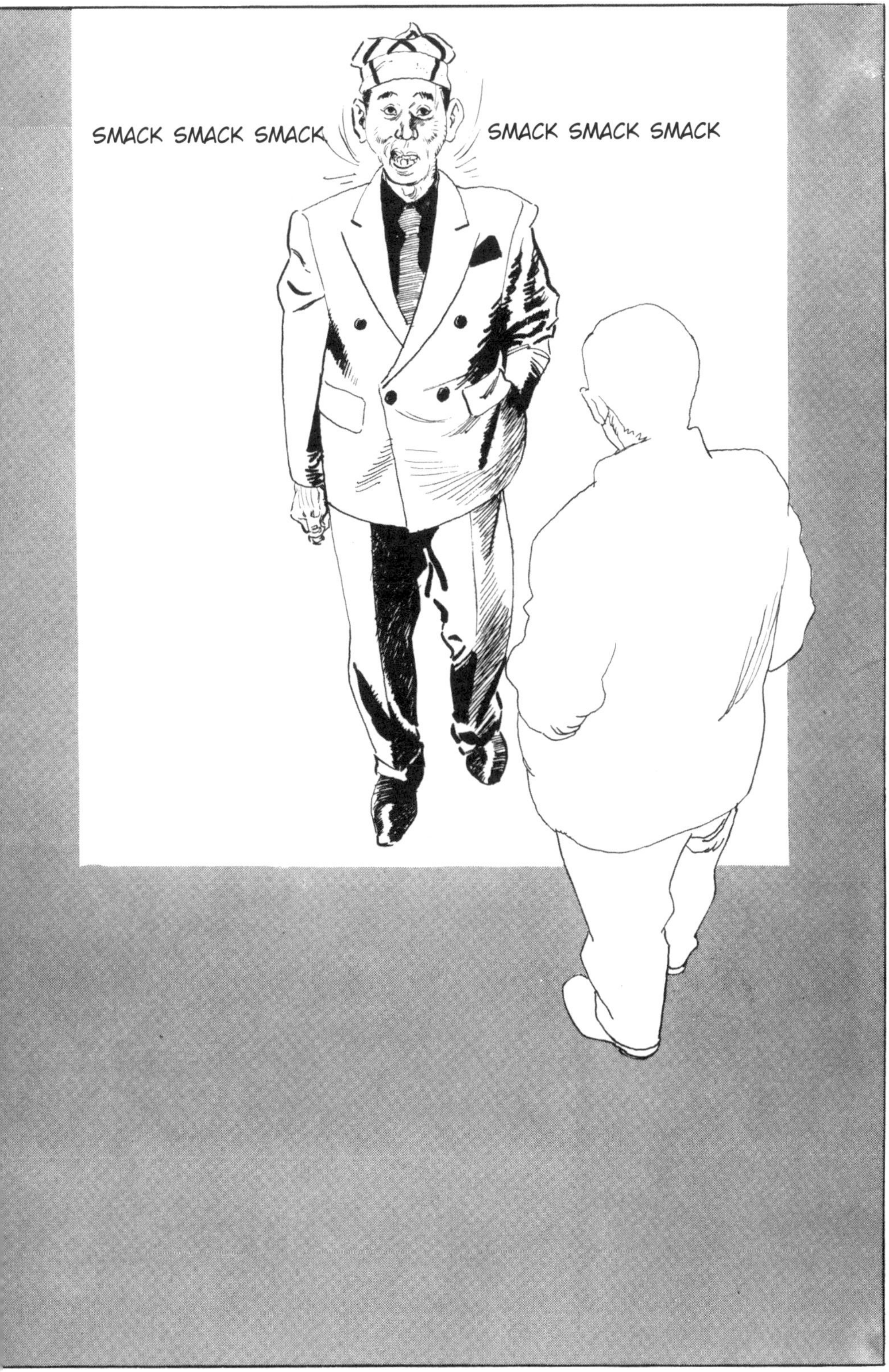
SMACK SMACK SMACK
SMACK SMACK SMACK

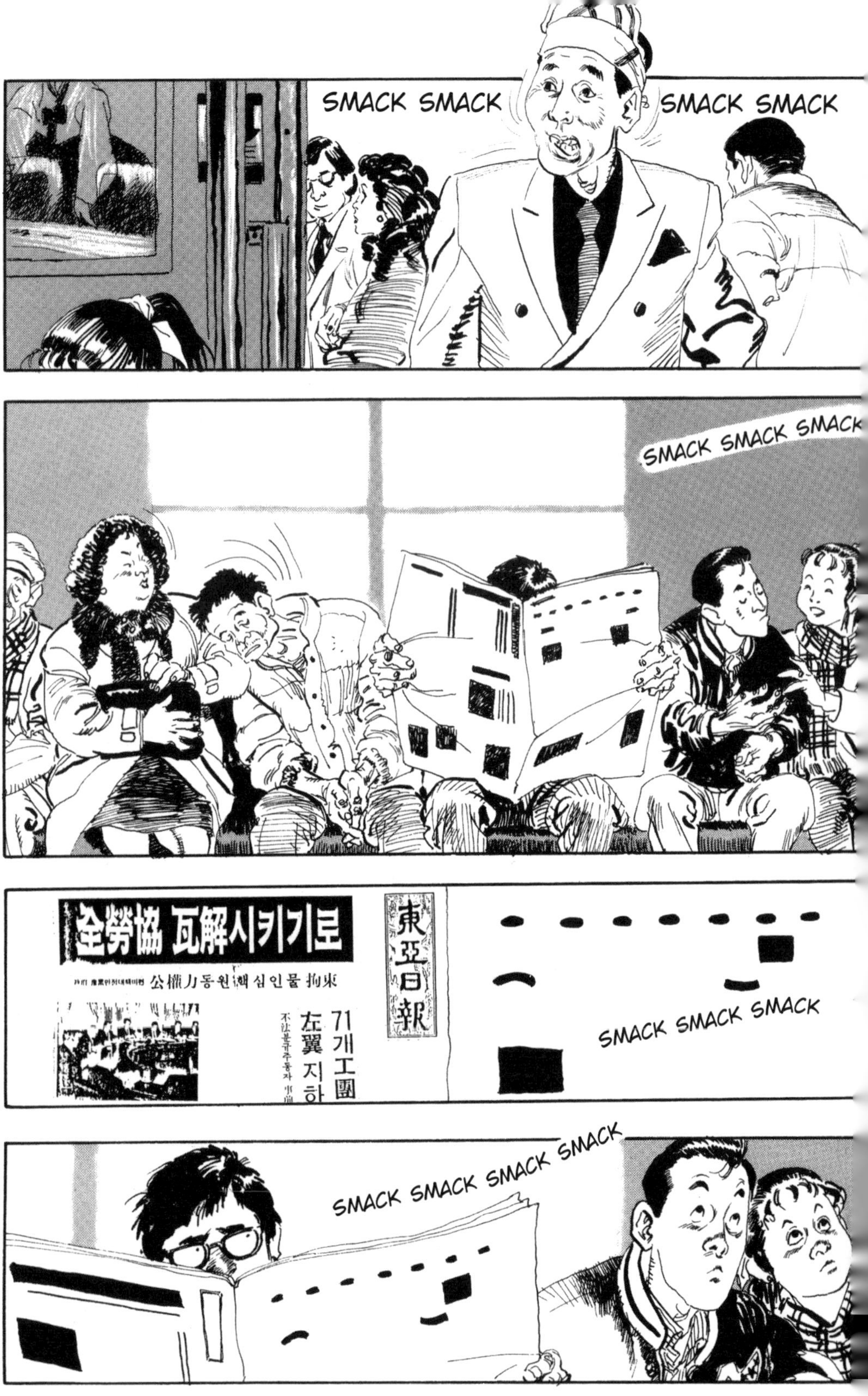
SMACK SMACK
SMACK SMACK
SMACK SMACK SMACK
全勞協 瓦解시키기로
公權力동원 핵심인물 拘束
東亞日報
71개工團
左翼 지하
SMACK SMACK SMACK
SMACK SMACK SMACK SMACK

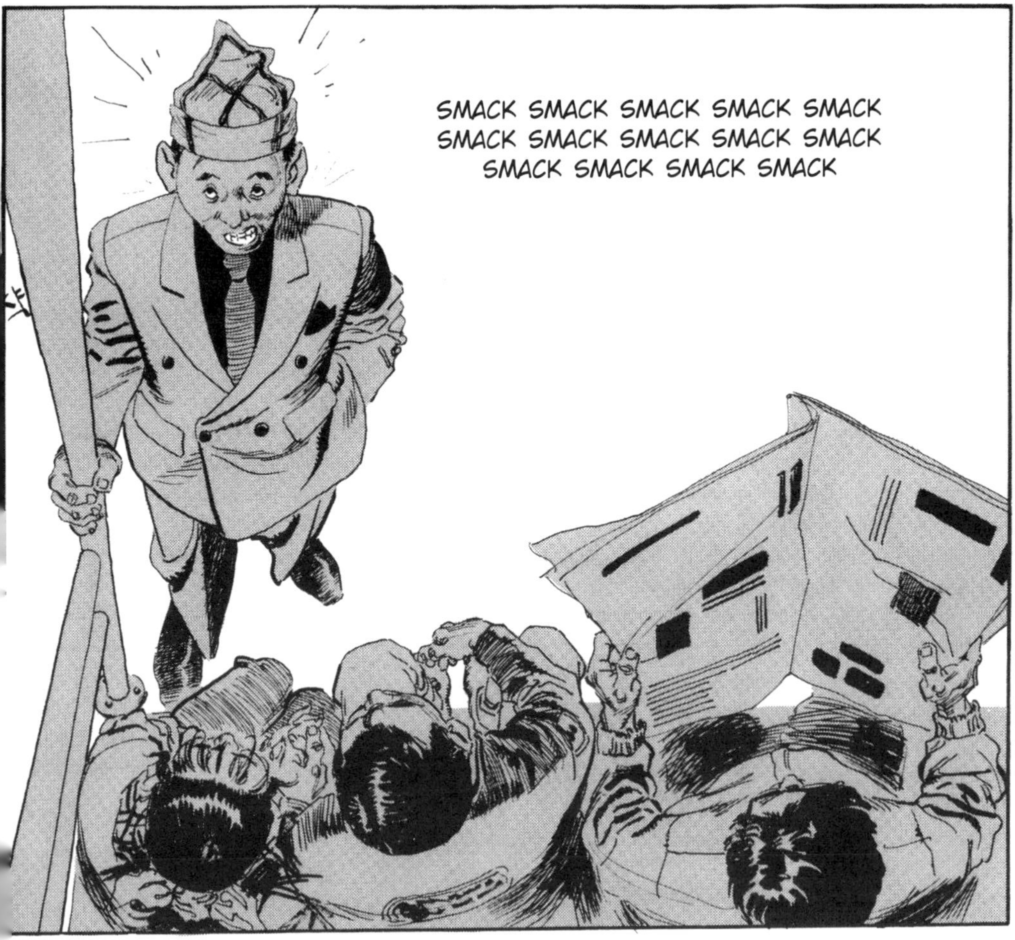
SMACK SMACK SMACK SMACK SMACK
SMACK SMACK SMACK SMACK SMACK
SMACK SMACK SMACK SMACK

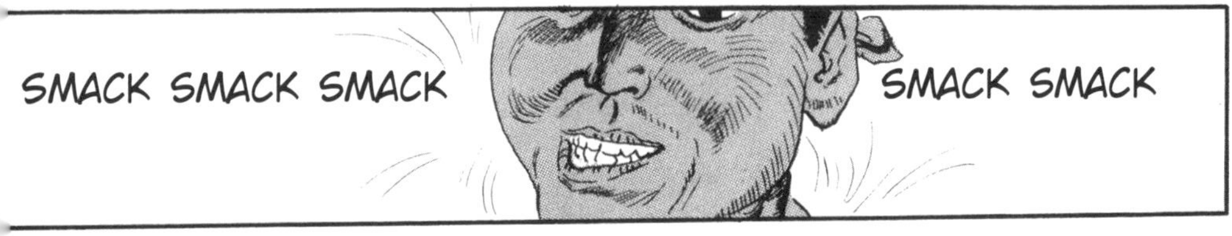
SMACK SMACK SMACK
SMACK SMACK

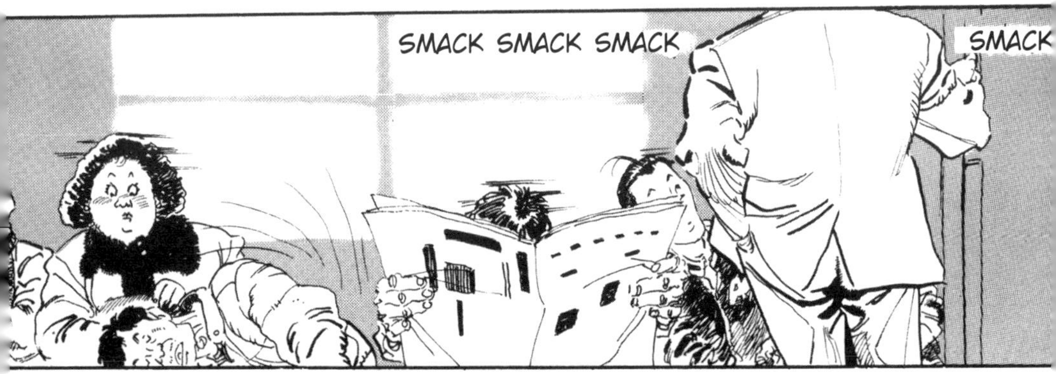
SMACK SMACK SMACK
SMACK

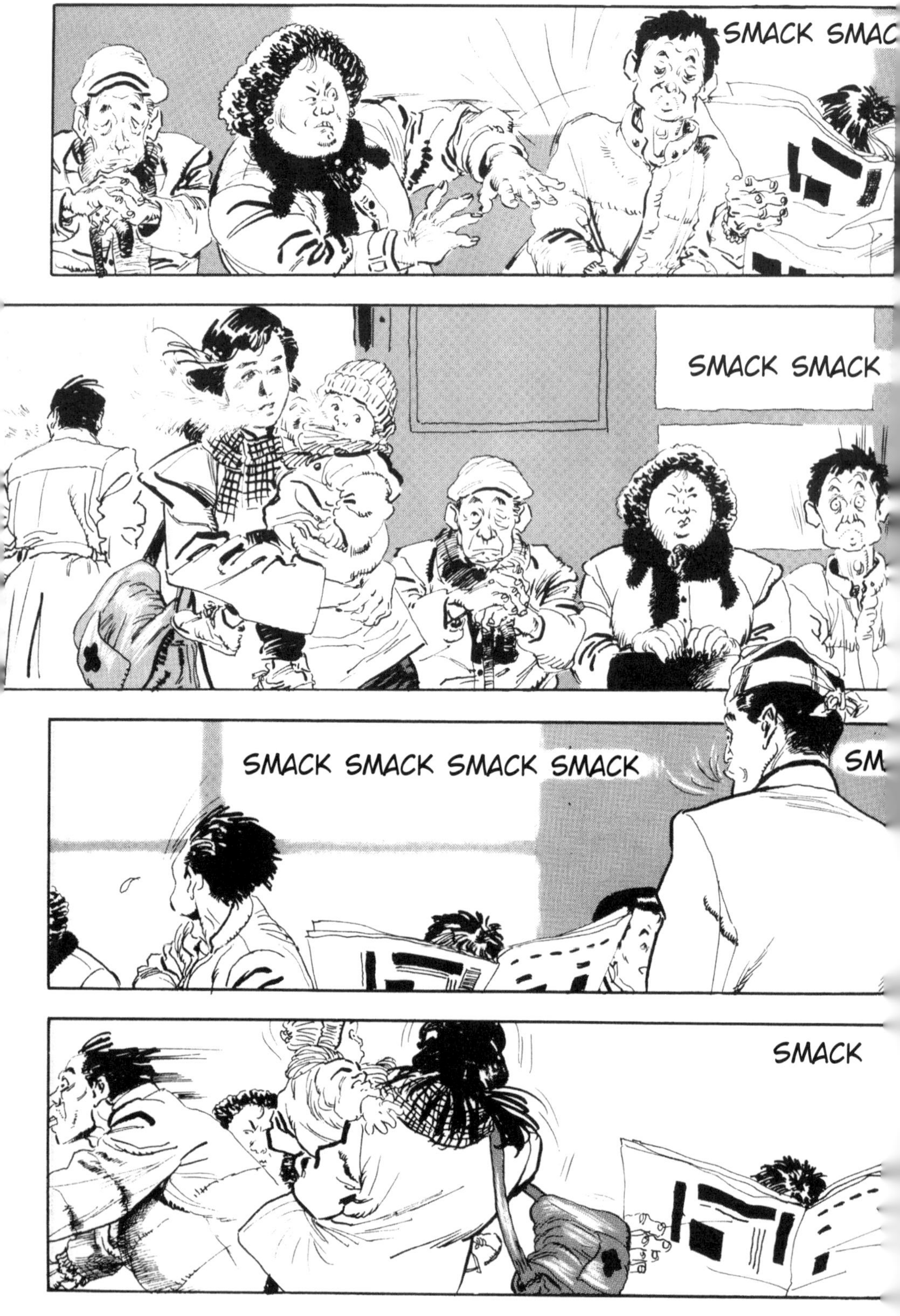
SMACK SMAC
SMACK SMACK
SMACK SMACK SMACK SMACK
SM
SMACK

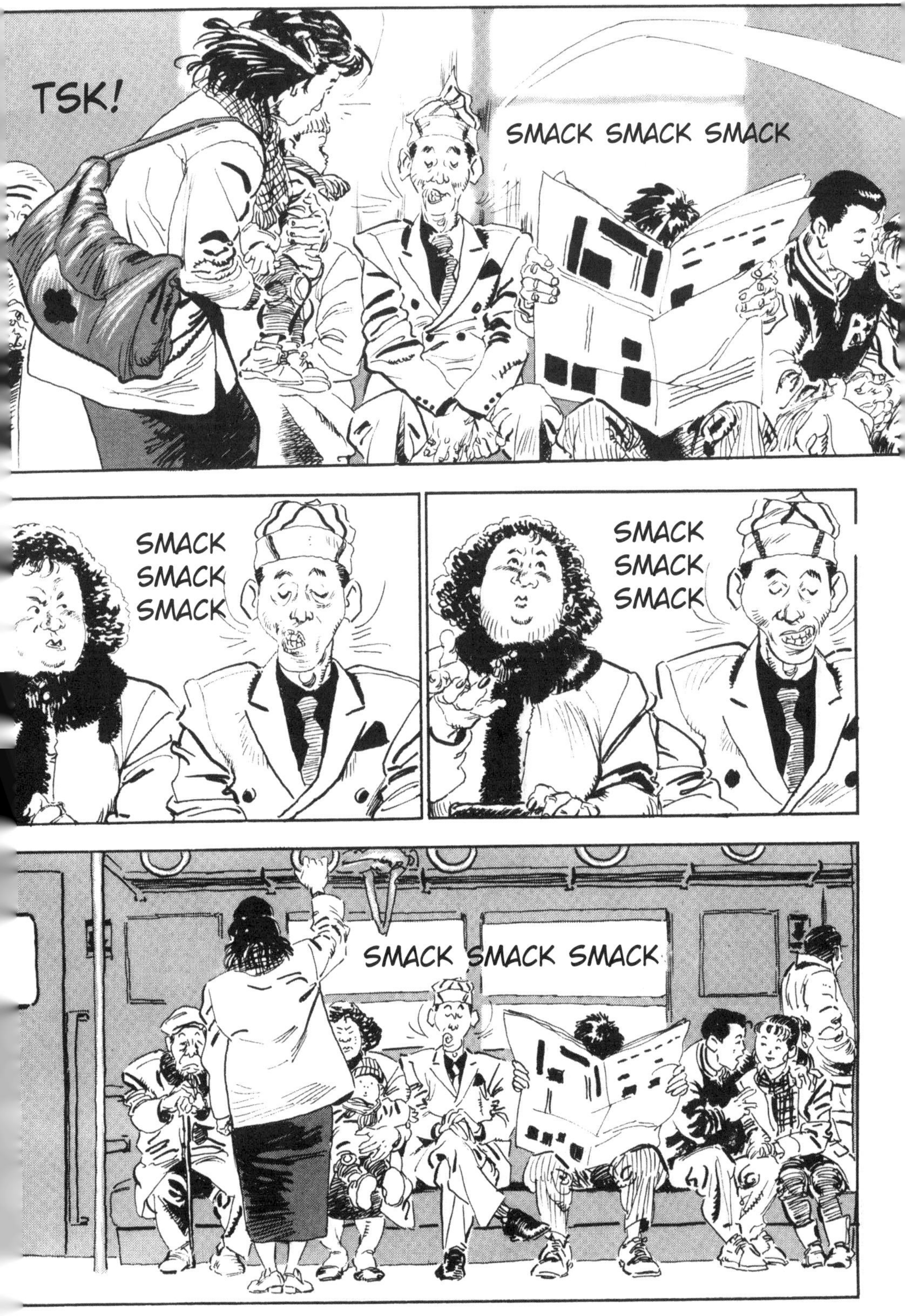
TSK!
SMACK SMACK SMACK
SMACK SMACK SMACK
SMACK SMACK SMACK
SMACK SMACK SMACK

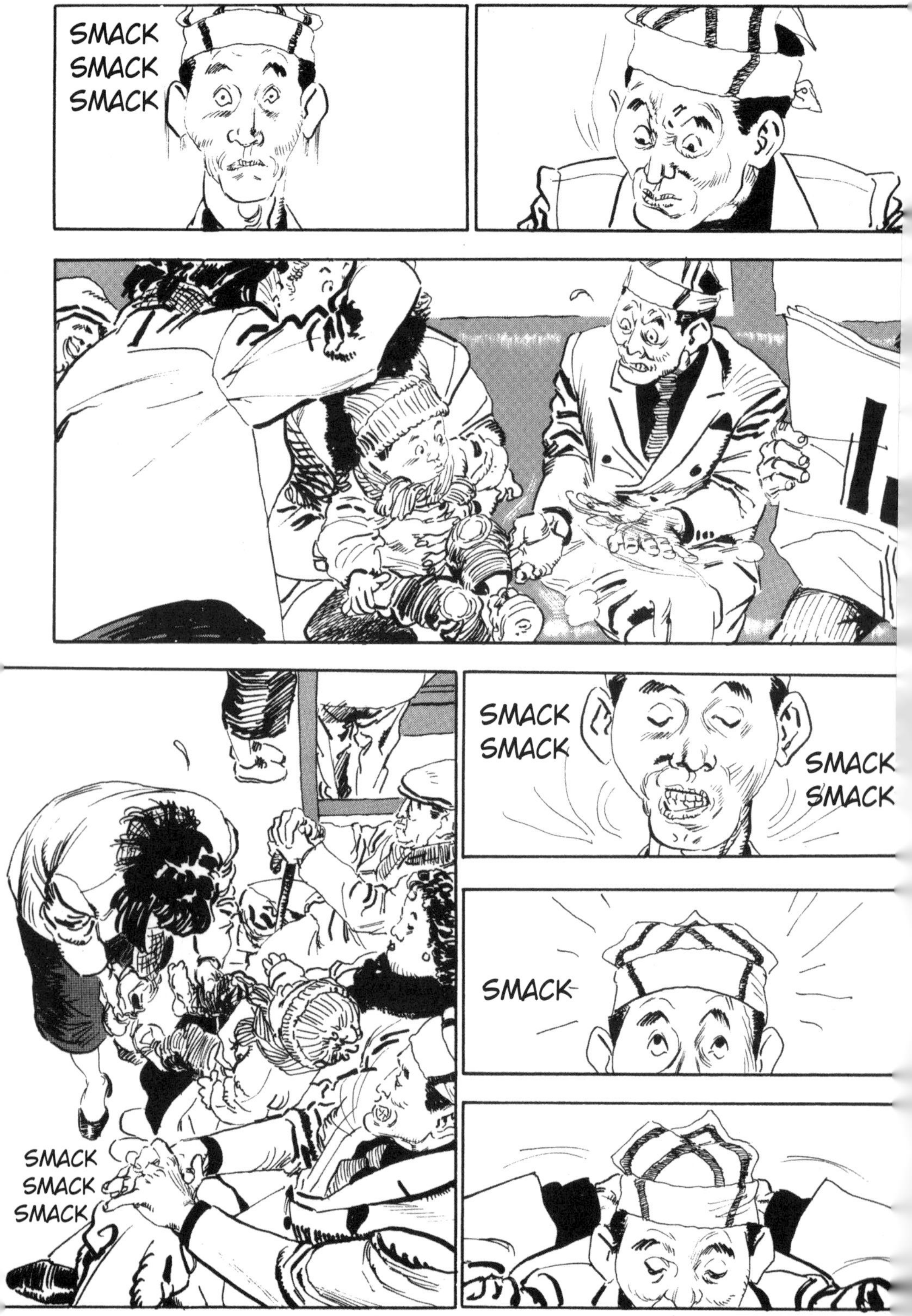
SMACK
SMACK
SMACK
SMACK
SMACK
SMACK
SMACK
SMACK
SMACK
SMACK
SMACK
SMACK

SMACK
SMACK
SMACK

SMACK
SMACK
SMACK

SMACK

SMACK
SMACK
SMACK

SMACK SMACK SMACK

쫙쫙

SMACK
SMACK
SMACK

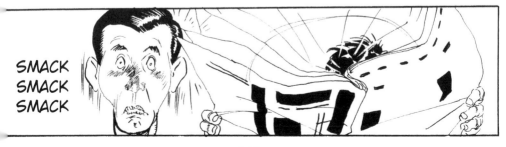

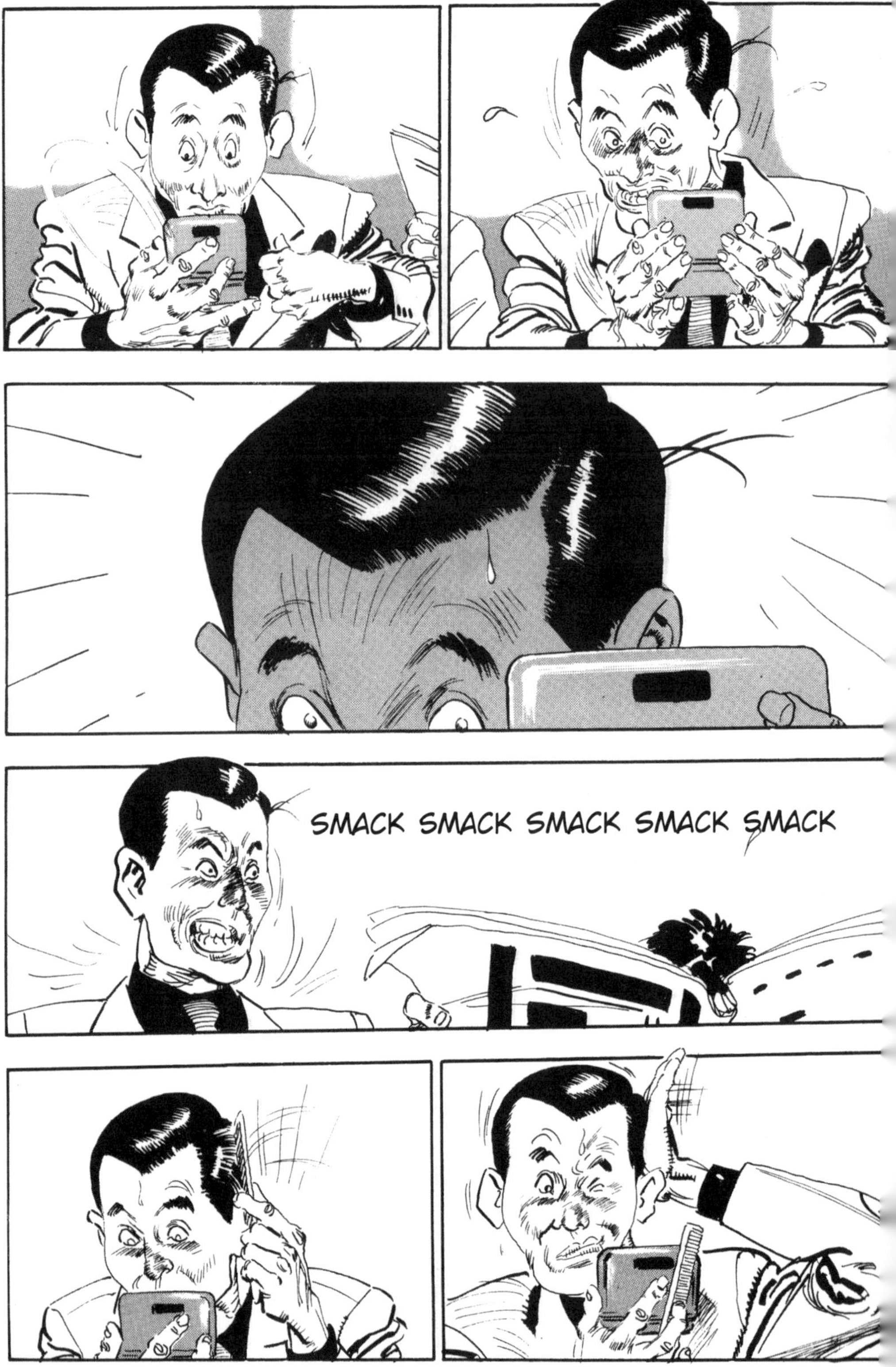
SMACK SMACK SMACK SMACK SMACK

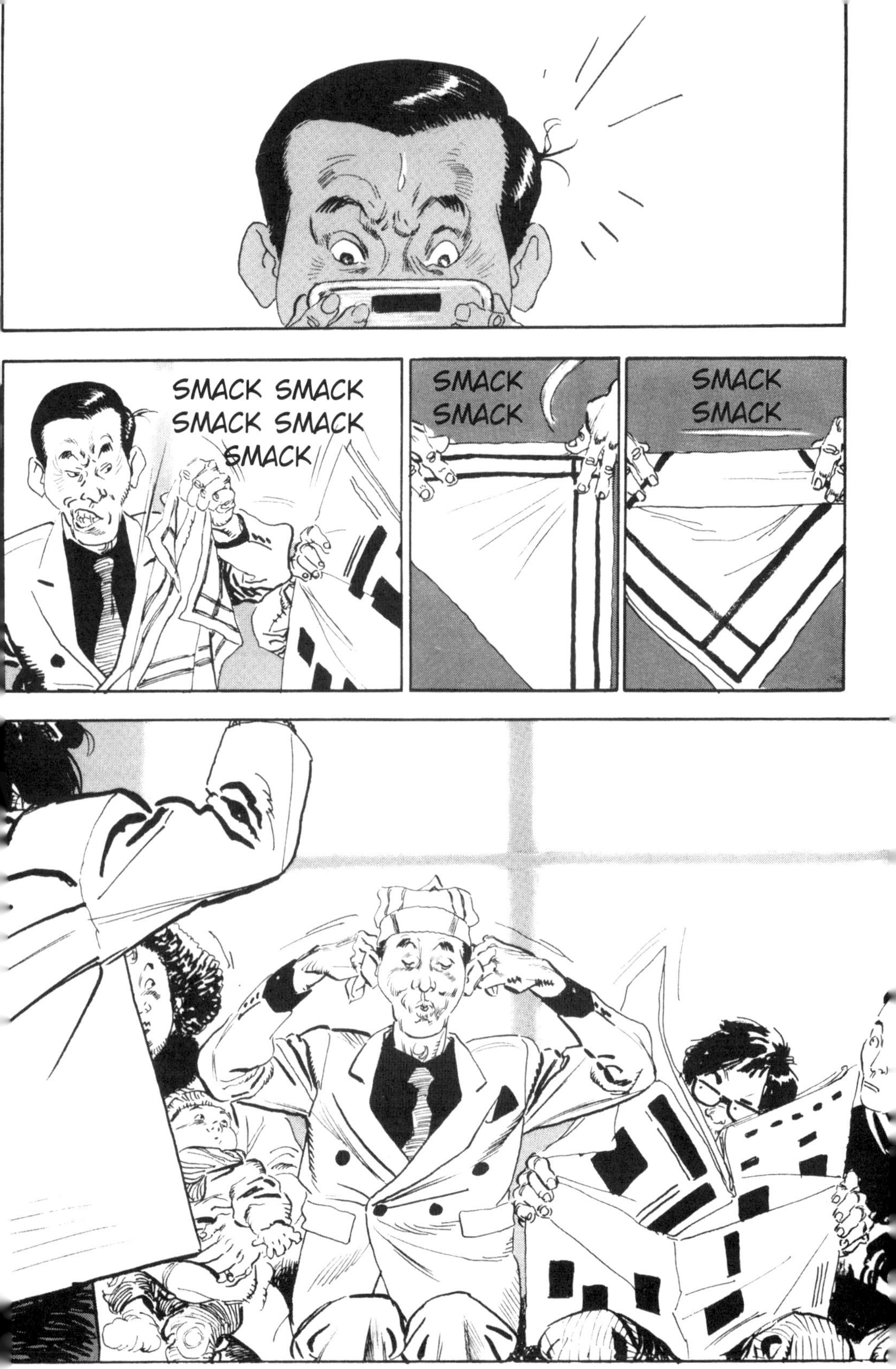
SMACK SMACK
SMACK SMACK
SMACK
SMACK
SMACK
SMACK
SMACK

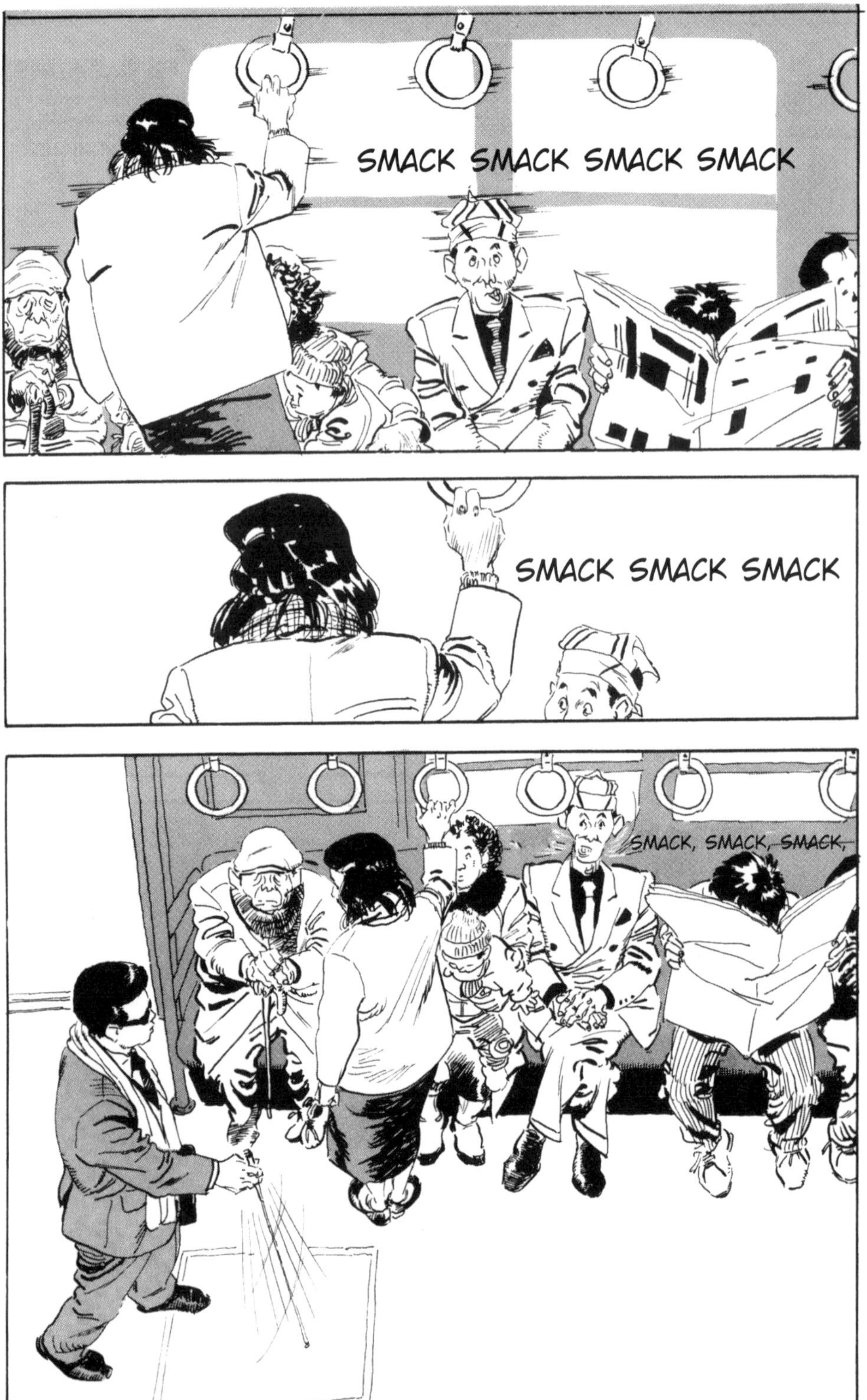
SMACK SMACK SMACK SMACK
SMACK SMACK SMACK
SMACK, SMACK, SMACK,

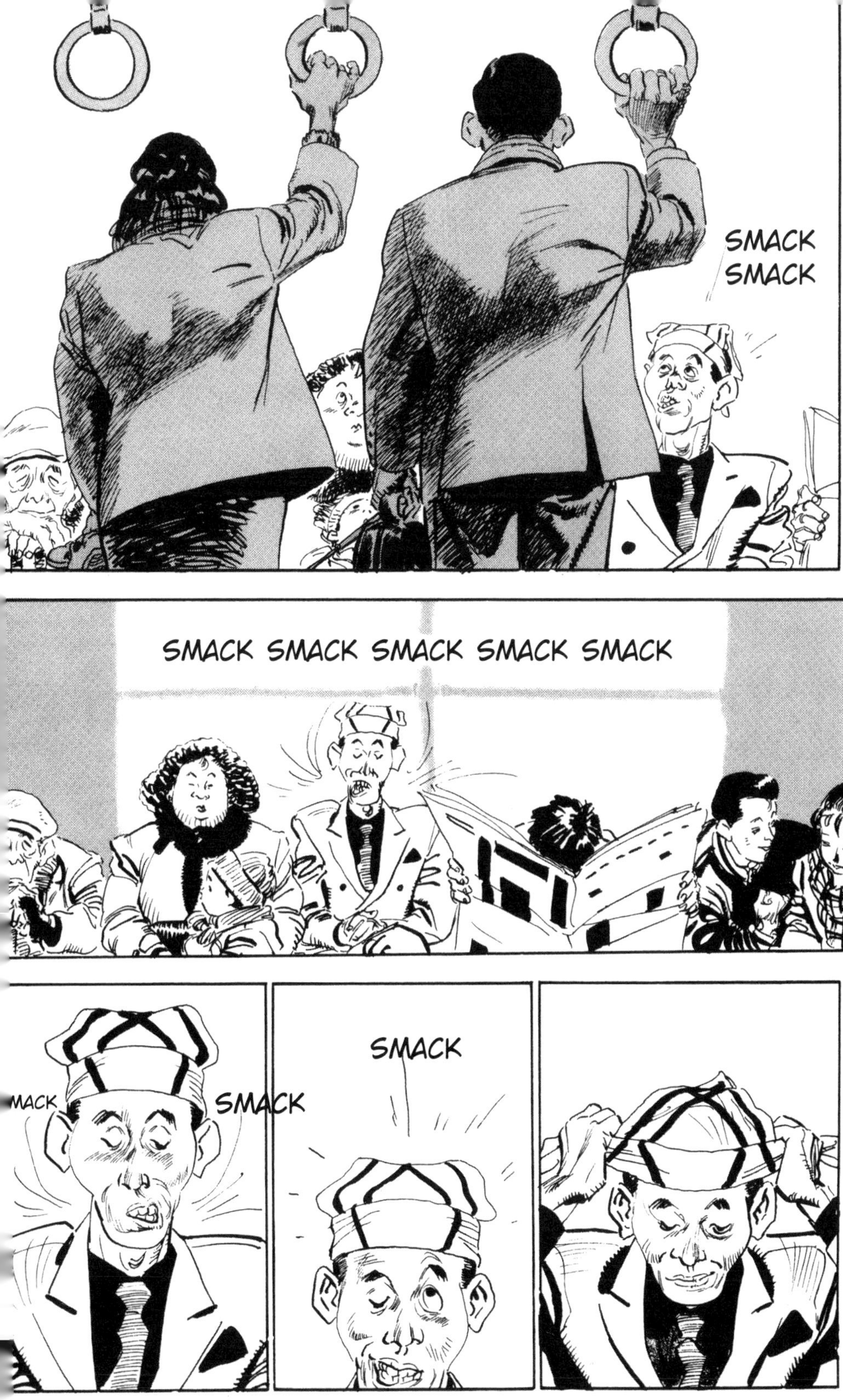
SMACK
SMACK
SMACK SMACK SMACK SMACK SMACK
MACK
SMACK
SMACK

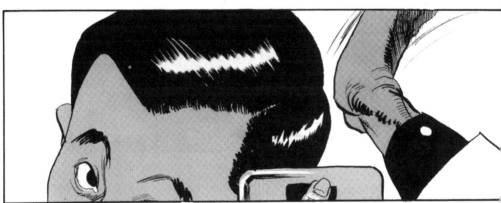

SMACK
SMACK
SMACK

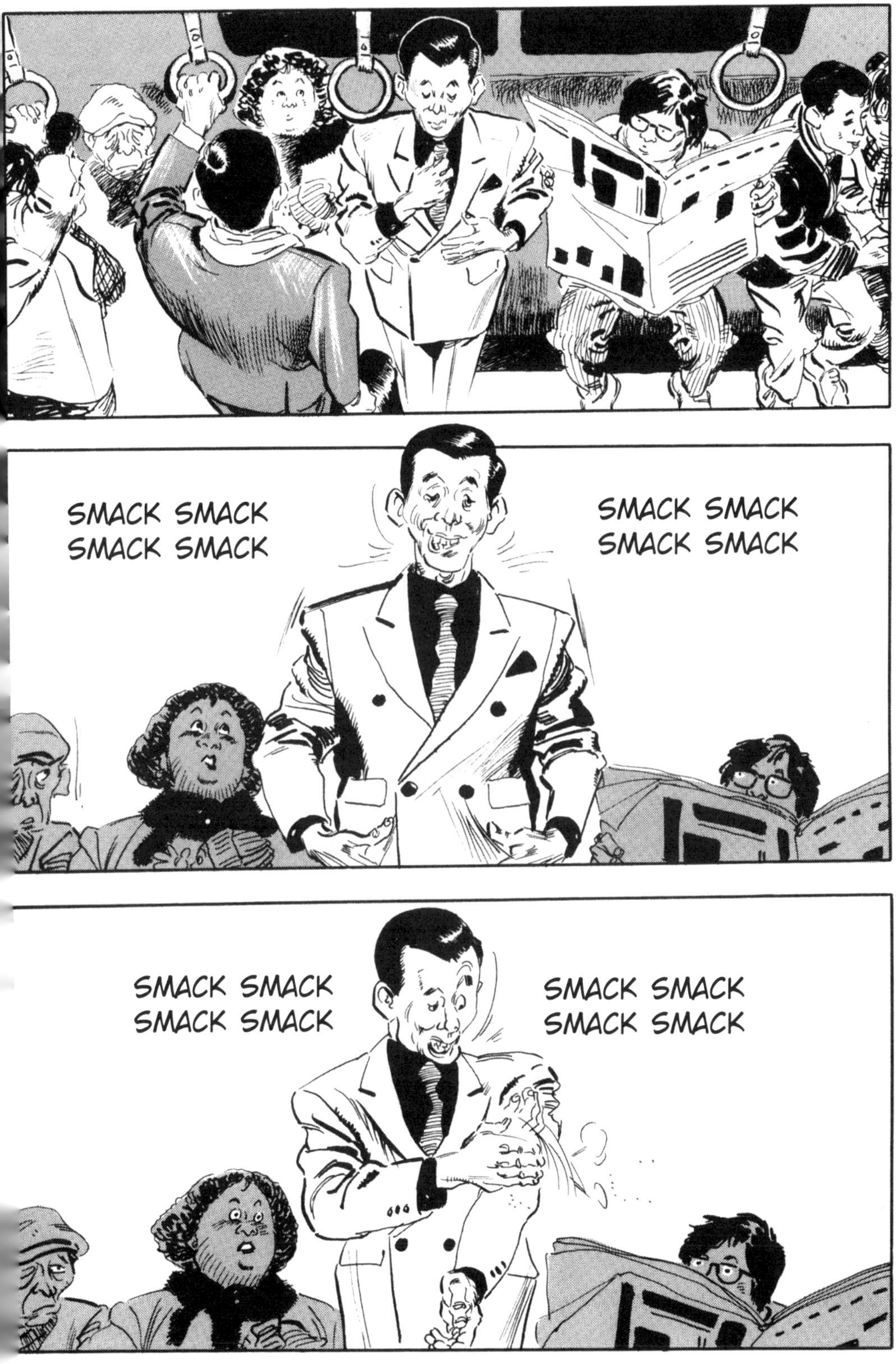
SMACK SMACK
SMACK SMACK
SMACK SMACK
SMACK SMACK
SMACK SMACK
SMACK SMACK
SMACK SMACK
SMACK SMACK

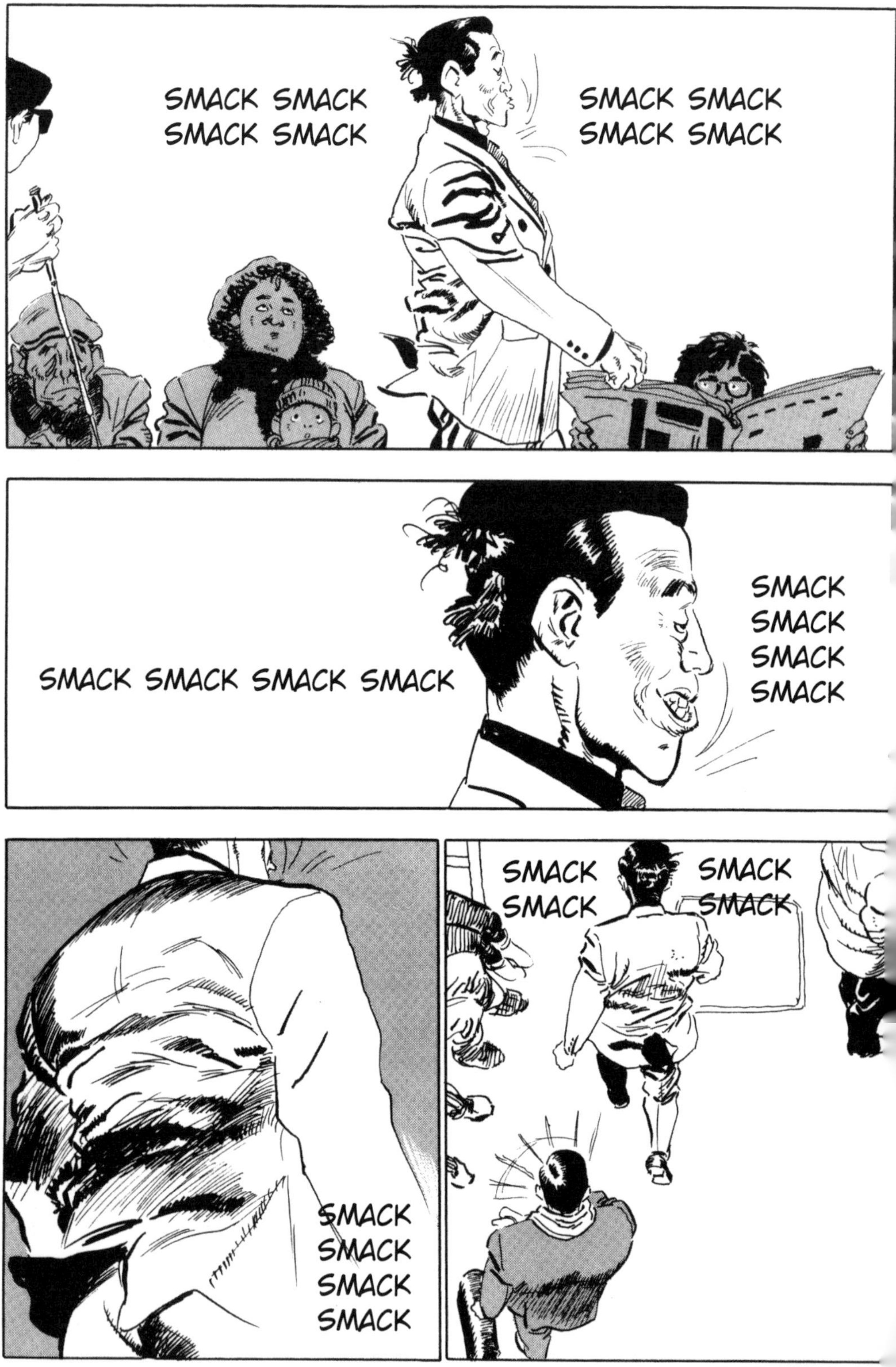
SMACK SMACK
SMACK SMACK
SMACK SMACK
SMACK SMACK
SMACK SMACK SMACK SMACK
SMACK
SMACK
SMACK
SMACK
SMACK
SMACK
SMACK
SMACK
SMACK
SMACK
SMACK
SMACK

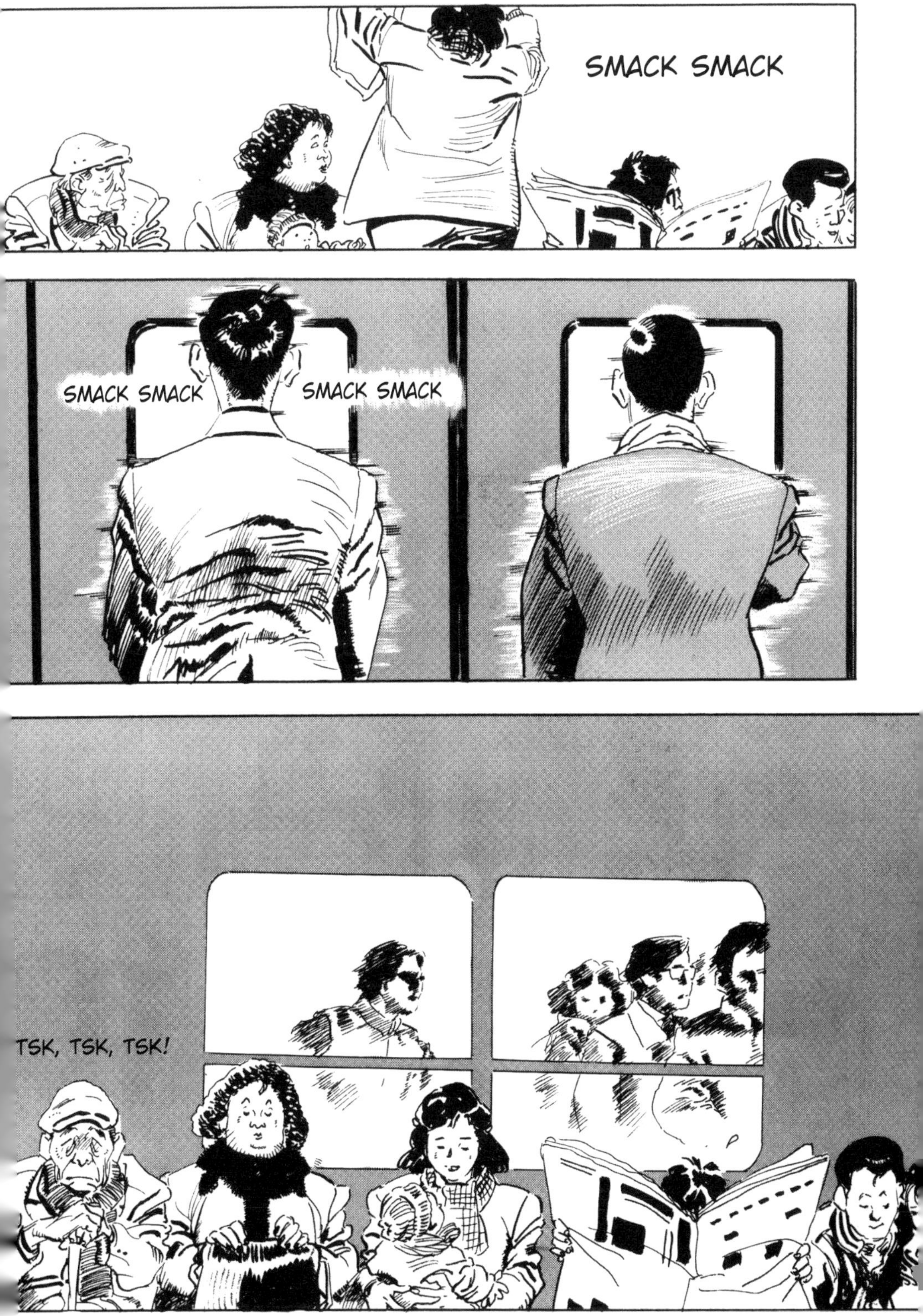
SMACK SMACK
SMACK SMACK
SMACK SMACK
TSK, TSK, TSK!

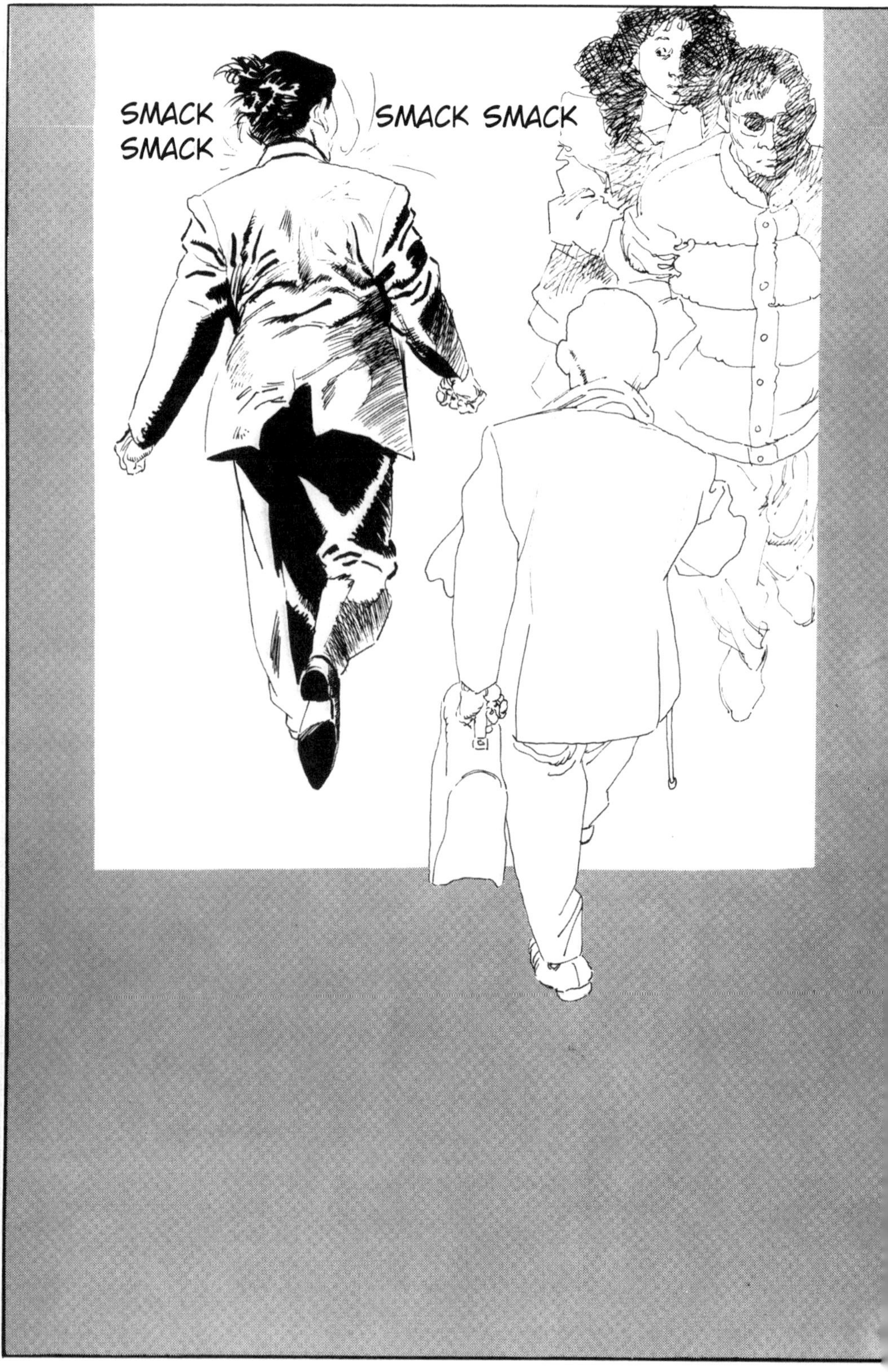
SMACK SMACK
SMACK SMACK

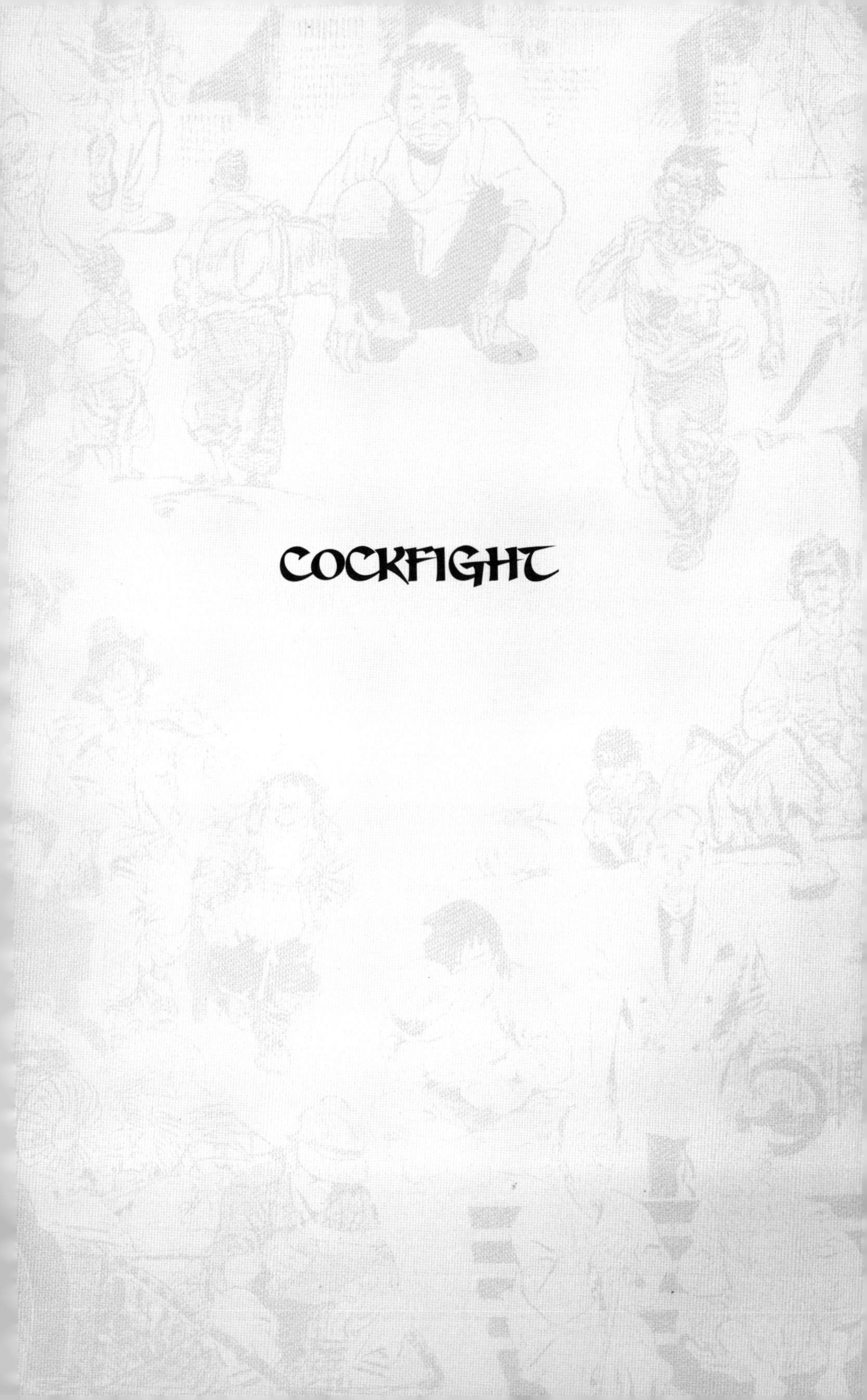

COCKFIGHT

AHN HOI-NAM
APRIL 1993

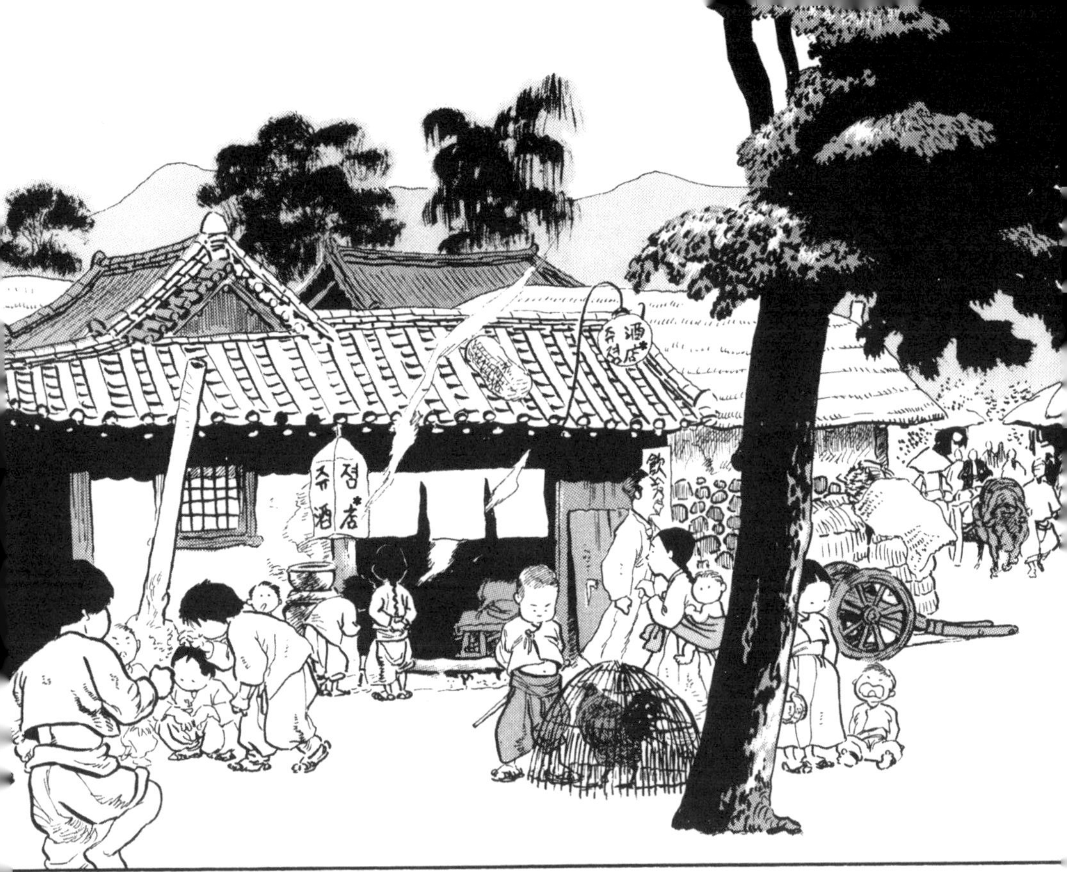
주점*
酒店

*TAVERN

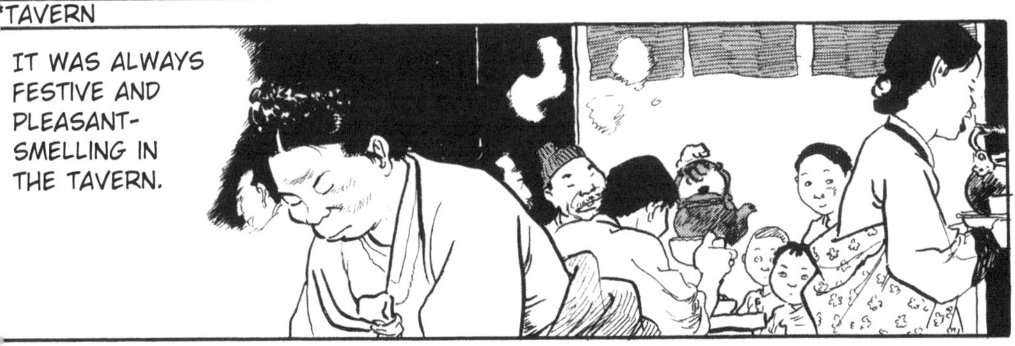
IT WAS ALWAYS FESTIVE AND PLEASANT-SMELLING IN THE TAVERN.

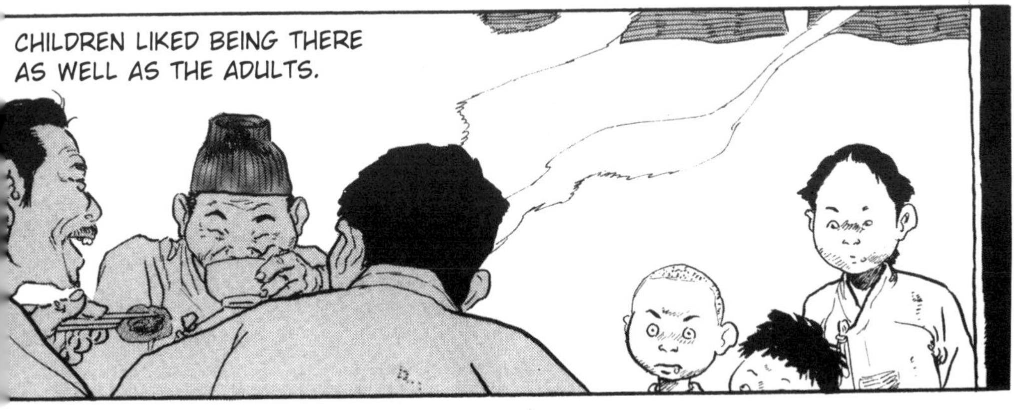
CHILDREN LIKED BEING THERE AS WELL AS THE ADULTS.

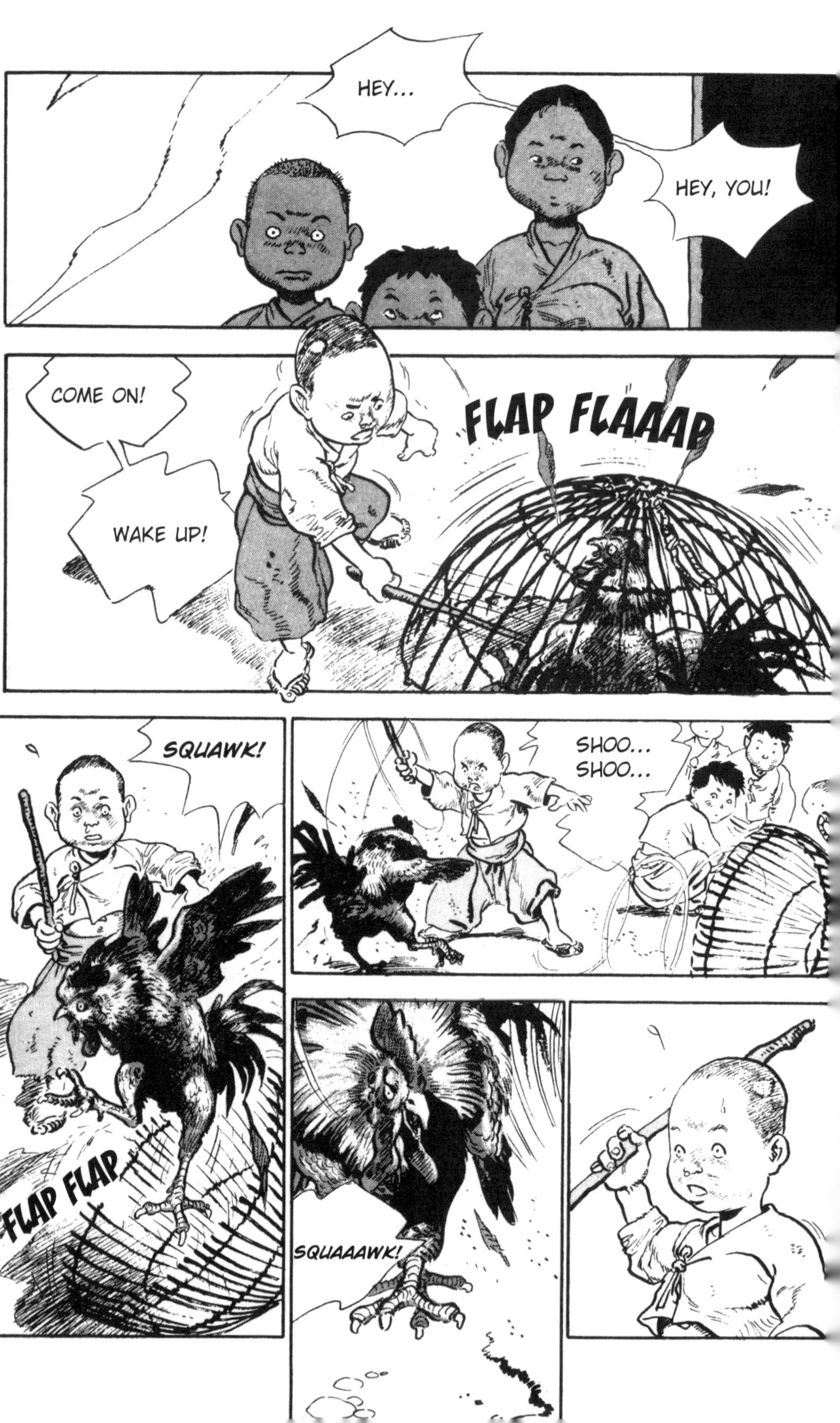
HEY...
HEY, YOU!
COME ON!
WAKE UP!
FLAP FLAAAP
SQUAWK!
FLAP FLAP
SHOO...
SHOO...
SQUAAAWK!

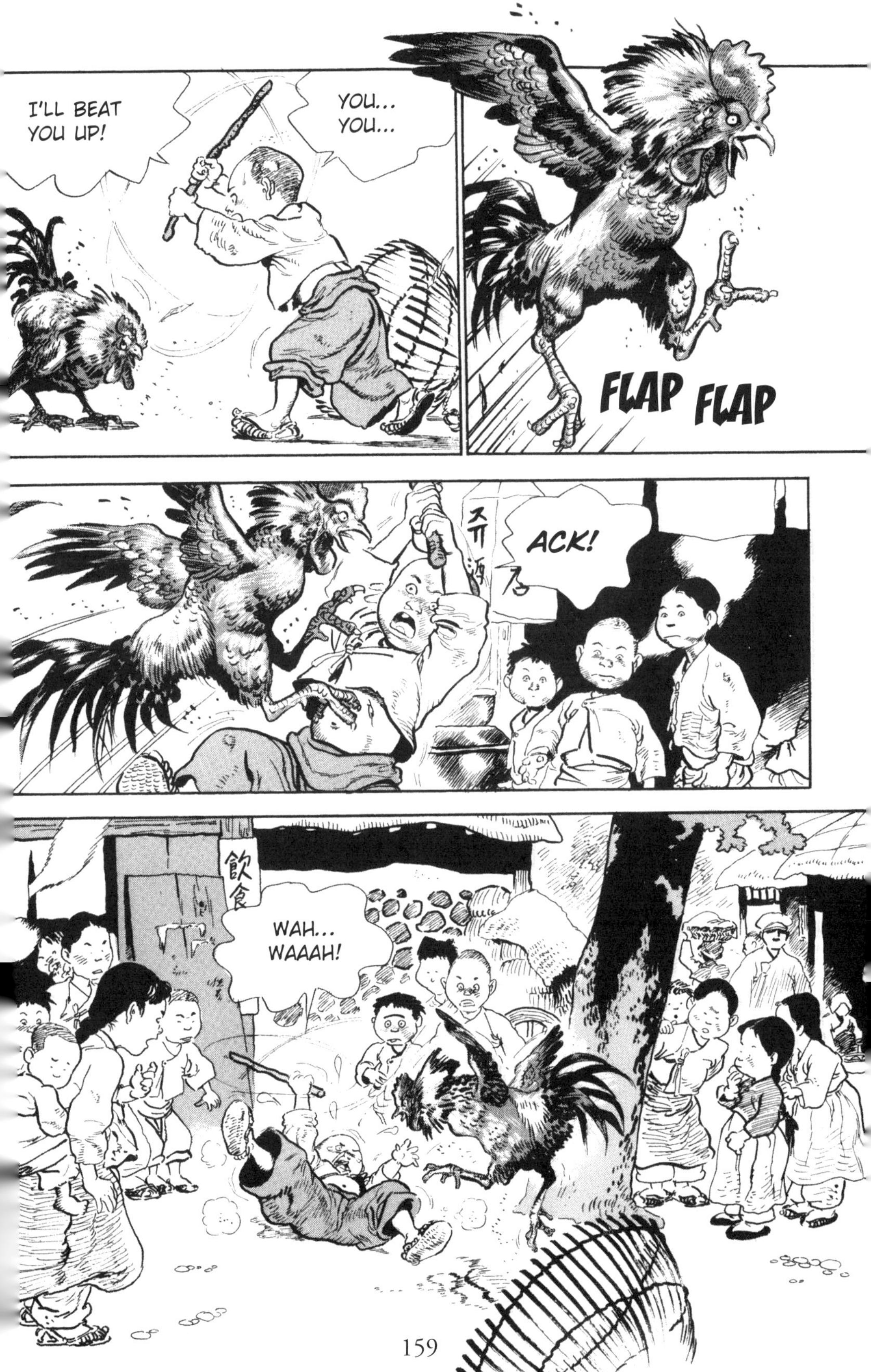
YOU... YOU...
I'LL BEAT YOU UP!
FLAP FLAP
ACK!
飮食
WAH... WAAAH!

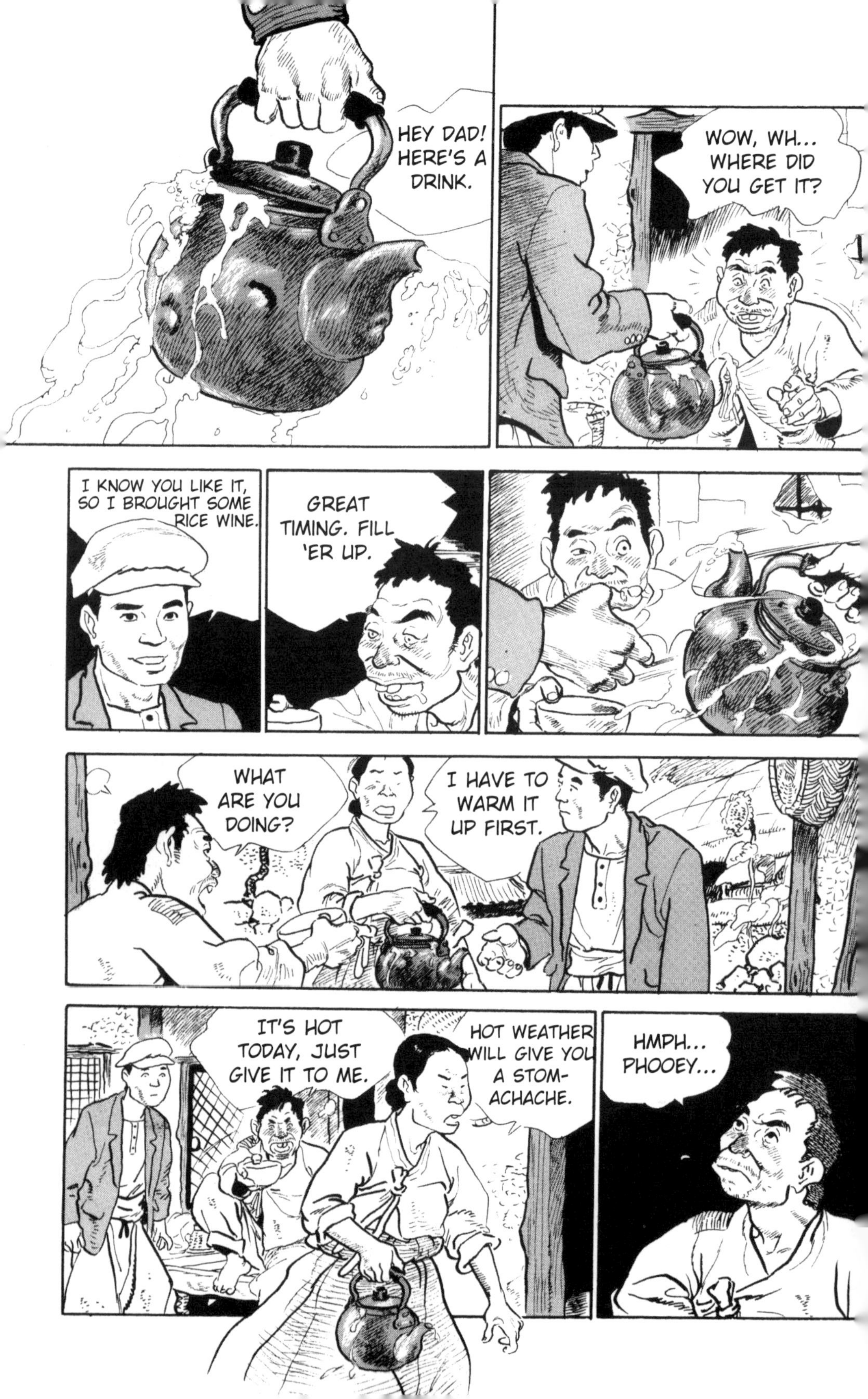
HEY DAD! HERE'S A DRINK.
WOW, WH... WHERE DID YOU GET IT?
I KNOW YOU LIKE IT, SO I BROUGHT SOME RICE WINE.
GREAT TIMING. FILL 'ER UP.
WHAT ARE YOU DOING?
I HAVE TO WARM IT UP FIRST.
IT'S HOT TODAY, JUST GIVE IT TO ME.
HOT WEATHER WILL GIVE YOU A STOM-ACHACHE.
HMPH... PHOOEY...

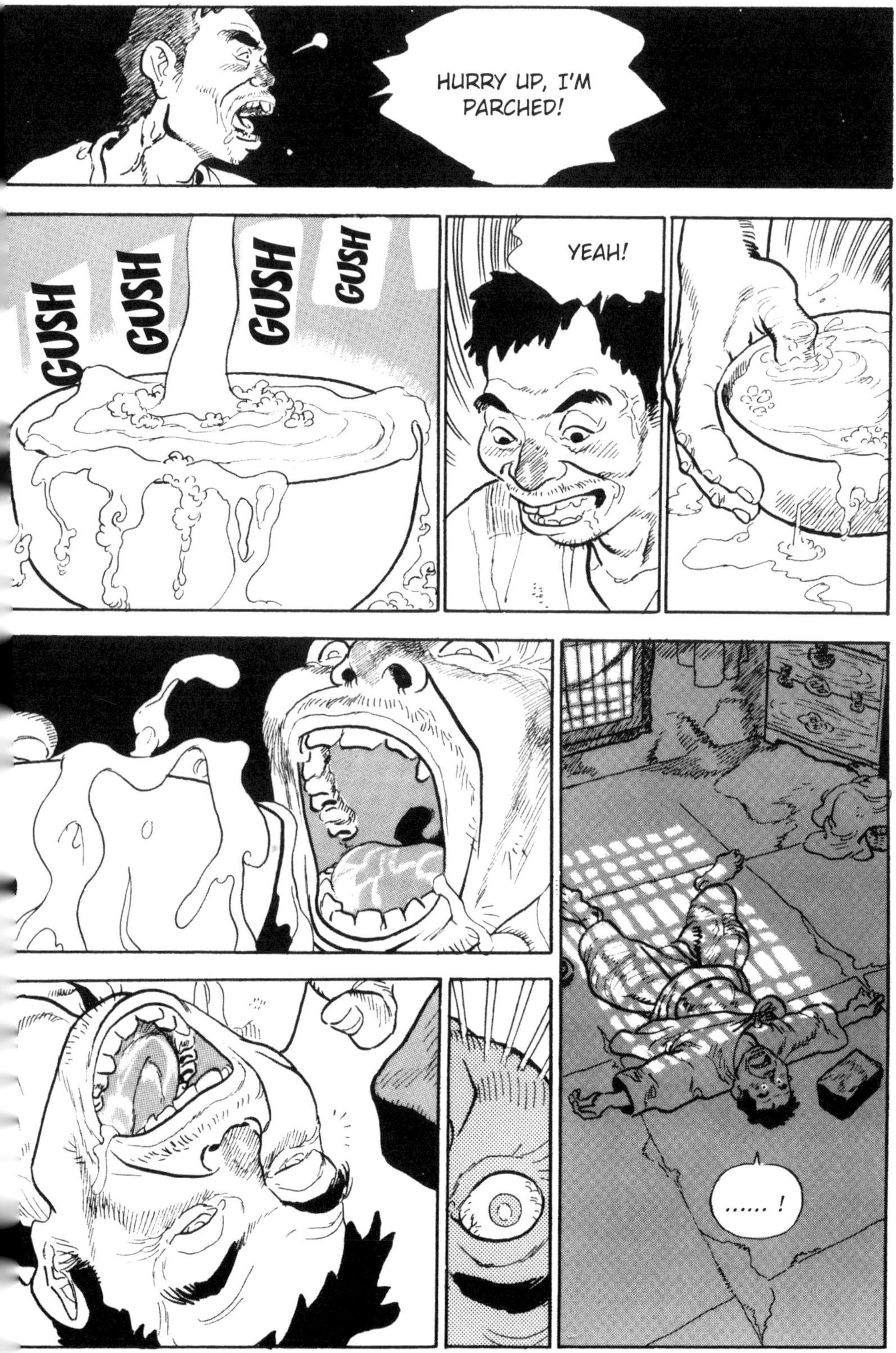
HURRY UP, I'M PARCHED!
GUSH
GUSH
GUSH
GUSH
YEAH!
...... !

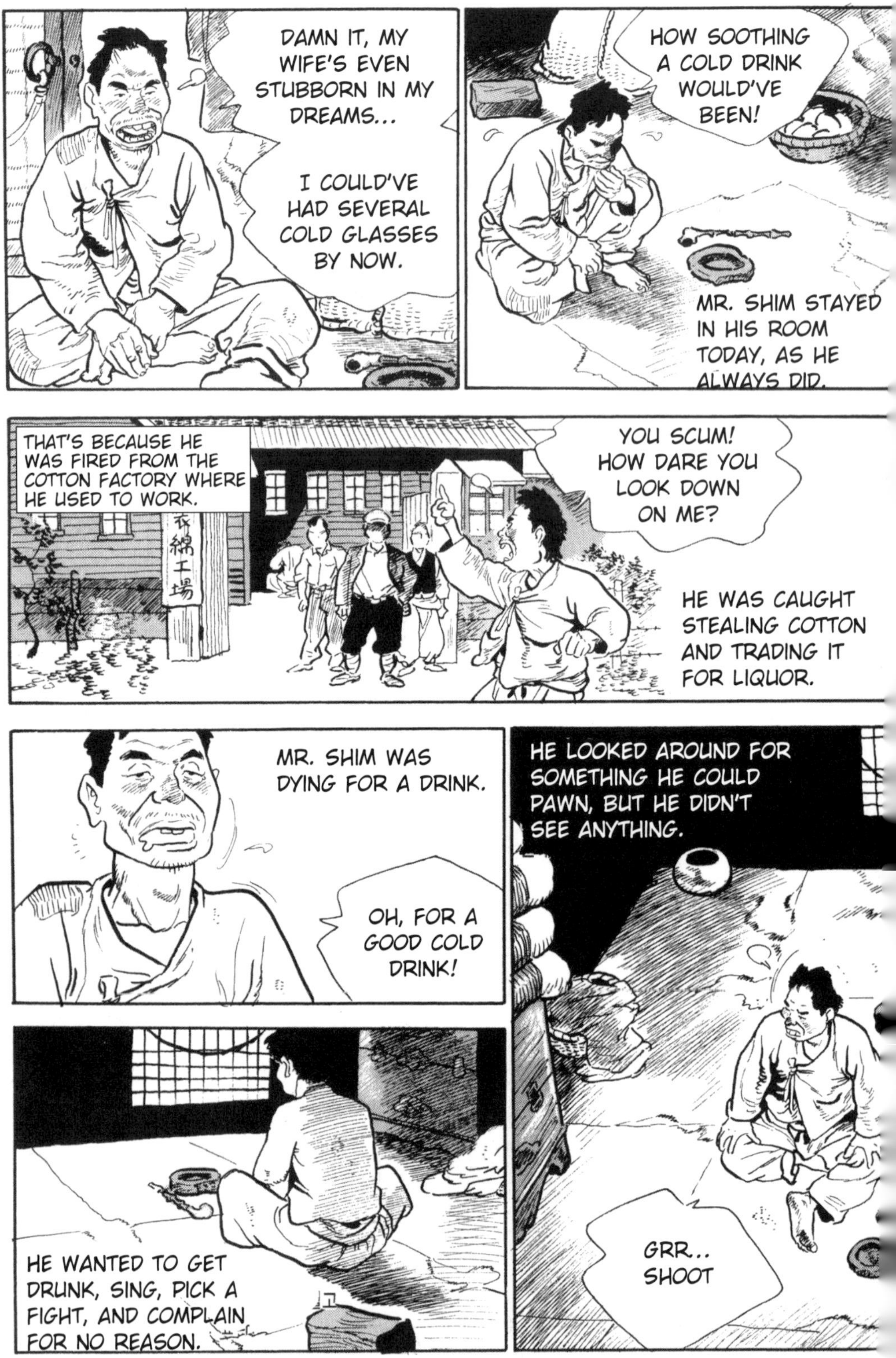
DAMN IT, MY WIFE'S EVEN STUBBORN IN MY DREAMS...
I COULD'VE HAD SEVERAL COLD GLASSES BY NOW.
HOW SOOTHING A COLD DRINK WOULD'VE BEEN!
MR. SHIM STAYED IN HIS ROOM TODAY, AS HE ALWAYS DID.
THAT'S BECAUSE HE WAS FIRED FROM THE COTTON FACTORY WHERE HE USED TO WORK.
YOU SCUM! HOW DARE YOU LOOK DOWN ON ME?
HE WAS CAUGHT STEALING COTTON AND TRADING IT FOR LIQUOR.
MR. SHIM WAS DYING FOR A DRINK.
OH, FOR A GOOD COLD DRINK!
HE WANTED TO GET DRUNK, SING, PICK A FIGHT, AND COMPLAIN FOR NO REASON.
HE LOOKED AROUND FOR SOMETHING HE COULD PAWN, BUT HE DIDN'T SEE ANYTHING.
GRR... SHOOT

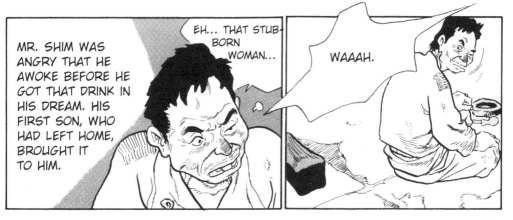

MR. SHIM WAS ANGRY THAT HE AWOKE BEFORE HE GOT THAT DRINK IN HIS DREAM. HIS FIRST SON, WHO HAD LEFT HOME, BROUGHT IT TO HIM.

EH... THAT STUBBORN WOMAN...

WAAAH.

WHAT'S WRONG, KID?

WAAH! I FOUGHT A ROOSTER.

YOU DID WHAT?

I FOUGHT A ROOSTER, WAAH WAAH.

HEY, THERE'S A SCRATCH ON YOUR FACE...

YOU KNOW, SNIFF, IT WAS THAT COCK AT THE TAVERN, SNIFF...

WAAH WAAH WAAH...

WHAT'D YOU SAY?

THAT NO GOOD LITTLE...

PTOOIE!

PTOOIE!

WAAH WAAH WAAH.

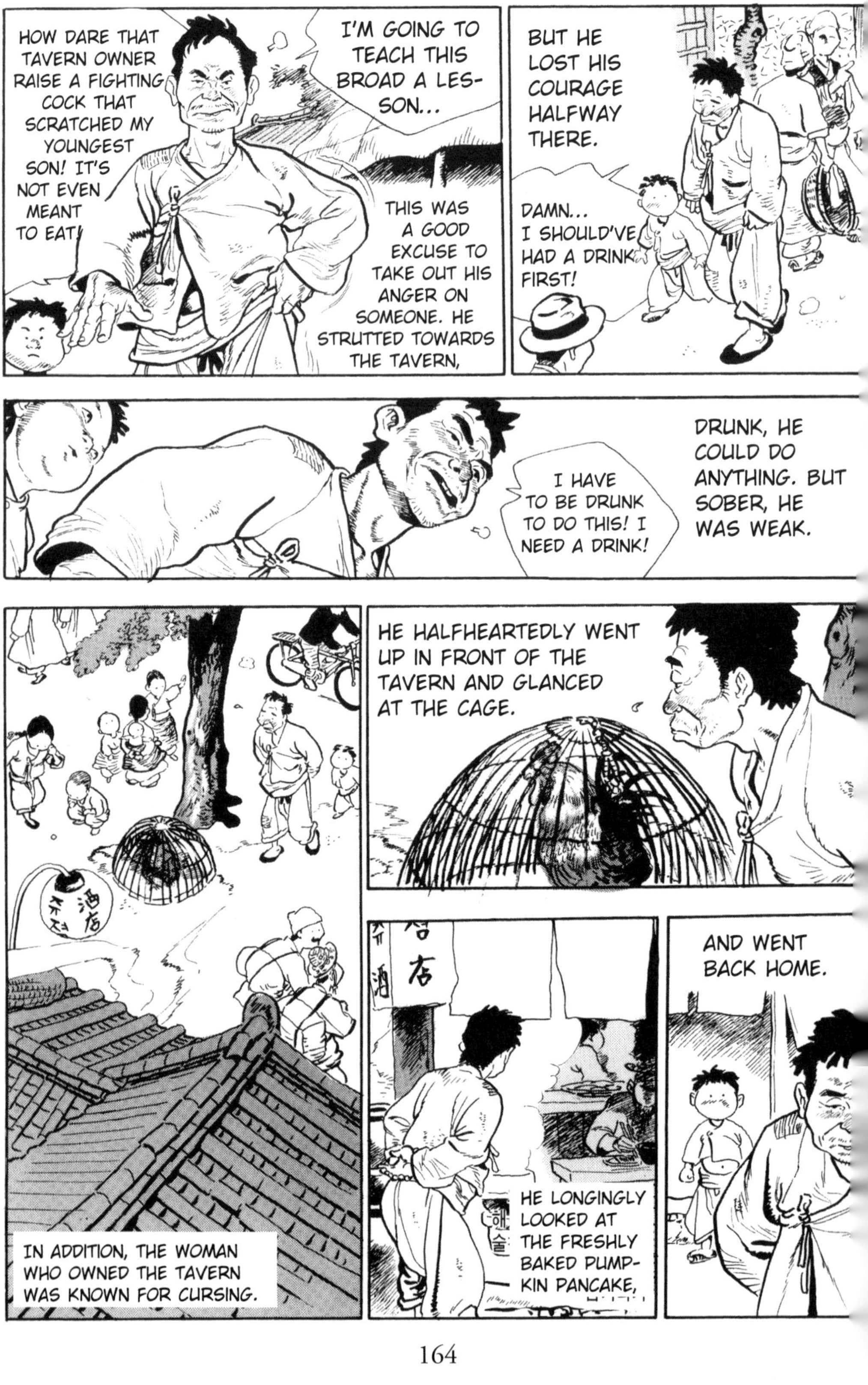
HOW DARE THAT TAVERN OWNER RAISE A FIGHTING COCK THAT SCRATCHED MY YOUNGEST SON! IT'S NOT EVEN MEANT TO EAT!
I'M GOING TO TEACH THIS BROAD A LES-SON...
THIS WAS A GOOD EXCUSE TO TAKE OUT HIS ANGER ON SOMEONE. HE STRUTTED TOWARDS THE TAVERN,
BUT HE LOST HIS COURAGE HALFWAY THERE.
DAMN... I SHOULD'VE HAD A DRINK FIRST!
I HAVE TO BE DRUNK TO DO THIS! I NEED A DRINK!
DRUNK, HE COULD DO ANYTHING. BUT SOBER, HE WAS WEAK.
酒店
IN ADDITION, THE WOMAN WHO OWNED THE TAVERN WAS KNOWN FOR CURSING.
HE HALFHEARTEDLY WENT UP IN FRONT OF THE TAVERN AND GLANCED AT THE CAGE.
酒店
HE LONGINGLY LOOKED AT THE FRESHLY BAKED PUMP-KIN PANCAKE,
AND WENT BACK HOME.

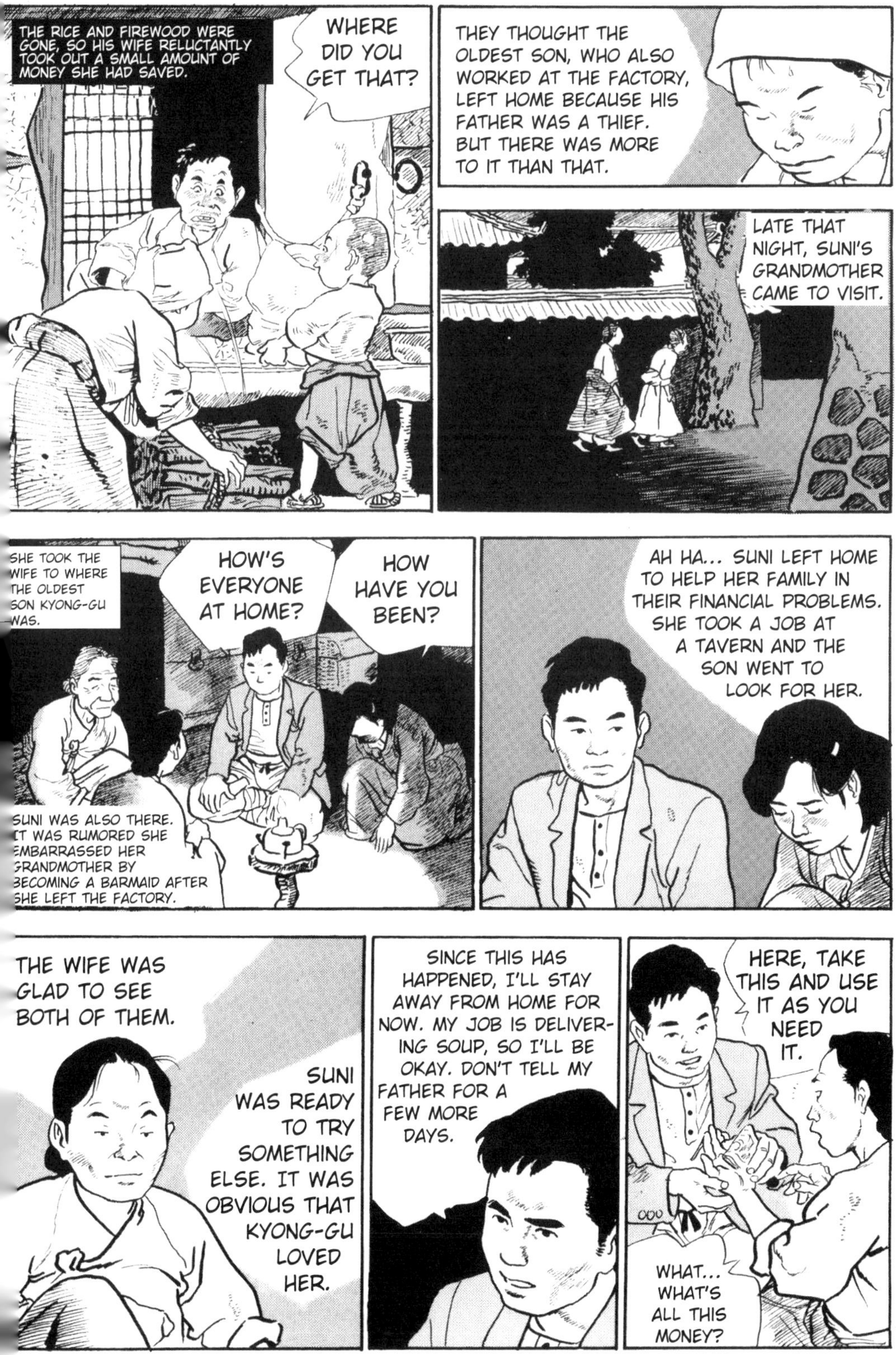
THE RICE AND FIREWOOD WERE GONE, SO HIS WIFE RELUCTANTLY TOOK OUT A SMALL AMOUNT OF MONEY SHE HAD SAVED.
WHERE DID YOU GET THAT?
THEY THOUGHT THE OLDEST SON, WHO ALSO WORKED AT THE FACTORY, LEFT HOME BECAUSE HIS FATHER WAS A THIEF. BUT THERE WAS MORE TO IT THAN THAT.
LATE THAT NIGHT, SUNI'S GRANDMOTHER CAME TO VISIT.
SHE TOOK THE WIFE TO WHERE THE OLDEST SON KYONG-GU WAS.
HOW'S EVERYONE AT HOME?
HOW HAVE YOU BEEN?
SUNI WAS ALSO THERE. IT WAS RUMORED SHE EMBARRASSED HER GRANDMOTHER BY BECOMING A BARMAID AFTER SHE LEFT THE FACTORY.
AH HA... SUNI LEFT HOME TO HELP HER FAMILY IN THEIR FINANCIAL PROBLEMS. SHE TOOK A JOB AT A TAVERN AND THE SON WENT TO LOOK FOR HER.
THE WIFE WAS GLAD TO SEE BOTH OF THEM.
SUNI WAS READY TO TRY SOMETHING ELSE. IT WAS OBVIOUS THAT KYONG-GU LOVED HER.
SINCE THIS HAS HAPPENED, I'LL STAY AWAY FROM HOME FOR NOW. MY JOB IS DELIVERING SOUP, SO I'LL BE OKAY. DON'T TELL MY FATHER FOR A FEW MORE DAYS.
HERE, TAKE THIS AND USE IT AS YOU NEED IT.
WHAT... WHAT'S ALL THIS MONEY?

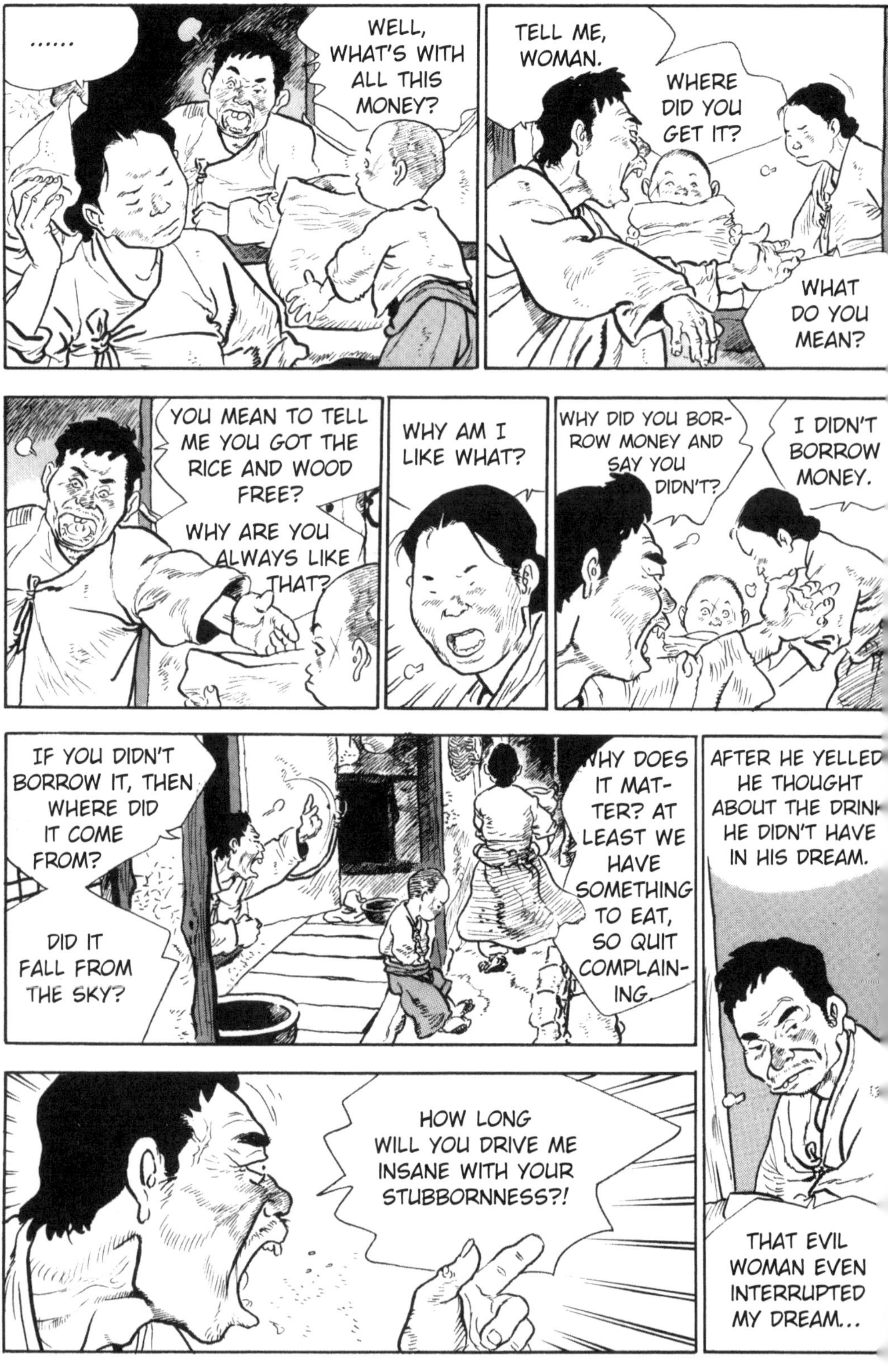
......
WELL, WHAT'S WITH ALL THIS MONEY?
TELL ME, WOMAN.
WHERE DID YOU GET IT?
WHAT DO YOU MEAN?
YOU MEAN TO TELL ME YOU GOT THE RICE AND WOOD FREE?
WHY ARE YOU ALWAYS LIKE THAT?
WHY AM I LIKE WHAT?
WHY DID YOU BORROW MONEY AND SAY YOU DIDN'T?
I DIDN'T BORROW MONEY.
IF YOU DIDN'T BORROW IT, THEN WHERE DID IT COME FROM?
DID IT FALL FROM THE SKY?
WHY DOES IT MATTER? AT LEAST WE HAVE SOMETHING TO EAT, SO QUIT COMPLAINING.
AFTER HE YELLED HE THOUGHT ABOUT THE DRINK HE DIDN'T HAVE IN HIS DREAM.
HOW LONG WILL YOU DRIVE ME INSANE WITH YOUR STUBBORNNESS?!
THAT EVIL WOMAN EVEN INTERRUPTED MY DREAM...

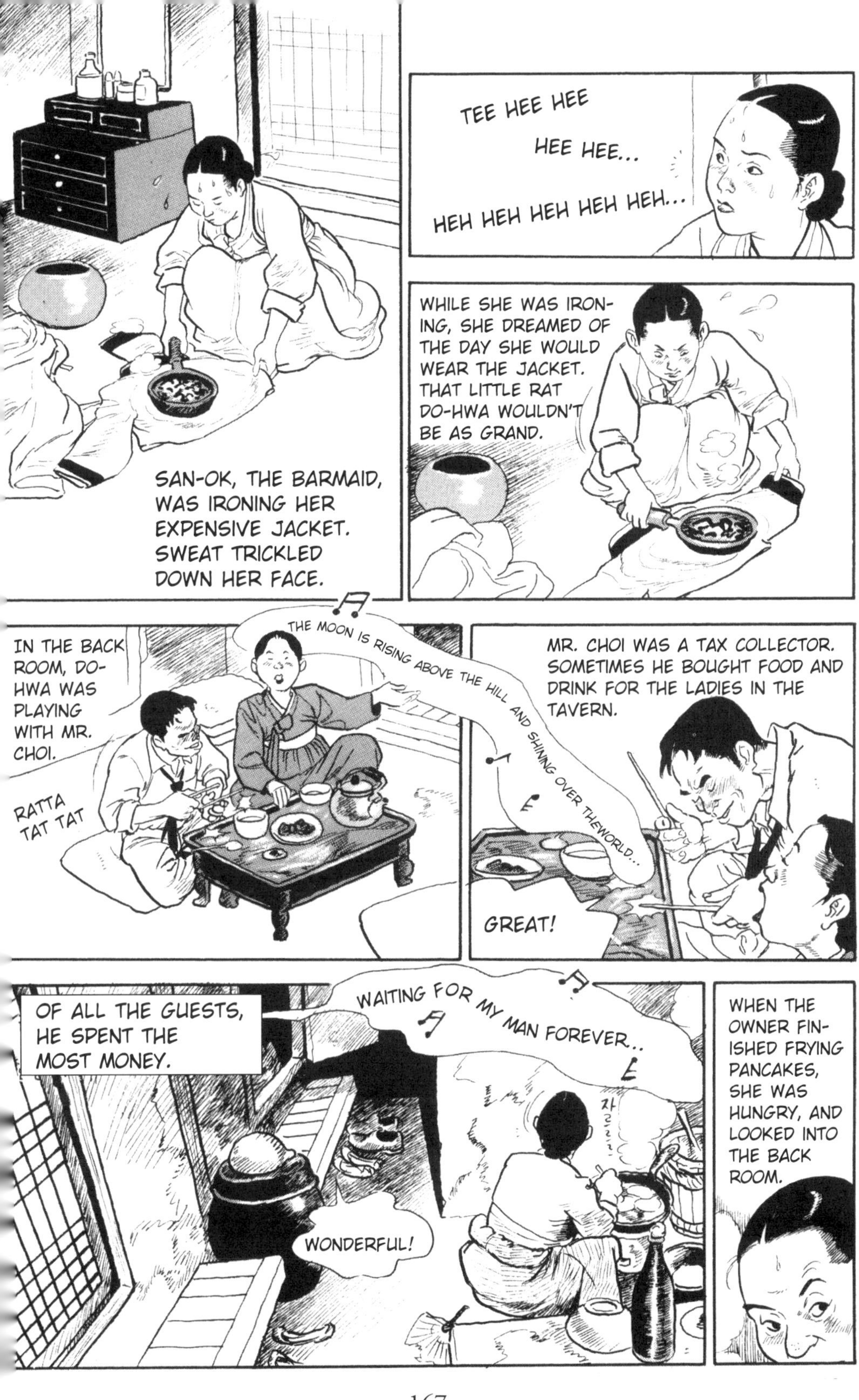
SAN-OK, THE BARMAID, WAS IRONING HER EXPENSIVE JACKET. SWEAT TRICKLED DOWN HER FACE.
TEE HEE HEE
HEE HEE...
HEH HEH HEH HEH HEH...
WHILE SHE WAS IRONING, SHE DREAMED OF THE DAY SHE WOULD WEAR THE JACKET. THAT LITTLE RAT DO-HWA WOULDN'T BE AS GRAND.
IN THE BACK ROOM, DO-HWA WAS PLAYING WITH MR. CHOI.
THE MOON IS RISING ABOVE THE HILL AND SHINING OVER THEWORLD...
RATTA TAT TAT
MR. CHOI WAS A TAX COLLECTOR. SOMETIMES HE BOUGHT FOOD AND DRINK FOR THE LADIES IN THE TAVERN.
GREAT!
OF ALL THE GUESTS, HE SPENT THE MOST MONEY.
WAITING FOR MY MAN FOREVER...
자글글글
WONDERFUL!
WHEN THE OWNER FINISHED FRYING PANCAKES, SHE WAS HUNGRY, AND LOOKED INTO THE BACK ROOM.

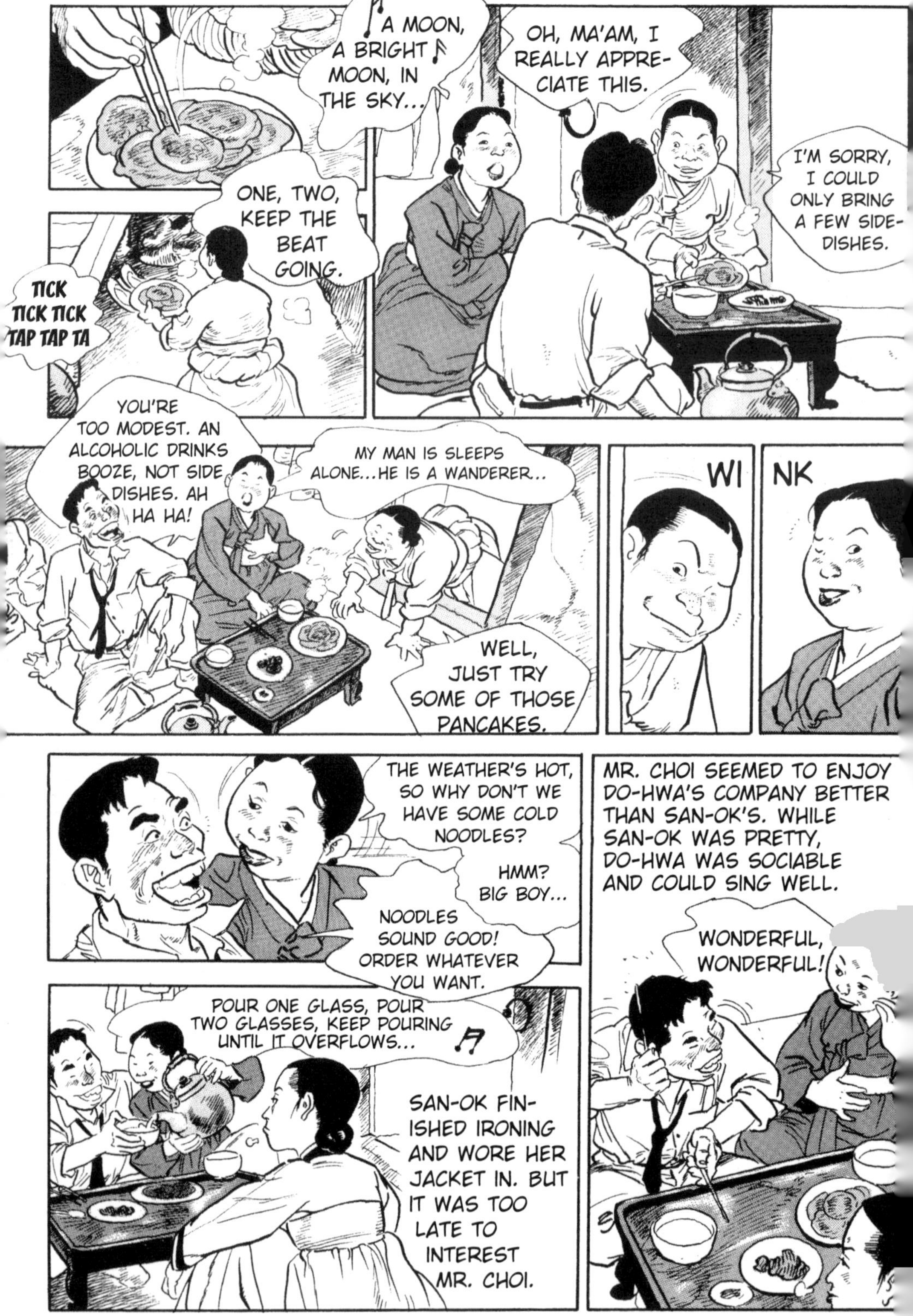
A MOON, A BRIGHT MOON, IN THE SKY...
OH, MA'AM, I REALLY APPRECIATE THIS.
I'M SORRY, I COULD ONLY BRING A FEW SIDE-DISHES.
ONE, TWO, KEEP THE BEAT GOING.
TICK TICK TICK TAP TAP TA
YOU'RE TOO MODEST. AN ALCOHOLIC DRINKS BOOZE, NOT SIDE DISHES. AH HA HA!
MY MAN IS SLEEPS ALONE...HE IS A WANDERER...
WELL, JUST TRY SOME OF THOSE PANCAKES.
WI NK
THE WEATHER'S HOT, SO WHY DON'T WE HAVE SOME COLD NOODLES?
HMM? BIG BOY...
NOODLES SOUND GOOD! ORDER WHATEVER YOU WANT.
MR. CHOI SEEMED TO ENJOY DO-HWA'S COMPANY BETTER THAN SAN-OK'S. WHILE SAN-OK WAS PRETTY, DO-HWA WAS SOCIABLE AND COULD SING WELL.
WONDERFUL, WONDERFUL!
POUR ONE GLASS, POUR TWO GLASSES, KEEP POURING UNTIL IT OVERFLOWS...
SAN-OK FINISHED IRONING AND WORE HER JACKET IN. BUT IT WAS TOO LATE TO INTEREST MR. CHOI.

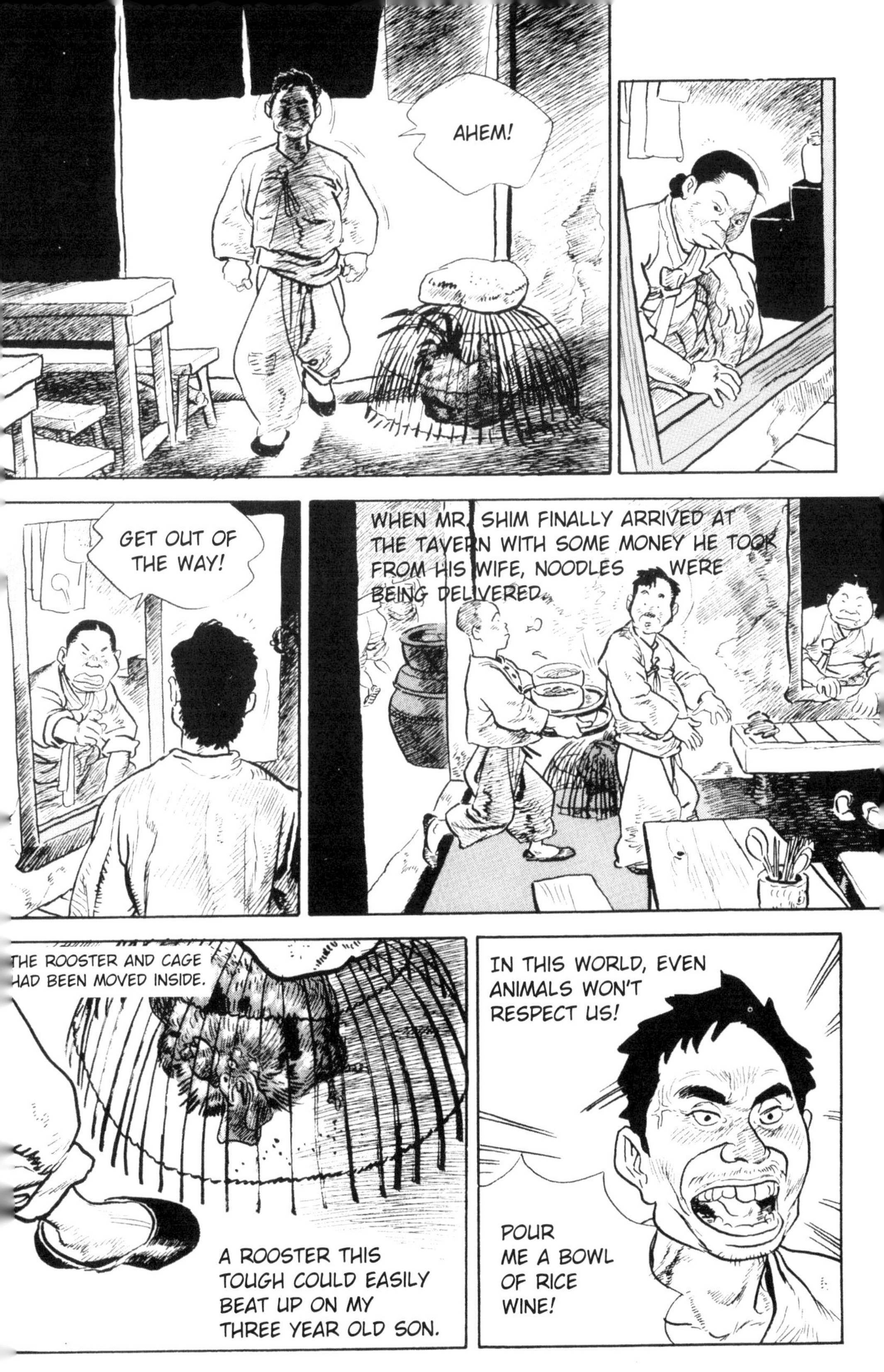

AHEM!
GET OUT OF THE WAY!
WHEN MR. SHIM FINALLY ARRIVED AT THE TAVERN WITH SOME MONEY HE TOOK FROM HIS WIFE, NOODLES WERE BEING DELIVERED.
THE ROOSTER AND CAGE HAD BEEN MOVED INSIDE.
A ROOSTER THIS TOUGH COULD EASILY BEAT UP ON MY THREE YEAR OLD SON.
IN THIS WORLD, EVEN ANIMALS WON'T RESPECT US!
POUR ME A BOWL OF RICE WINE!

THE OWNER AND SAN-OK WERE EATING NOODLES. ALL THE WHILE SAN-OK WAS POURING LIQUOR FOR THEIR GUEST.

GULP! GULP!

AAAH...

MR. SHIM GULPED DOWN THE BOOZE, AND THEN GRABBED SOME PANCAKES.

WHERE'S DO-HWA?

WHAT'S IT TO YOU?

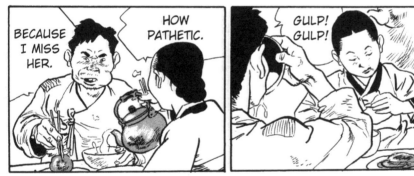

BECAUSE I MISS HER.

HOW PATHETIC.

GULP! GULP!

SAN-OK WAS WORRIED THE NOODLES MIGHT SPLATTER HER JACKET.

AHH...

SLAM

CHOMP, CHOMP.

THE MORE HE DRANK, THE MORE HIS NOSTRILS FLARED.

170

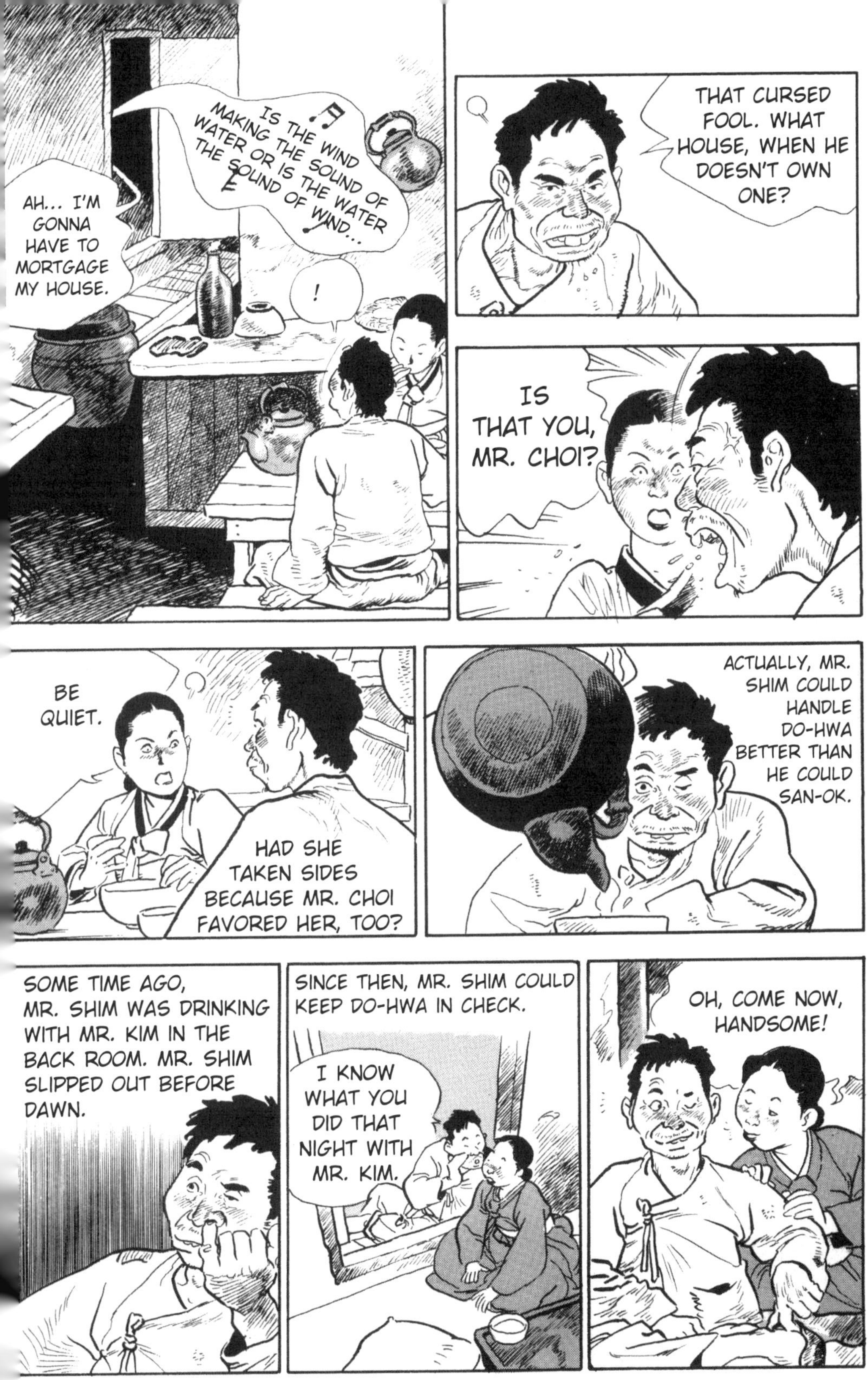

IS THE WIND MAKING THE SOUND OF WATER OR IS THE WATER THE SOUND OF WIND...
AH... I'M GONNA HAVE TO MORTGAGE MY HOUSE.
!
THAT CURSED FOOL. WHAT HOUSE, WHEN HE DOESN'T OWN ONE?
IS THAT YOU, MR. CHOI?
BE QUIET.
HAD SHE TAKEN SIDES BECAUSE MR. CHOI FAVORED HER, TOO?
ACTUALLY, MR. SHIM COULD HANDLE DO-HWA BETTER THAN HE COULD SAN-OK.
SOME TIME AGO, MR. SHIM WAS DRINKING WITH MR. KIM IN THE BACK ROOM. MR. SHIM SLIPPED OUT BEFORE DAWN.
SINCE THEN, MR. SHIM COULD KEEP DO-HWA IN CHECK.
I KNOW WHAT YOU DID THAT NIGHT WITH MR. KIM.
OH, COME NOW, HANDSOME!

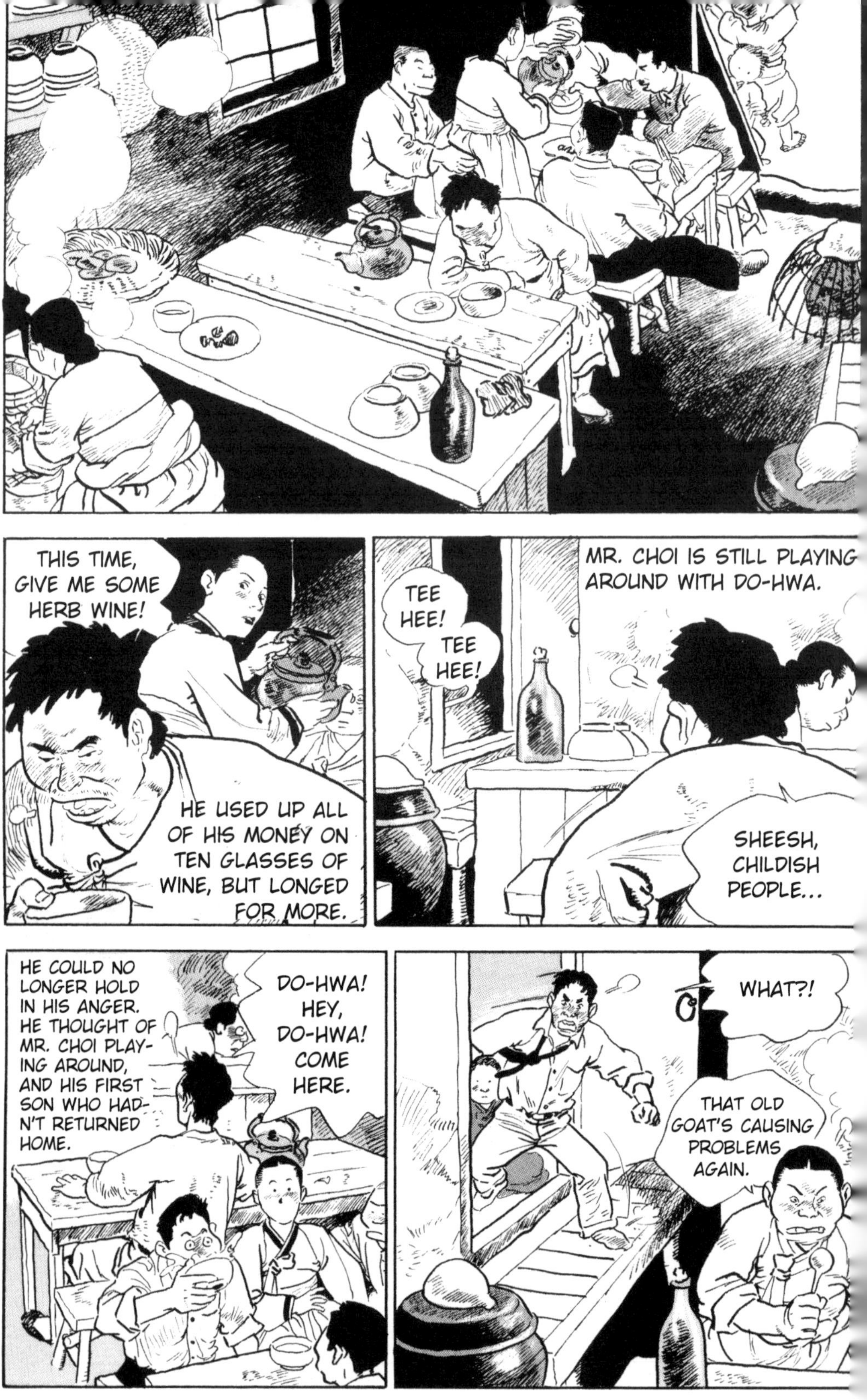
THIS TIME, GIVE ME SOME HERB WINE!
HE USED UP ALL OF HIS MONEY ON TEN GLASSES OF WINE, BUT LONGED FOR MORE.
MR. CHOI IS STILL PLAYING AROUND WITH DO-HWA.
TEE HEE!
TEE HEE!
SHEESH, CHILDISH PEOPLE...
HE COULD NO LONGER HOLD IN HIS ANGER. HE THOUGHT OF MR. CHOI PLAYING AROUND, AND HIS FIRST SON WHO HADN'T RETURNED HOME.
DO-HWA! HEY, DO-HWA! COME HERE.
WHAT?!
THAT OLD GOAT'S CAUSING PROBLEMS AGAIN.

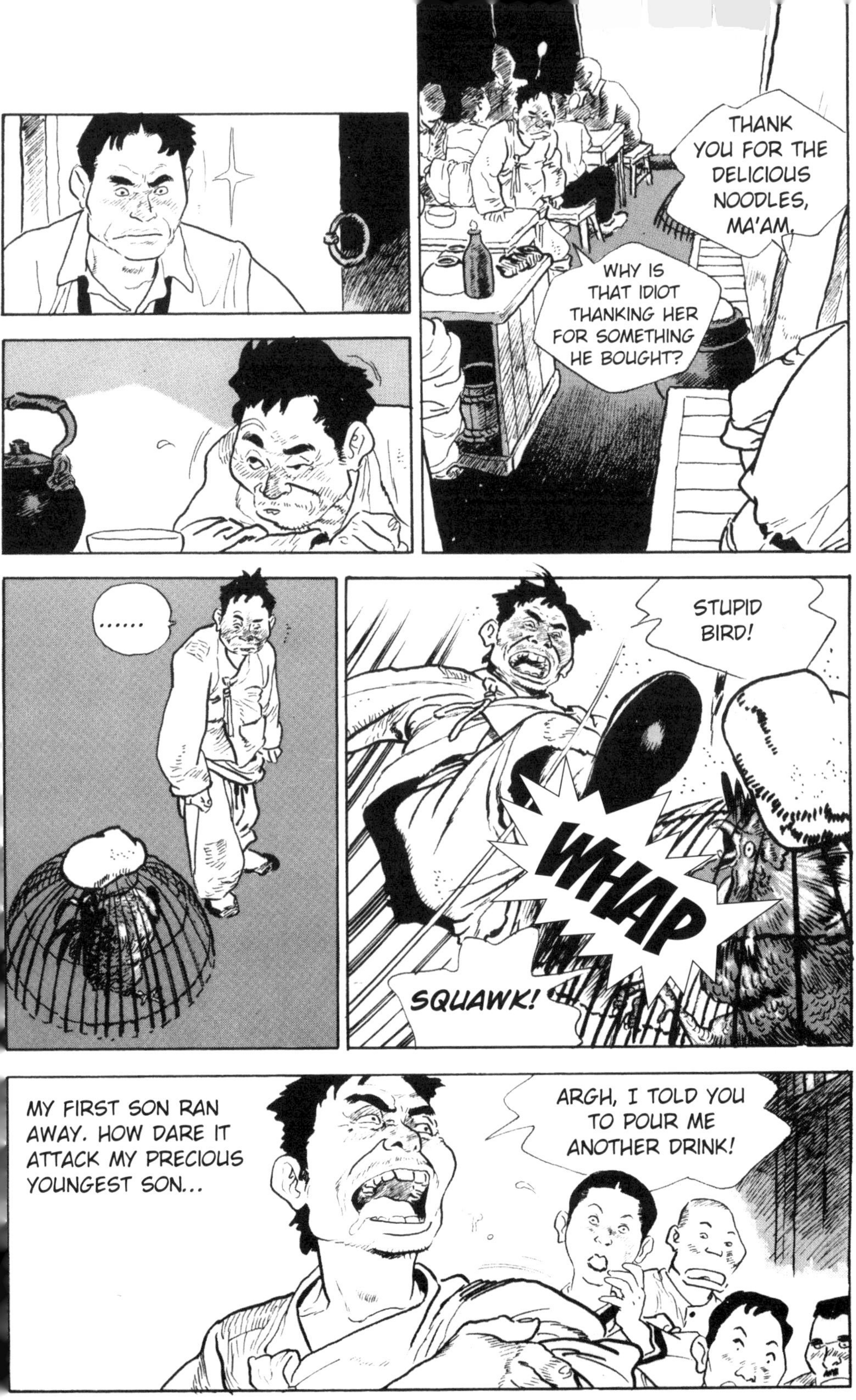
THANK YOU FOR THE DELICIOUS NOODLES, MA'AM.
WHY IS THAT IDIOT THANKING HER FOR SOMETHING HE BOUGHT?
......
STUPID BIRD!
WHAP
SQUAWK!
MY FIRST SON RAN AWAY. HOW DARE IT ATTACK MY PRECIOUS YOUNGEST SON...
ARGH, I TOLD YOU TO POUR ME ANOTHER DRINK!

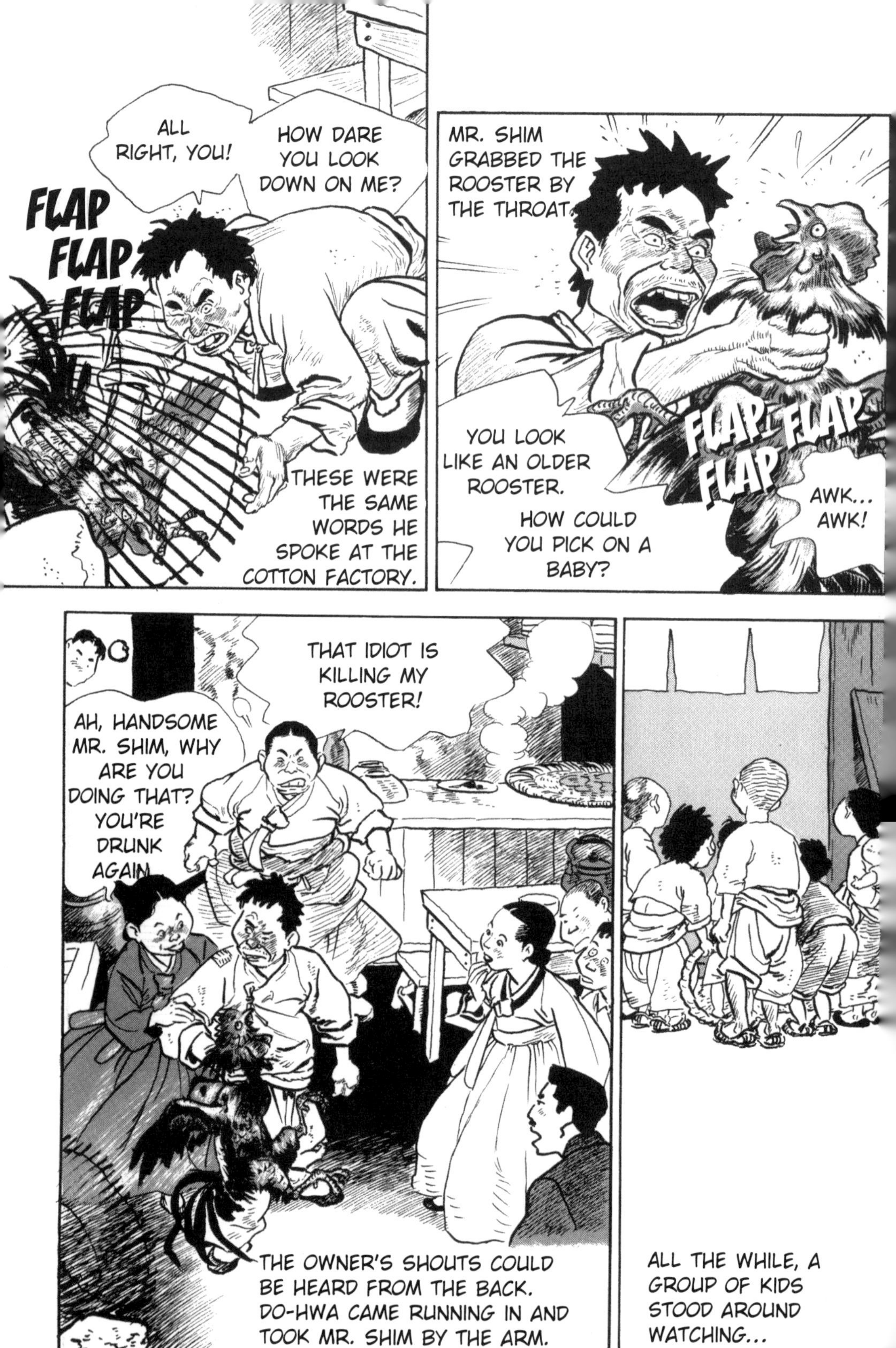
ALL RIGHT, YOU!
HOW DARE YOU LOOK DOWN ON ME?
FLAP FLAP FLAP
THESE WERE THE SAME WORDS HE SPOKE AT THE COTTON FACTORY.
MR. SHIM GRABBED THE ROOSTER BY THE THROAT.
YOU LOOK LIKE AN OLDER ROOSTER.
HOW COULD YOU PICK ON A BABY?
FLAP FLAP FLAP
AWK... AWK!
THAT IDIOT IS KILLING MY ROOSTER!
AH, HANDSOME MR. SHIM, WHY ARE YOU DOING THAT? YOU'RE DRUNK AGAIN
THE OWNER'S SHOUTS COULD BE HEARD FROM THE BACK. DO-HWA CAME RUNNING IN AND TOOK MR. SHIM BY THE ARM.
ALL THE WHILE, A GROUP OF KIDS STOOD AROUND WATCHING...

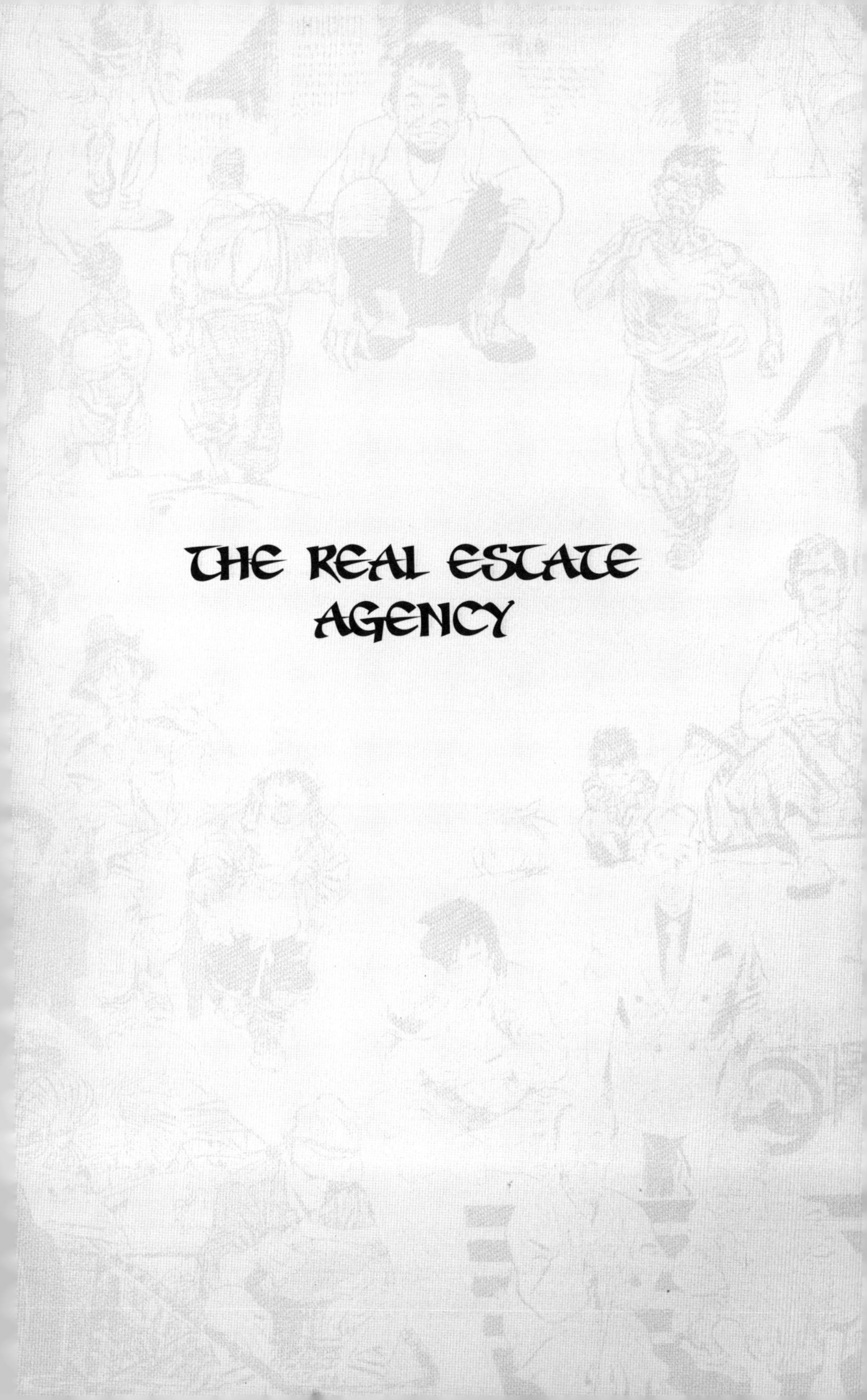

THE REAL ESTATE AGENCY

LEE TAE-JUN
JANUARY 1993

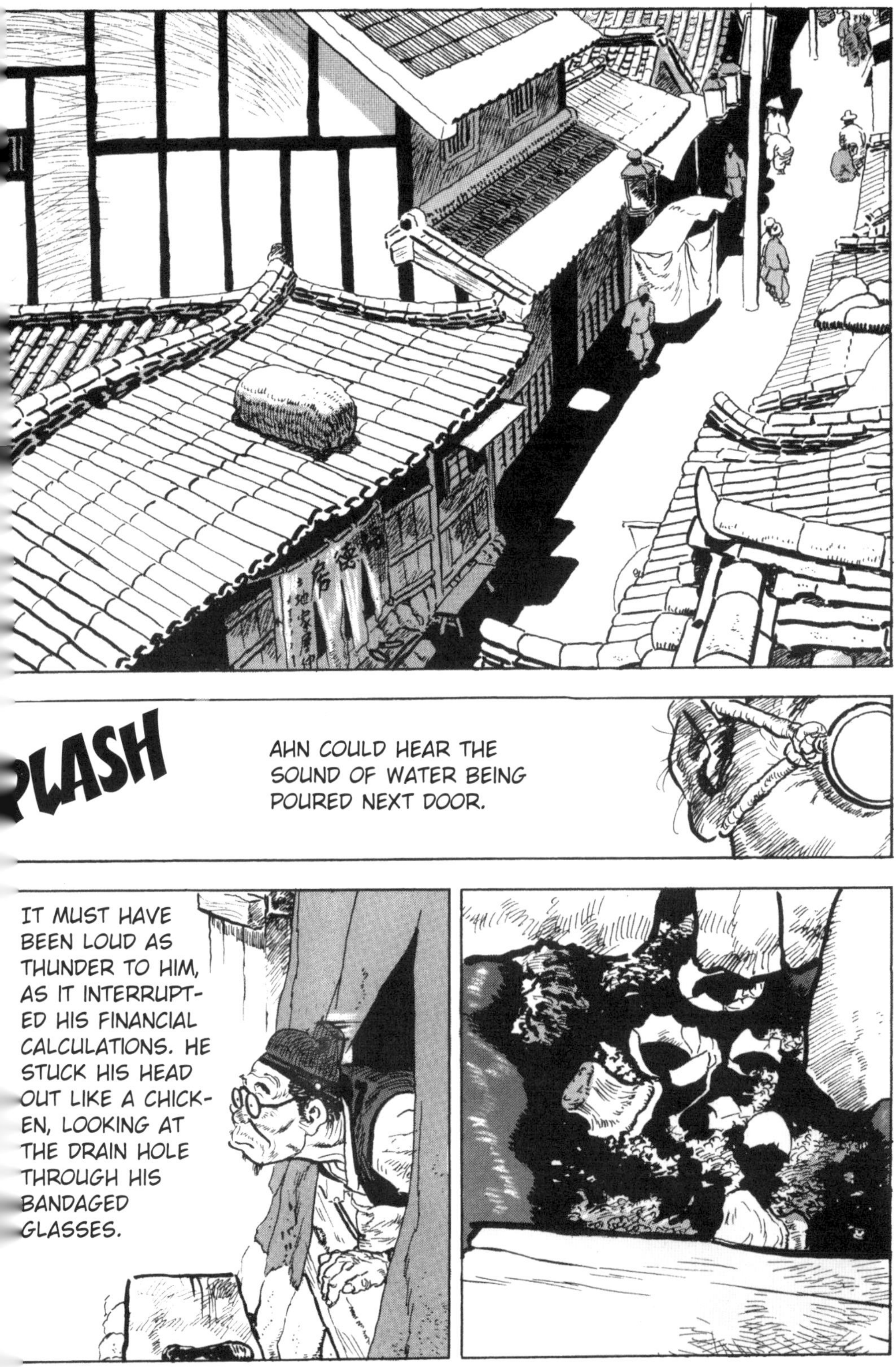
PLASH
AHN COULD HEAR THE SOUND OF WATER BEING POURED NEXT DOOR.
IT MUST HAVE BEEN LOUD AS THUNDER TO HIM, AS IT INTERRUPTED HIS FINANCIAL CALCULATIONS. HE STUCK HIS HEAD OUT LIKE A CHICKEN, LOOKING AT THE DRAIN HOLE THROUGH HIS BANDAGED GLASSES.

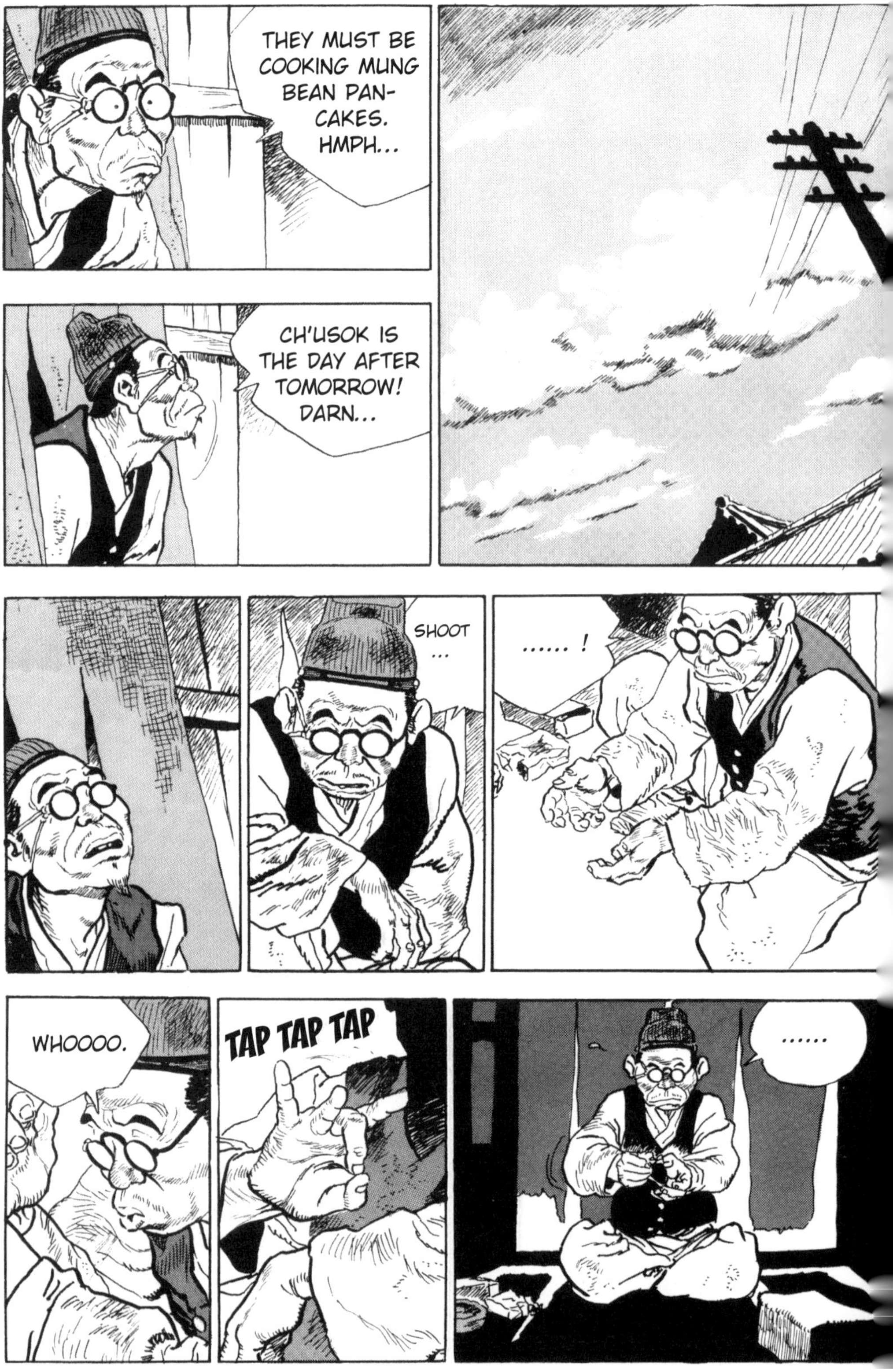
THEY MUST BE COOKING MUNG BEAN PAN-CAKES. HMPH...
CH'USOK IS THE DAY AFTER TOMORROW! DARN...
SHOOT ...
...... !
WHOOOO.
TAP TAP TAP
......

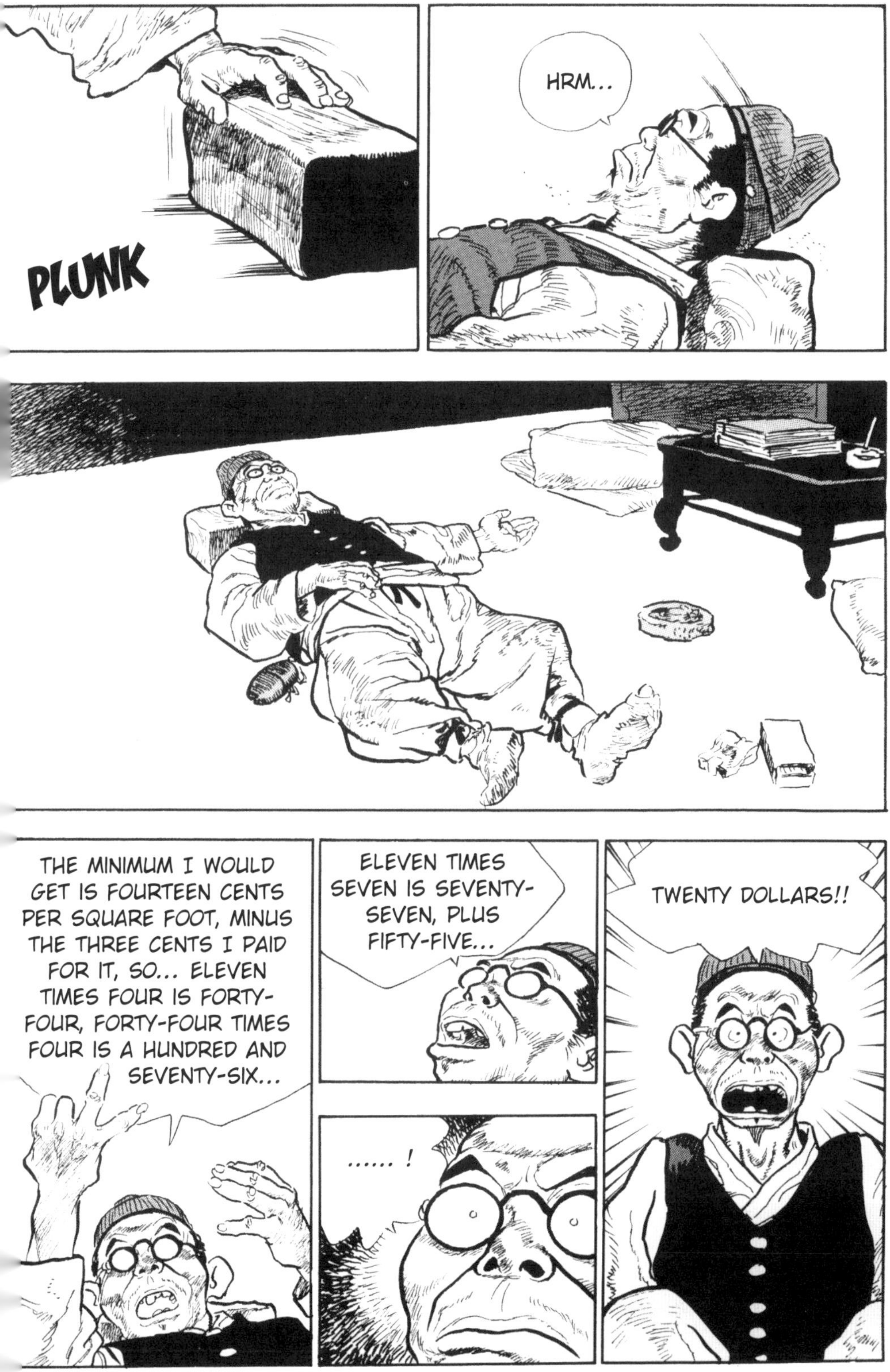
PLUNK
HRM...
THE MINIMUM I WOULD GET IS FOURTEEN CENTS PER SQUARE FOOT, MINUS THE THREE CENTS I PAID FOR IT, SO... ELEVEN TIMES FOUR IS FORTY-FOUR, FORTY-FOUR TIMES FOUR IS A HUNDRED AND SEVENTY-SIX...
ELEVEN TIMES SEVEN IS SEVENTY-SEVEN, PLUS FIFTY-FIVE...
...... !
TWENTY DOLLARS!!

GULP!

CRINKLE

I INVEST A DOLLAR AND GET TWENTY DOLLARS... IF I INVESTED TEN DOLLARS...

......!

CRUNCH

CRUNCH

WHEW...

SMAK

FUMBLE FUMBLE

......

HE ONLY HAD ONE CENT.

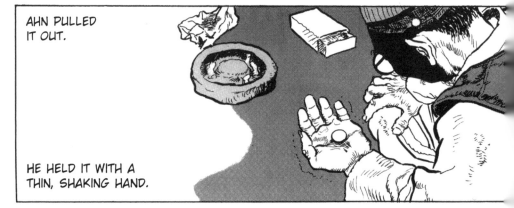

AHN PULLED IT OUT.

HE HELD IT WITH A THIN, SHAKING HAND.

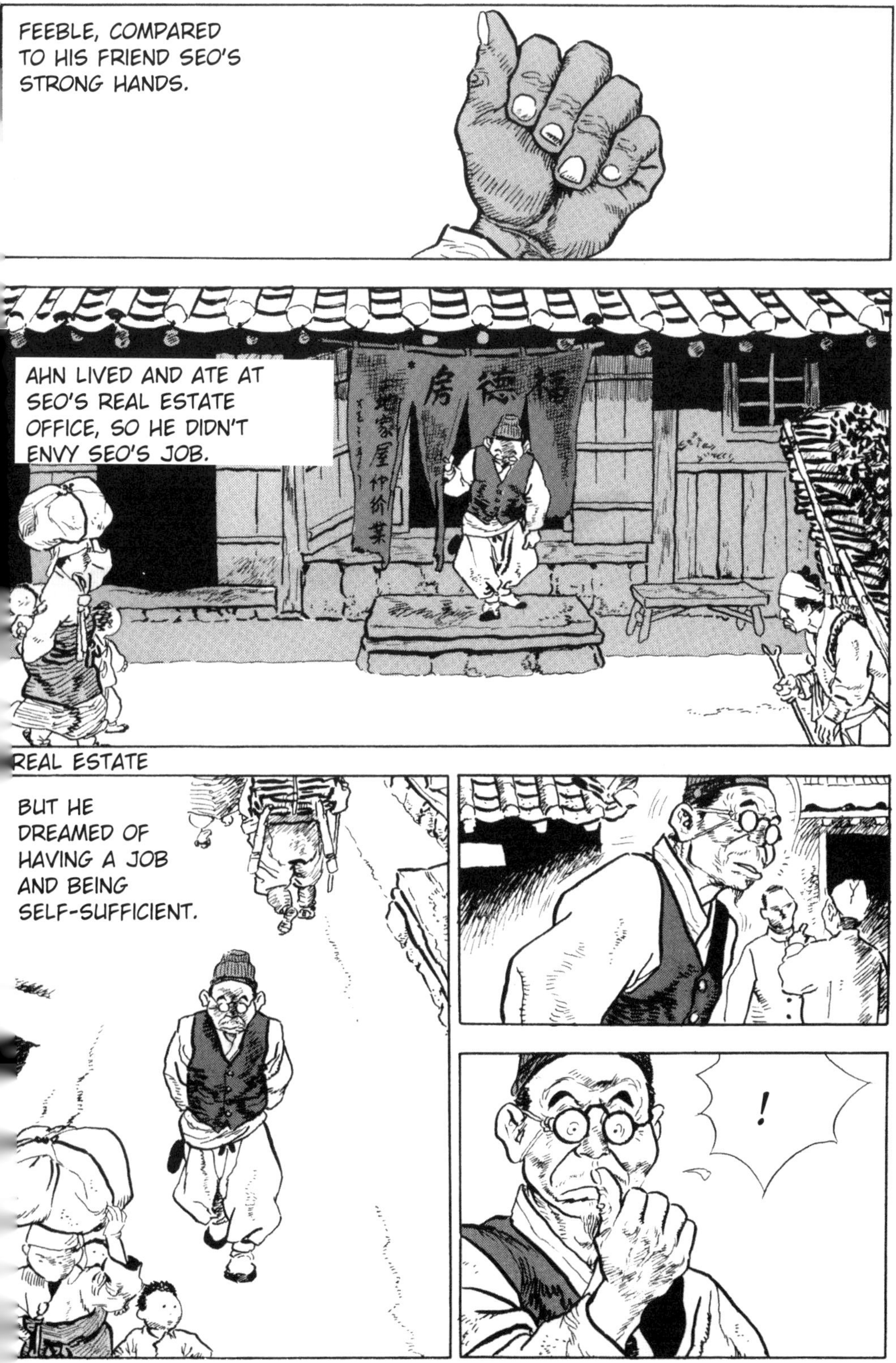

FEEBLE, COMPARED TO HIS FRIEND SEO'S STRONG HANDS.
AHN LIVED AND ATE AT SEO'S REAL ESTATE OFFICE, SO HE DIDN'T ENVY SEO'S JOB.
REAL ESTATE
BUT HE DREAMED OF HAVING A JOB AND BEING SELF-SUFFICIENT.
!

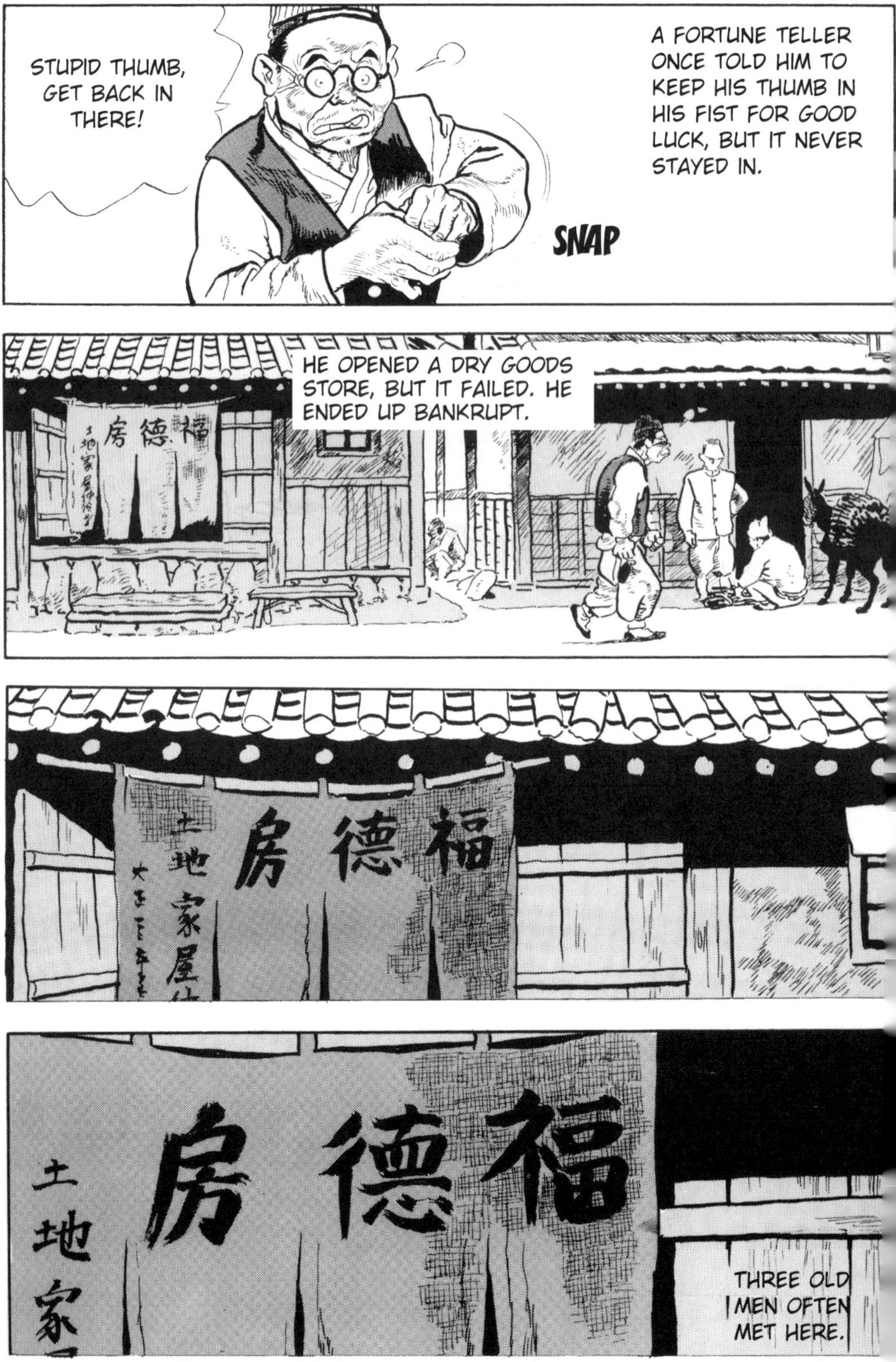
STUPID THUMB, GET BACK IN THERE!
A FORTUNE TELLER ONCE TOLD HIM TO KEEP HIS THUMB IN HIS FIST FOR GOOD LUCK, BUT IT NEVER STAYED IN.
SNAP
HE OPENED A DRY GOODS STORE, BUT IT FAILED. HE ENDED UP BANKRUPT.
福德房
土地家
THREE OLD MEN OFTEN MET HERE.

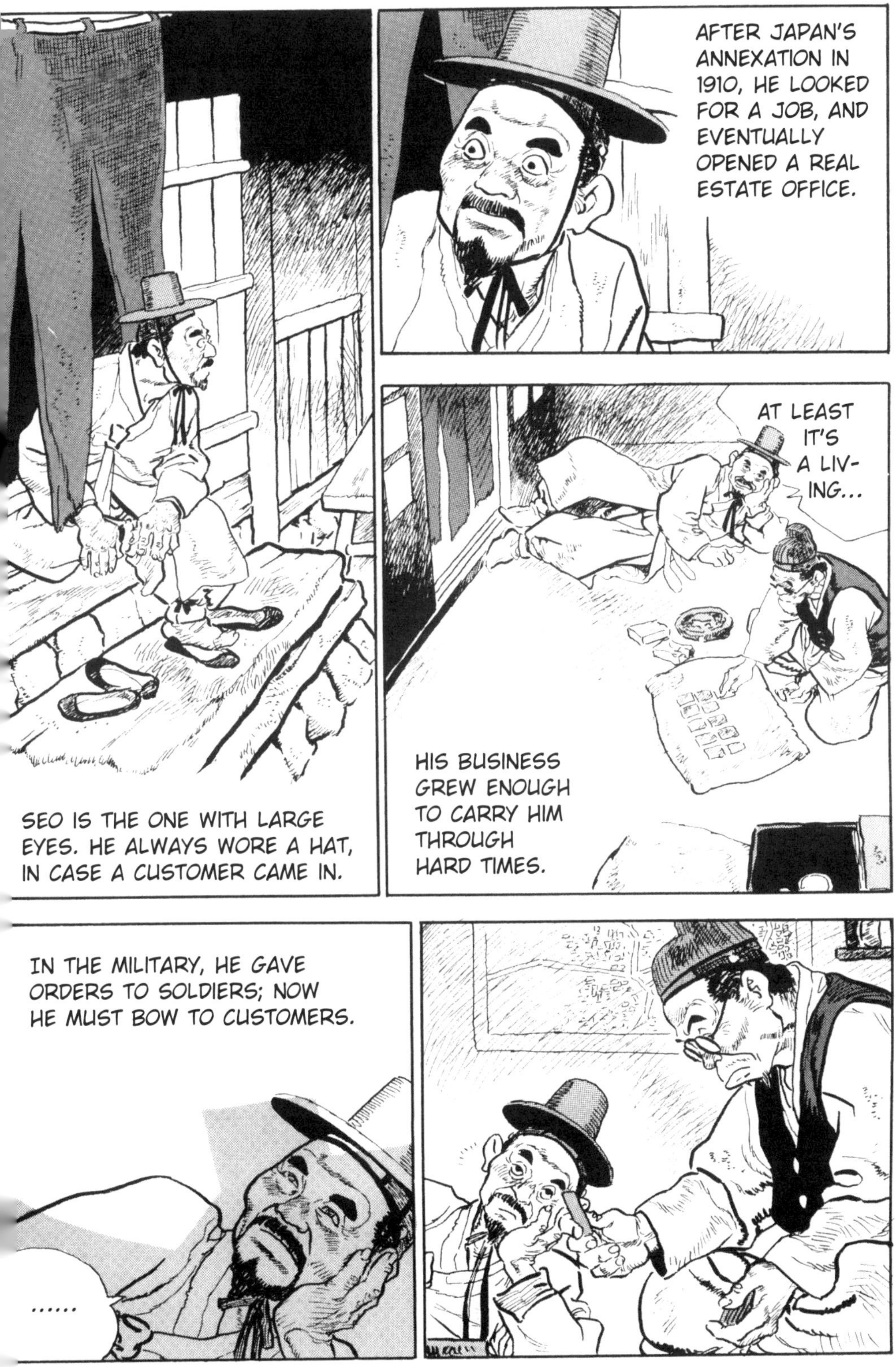
SEO IS THE ONE WITH LARGE EYES. HE ALWAYS WORE A HAT, IN CASE A CUSTOMER CAME IN.
AFTER JAPAN'S ANNEXATION IN 1910, HE LOOKED FOR A JOB, AND EVENTUALLY OPENED A REAL ESTATE OFFICE.
AT LEAST IT'S A LIV-ING...
HIS BUSINESS GREW ENOUGH TO CARRY HIM THROUGH HARD TIMES.
IN THE MILITARY, HE GAVE ORDERS TO SOLDIERS; NOW HE MUST BOW TO CUSTOMERS.
......

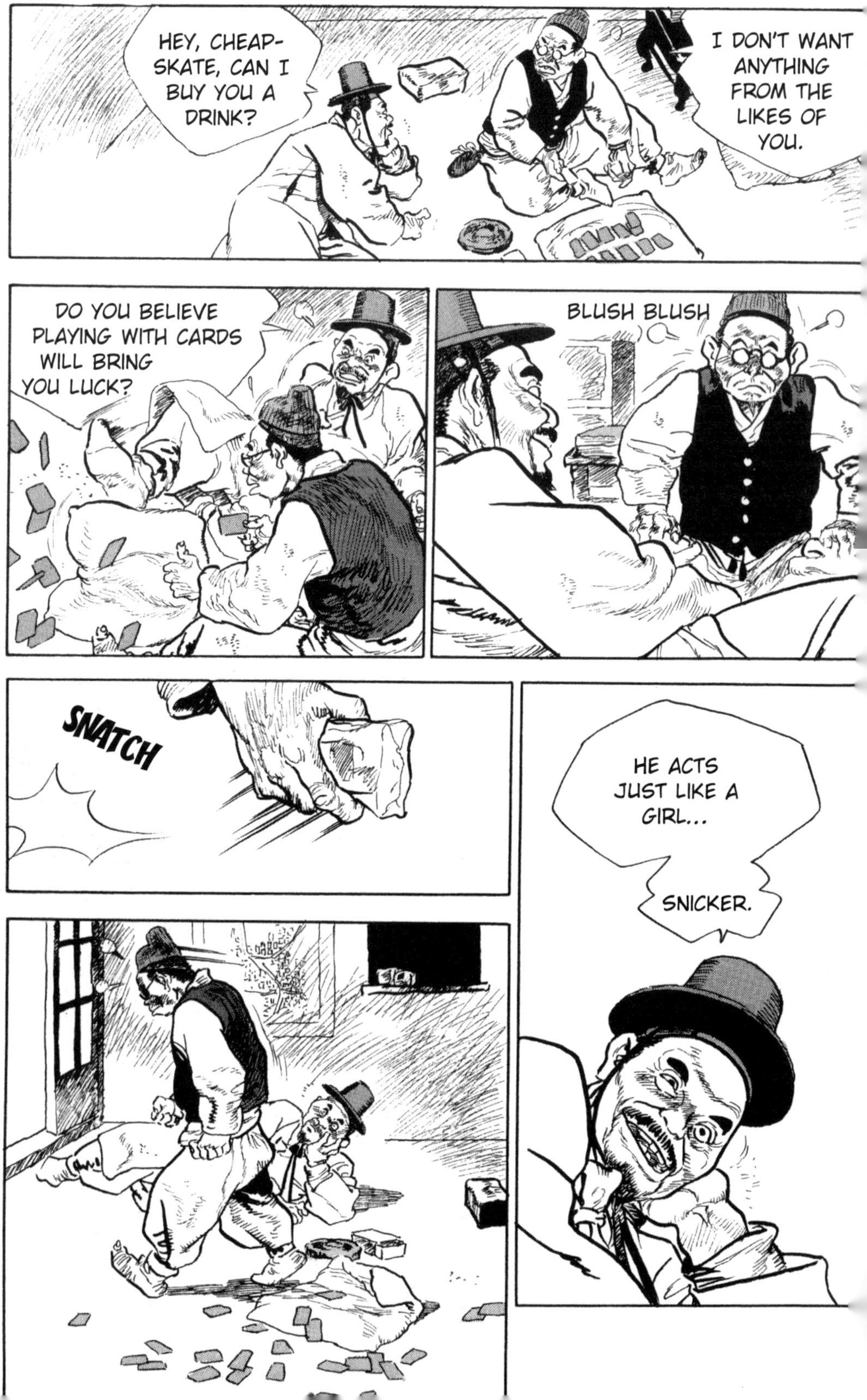
HEY, CHEAP-SKATE, CAN I BUY YOU A DRINK?
I DON'T WANT ANYTHING FROM THE LIKES OF YOU.
DO YOU BELIEVE PLAYING WITH CARDS WILL BRING YOU LUCK?
BLUSH BLUSH
SNATCH
HE ACTS JUST LIKE A GIRL...
SNICKER.

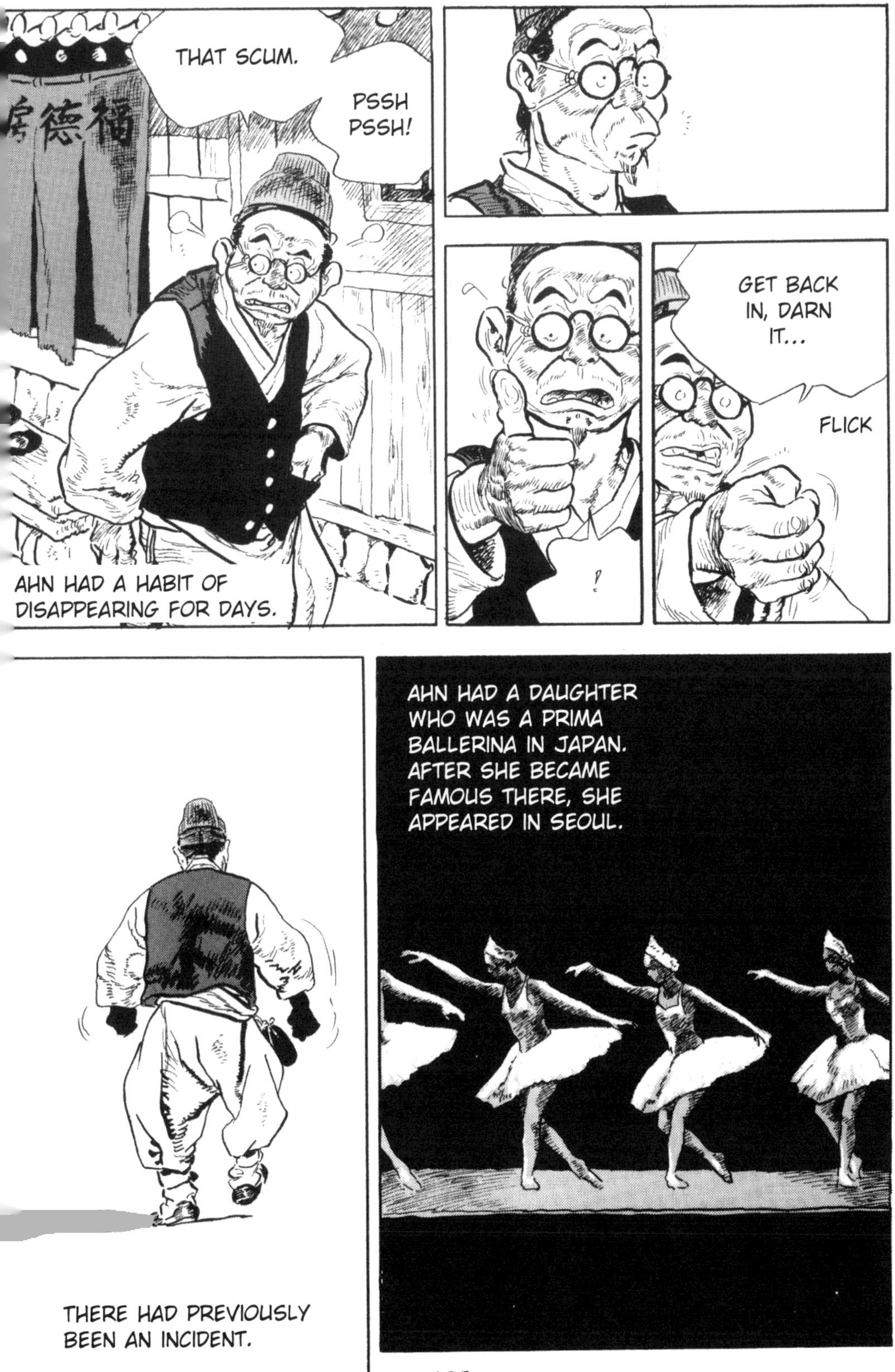
THAT SCUM.
PSSH PSSH!
AHN HAD A HABIT OF DISAPPEARING FOR DAYS.
GET BACK IN, DARN IT...
FLICK
THERE HAD PREVIOUSLY BEEN AN INCIDENT.
AHN HAD A DAUGHTER WHO WAS A PRIMA BALLERINA IN JAPAN. AFTER SHE BECAME FAMOUS THERE, SHE APPEARED IN SEOUL.

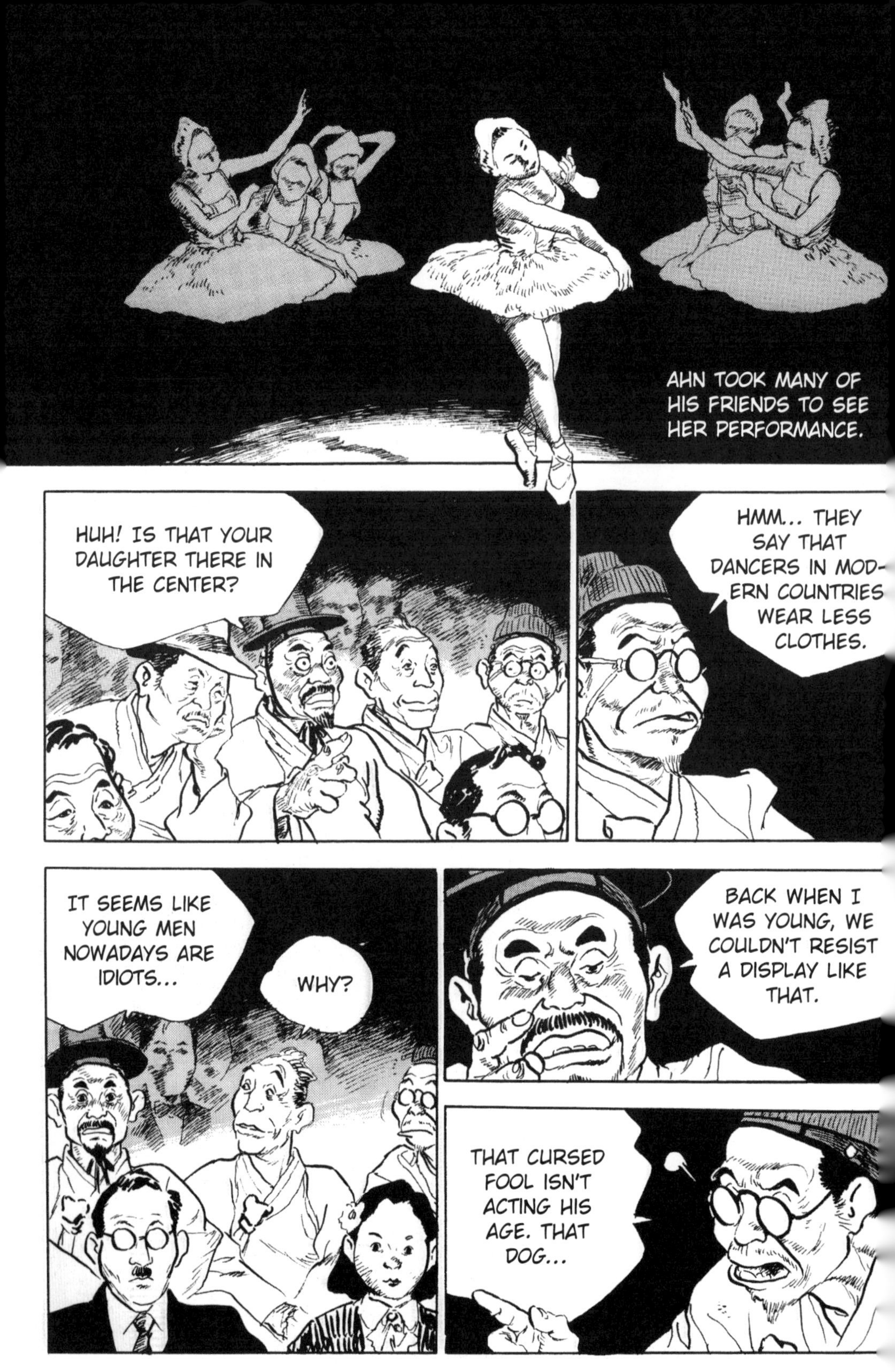
AHN TOOK MANY OF HIS FRIENDS TO SEE HER PERFORMANCE.
HUH! IS THAT YOUR DAUGHTER THERE IN THE CENTER?
HMM... THEY SAY THAT DANCERS IN MOD-ERN COUNTRIES WEAR LESS CLOTHES.
IT SEEMS LIKE YOUNG MEN NOWADAYS ARE IDIOTS...
WHY?
BACK WHEN I WAS YOUNG, WE COULDN'T RESIST A DISPLAY LIKE THAT.
THAT CURSED FOOL ISN'T ACTING HIS AGE. THAT DOG...

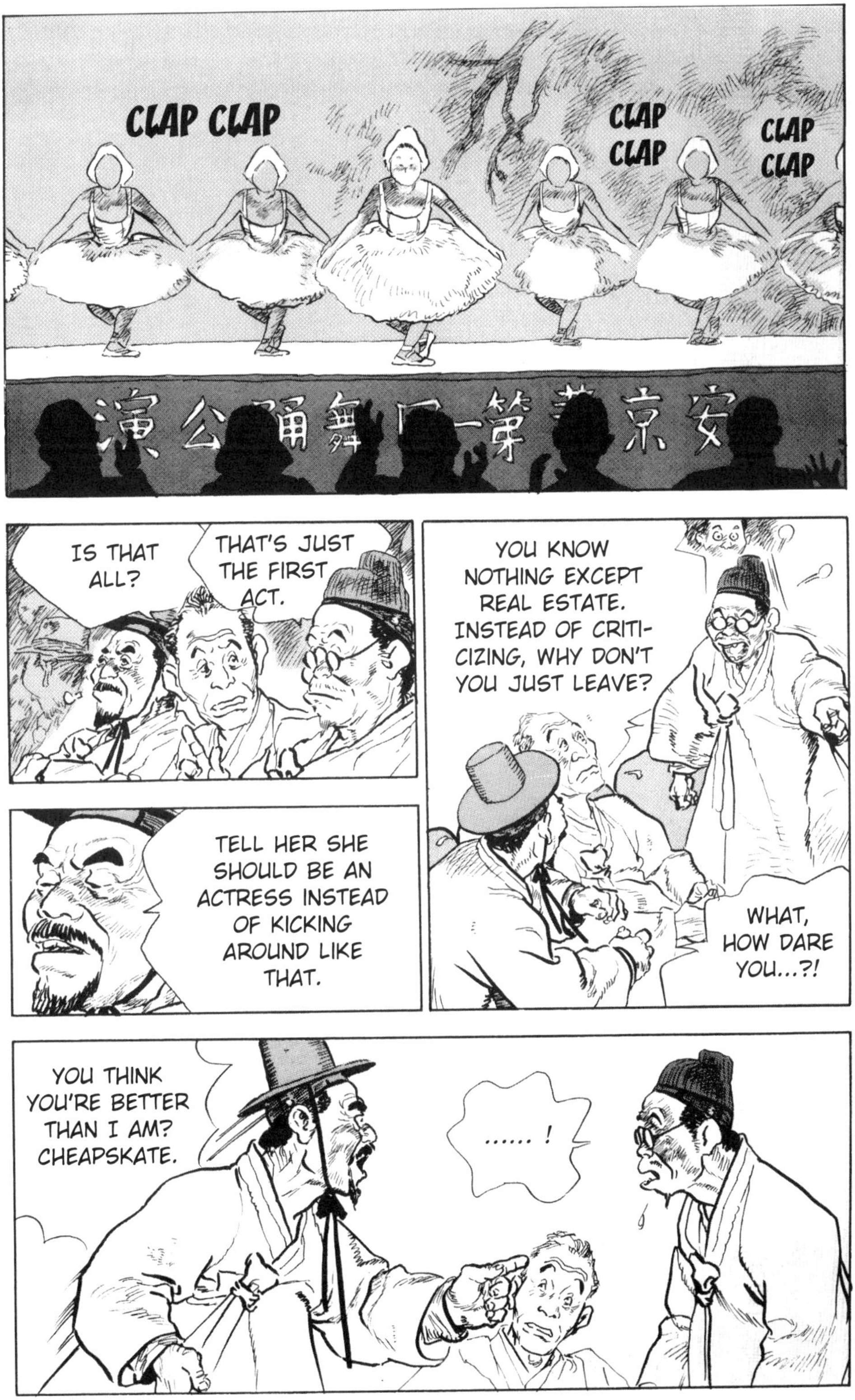

CLAP CLAP
CLAP CLAP
CLAP CLAP
IS THAT ALL?
THAT'S JUST THE FIRST ACT.
YOU KNOW NOTHING EXCEPT REAL ESTATE. INSTEAD OF CRITI-CIZING, WHY DON'T YOU JUST LEAVE?
TELL HER SHE SHOULD BE AN ACTRESS INSTEAD OF KICKING AROUND LIKE THAT.
WHAT, HOW DARE YOU...?!
YOU THINK YOU'RE BETTER THAN I AM? CHEAPSKATE.
...... !

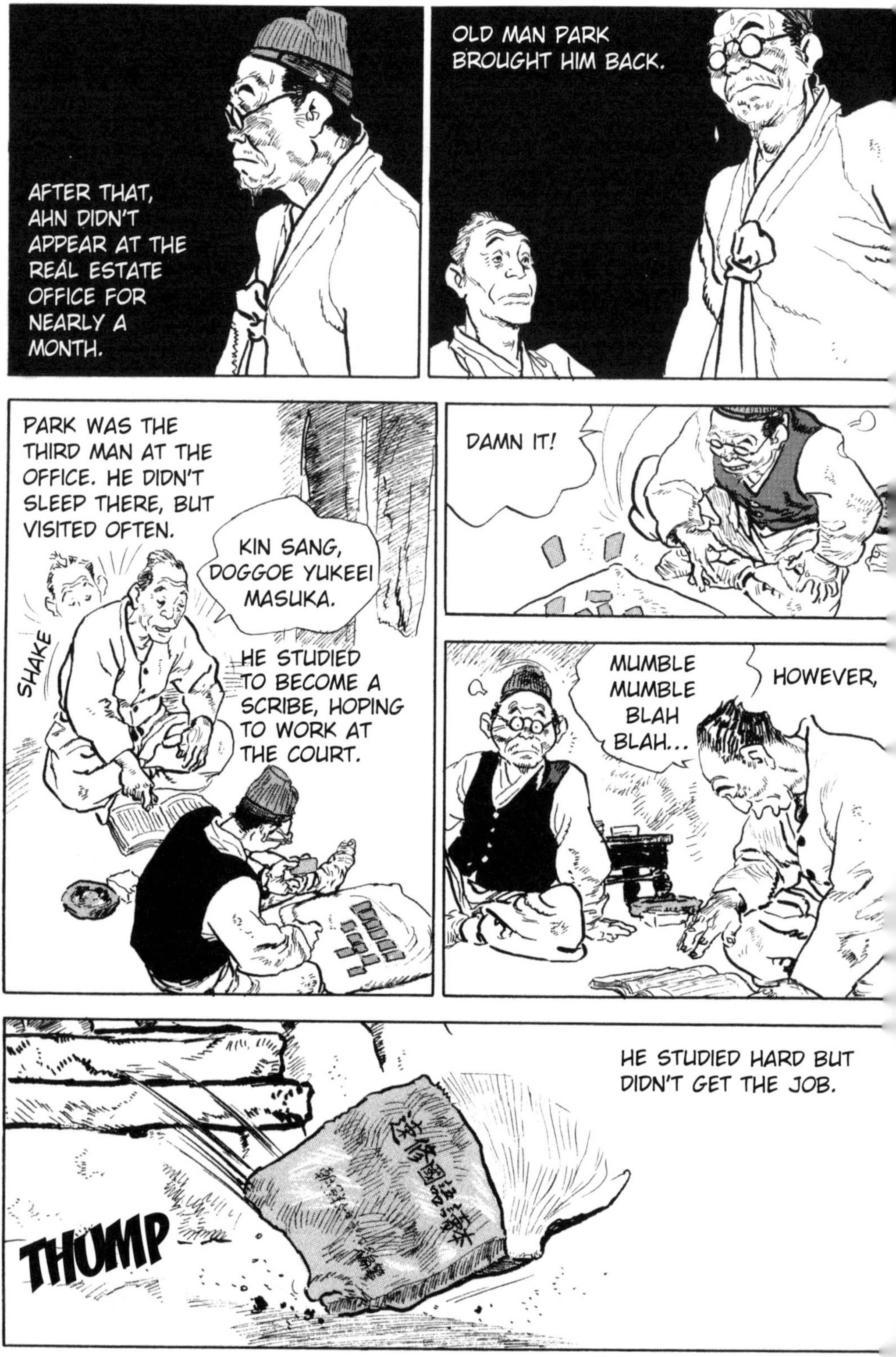
AFTER THAT, AHN DIDN'T APPEAR AT THE REAL ESTATE OFFICE FOR NEARLY A MONTH.
OLD MAN PARK BROUGHT HIM BACK.
PARK WAS THE THIRD MAN AT THE OFFICE. HE DIDN'T SLEEP THERE, BUT VISITED OFTEN.
KIN SANG, DOGGOE YUKEEI MASUKA.
SHAKE
HE STUDIED TO BECOME A SCRIBE, HOPING TO WORK AT THE COURT.
DAMN IT!
MUMBLE MUMBLE BLAH BLAH...
HOWEVER,
HE STUDIED HARD BUT DIDN'T GET THE JOB.
THUMP

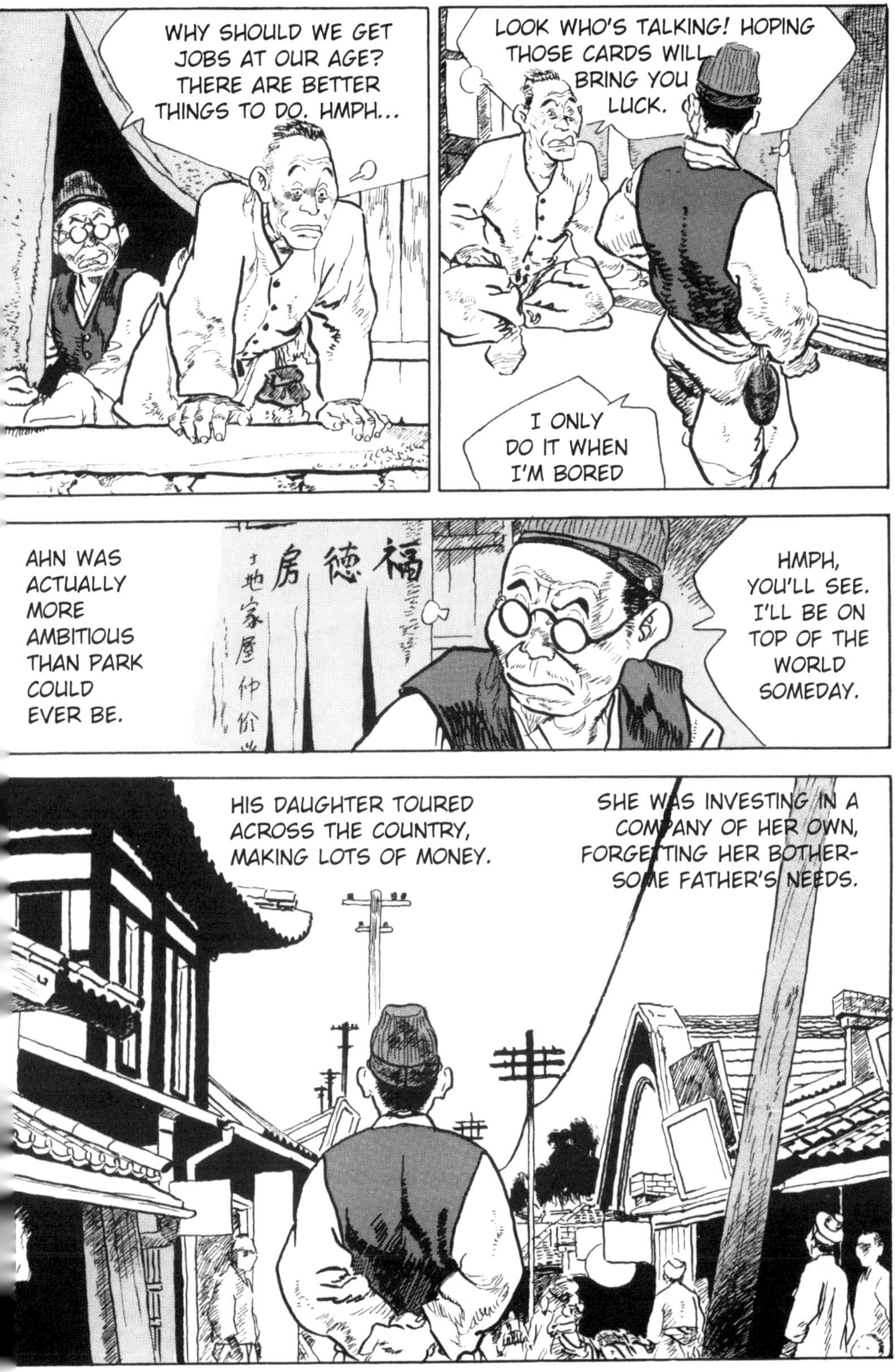
WHY SHOULD WE GET JOBS AT OUR AGE? THERE ARE BETTER THINGS TO DO. HMPH...
LOOK WHO'S TALKING! HOPING THOSE CARDS WILL BRING YOU LUCK.
I ONLY DO IT WHEN I'M BORED
AHN WAS ACTUALLY MORE AMBITIOUS THAN PARK COULD EVER BE.
福徳房
HMPH, YOU'LL SEE. I'LL BE ON TOP OF THE WORLD SOMEDAY.
HIS DAUGHTER TOURED ACROSS THE COUNTRY, MAKING LOTS OF MONEY.
SHE WAS INVESTING IN A COMPANY OF HER OWN, FORGETTING HER BOTHER-SOME FATHER'S NEEDS.

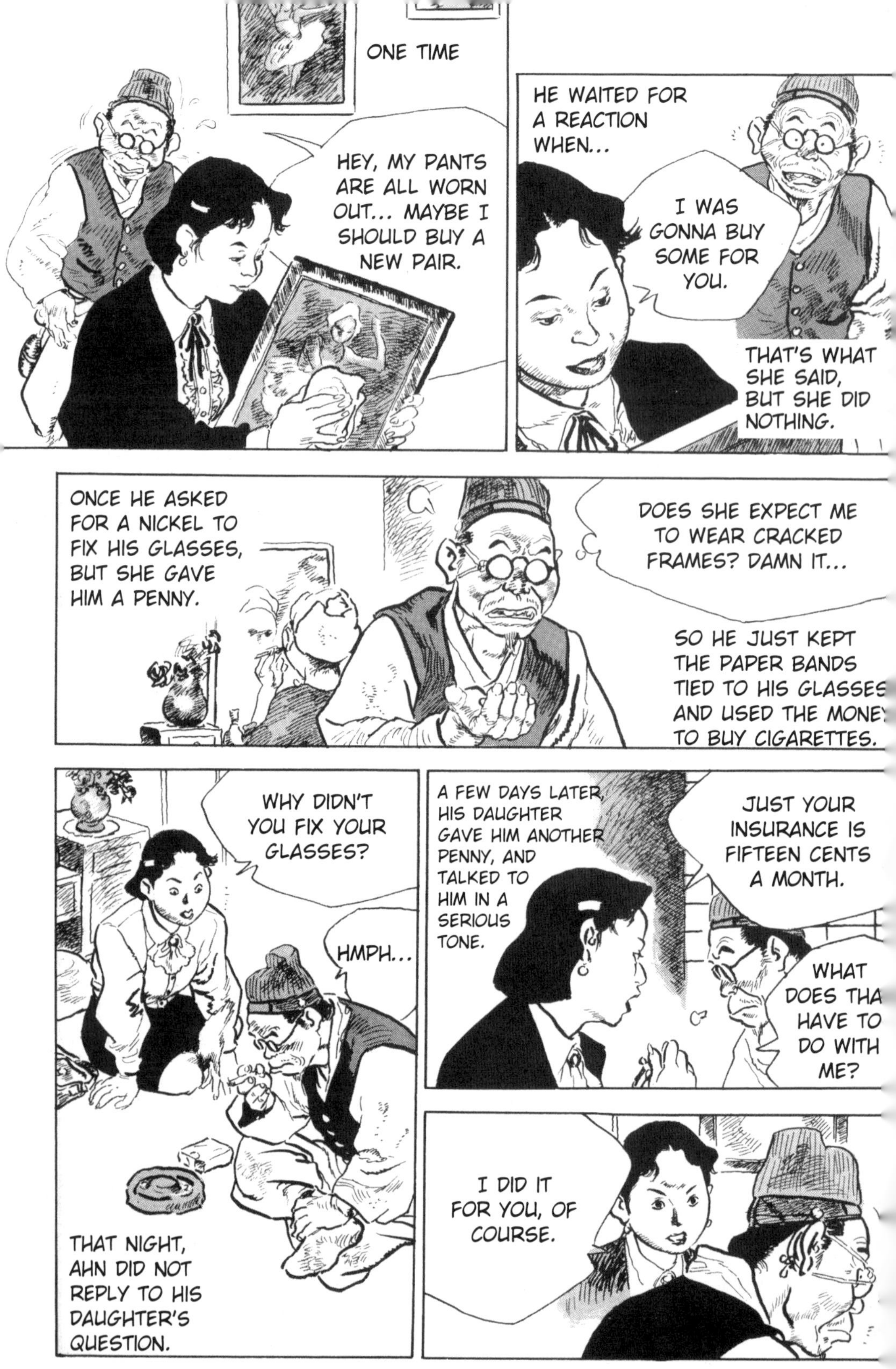
ONE TIME
HEY, MY PANTS ARE ALL WORN OUT... MAYBE I SHOULD BUY A NEW PAIR.
HE WAITED FOR A REACTION WHEN...
I WAS GONNA BUY SOME FOR YOU.
THAT'S WHAT SHE SAID, BUT SHE DID NOTHING.
ONCE HE ASKED FOR A NICKEL TO FIX HIS GLASSES, BUT SHE GAVE HIM A PENNY.
DOES SHE EXPECT ME TO WEAR CRACKED FRAMES? DAMN IT...
SO HE JUST KEPT THE PAPER BANDS TIED TO HIS GLASSES AND USED THE MONEY TO BUY CIGARETTES.
WHY DIDN'T YOU FIX YOUR GLASSES?
HMPH...
THAT NIGHT, AHN DID NOT REPLY TO HIS DAUGHTER'S QUESTION.
A FEW DAYS LATER, HIS DAUGHTER GAVE HIM ANOTHER PENNY, AND TALKED TO HIM IN A SERIOUS TONE.
JUST YOUR INSURANCE IS FIFTEEN CENTS A MONTH.
WHAT DOES THA HAVE TO DO WITH ME?
I DID IT FOR YOU, OF COURSE.

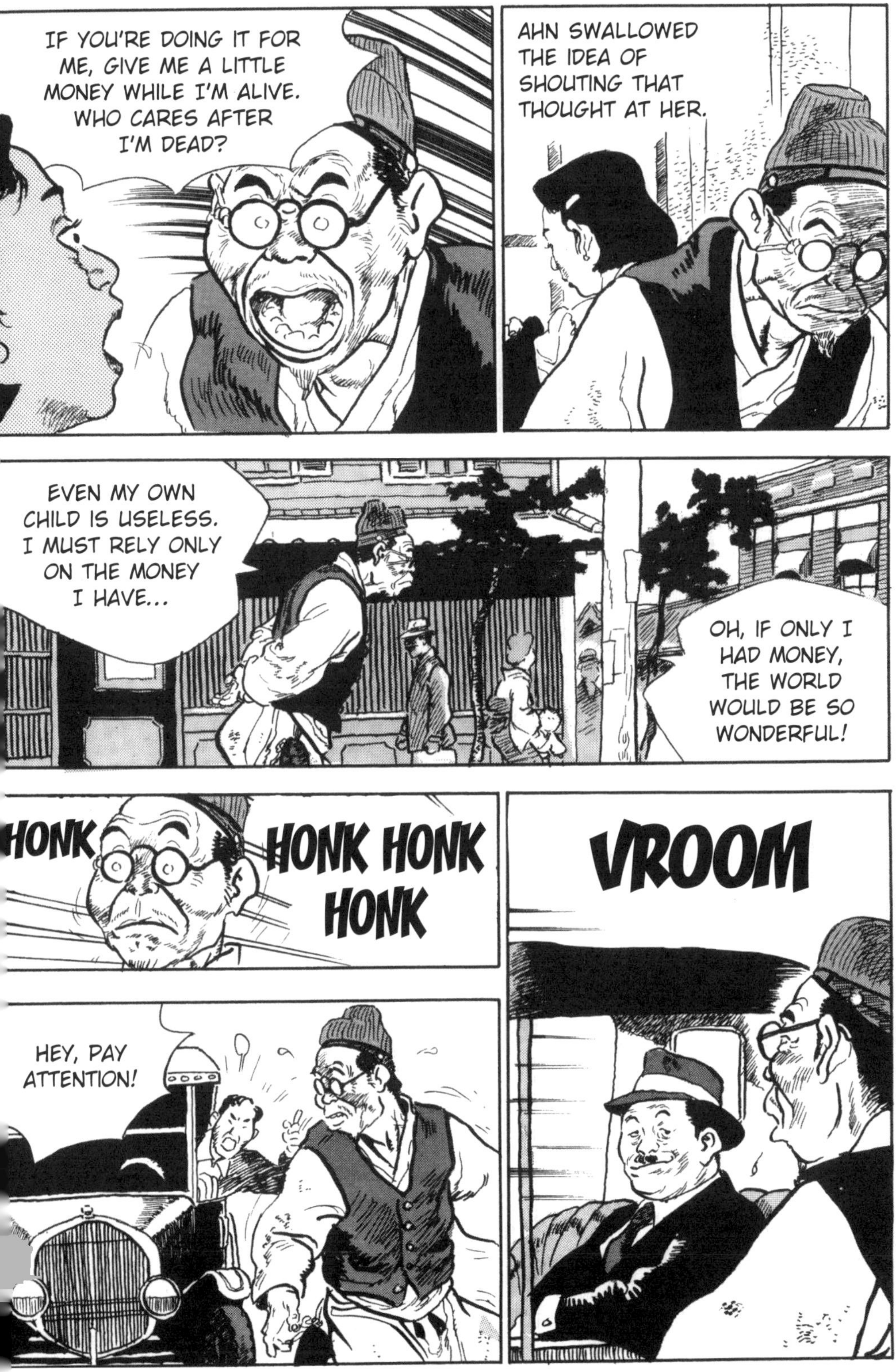
IF YOU'RE DOING IT FOR ME, GIVE ME A LITTLE MONEY WHILE I'M ALIVE. WHO CARES AFTER I'M DEAD?
AHN SWALLOWED THE IDEA OF SHOUTING THAT THOUGHT AT HER.
EVEN MY OWN CHILD IS USELESS. I MUST RELY ONLY ON THE MONEY I HAVE...
OH, IF ONLY I HAD MONEY, THE WORLD WOULD BE SO WONDERFUL!
HONK
HONK HONK HONK
VROOM
HEY, PAY ATTENTION!

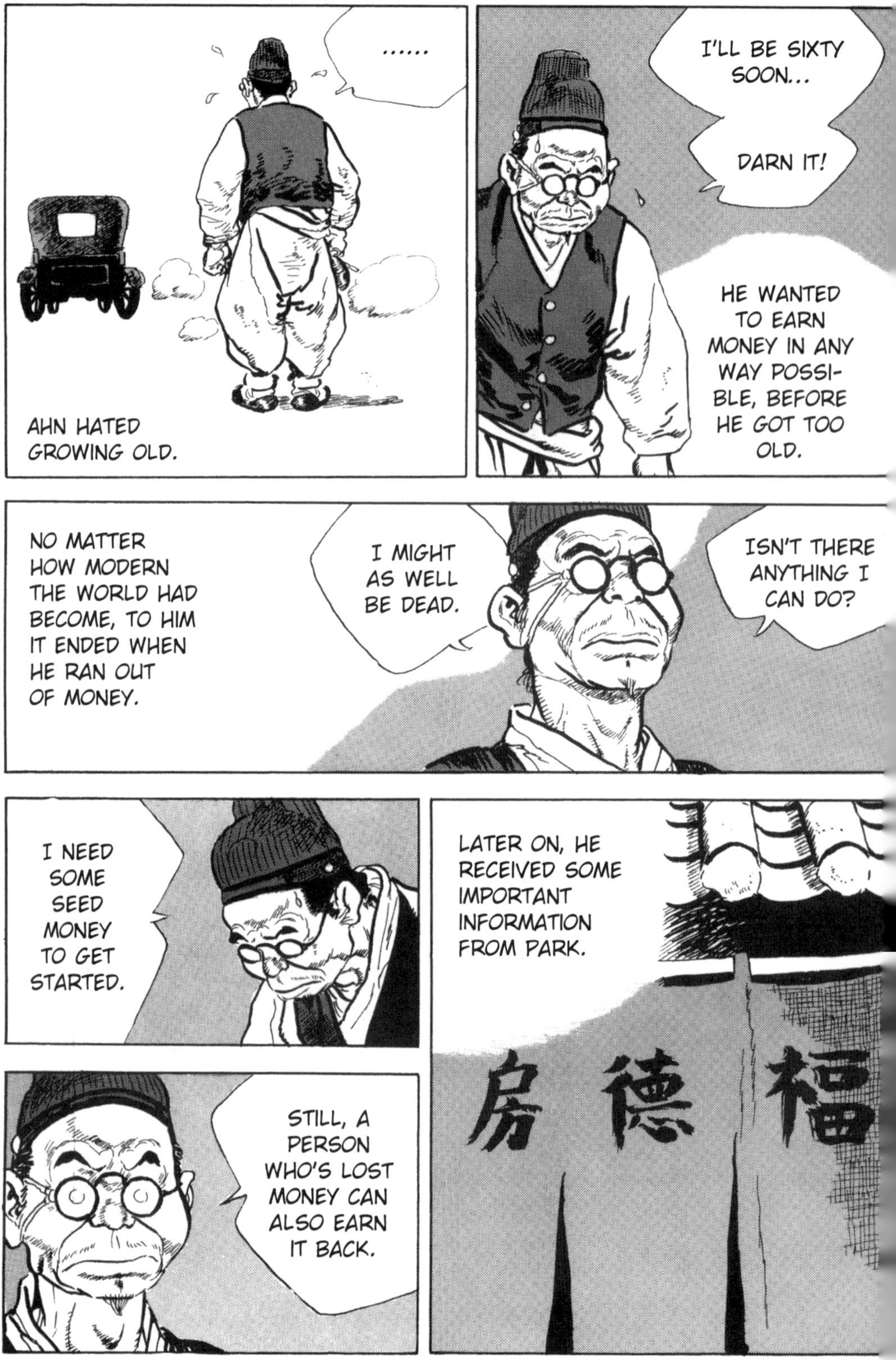
......
AHN HATED GROWING OLD.
I'LL BE SIXTY SOON...
DARN IT!
HE WANTED TO EARN MONEY IN ANY WAY POSSIBLE, BEFORE HE GOT TOO OLD.
NO MATTER HOW MODERN THE WORLD HAD BECOME, TO HIM IT ENDED WHEN HE RAN OUT OF MONEY.
I MIGHT AS WELL BE DEAD.
ISN'T THERE ANYTHING I CAN DO?
I NEED SOME SEED MONEY TO GET STARTED.
STILL, A PERSON WHO'S LOST MONEY CAN ALSO EARN IT BACK.
LATER ON, HE RECEIVED SOME IMPORTANT INFORMATION FROM PARK.
房德福

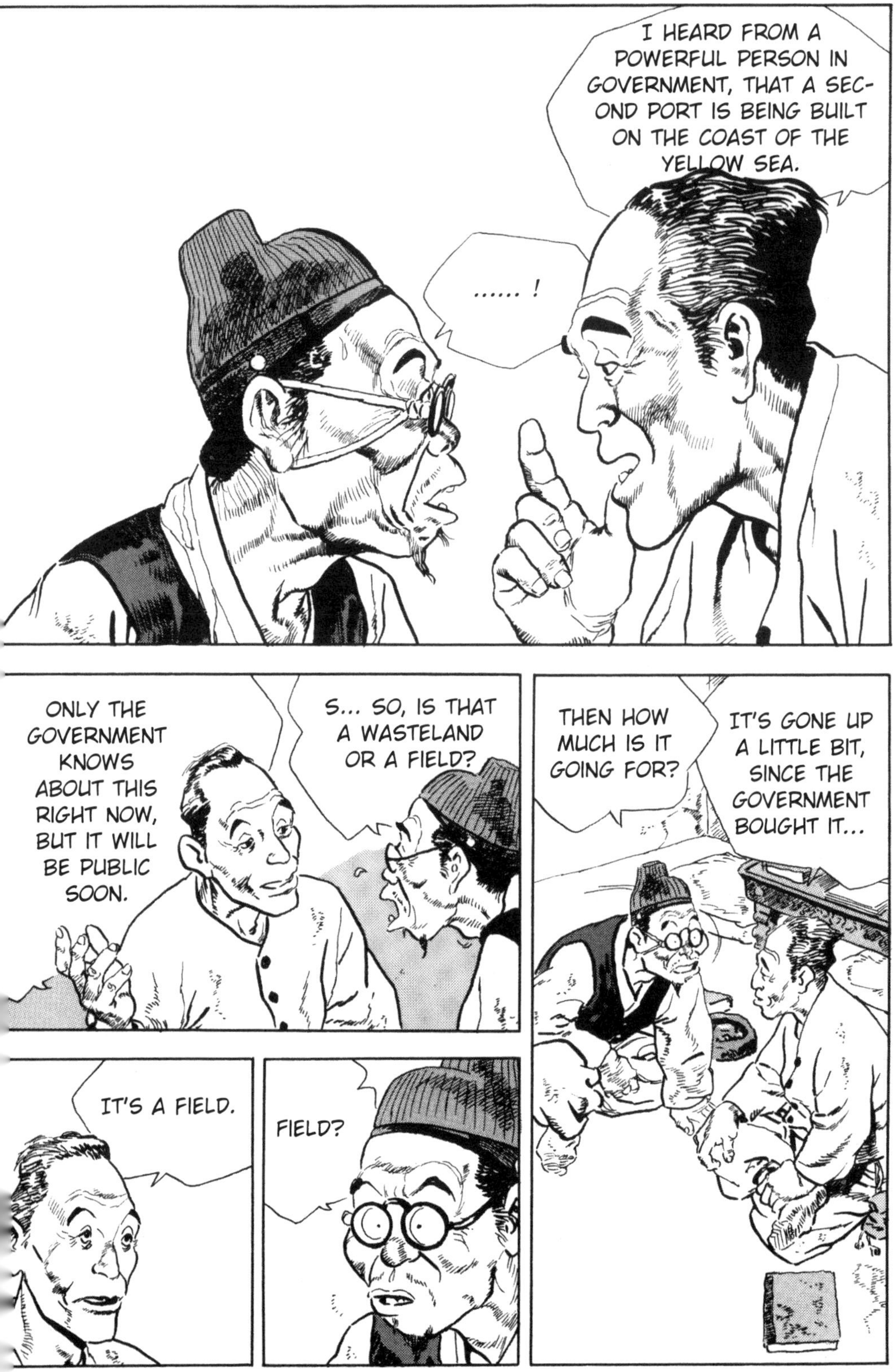
I HEARD FROM A POWERFUL PERSON IN GOVERNMENT, THAT A SEC-OND PORT IS BEING BUILT ON THE COAST OF THE YELLOW SEA.
...... !
ONLY THE GOVERNMENT KNOWS ABOUT THIS RIGHT NOW, BUT IT WILL BE PUBLIC SOON.
S... SO, IS THAT A WASTELAND OR A FIELD?
IT'S A FIELD.
FIELD?
THEN HOW MUCH IS IT GOING FOR?
IT'S GONE UP A LITTLE BIT, SINCE THE GOVERNMENT BOUGHT IT...

STILL, THE LOCALS DON'T KNOW WHY THE GOVERNMENT IS BUYING THE LAND...

OH?

THAT'S WHY THE PRICE DIDN'T RISE ALL THAT MUCH... ONE COULD BUY IT CHEAP.

BUT IT'S JUST A PIE IN THE SKY FOR US...

HMM...

AHN'S TEMPLES THROBBED.

IF IT'S REAL, WHOEVER GOT TO IT FIRST WOULD GET MORE OUT OF IT.

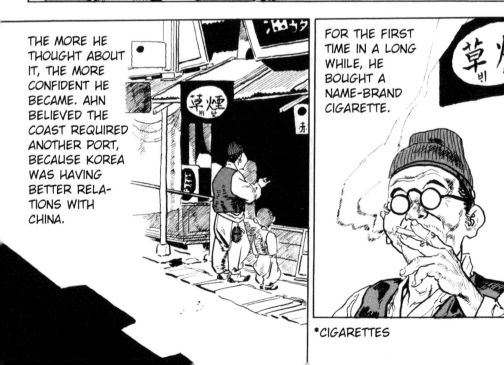

THE MORE HE THOUGHT ABOUT IT, THE MORE CONFIDENT HE BECAME. AHN BELIEVED THE COAST REQUIRED ANOTHER PORT, BECAUSE KOREA WAS HAVING BETTER RELA-TIONS WITH CHINA.

FOR THE FIRST TIME IN A LONG WHILE, HE BOUGHT A NAME-BRAND CIGARETTE.

*CIGARETTES

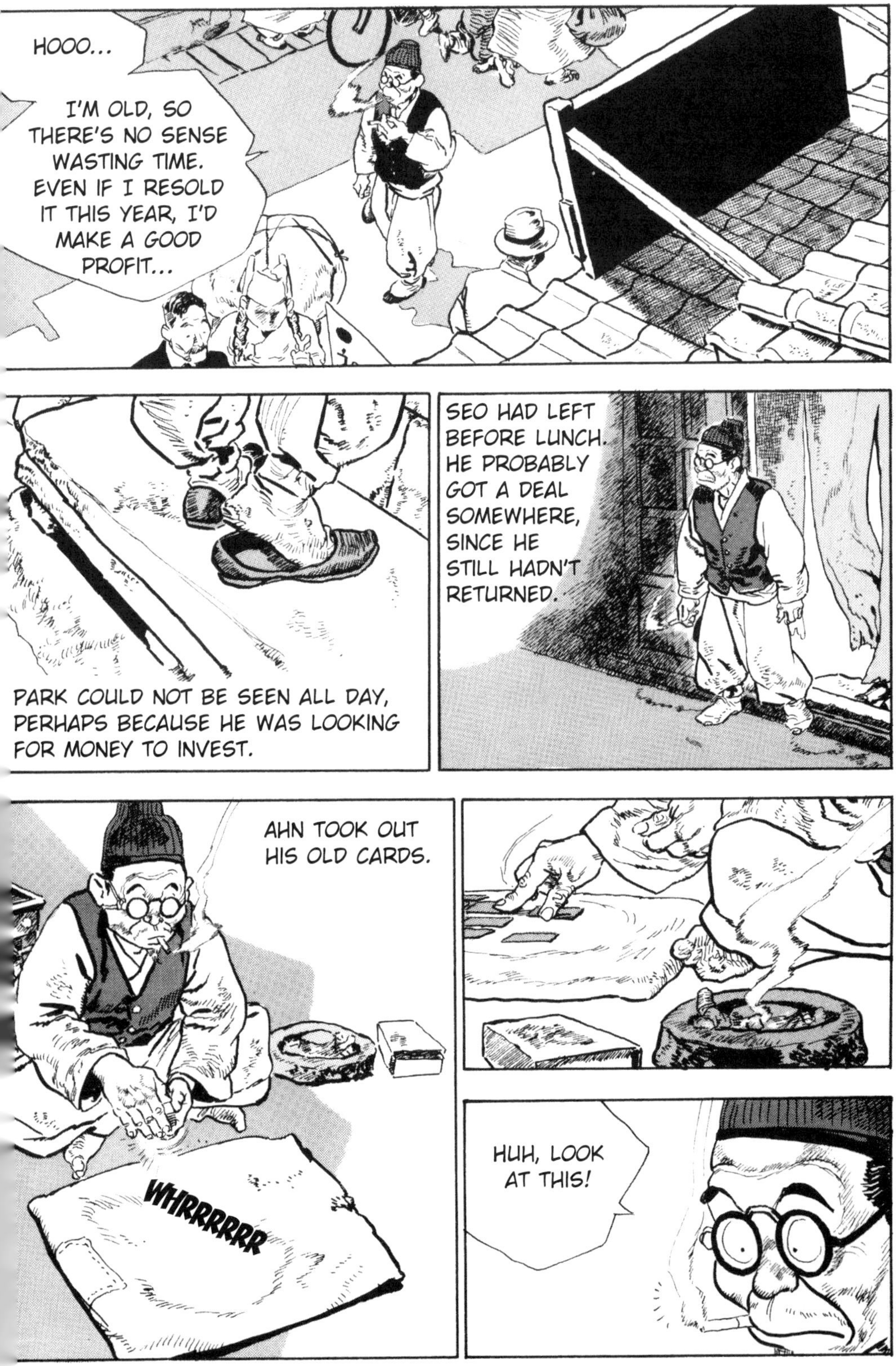
HOOO...
I'M OLD, SO THERE'S NO SENSE WASTING TIME. EVEN IF I RESOLD IT THIS YEAR, I'D MAKE A GOOD PROFIT...
PARK COULD NOT BE SEEN ALL DAY, PERHAPS BECAUSE HE WAS LOOKING FOR MONEY TO INVEST.
SEO HAD LEFT BEFORE LUNCH. HE PROBABLY GOT A DEAL SOMEWHERE, SINCE HE STILL HADN'T RETURNED.
AHN TOOK OUT HIS OLD CARDS.
WHRRRRRR
HUH, LOOK AT THIS!

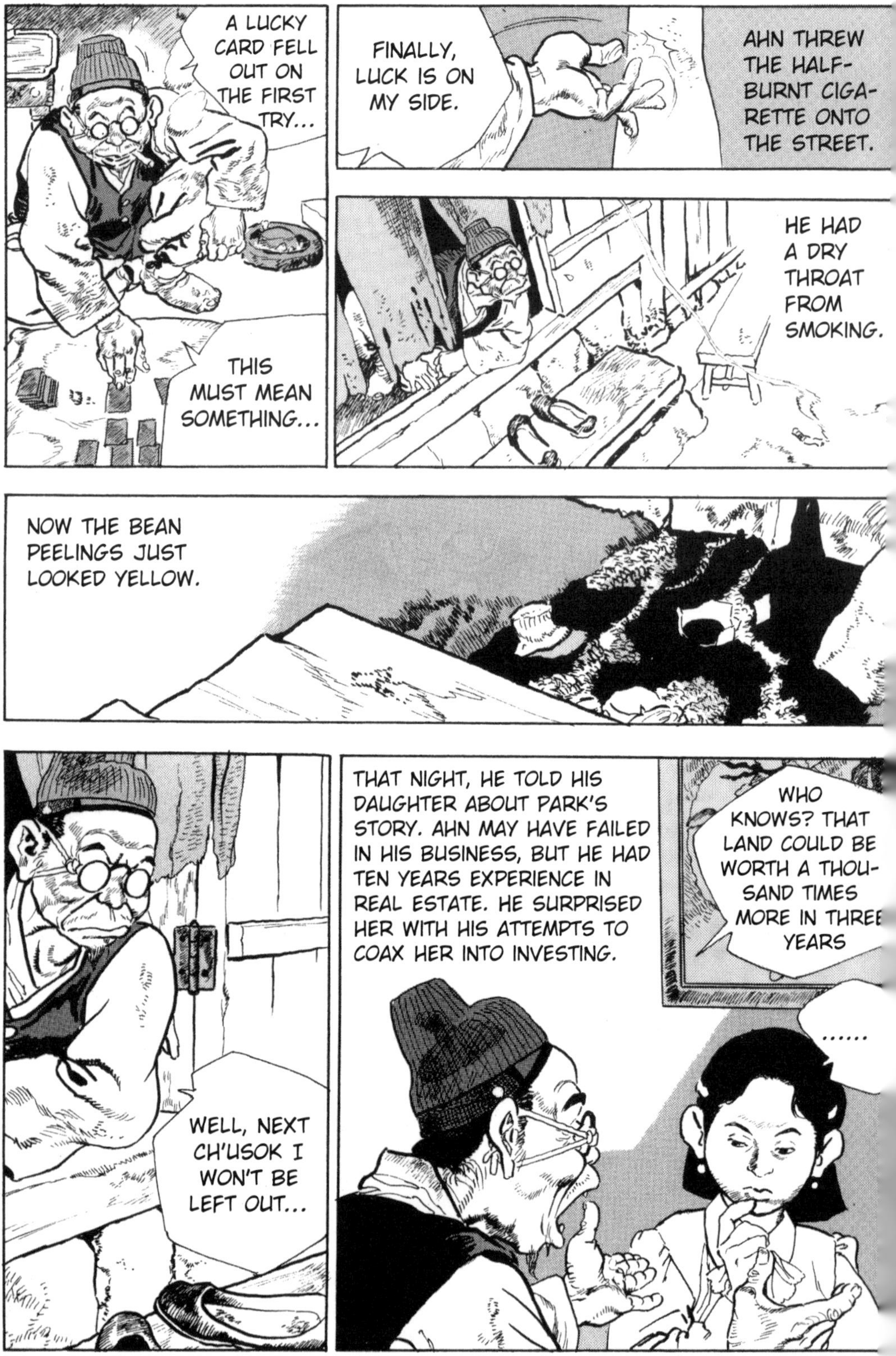
A LUCKY CARD FELL OUT ON THE FIRST TRY...
THIS MUST MEAN SOMETHING...
FINALLY, LUCK IS ON MY SIDE.
AHN THREW THE HALF-BURNT CIGARETTE ONTO THE STREET.
HE HAD A DRY THROAT FROM SMOKING.
NOW THE BEAN PEELINGS JUST LOOKED YELLOW.
WELL, NEXT CH'USOK I WON'T BE LEFT OUT...
THAT NIGHT, HE TOLD HIS DAUGHTER ABOUT PARK'S STORY. AHN MAY HAVE FAILED IN HIS BUSINESS, BUT HE HAD TEN YEARS EXPERIENCE IN REAL ESTATE. HE SURPRISED HER WITH HIS ATTEMPTS TO COAX HER INTO INVESTING.
WHO KNOWS? THAT LAND COULD BE WORTH A THOUSAND TIMES MORE IN THREE YEARS
......

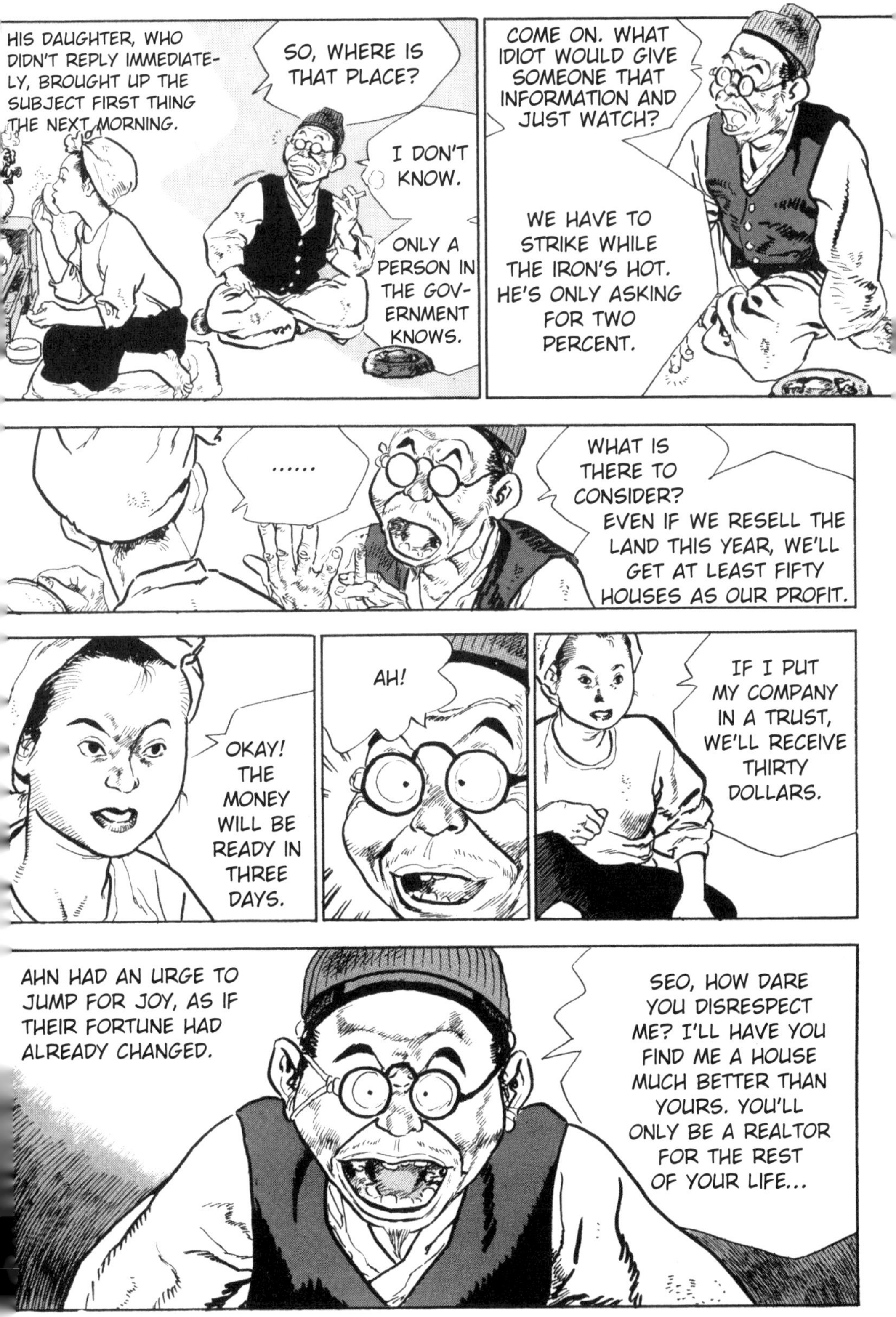
HIS DAUGHTER, WHO DIDN'T REPLY IMMEDIATE-LY, BROUGHT UP THE SUBJECT FIRST THING THE NEXT MORNING.
SO, WHERE IS THAT PLACE?
I DON'T KNOW.
ONLY A PERSON IN THE GOV-ERNMENT KNOWS.
COME ON. WHAT IDIOT WOULD GIVE SOMEONE THAT INFORMATION AND JUST WATCH?
WE HAVE TO STRIKE WHILE THE IRON'S HOT. HE'S ONLY ASKING FOR TWO PERCENT.
......
WHAT IS THERE TO CONSIDER?
EVEN IF WE RESELL THE LAND THIS YEAR, WE'LL GET AT LEAST FIFTY HOUSES AS OUR PROFIT.
OKAY! THE MONEY WILL BE READY IN THREE DAYS.
AH!
IF I PUT MY COMPANY IN A TRUST, WE'LL RECEIVE THIRTY DOLLARS.
AHN HAD AN URGE TO JUMP FOR JOY, AS IF THEIR FORTUNE HAD ALREADY CHANGED.
SEO, HOW DARE YOU DISRESPECT ME? I'LL HAVE YOU FIND ME A HOUSE MUCH BETTER THAN YOURS. YOU'LL ONLY BE A REALTOR FOR THE REST OF YOUR LIFE...

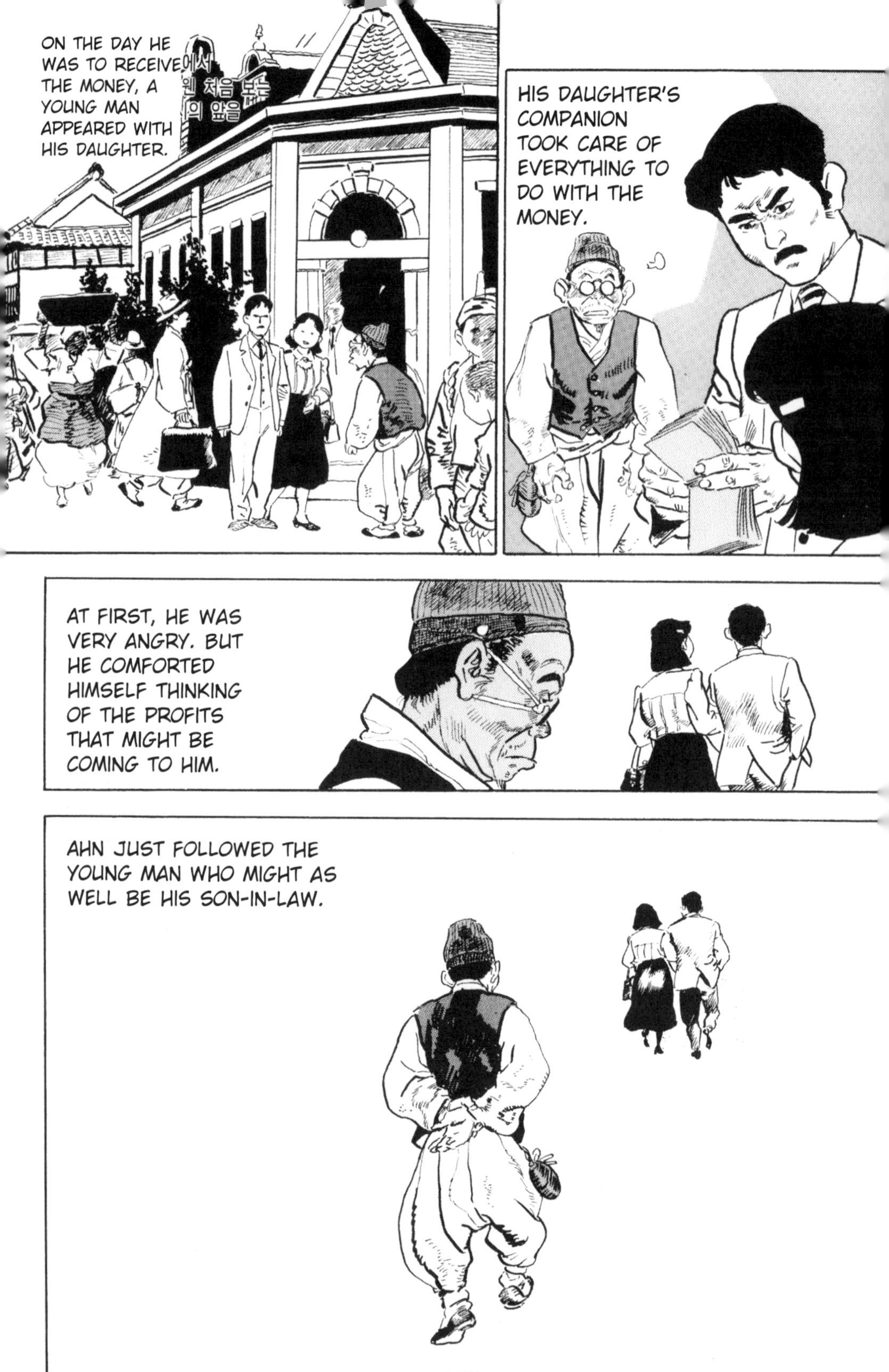
ON THE DAY HE WAS TO RECEIVE THE MONEY, A YOUNG MAN APPEARED WITH HIS DAUGHTER.
HIS DAUGHTER'S COMPANION TOOK CARE OF EVERYTHING TO DO WITH THE MONEY.
AT FIRST, HE WAS VERY ANGRY. BUT HE COMFORTED HIMSELF THINKING OF THE PROFITS THAT MIGHT BE COMING TO HIM.
AHN JUST FOLLOWED THE YOUNG MAN WHO MIGHT AS WELL BE HIS SON-IN-LAW.

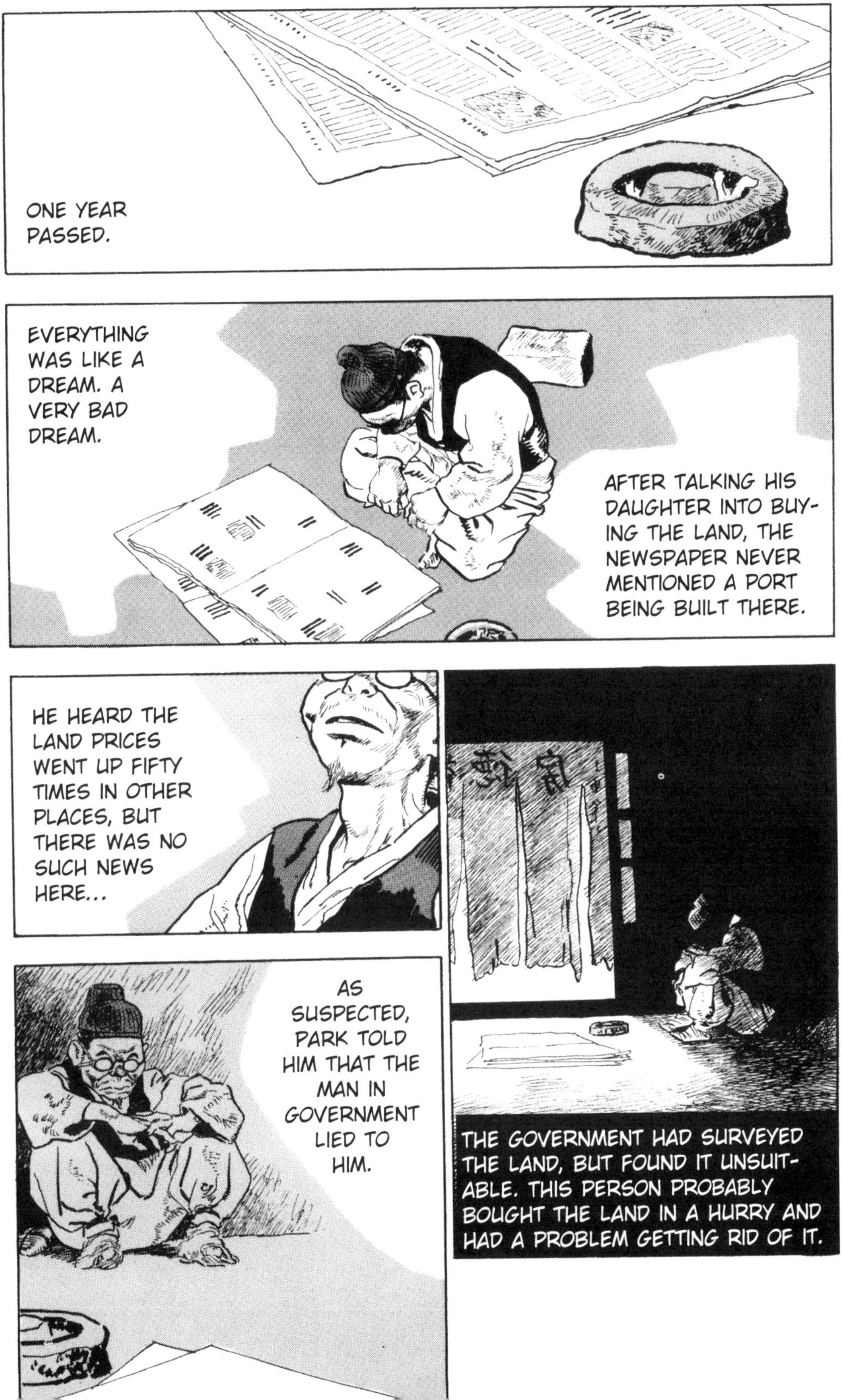
ONE YEAR PASSED.
EVERYTHING WAS LIKE A DREAM. A VERY BAD DREAM.
AFTER TALKING HIS DAUGHTER INTO BUY-ING THE LAND, THE NEWSPAPER NEVER MENTIONED A PORT BEING BUILT THERE.
HE HEARD THE LAND PRICES WENT UP FIFTY TIMES IN OTHER PLACES, BUT THERE WAS NO SUCH NEWS HERE...
AS SUSPECTED, PARK TOLD HIM THAT THE MAN IN GOVERNMENT LIED TO HIM.
THE GOVERNMENT HAD SURVEYED THE LAND, BUT FOUND IT UNSUIT-ABLE. THIS PERSON PROBABLY BOUGHT THE LAND IN A HURRY AND HAD A PROBLEM GETTING RID OF IT.

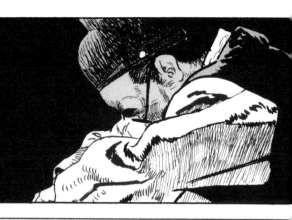

EVEN THOUGH HE DIDN'T GET TO TOUCH A SINGLE CENT, HE GOT ALL THE BLAME. HE DIDN'T DARE GO INSIDE TO EAT.

CAN YOU EVEN ALIENATE FAMILY MEMBERS, WHEN IT COMES TO MONEY?

AHN ONLY GRIEVED. HE MISSED ALCOHOL AND CIGARETTES MORE THAN HE DID FOOD. OF COURSE, HIS GLASSES WERE STILL NOT FIXED.

THERE WAS NO WAY HE COULD GET EVEN A PENNY FROM HIS DAUGHTER.

THE WEATHER LEADING UP TO CH'USOK WAS CLEAR, JUST AS IN ALL OTHER YEARS.

THIS TIME, HOWEVER, HE WIPED AWAY HIS TEARS WITH THE DUSTY SLEEVE.

ONCE AGAIN, AHN THOUGHT ABOUT HIS DIRTY OLD SHIRT.

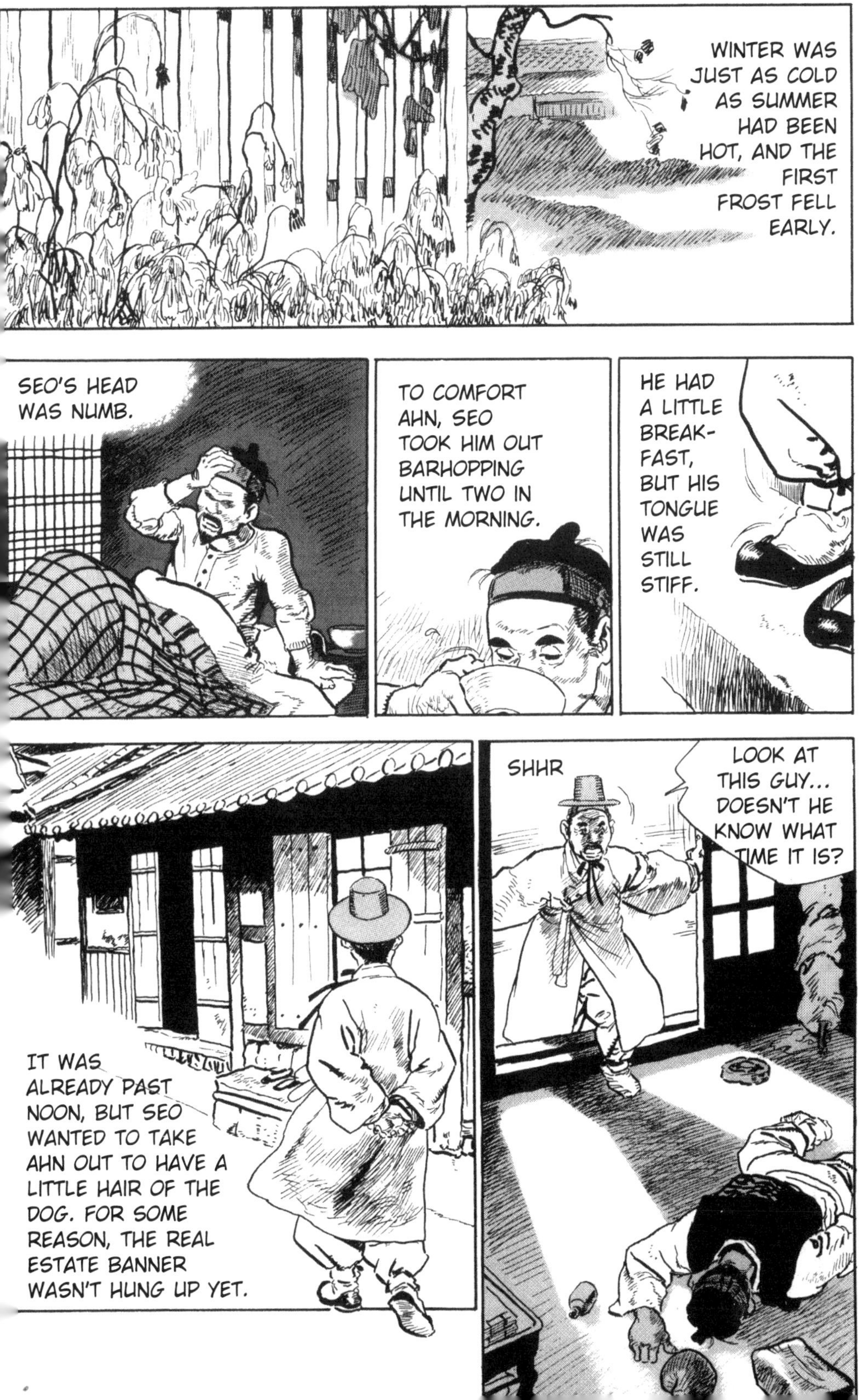
WINTER WAS JUST AS COLD AS SUMMER HAD BEEN HOT, AND THE FIRST FROST FELL EARLY.
SEO'S HEAD WAS NUMB.
TO COMFORT AHN, SEO TOOK HIM OUT BARHOPPING UNTIL TWO IN THE MORNING.
HE HAD A LITTLE BREAK-FAST, BUT HIS TONGUE WAS STILL STIFF.
IT WAS ALREADY PAST NOON, BUT SEO WANTED TO TAKE AHN OUT TO HAVE A LITTLE HAIR OF THE DOG. FOR SOME REASON, THE REAL ESTATE BANNER WASN'T HUNG UP YET.
SHHR
LOOK AT THIS GUY... DOESN'T HE KNOW WHAT TIME IT IS?

WHAT...?

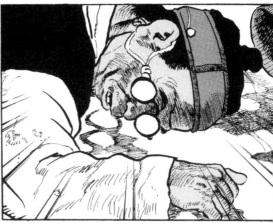

HUH...

DRUGS!

OH NO, HE'S DEAD...!

SEO THOUGHT OF GOING TO THE POLICE STATION, BUT FIGURED HE SHOULD TELL AHN'S DAUGHTER FIRST. HE WENT TO HER PLACE OF BUSINESS AND BROUGHT HER BACK WITH HIM.

SOB...

SOOOOOB..

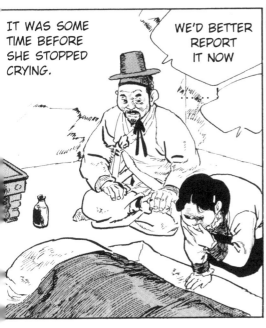

IT WAS SOME TIME BEFORE SHE STOPPED CRYING.

WE'D BETTER REPORT IT NOW

NO, PLEASE, DON'T.

WHAT DO YOU MEAN, DON'T?

WELL...

WELL?

THINK ABOUT MY HONOR...

HONOR?

LUDICROUS! HOW CAN YOU THINK ABOUT HONOR, WHEN YOU CAUSED YOUR FATHER TO PASS AWAY IN THE FIRST PLACE?

......

GRUMBLE...

WHOOSH

OH, PLEASE SAVE ME.

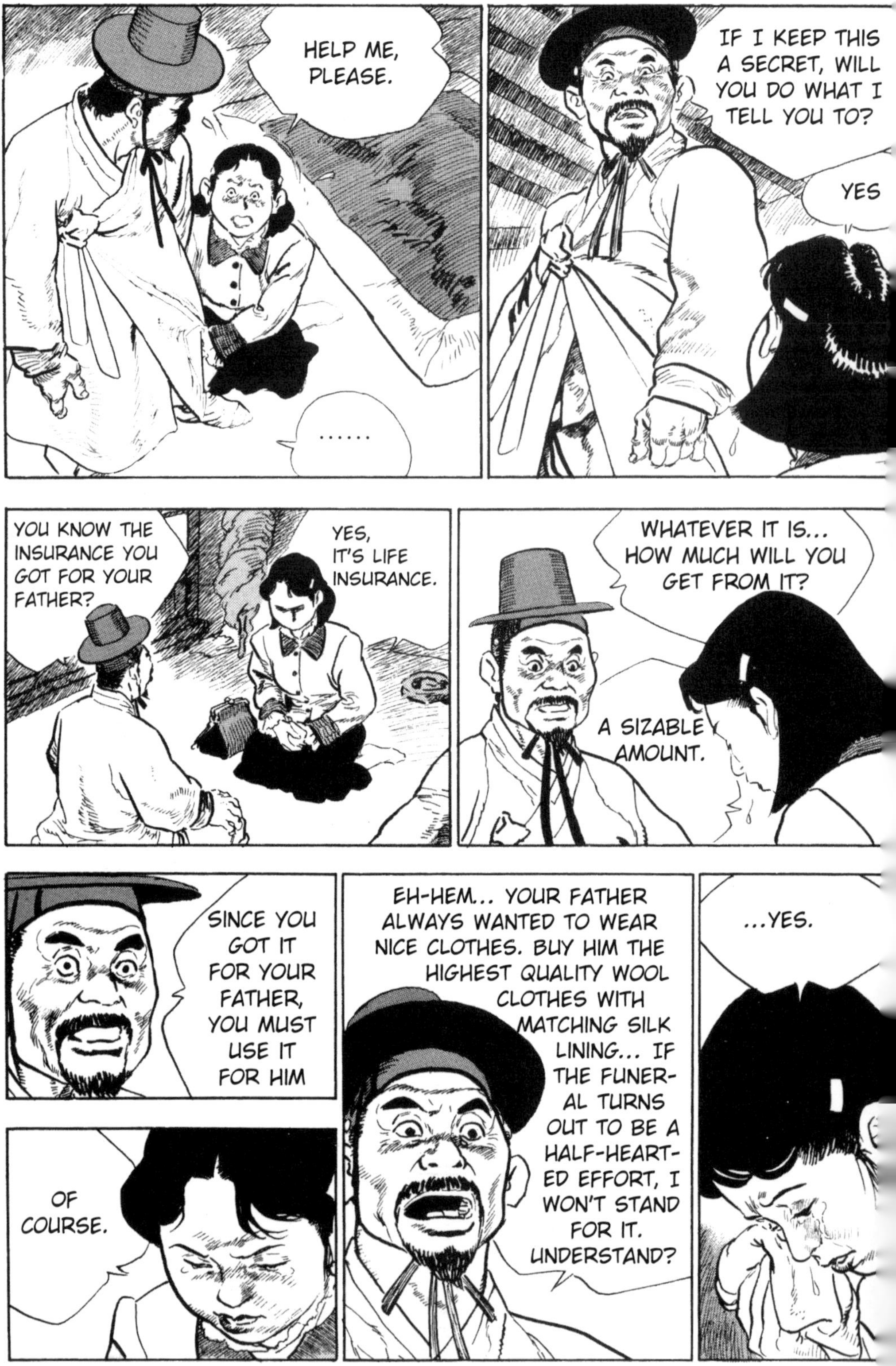
HELP ME, PLEASE.
......
IF I KEEP THIS A SECRET, WILL YOU DO WHAT I TELL YOU TO?
YES
YOU KNOW THE INSURANCE YOU GOT FOR YOUR FATHER?
YES, IT'S LIFE INSURANCE.
WHATEVER IT IS... HOW MUCH WILL YOU GET FROM IT?
A SIZABLE AMOUNT.
SINCE YOU GOT IT FOR YOUR FATHER, YOU MUST USE IT FOR HIM
OF COURSE.
EH-HEM... YOUR FATHER ALWAYS WANTED TO WEAR NICE CLOTHES. BUY HIM THE HIGHEST QUALITY WOOL CLOTHES WITH MATCHING SILK LINING... IF THE FUNER-AL TURNS OUT TO BE A HALF-HEART-ED EFFORT, I WON'T STAND FOR IT. UNDERSTAND?
...YES.

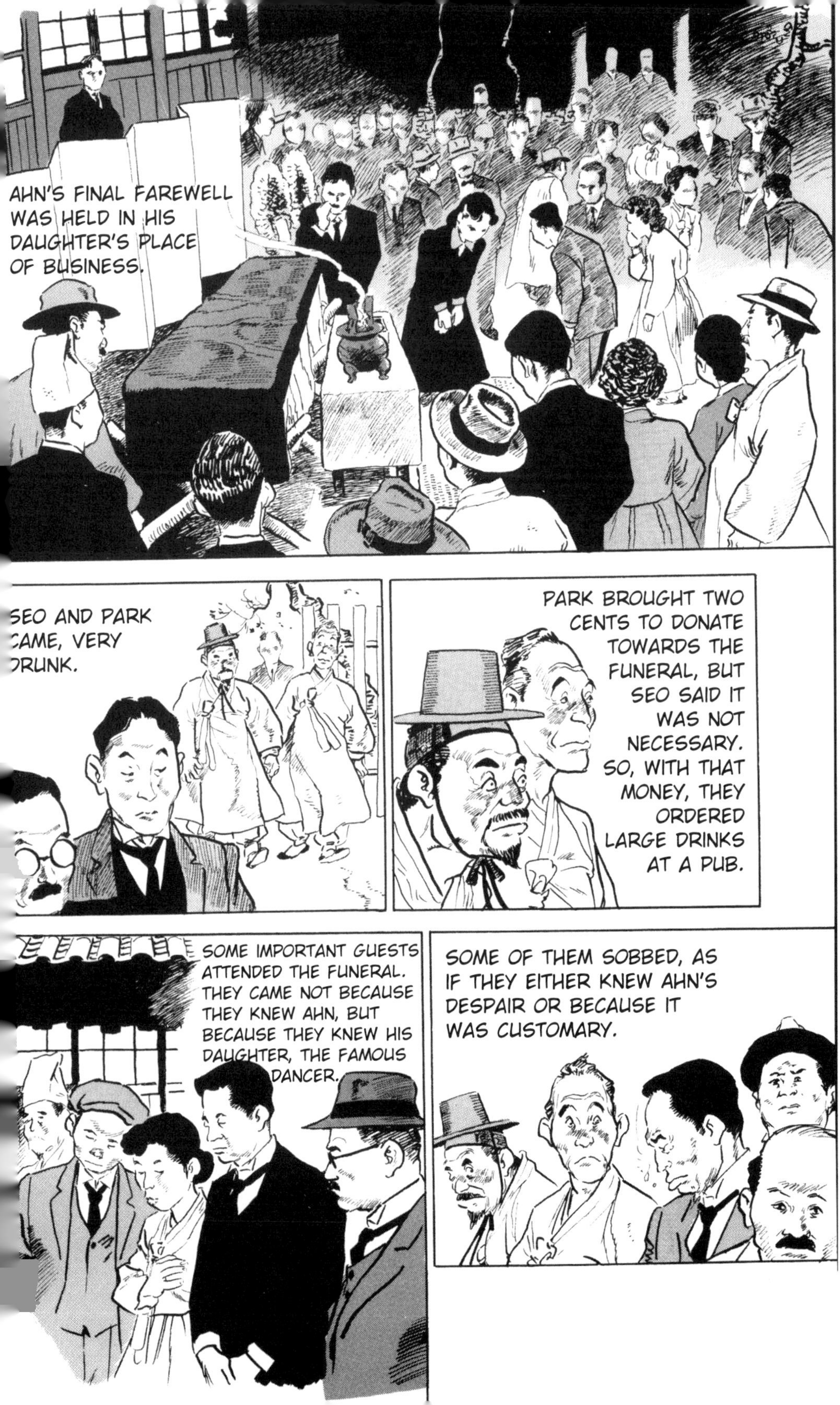
AHN'S FINAL FAREWELL WAS HELD IN HIS DAUGHTER'S PLACE OF BUSINESS.
SEO AND PARK CAME, VERY DRUNK.
PARK BROUGHT TWO CENTS TO DONATE TOWARDS THE FUNERAL, BUT SEO SAID IT WAS NOT NECESSARY. SO, WITH THAT MONEY, THEY ORDERED LARGE DRINKS AT A PUB.
SOME IMPORTANT GUESTS ATTENDED THE FUNERAL. THEY CAME NOT BECAUSE THEY KNEW AHN, BUT BECAUSE THEY KNEW HIS DAUGHTER, THE FAMOUS DANCER.
SOME OF THEM SOBBED, AS IF THEY EITHER KNEW AHN'S DESPAIR OR BECAUSE IT WAS CUSTOMARY.

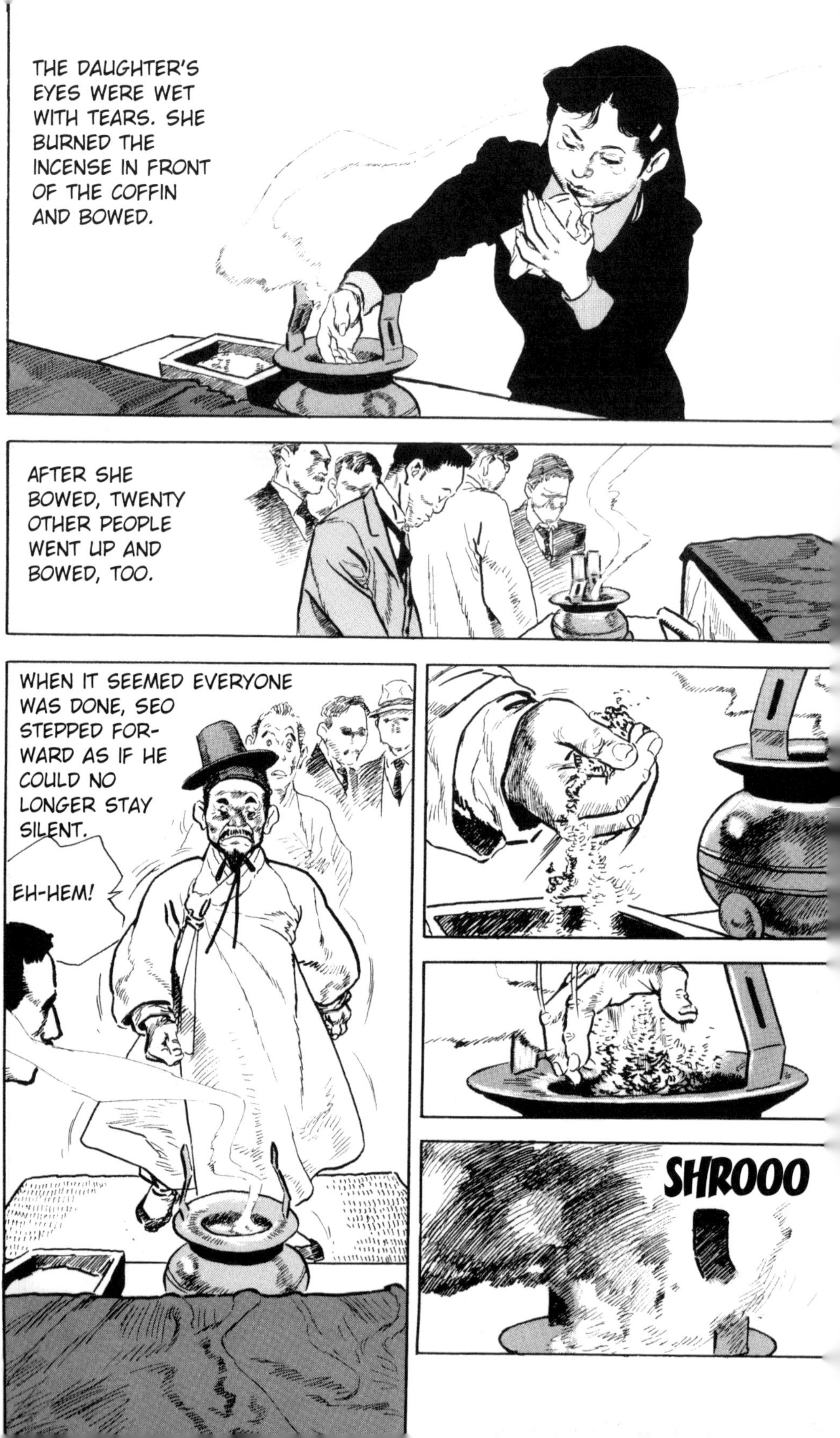
THE DAUGHTER'S EYES WERE WET WITH TEARS. SHE BURNED THE INCENSE IN FRONT OF THE COFFIN AND BOWED.
AFTER SHE BOWED, TWENTY OTHER PEOPLE WENT UP AND BOWED, TOO.
WHEN IT SEEMED EVERYONE WAS DONE, SEO STEPPED FOR-WARD AS IF HE COULD NO LONGER STAY SILENT.
EH-HEM!
SHROOO

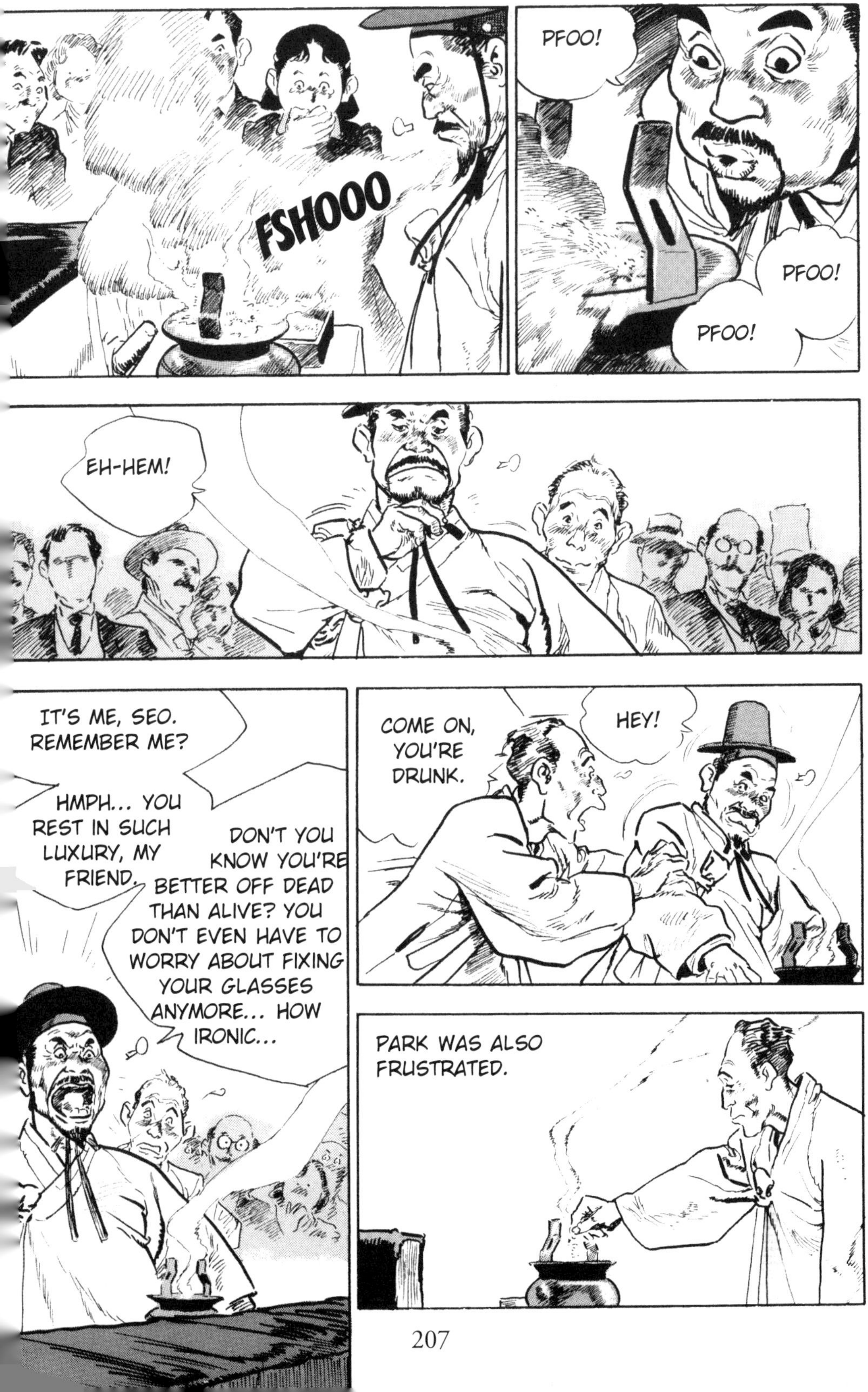
FSHOOO
PFOO!
PFOO!
PFOO!
EH-HEM!
IT'S ME, SEO. REMEMBER ME?
HMPH... YOU REST IN SUCH LUXURY, MY FRIEND.
DON'T YOU KNOW YOU'RE BETTER OFF DEAD THAN ALIVE? YOU DON'T EVEN HAVE TO WORRY ABOUT FIXING YOUR GLASSES ANYMORE... HOW IRONIC...
HEY!
COME ON, YOU'RE DRUNK.
PARK WAS ALSO FRUSTRATED.

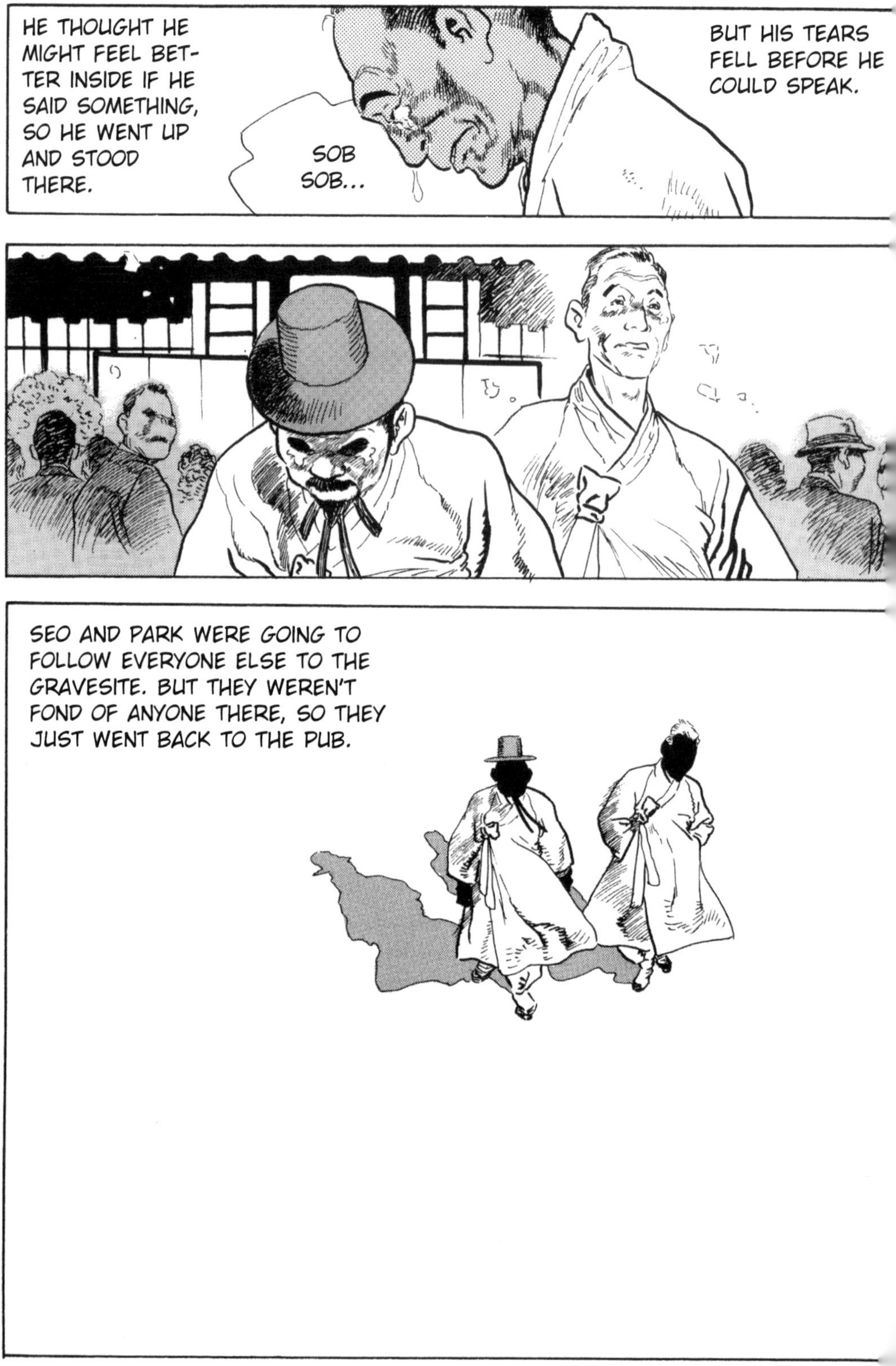
HE THOUGHT HE MIGHT FEEL BETTER INSIDE IF HE SAID SOMETHING, SO HE WENT UP AND STOOD THERE.
SOB SOB...
BUT HIS TEARS FELL BEFORE HE COULD SPEAK.
SEO AND PARK WERE GOING TO FOLLOW EVERYONE ELSE TO THE GRAVESITE. BUT THEY WEREN'T FOND OF ANYONE THERE, SO THEY JUST WENT BACK TO THE PUB.

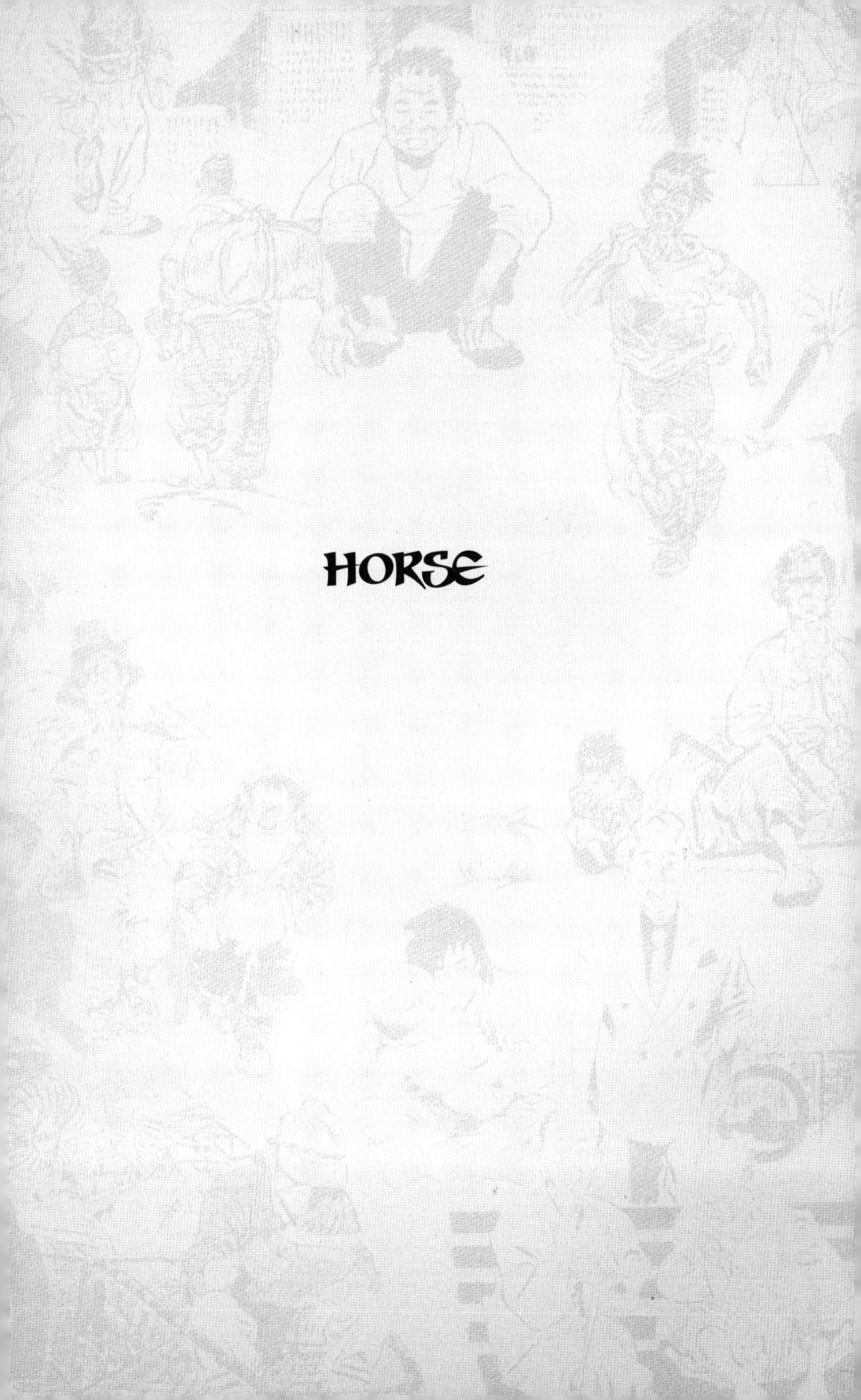

HORSE

AHN HOI-NAM
MAY 1993

A LARGE HERD
OF HORSES
MIGRATED FROM
THE NORTH.

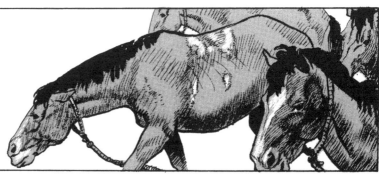

THEY HAD BEEN ABANDONED
BY THE JAPANESE ARMY
AFTER THEY LOST THE WAR.

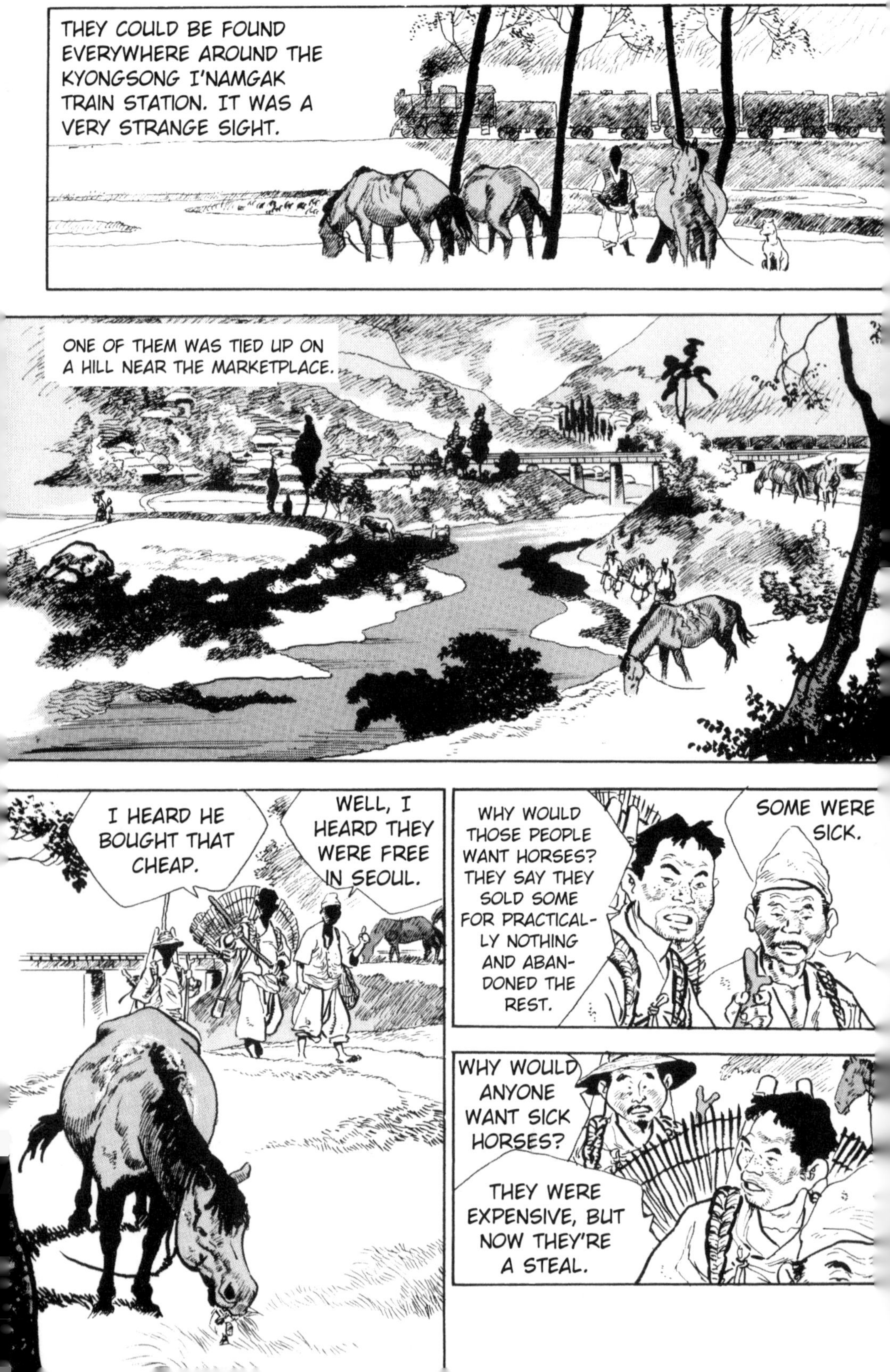
THEY COULD BE FOUND EVERYWHERE AROUND THE KYONGSONG I'NAMGAK TRAIN STATION. IT WAS A VERY STRANGE SIGHT.
ONE OF THEM WAS TIED UP ON A HILL NEAR THE MARKETPLACE.
I HEARD HE BOUGHT THAT CHEAP.
WELL, I HEARD THEY WERE FREE IN SEOUL.
WHY WOULD THOSE PEOPLE WANT HORSES? THEY SAY THEY SOLD SOME FOR PRACTICALLY NOTHING AND ABANDONED THE REST.
SOME WERE SICK.
WHY WOULD ANYONE WANT SICK HORSES?
THEY WERE EXPENSIVE, BUT NOW THEY'RE A STEAL.

SO YOU CAN STILL SELL THEM FOR MEAT AND GET YOUR MONEY BACK.

THAT'S RIGHT!

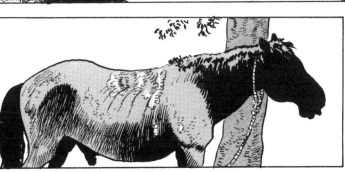

THE HORSES LOOKED UGLY. THEIR FUR HAD BEEN WORN OFF BY THE SADDLES. THEY ALMOST RESEMBLED THE JAPANESE SOLDIERS WHO HAD DISARMED IN SURRENDER.

THESE FORMERLY MAJESTIC CREATURES WERE NOW PITIFULLY WEAK, AS THEY ROAMED ABOUT THE HILLSIDE.

HMPH, YOU AND THE JAPS BOTH GOT WHAT WAS COMING TO YOU!

YOU DESERVE THE SAME FATE AS THE JAPS!

DUK-MAN WAS CAPTURED BY THE JAPANESE AND RECENTLY RELEASED. HE VENTED HIS ANGER ON THE HORSE.

HE SEEMED TO FEEL BETTER AFTER YELLING.

HMPH...

HE THOUGHT HE COULD SMELL THE DIRTY STENCH OF THE JAPANESE ON THE HORSES.

THAT'S WHY HE SHOOK HIS FIST AT THE HORSE EVERY CHANCE HE GOT.

HEY, AREN'T YOU DUK-MAN? IT'S SO GOOD TO SEE YOU AGAIN...

...... !

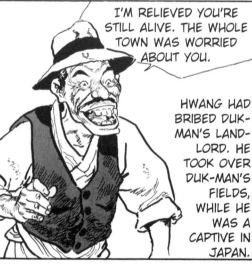

I'M RELIEVED YOU'RE STILL ALIVE. THE WHOLE TOWN WAS WORRIED ABOUT YOU.

HWANG HAD BRIBED DUK-MAN'S LAND-LORD. HE TOOK OVER DUK-MAN'S FIELDS, WHILE HE WAS A CAPTIVE IN JAPAN.

DUK-MAN'S WIFE HAD SENT HIM THE NEWS. HE CRIED ALL DAY AND DIDN'T DO ANY WORK.

HMPH! I'LL BET.

HWANG EVADED THE DRAFT BY BROWN-NOSING GOV-ERNMENT OFFICIALS. HE AMASSED A FORTUNE BY CONFISCATING PROPERTY. NOW HE WAS TRYING TO GET CLOSE TO DUK-MAN.

214

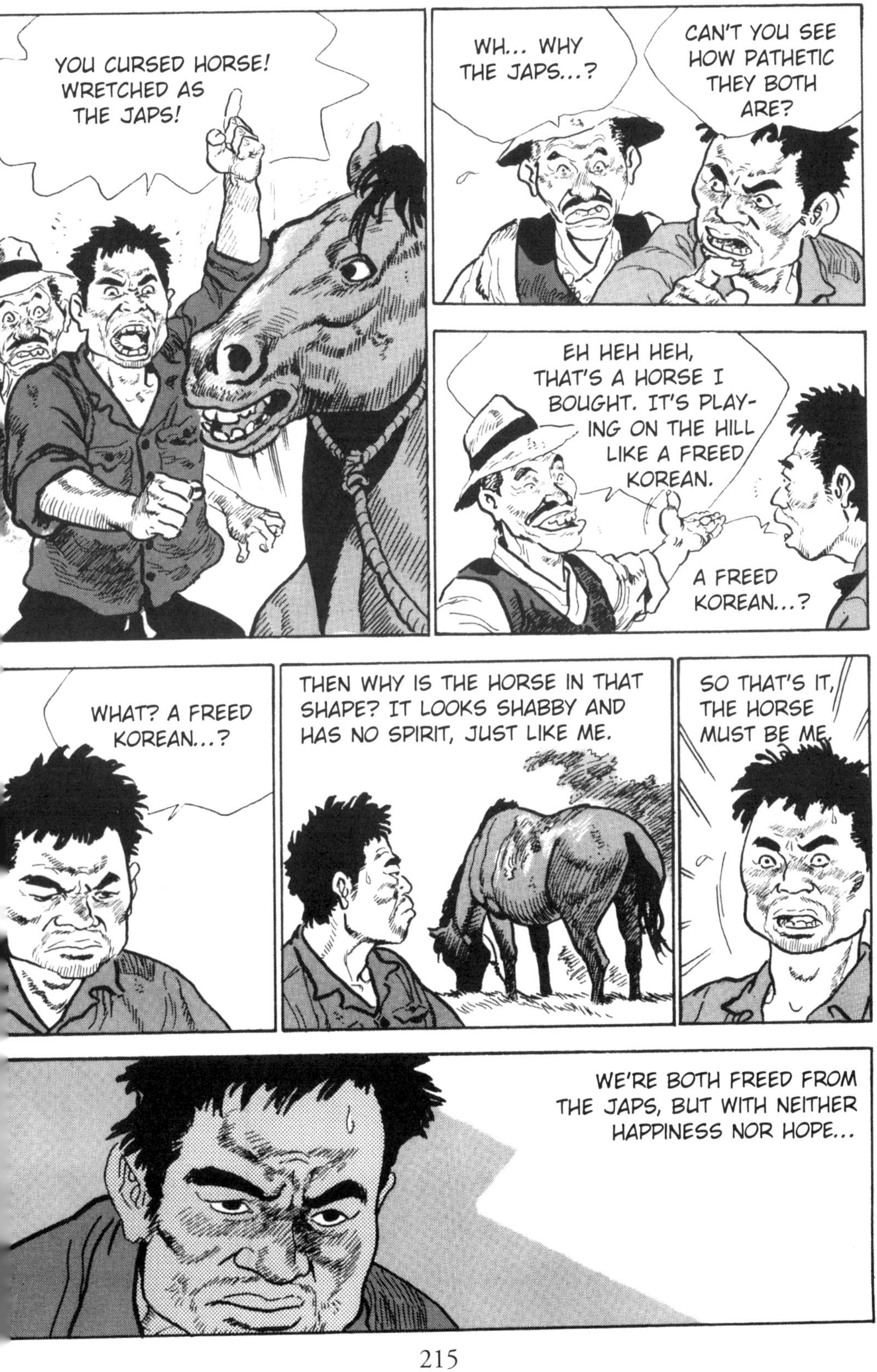
YOU CURSED HORSE! WRETCHED AS THE JAPS!
WH... WHY THE JAPS...?
CAN'T YOU SEE HOW PATHETIC THEY BOTH ARE?
EH HEH HEH, THAT'S A HORSE I BOUGHT. IT'S PLAY-ING ON THE HILL LIKE A FREED KOREAN.
A FREED KOREAN...?
WHAT? A FREED KOREAN...?
THEN WHY IS THE HORSE IN THAT SHAPE? IT LOOKS SHABBY AND HAS NO SPIRIT, JUST LIKE ME.
SO THAT'S IT, THE HORSE MUST BE ME.
WE'RE BOTH FREED FROM THE JAPS, BUT WITH NEITHER HAPPINESS NOR HOPE...

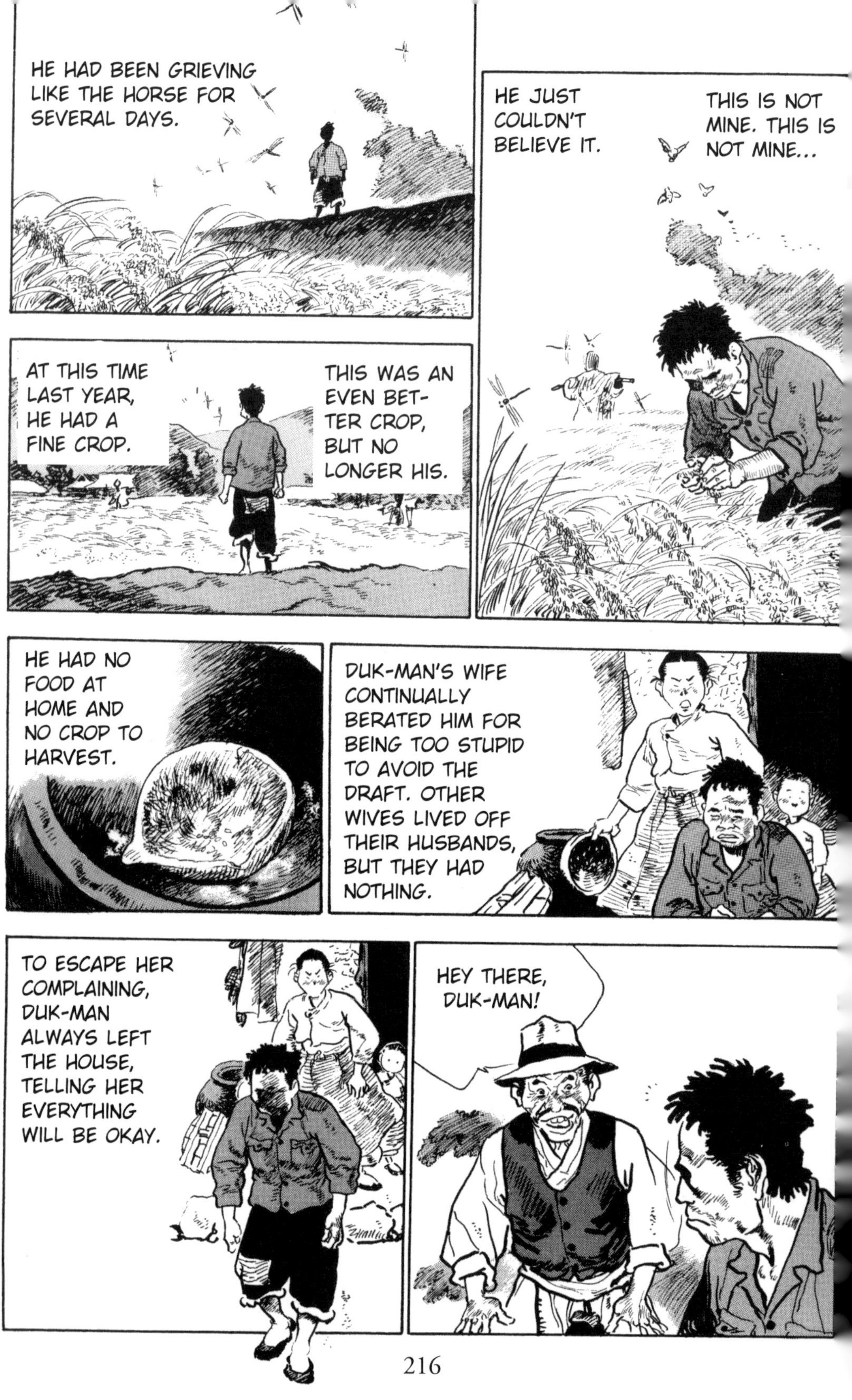
HE HAD BEEN GRIEVING LIKE THE HORSE FOR SEVERAL DAYS.
HE JUST COULDN'T BELIEVE IT.
THIS IS NOT MINE. THIS IS NOT MINE...
AT THIS TIME LAST YEAR, HE HAD A FINE CROP.
THIS WAS AN EVEN BET-TER CROP, BUT NO LONGER HIS.
HE HAD NO FOOD AT HOME AND NO CROP TO HARVEST.
DUK-MAN'S WIFE CONTINUALLY BERATED HIM FOR BEING TOO STUPID TO AVOID THE DRAFT. OTHER WIVES LIVED OFF THEIR HUSBANDS, BUT THEY HAD NOTHING.
TO ESCAPE HER COMPLAINING, DUK-MAN ALWAYS LEFT THE HOUSE, TELLING HER EVERYTHING WILL BE OKAY.
HEY THERE, DUK-MAN!

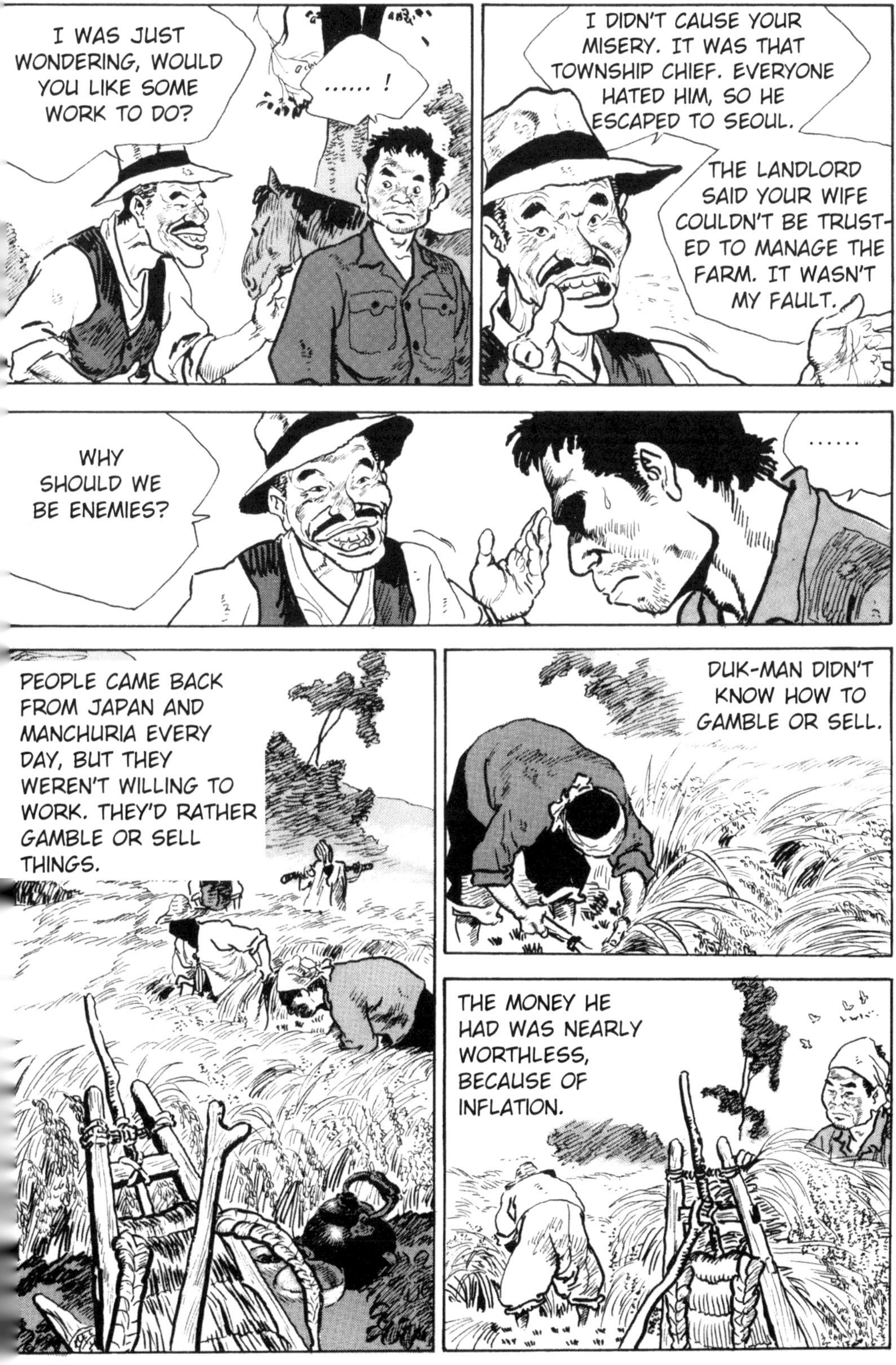
I WAS JUST WONDERING, WOULD YOU LIKE SOME WORK TO DO?
...... !
I DIDN'T CAUSE YOUR MISERY. IT WAS THAT TOWNSHIP CHIEF. EVERYONE HATED HIM, SO HE ESCAPED TO SEOUL.
THE LANDLORD SAID YOUR WIFE COULDN'T BE TRUST-ED TO MANAGE THE FARM. IT WASN'T MY FAULT.
WHY SHOULD WE BE ENEMIES?
......
PEOPLE CAME BACK FROM JAPAN AND MANCHURIA EVERY DAY, BUT THEY WEREN'T WILLING TO WORK. THEY'D RATHER GAMBLE OR SELL THINGS.
DUK-MAN DIDN'T KNOW HOW TO GAMBLE OR SELL.
THE MONEY HE HAD WAS NEARLY WORTHLESS, BECAUSE OF INFLATION.

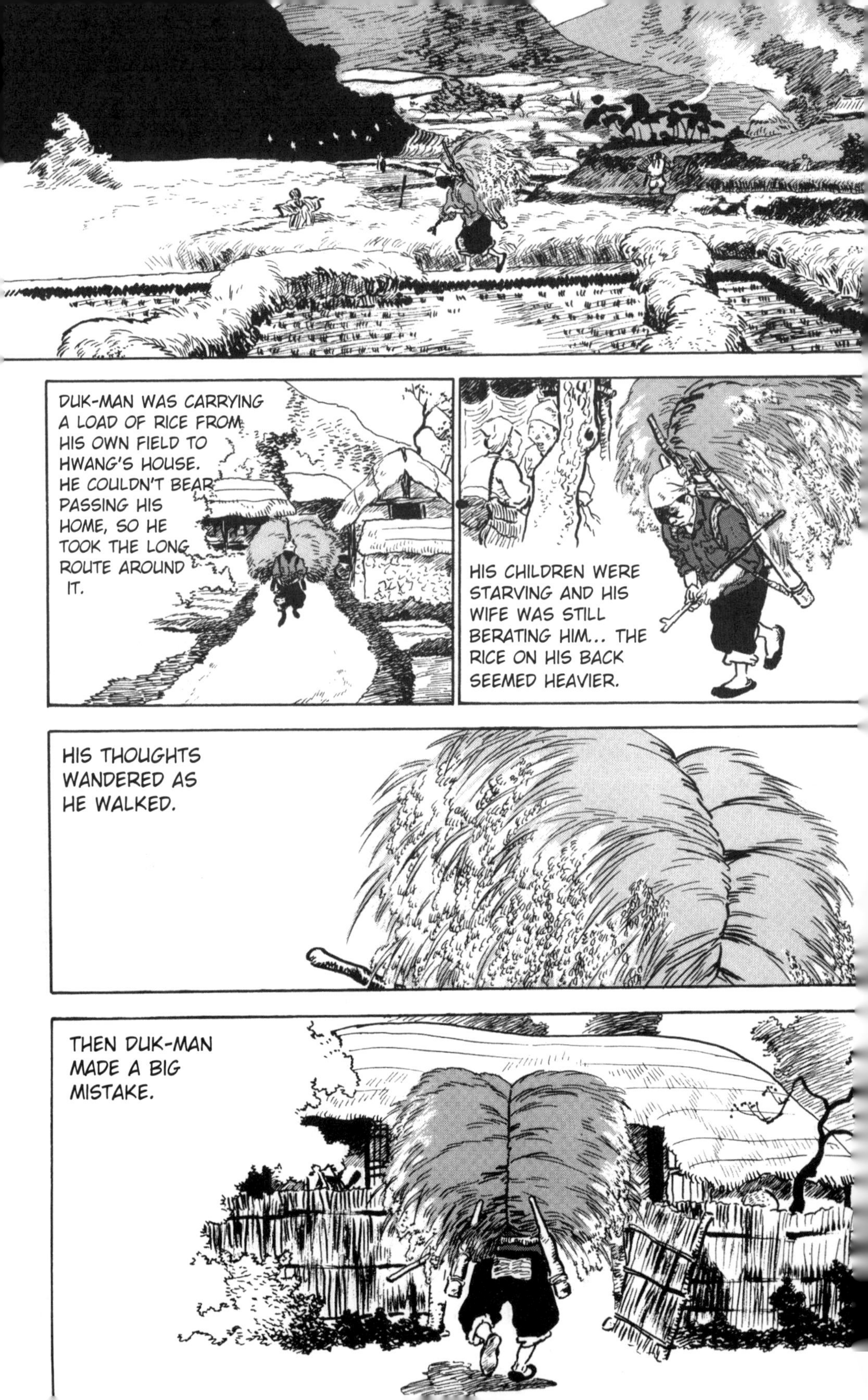
DUK-MAN WAS CARRYING A LOAD OF RICE FROM HIS OWN FIELD TO HWANG'S HOUSE. HE COULDN'T BEAR PASSING HIS HOME, SO HE TOOK THE LONG ROUTE AROUND IT.
HIS CHILDREN WERE STARVING AND HIS WIFE WAS STILL BERATING HIM... THE RICE ON HIS BACK SEEMED HEAVIER.
HIS THOUGHTS WANDERED AS HE WALKED.
THEN DUK-MAN MADE A BIG MISTAKE.

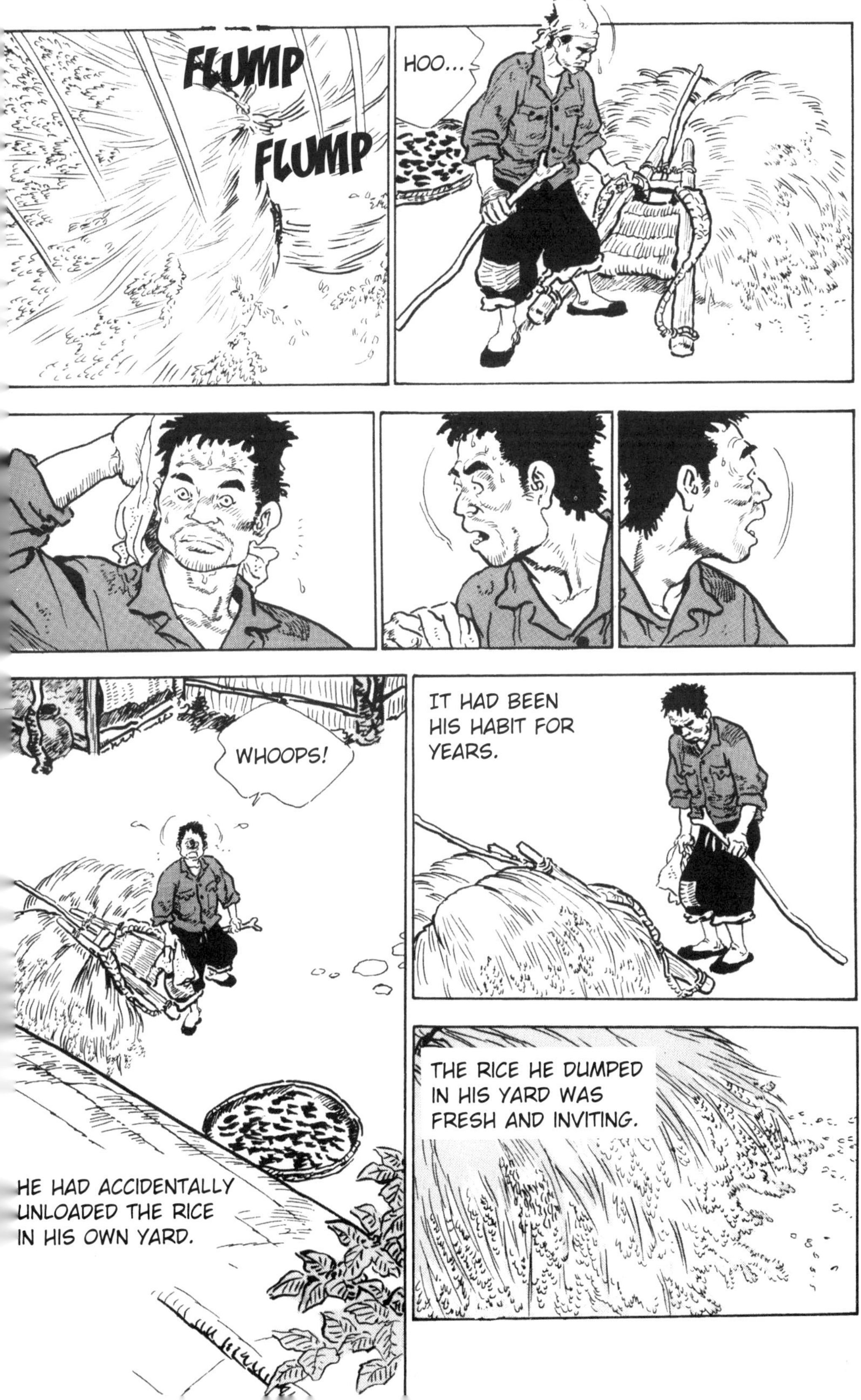

FLUMP
FLUMP
HOO...
WHOOPS!
HE HAD ACCIDENTALLY UNLOADED THE RICE IN HIS OWN YARD.
IT HAD BEEN HIS HABIT FOR YEARS.
THE RICE HE DUMPED IN HIS YARD WAS FRESH AND INVITING.

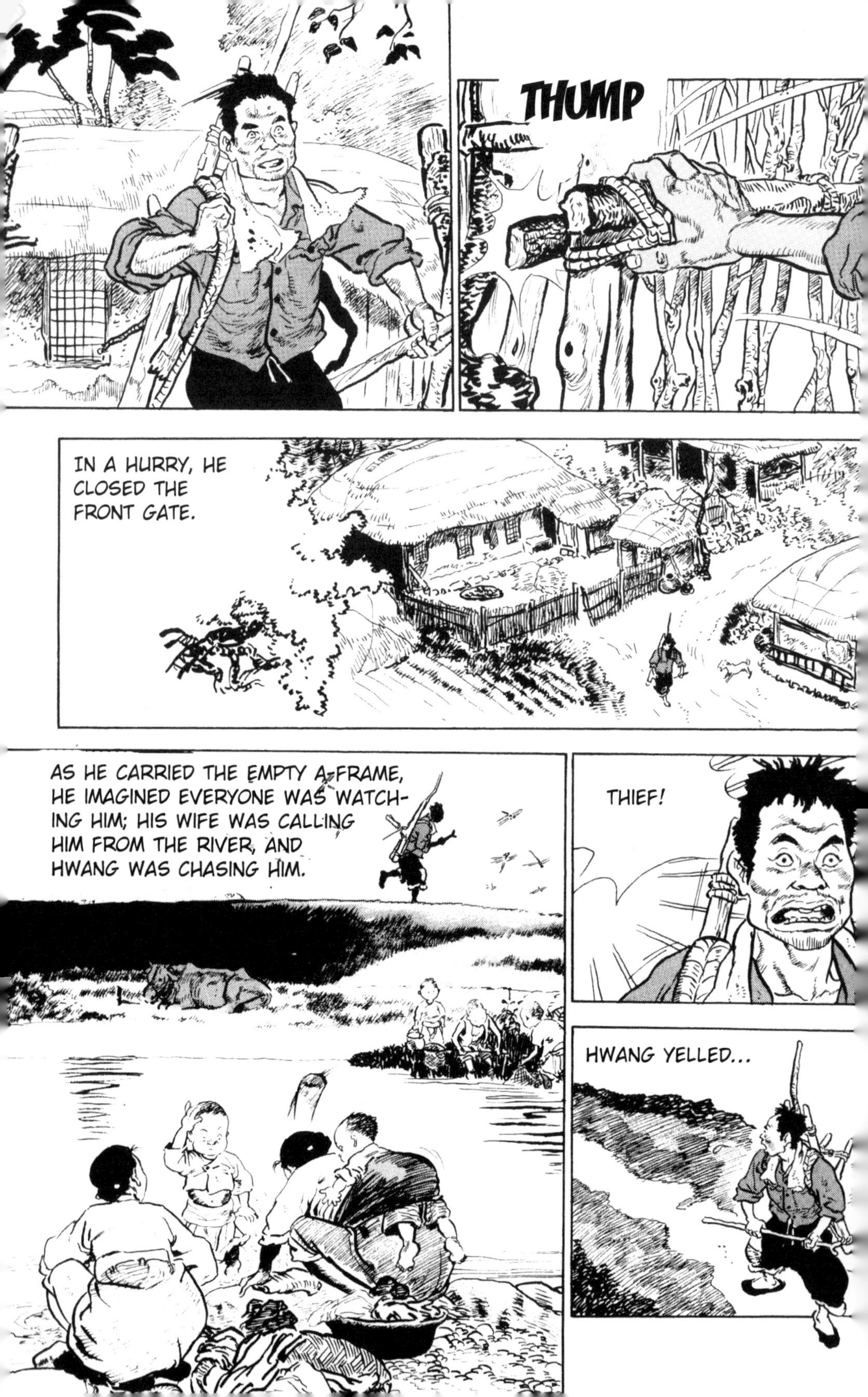
THUMP
IN A HURRY, HE CLOSED THE FRONT GATE.
AS HE CARRIED THE EMPTY A-FRAME, HE IMAGINED EVERYONE WAS WATCHING HIM; HIS WIFE WAS CALLING HIM FROM THE RIVER, AND HWANG WAS CHASING HIM.
THIEF!
HWANG YELLED...

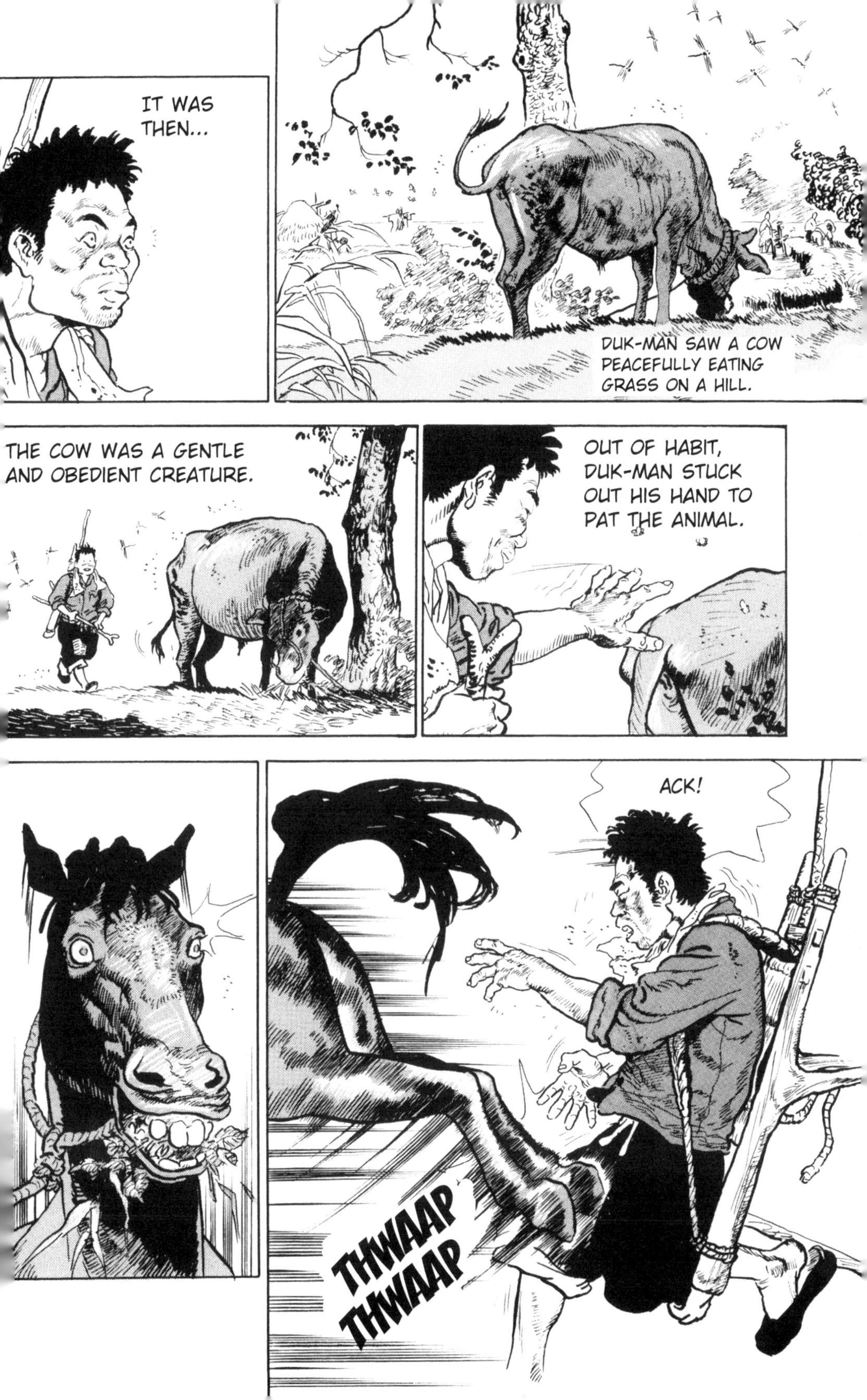
IT WAS THEN...
DUK-MAN SAW A COW PEACEFULLY EATING GRASS ON A HILL.
THE COW WAS A GENTLE AND OBEDIENT CREATURE.
OUT OF HABIT, DUK-MAN STUCK OUT HIS HAND TO PAT THE ANIMAL.
ACK!
THWAAP THWAAP

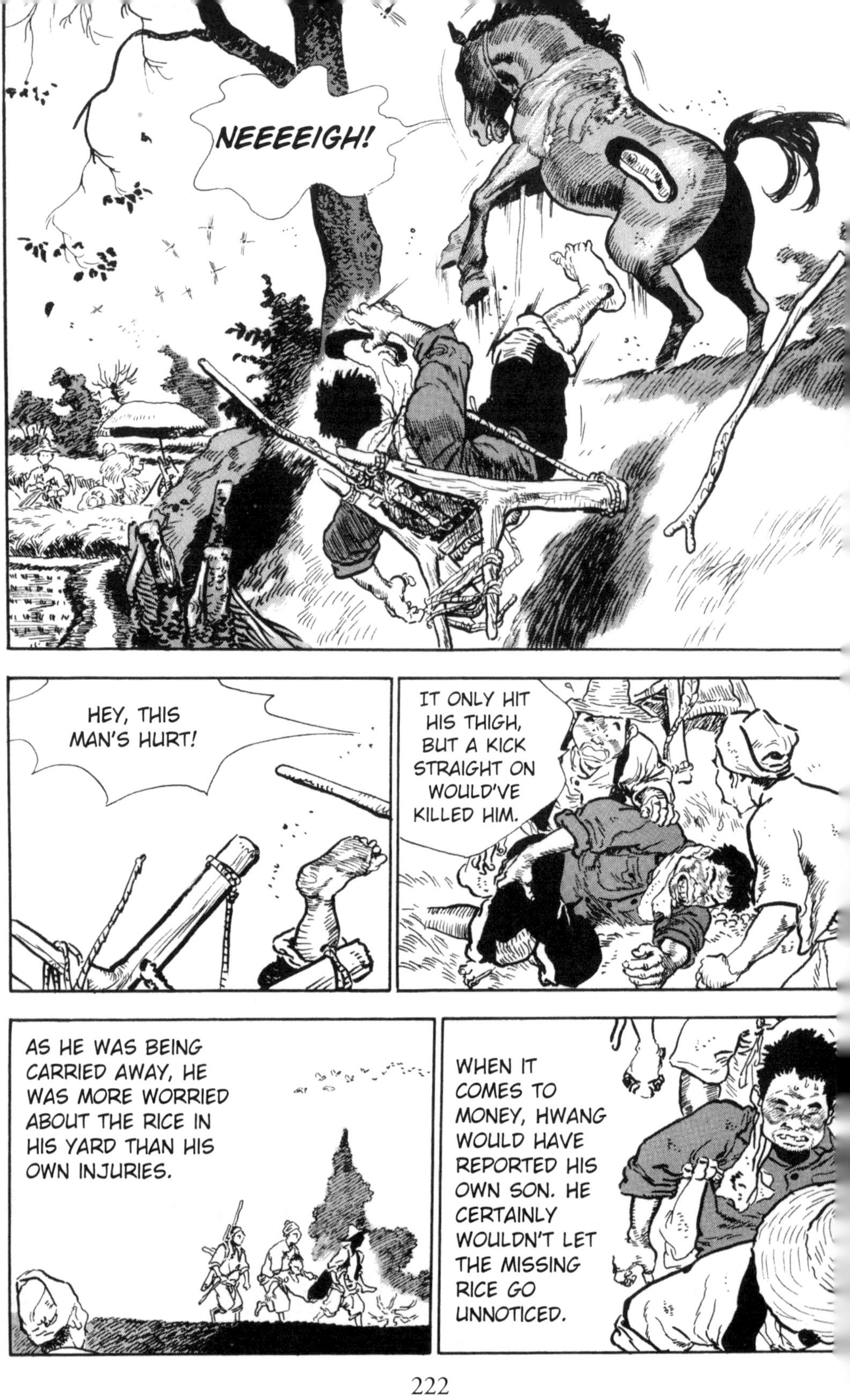
NEEEEIGH!
HEY, THIS MAN'S HURT!
IT ONLY HIT HIS THIGH, BUT A KICK STRAIGHT ON WOULD'VE KILLED HIM.
AS HE WAS BEING CARRIED AWAY, HE WAS MORE WORRIED ABOUT THE RICE IN HIS YARD THAN HIS OWN INJURIES.
WHEN IT COMES TO MONEY, HWANG WOULD HAVE REPORTED HIS OWN SON. HE CERTAINLY WOULDN'T LET THE MISSING RICE GO UNNOTICED.

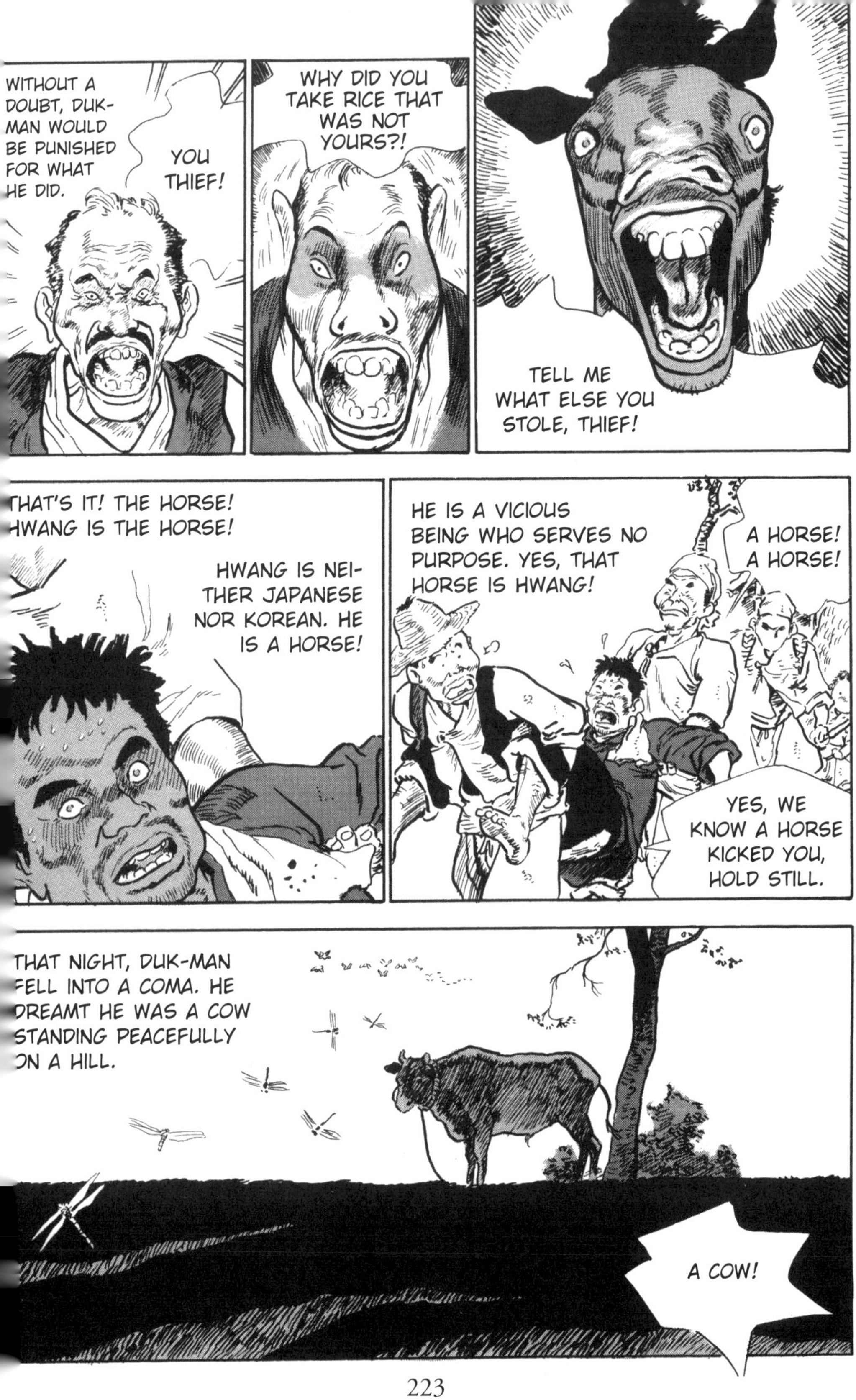

WITHOUT A DOUBT, DUK-MAN WOULD BE PUNISHED FOR WHAT HE DID.
YOU THIEF!
WHY DID YOU TAKE RICE THAT WAS NOT YOURS?!
TELL ME WHAT ELSE YOU STOLE, THIEF!
THAT'S IT! THE HORSE! HWANG IS THE HORSE!
HWANG IS NEITHER JAPANESE NOR KOREAN. HE IS A HORSE!
HE IS A VICIOUS BEING WHO SERVES NO PURPOSE. YES, THAT HORSE IS HWANG!
A HORSE! A HORSE!
YES, WE KNOW A HORSE KICKED YOU, HOLD STILL.
THAT NIGHT, DUK-MAN FELL INTO A COMA. HE DREAMT HE WAS A COW STANDING PEACEFULLY ON A HILL.
A COW!

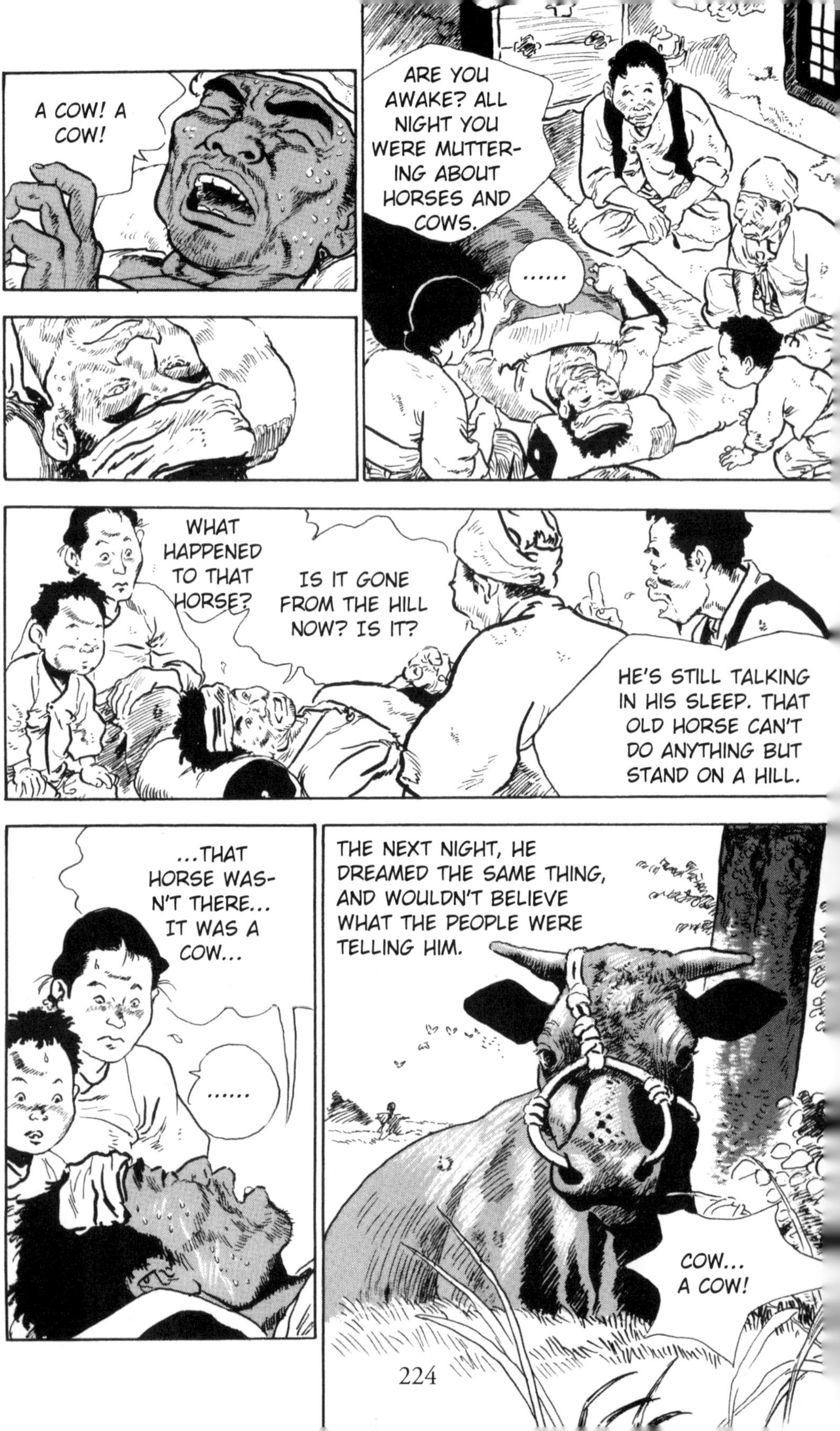
A COW! A COW!
ARE YOU AWAKE? ALL NIGHT YOU WERE MUTTERING ABOUT HORSES AND COWS.
......
WHAT HAPPENED TO THAT HORSE?
IS IT GONE FROM THE HILL NOW? IS IT?
HE'S STILL TALKING IN HIS SLEEP. THAT OLD HORSE CAN'T DO ANYTHING BUT STAND ON A HILL.
...THAT HORSE WASN'T THERE... IT WAS A COW...
......
THE NEXT NIGHT, HE DREAMED THE SAME THING, AND WOULDN'T BELIEVE WHAT THE PEOPLE WERE TELLING HIM.
COW... A COW!

NO ONE MEN-TIONED THE RICE IN HIS YARD. THEY ONLY DISCUSSED HWANG'S HORSE.

HE WAS CERTAIN THAT THERE WAS ONLY A COW ON THAT HILL.

THAT HORSE IS A MENACE TO US. IT BITES AND KICKS WHEN WE GO NEAR.

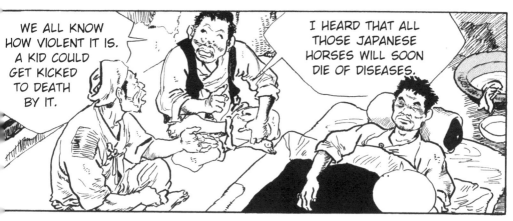

WE ALL KNOW HOW VIOLENT IT IS. A KID COULD GET KICKED TO DEATH BY IT.

I HEARD THAT ALL THOSE JAPANESE HORSES WILL SOON DIE OF DISEASES.

ONE AFTERNOON, DUK-MAN WENT OUT TO SIT IN THE SUN.

THE HORSE IS RUNNING AWAY!

CLIPPITY-CLOP CLIPPITY-CLOP

225

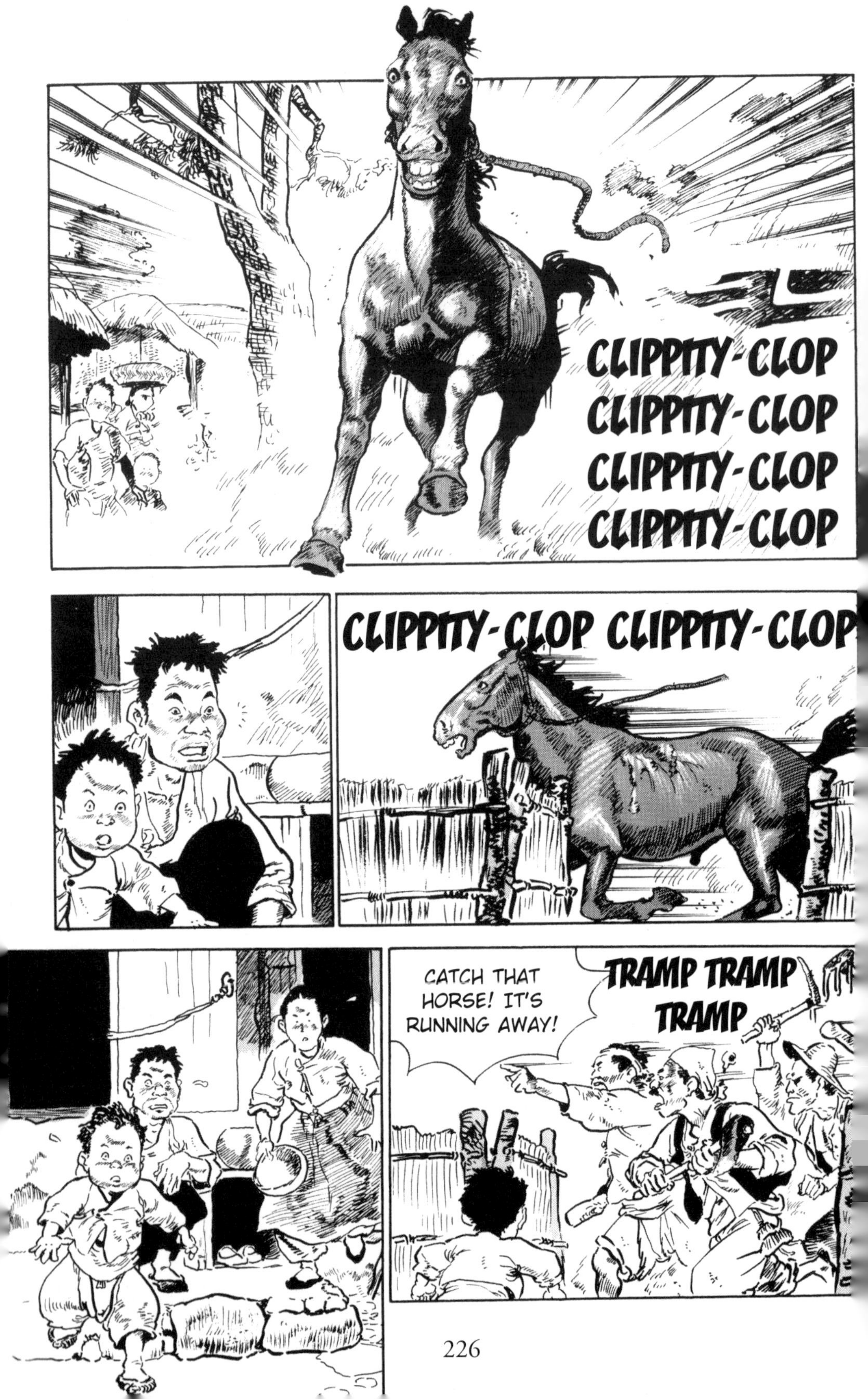
CLIPPITY-CLOP
CLIPPITY-CLOP
CLIPPITY-CLOP
CLIPPITY-CLOP
CLIPPITY-CLOP CLIPPITY-CLOP
CATCH THAT HORSE! IT'S RUNNING AWAY!
TRAMP TRAMP TRAMP

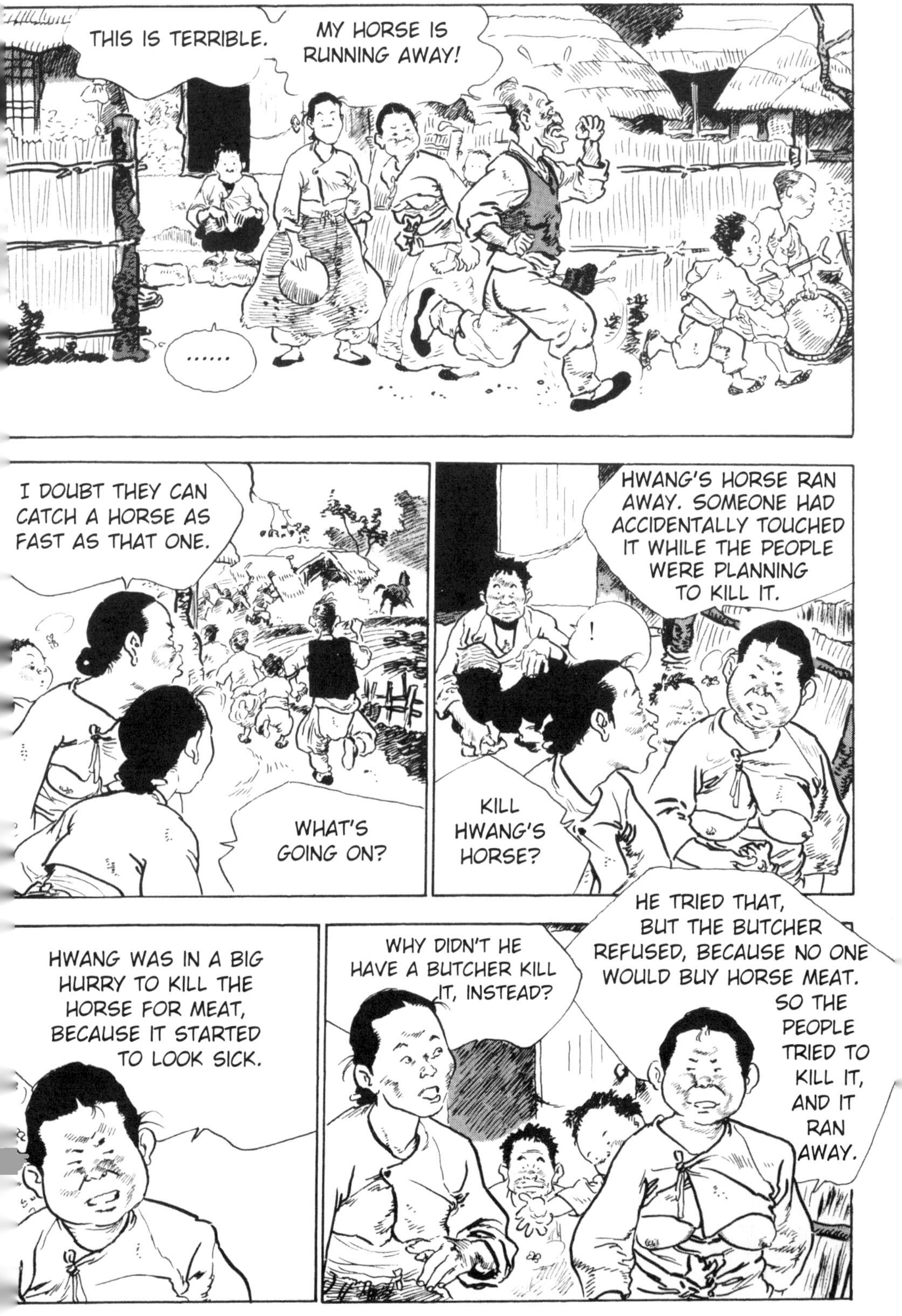

THIS IS TERRIBLE.
MY HORSE IS RUNNING AWAY!
......
I DOUBT THEY CAN CATCH A HORSE AS FAST AS THAT ONE.
WHAT'S GOING ON?
HWANG'S HORSE RAN AWAY. SOMEONE HAD ACCIDENTALLY TOUCHED IT WHILE THE PEOPLE WERE PLANNING TO KILL IT.
!
KILL HWANG'S HORSE?
HWANG WAS IN A BIG HURRY TO KILL THE HORSE FOR MEAT, BECAUSE IT STARTED TO LOOK SICK.
WHY DIDN'T HE HAVE A BUTCHER KILL IT, INSTEAD?
HE TRIED THAT, BUT THE BUTCHER REFUSED, BECAUSE NO ONE WOULD BUY HORSE MEAT.
SO THE PEOPLE TRIED TO KILL IT, AND IT RAN AWAY.

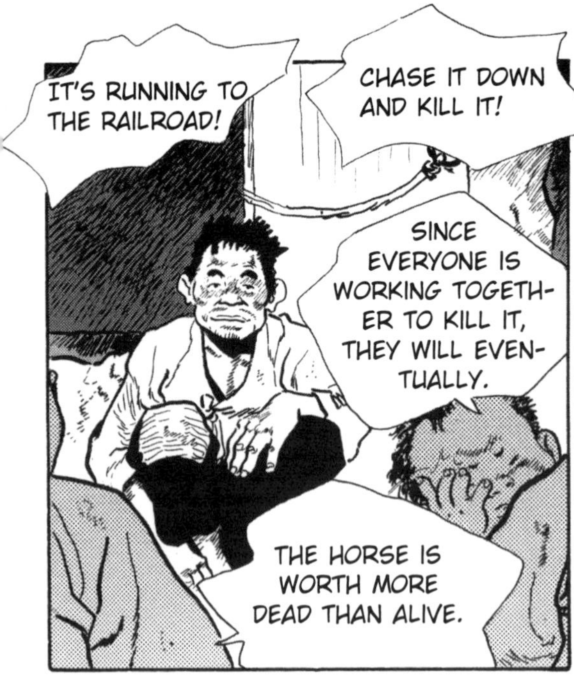
IT'S RUNNING TO THE RAILROAD!
CHASE IT DOWN AND KILL IT!
SINCE EVERYONE IS WORKING TOGETHER TO KILL IT, THEY WILL EVENTUALLY.
THE HORSE IS WORTH MORE DEAD THAN ALIVE.

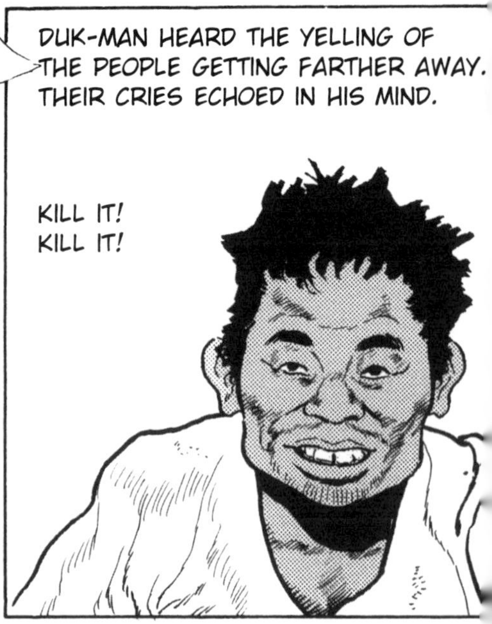
DUK-MAN HEARD THE YELLING OF THE PEOPLE GETTING FARTHER AWAY. THEIR CRIES ECHOED IN HIS MIND.
KILL IT!
KILL IT!

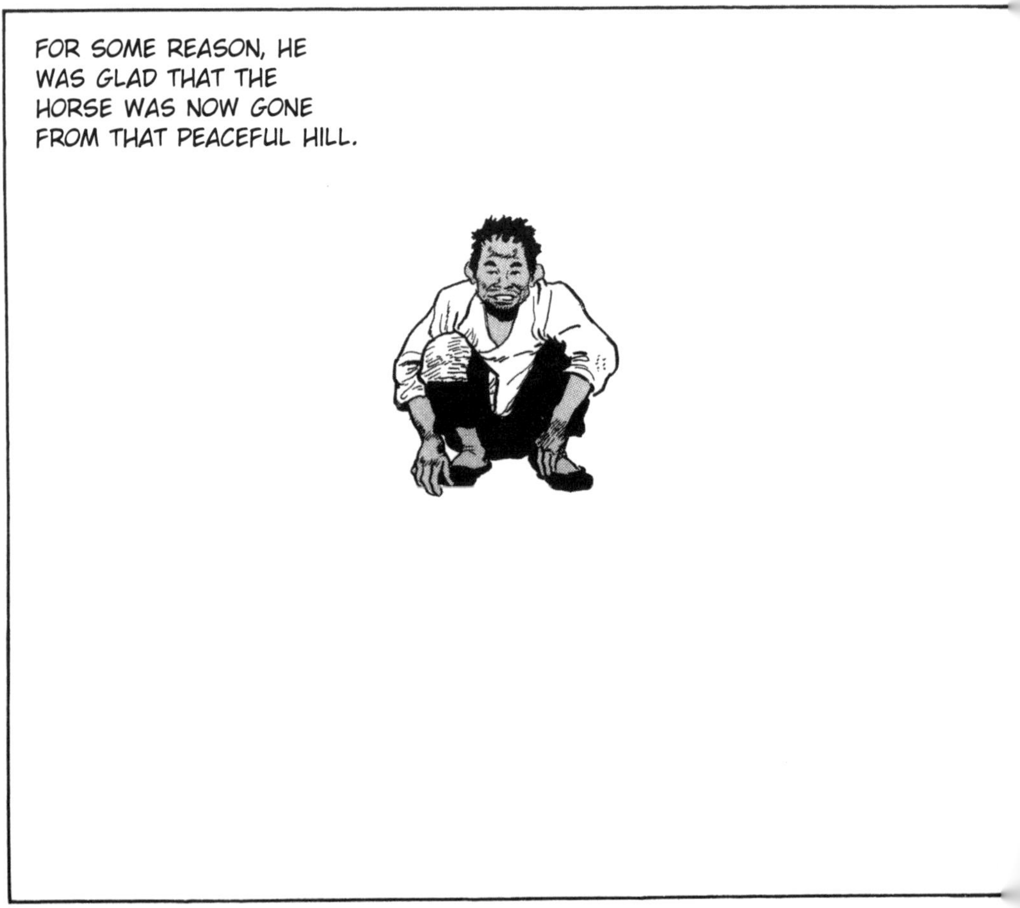
FOR SOME REASON, HE WAS GLAD THAT THE HORSE WAS NOW GONE FROM THAT PEACEFUL HILL.

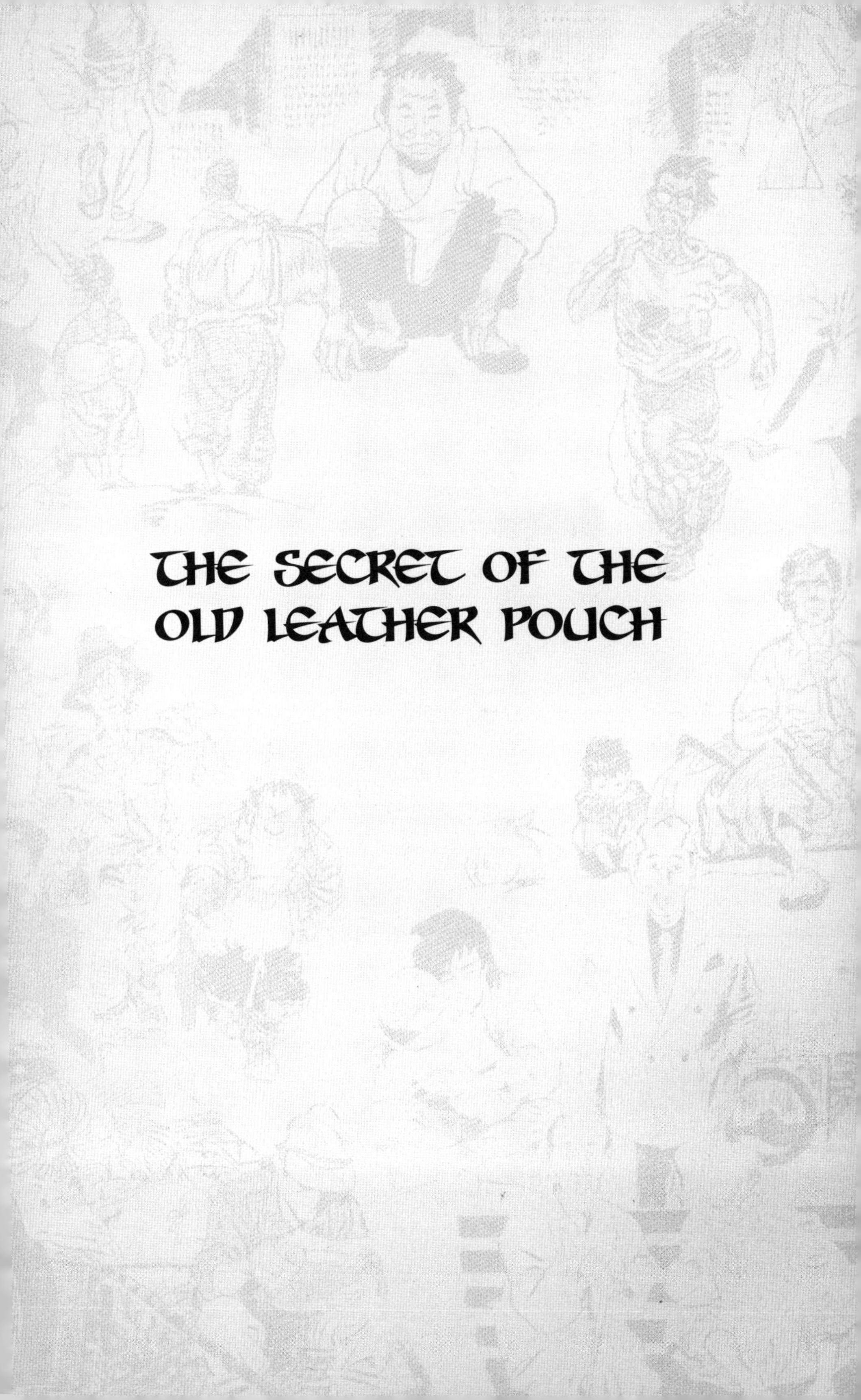

THE SECRET OF THE OLD LEATHER POUCH

SEYEONG O
SEPTEMBER 1990

WHAT LED GRANDPA
TO HIS DEATH?

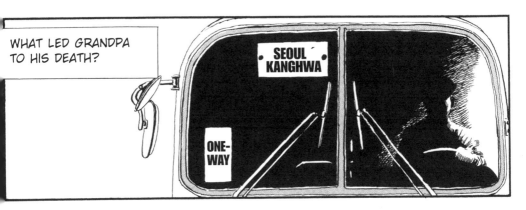

WHAT BOTHERED HIM
ALL THOSE YEARS?

WHY DID HE
CARRY THAT LOAD
TO THE END?

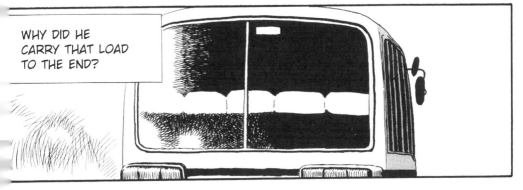

WHAT IS IN THAT OLD
LEATHER POUCH?

THERE USED TO BE AN OLD POUCH HANGING FROM GRANDPA'S WALL.

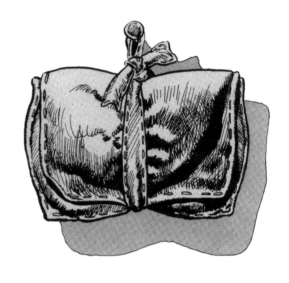

I DON'T KNOW HOW LONG IT'S BEEN THERE, BUT IT WAS THERE BEFORE I WAS BORN.

I WAS ALWAYS CURIOUS ABOUT WHAT WAS IN THE POUCH. BUT EVERYTIME I MENTIONED IT, FATHER GLARED AT ME AND GRANDPA SIGHED.

I FINALLY REALIZED IT WAS THE POUCH THAT MADE THE HOUSE GLOOMY ALL THOSE YEARS.

FATHER, IT'S TIME WE GET RID OF IT.

SHUT UP! YOU WORTHLESS IDIOT!

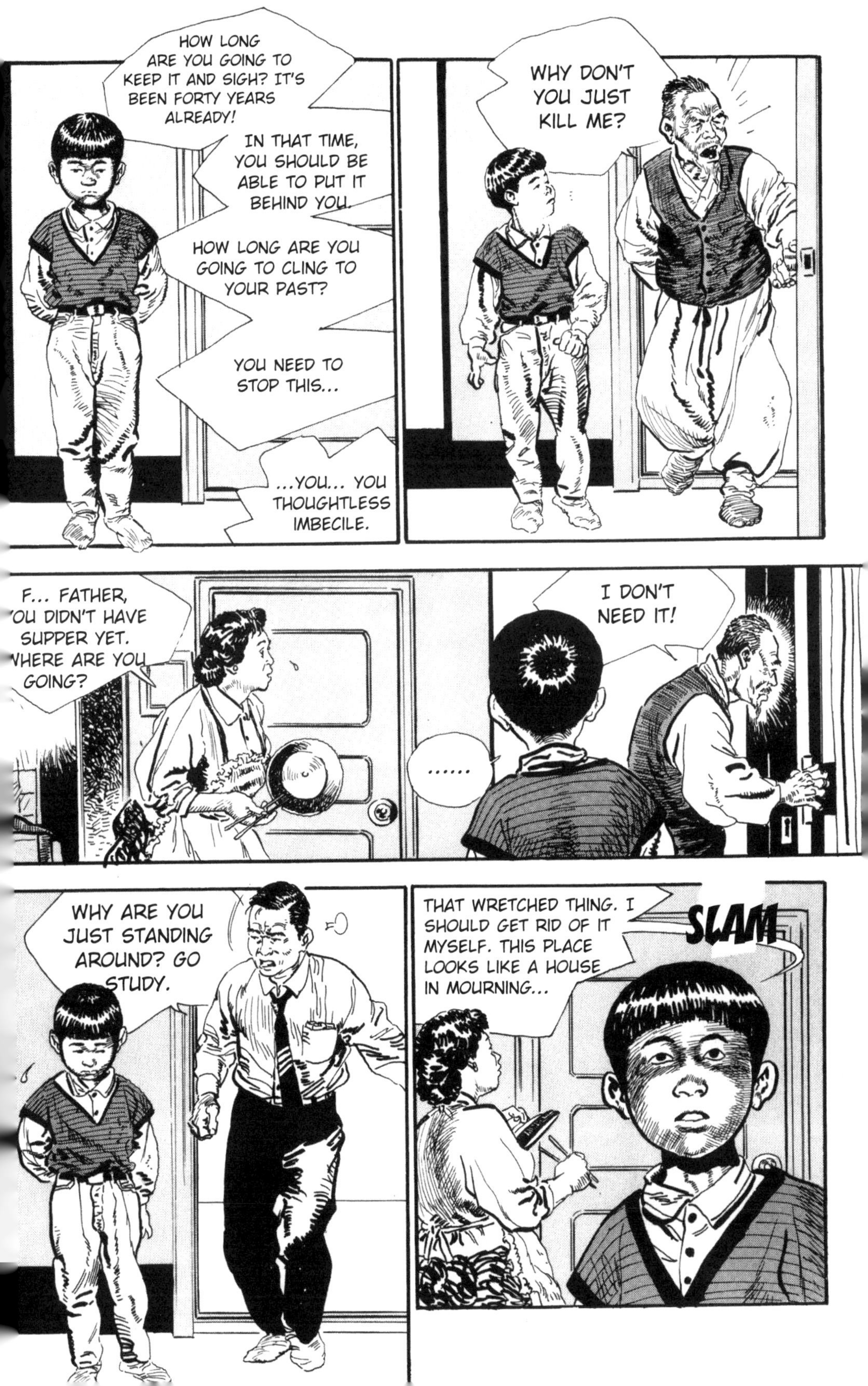
HOW LONG ARE YOU GOING TO KEEP IT AND SIGH? IT'S BEEN FORTY YEARS ALREADY!
IN THAT TIME, YOU SHOULD BE ABLE TO PUT IT BEHIND YOU.
HOW LONG ARE YOU GOING TO CLING TO YOUR PAST?
YOU NEED TO STOP THIS...
...YOU... YOU THOUGHTLESS IMBECILE.
WHY DON'T YOU JUST KILL ME?
F... FATHER, YOU DIDN'T HAVE SUPPER YET. WHERE ARE YOU GOING?
I DON'T NEED IT!
......
WHY ARE YOU JUST STANDING AROUND? GO STUDY.
THAT WRETCHED THING. I SHOULD GET RID OF IT MYSELF. THIS PLACE LOOKS LIKE A HOUSE IN MOURNING...
SLAM

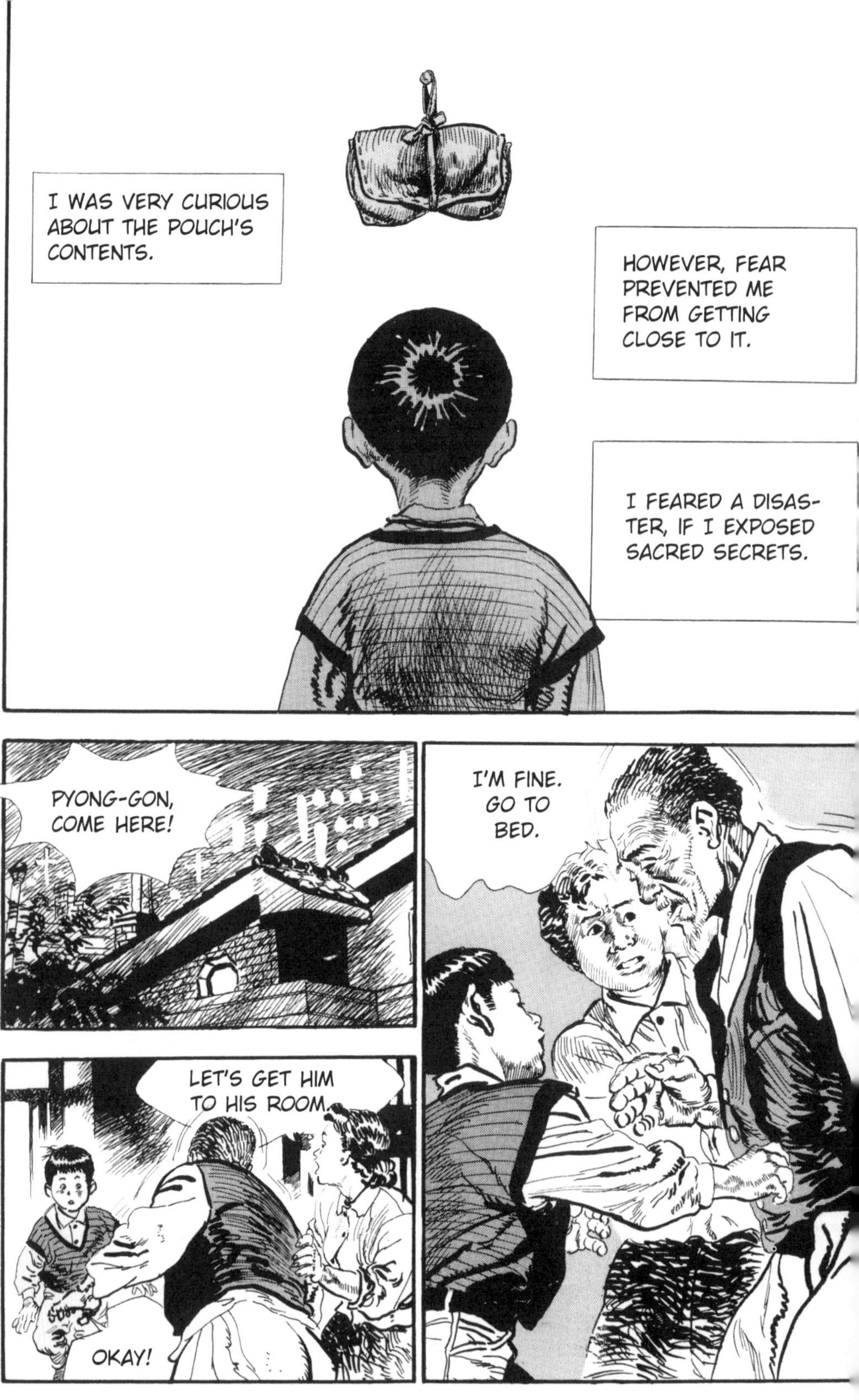
I WAS VERY CURIOUS ABOUT THE POUCH'S CONTENTS.
HOWEVER, FEAR PREVENTED ME FROM GETTING CLOSE TO IT.
I FEARED A DISASTER, IF I EXPOSED SACRED SECRETS.
PYONG-GON, COME HERE!
LET'S GET HIM TO HIS ROOM.
OKAY!
I'M FINE. GO TO BED.

ON THOSE DAYS, IT SEEMED GRANDPA'S CHEST HAD A POUCH-SIZED HOLE.

WHEEZE

ON MEMORIAL DAYS AND BIRTHDAYS,

ON NEW YEARS, CH'USOK AND OTHER NATIONAL HOLIDAYS,

GRANDPA SLEPT WITH THE POUCH HELD CLOSE TO HIS CHEST, TO FILL THAT HOLE.

MANY YEARS HAD PASSED WHEN SOMETHING IMPORTANT HAPPENED TO ALL OF US.

IT WAS A FEW DAYS BEFORE GRANDPA'S SEVENTIETH BIRTHDAY.

WHAT?

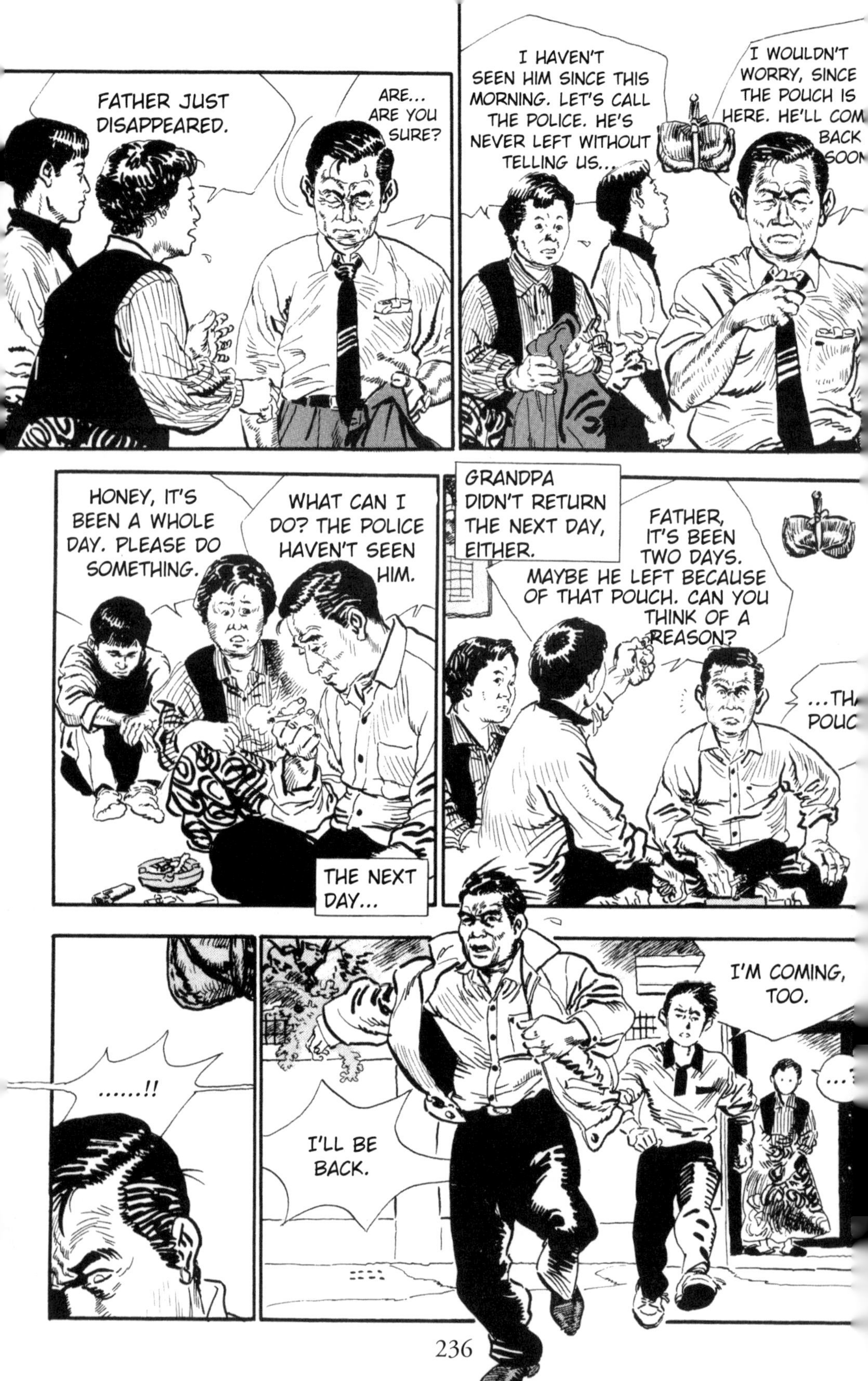
FATHER JUST DISAPPEARED.
ARE... ARE YOU SURE?
I HAVEN'T SEEN HIM SINCE THIS MORNING. LET'S CALL THE POLICE. HE'S NEVER LEFT WITHOUT TELLING US...
I WOULDN'T WORRY, SINCE THE POUCH IS HERE. HE'LL COM BACK SOON
HONEY, IT'S BEEN A WHOLE DAY. PLEASE DO SOMETHING.
WHAT CAN I DO? THE POLICE HAVEN'T SEEN HIM.
THE NEXT DAY...
GRANDPA DIDN'T RETURN THE NEXT DAY, EITHER.
FATHER, IT'S BEEN TWO DAYS.
MAYBE HE LEFT BECAUSE OF THAT POUCH. CAN YOU THINK OF A REASON?
...TH POUC
......!!
I'LL BE BACK.
I'M COMING, TOO.
...

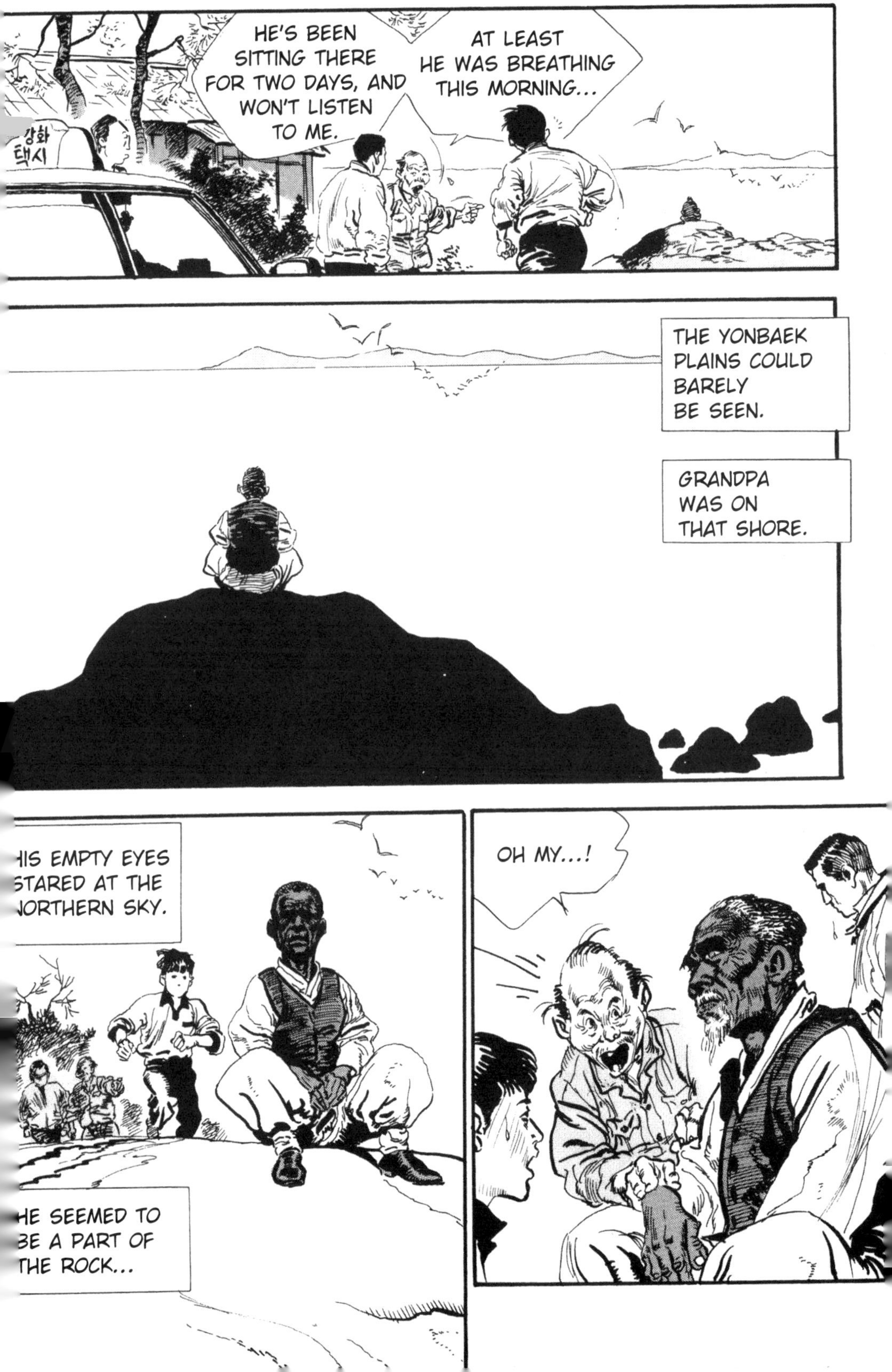

강화 택시
HE'S BEEN SITTING THERE FOR TWO DAYS, AND WON'T LISTEN TO ME.
AT LEAST HE WAS BREATHING THIS MORNING...
THE YONBAEK PLAINS COULD BARELY BE SEEN.
GRANDPA WAS ON THAT SHORE.
HIS EMPTY EYES STARED AT THE NORTHERN SKY.
HE SEEMED TO BE A PART OF THE ROCK...
OH MY...!

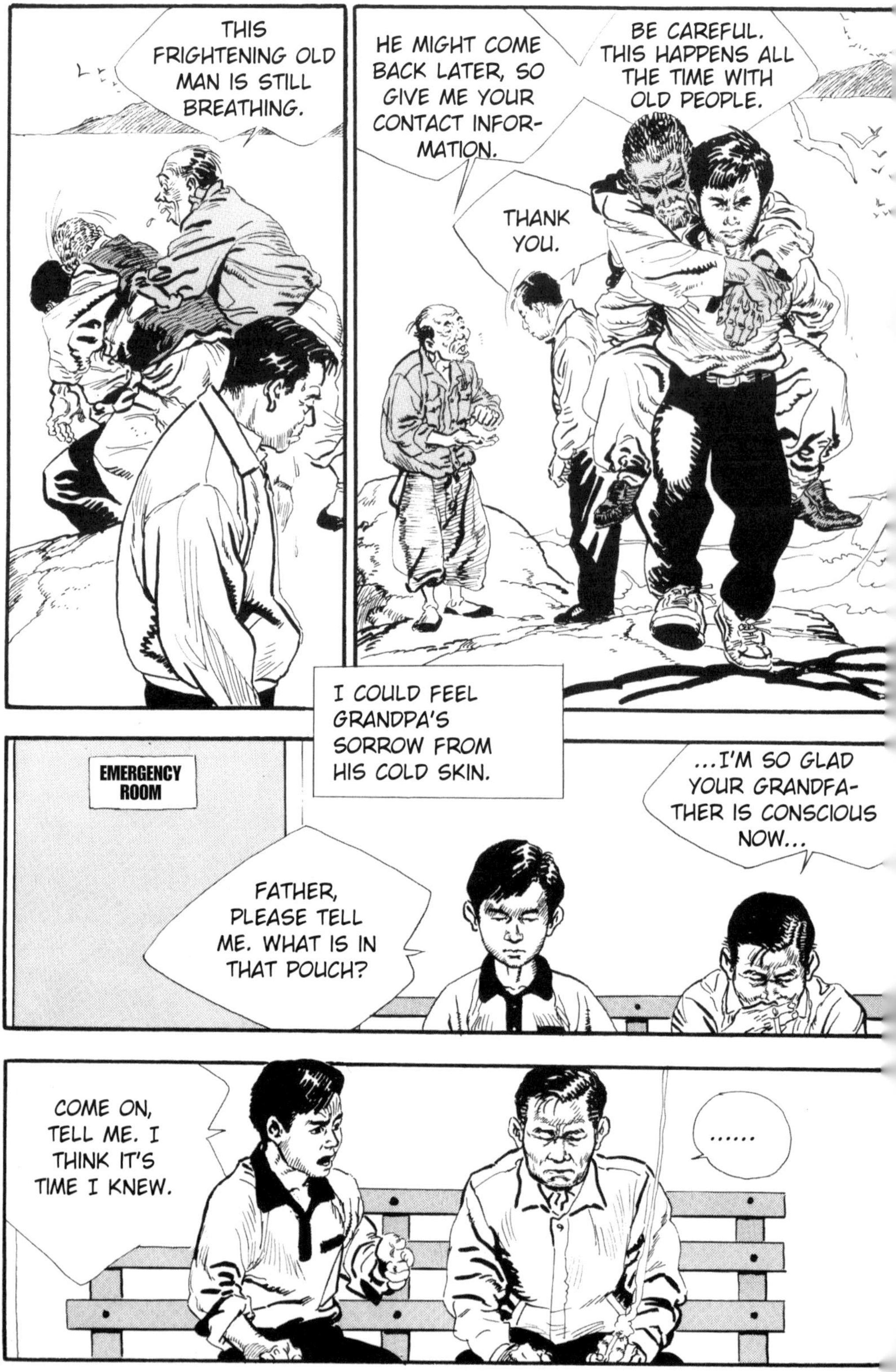
THIS FRIGHTENING OLD MAN IS STILL BREATHING.
HE MIGHT COME BACK LATER, SO GIVE ME YOUR CONTACT INFOR-MATION.
BE CAREFUL. THIS HAPPENS ALL THE TIME WITH OLD PEOPLE.
THANK YOU.
I COULD FEEL GRANDPA'S SORROW FROM HIS COLD SKIN.
EMERGENCY ROOM
...I'M SO GLAD YOUR GRANDFA-THER IS CONSCIOUS NOW...
FATHER, PLEASE TELL ME. WHAT IS IN THAT POUCH?
COME ON, TELL ME. I THINK IT'S TIME I KNEW.
......

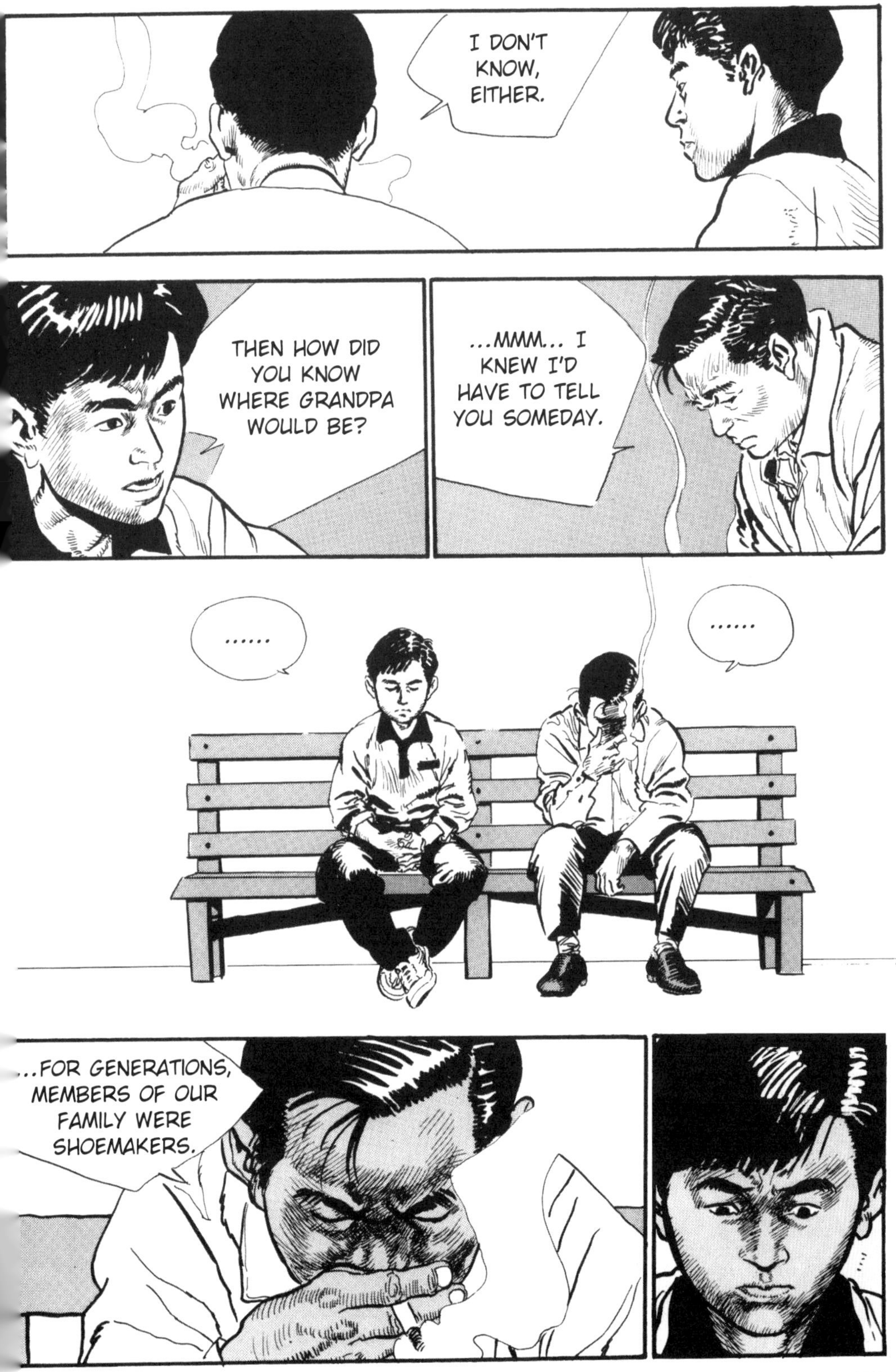
I DON'T KNOW, EITHER.
THEN HOW DID YOU KNOW WHERE GRANDPA WOULD BE?
...MMM... I KNEW I'D HAVE TO TELL YOU SOMEDAY.
......
......
...FOR GENERATIONS, MEMBERS OF OUR FAMILY WERE SHOEMAKERS.

THE POUCH WAS YOUR GREAT
GRANDFATHER'S. IT WAS PROBABLY
IN OUR FAMILY LONGER THAN THAT.

THE FIRST TIME I SAW IT, YOUR
GRANDFATHER WAS COMING HOME
FROM THE WAR WITH THE JAPANESE.

IT WAS HANGING ON HIS BELT.

FROM THAT DAY ON, HE ALWAYS
CARRIED IT.

IT WAS WITH HIM IN THE SUMMER, WHEN HE WORKED ON THE CROPS.

ALSO IN THE WINTER, WHEN HE SOLD HOMEMADE TOFU IN A TOWN FAR AWAY.

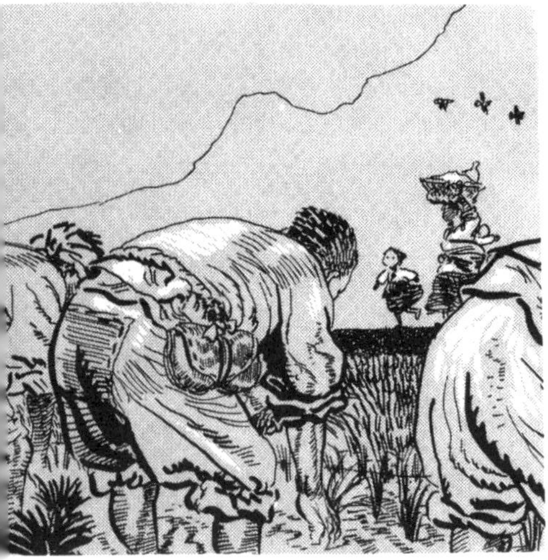

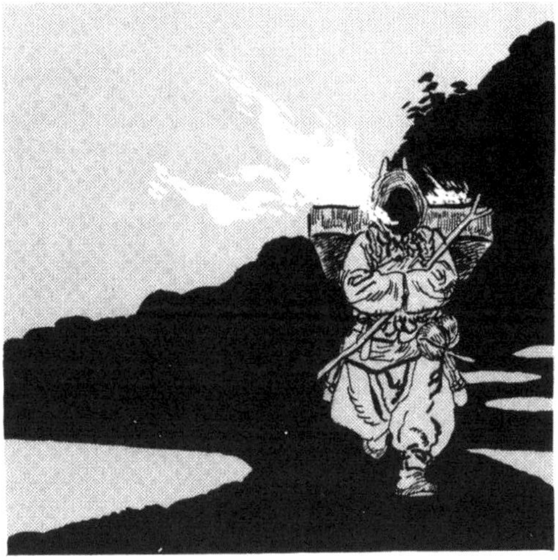

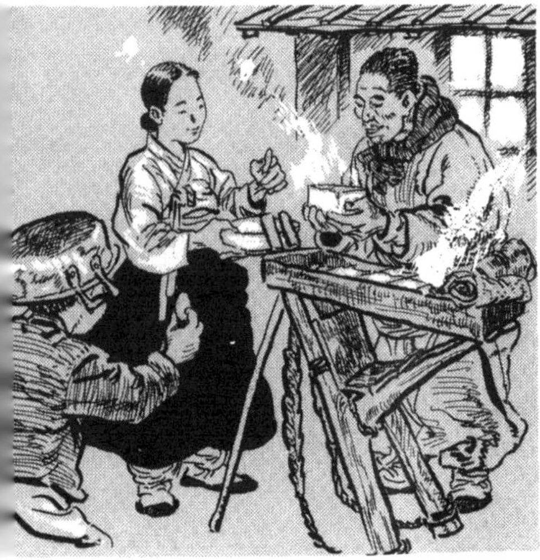

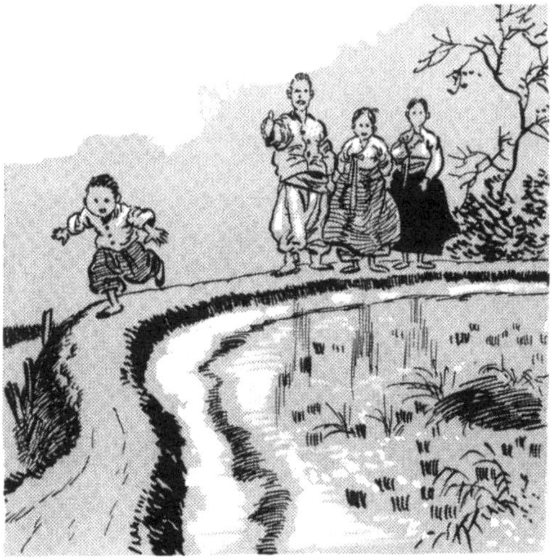

HE POUCH BECAME FULLER.

AFTER HE PURCHASED TWO FIELDS, IT WAS NO LONGER ON HIS BELT.

INSTEAD, IT GOT BIGGER, AND HE TIED IT TIGHT.

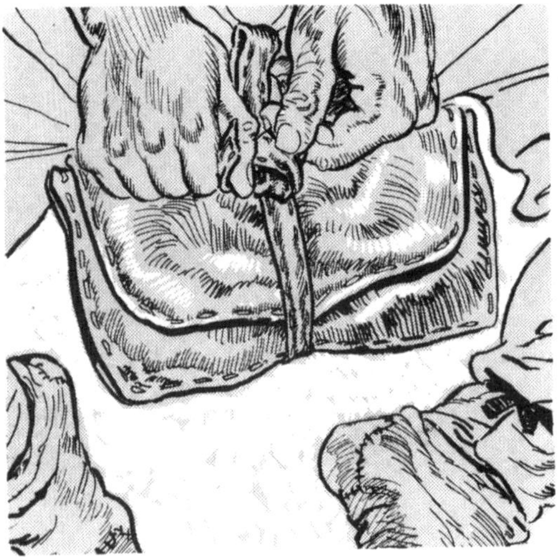

IN HONOR OF THREE GENERATIONS OF SINGLE SONS, MY GRANDMOTHER HUNG MY DRIED UMBILICAL CORD FROM THE WALL. THE POUCH WAS HUNG UP EVEN HIGHER THAN THAT.

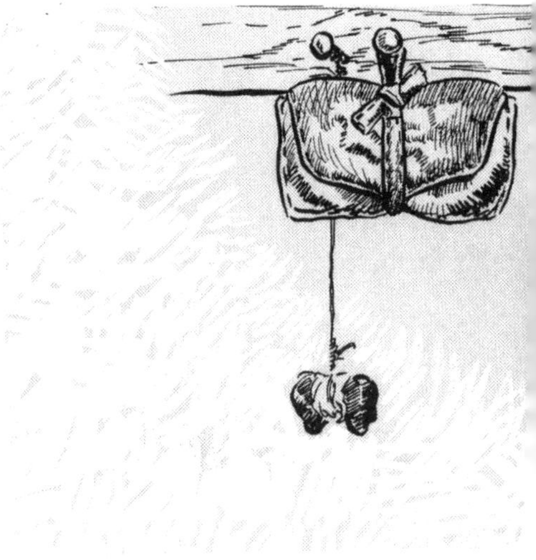

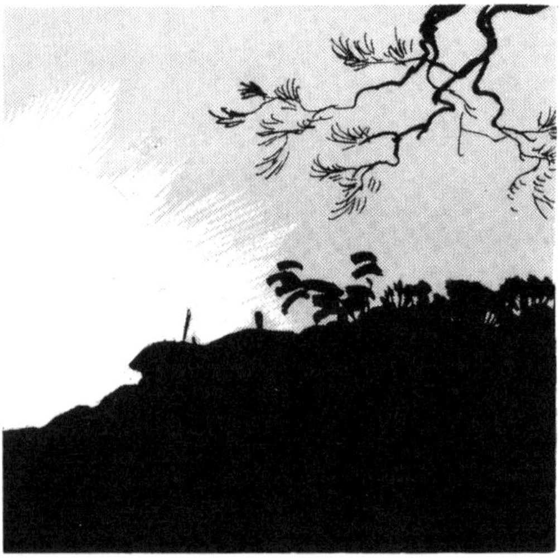

IN LESS THAN A YEAR, MISFORTUNE STRUCK.

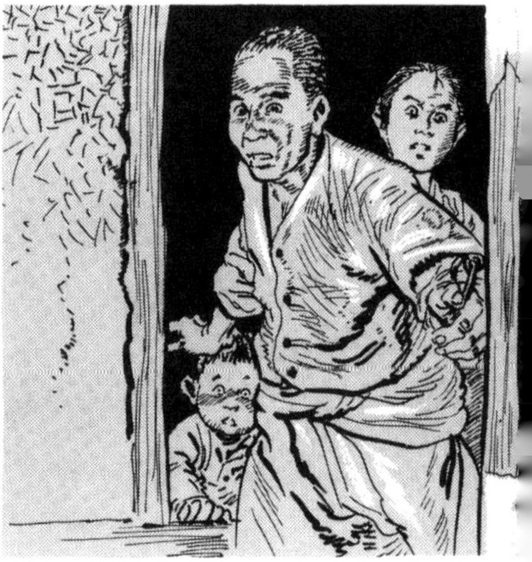

A WAR BEGAN.

MOST PEOPLE FLED THE TOWN, BUT MY FATHER WOULDN'T GO.

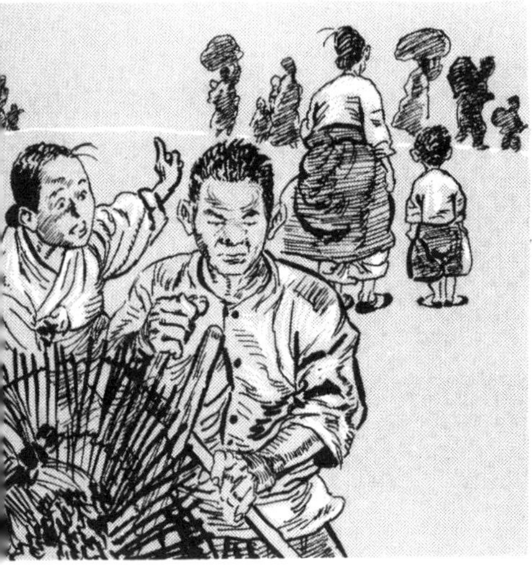

FOR THE FIRST TIME, HE WAS ABLE TO PLANT RICE ON HIS OWN LAND.

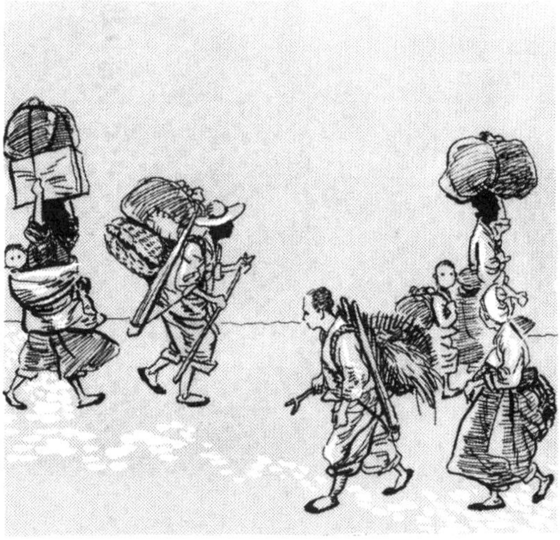

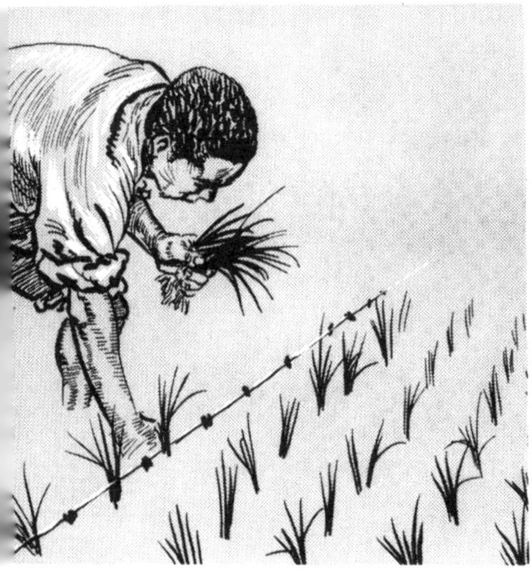

HOW COULD HE GIVE THIS UP?

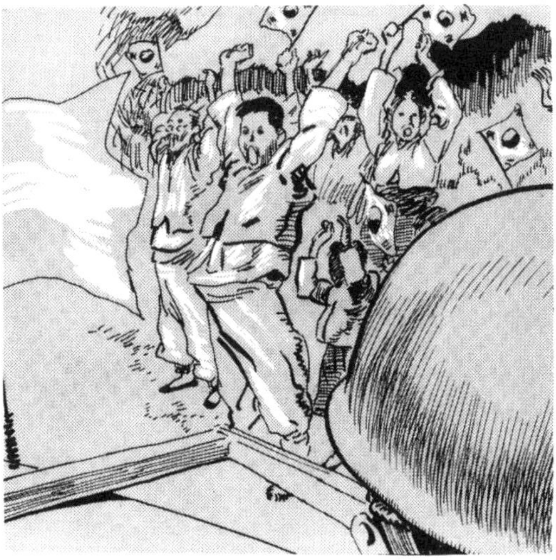

HOWEVER, WHEN OUR ARMY RETURNED, THEY THOUGHT WE WERE NORTH KOREAN SPIES.

MY PARENTS WERE TAKEN AWAY.

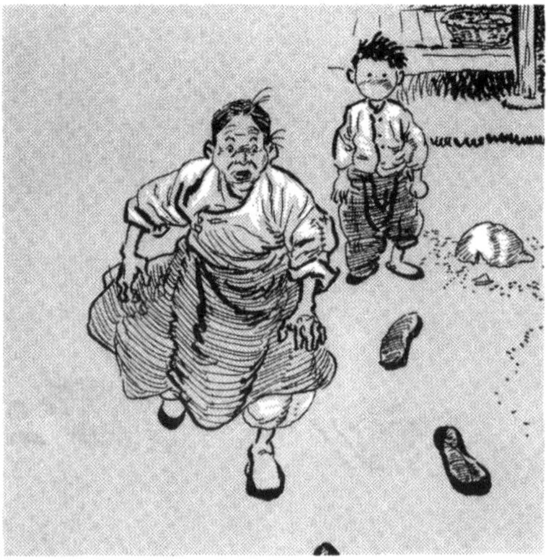

MY MOTHER COULD NOT STAND THE TORTURE AND DIED.

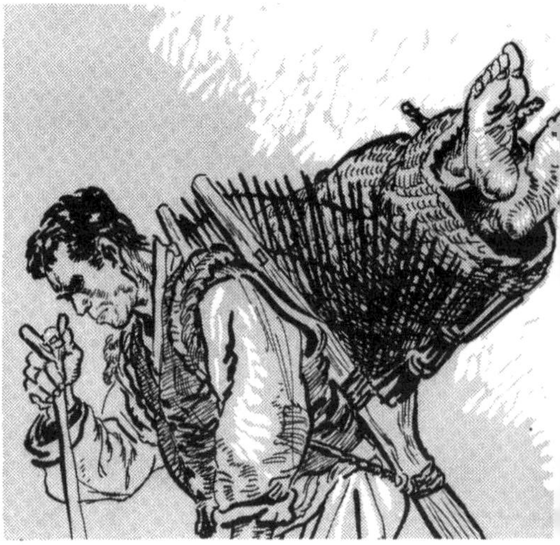

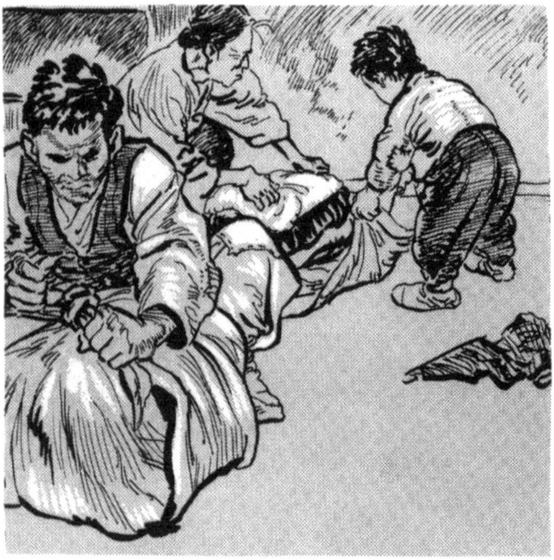

IN WINTER, THE ARMY RETREATED AGAIN. THIS TIME, MY FATHER PACKED OUR BELONGINGS.

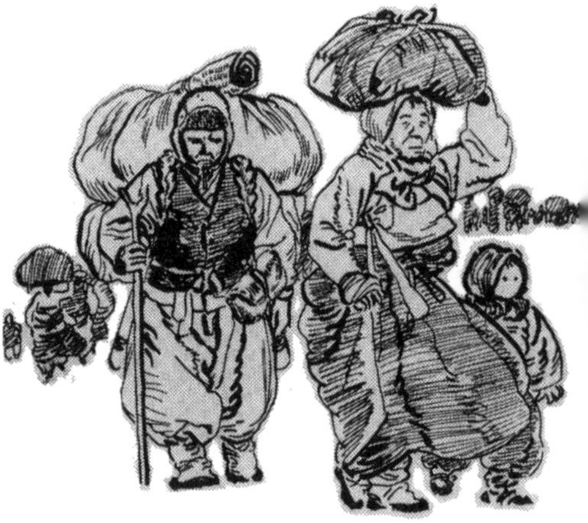

HE TOOK THE POUCH OFF THE WALL AN
TIED IT TO HIS BELT. MY GRANDMOTHER
DIDN'T WANT TO LEAVE, BUT HE MADE H
WALK AHEAD.

VE WERE BOMBED WHILE SEEKING REFUGE.

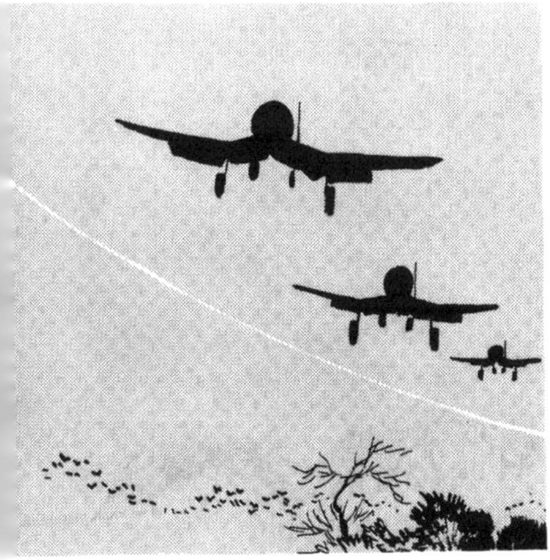

MY FATHER AND I HAD BEEN DIGGING THROUGH A RADISH HOLE TO FIND SOMETHING TO EAT.

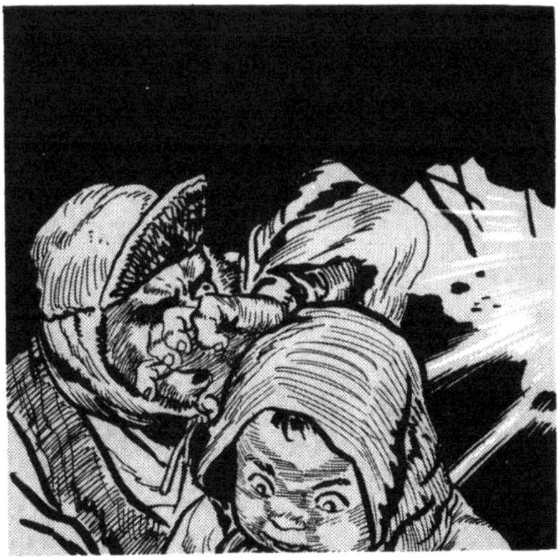

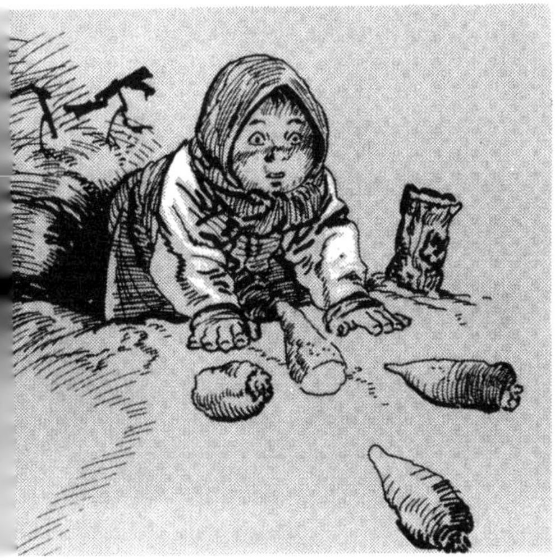

FTER BEING SURPRISED BY AN EXPLOION, I RECOVERED AND CAME OUT OF HE HOLE.

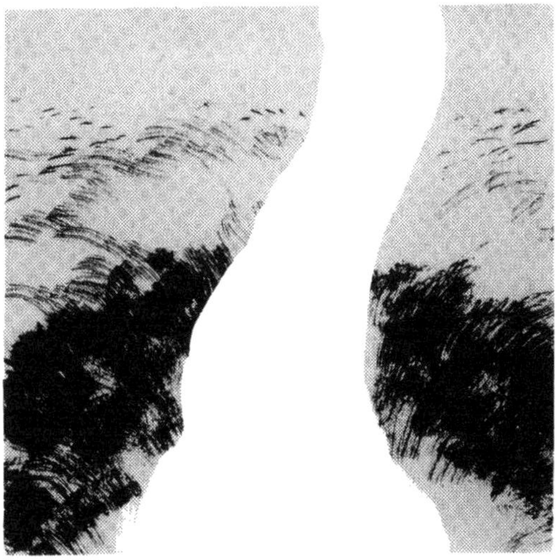

THERE WAS NOW A HUGE HOLE ON THE SPOT WHERE MY GRANDMOTHER HAD JUST BEEN SITTING.

MY FATHER WAS SHOCKED, AND HELD ONE OF MY GRANDMOTHER'S OLD SHOES.

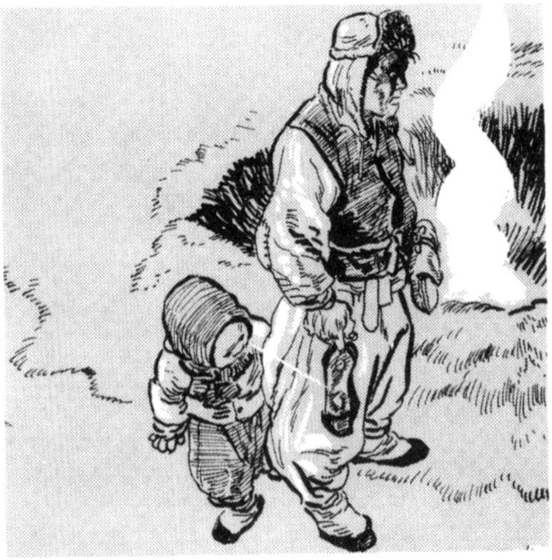

THAT'S WHEN THE POUCH BECAME AS STUFFED AS IT IS NOW.

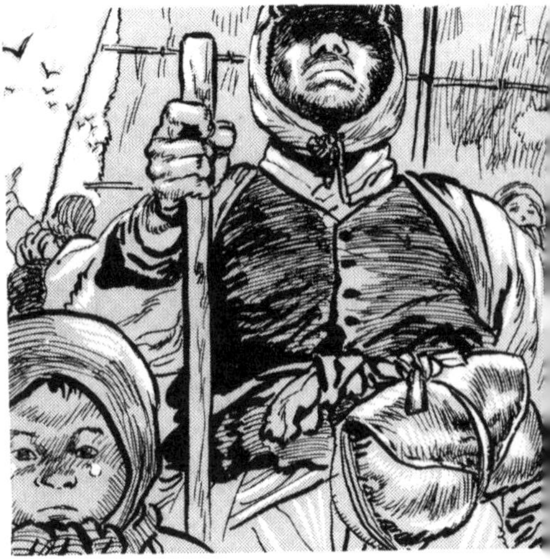

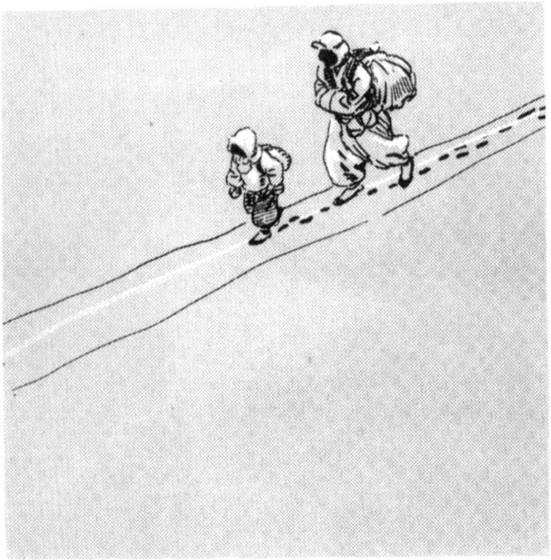

I WON'T TELL YOU ABOUT THE HARDSHIPS OF THAT WINTER...

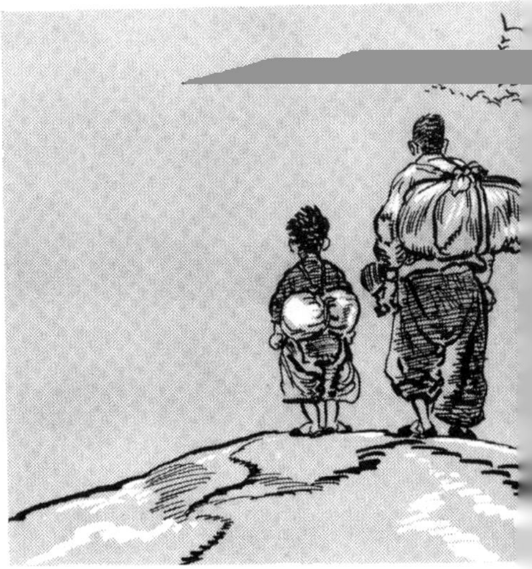

WE HAD NO PLACE TO GO. OUR TOWN HAD BEEN PART OF THE SOUTH BEFO THE WAR, BUT NOW IS PART OF THE NORTH.

DURING THAT TIME,

MY FATHER SAT ON THAT
ROCK FOR DAYS, JUST
LIKE HE DID YESTERDAY.

YOUR
GRANDFATHER
ALSO BECAME
ATTACHED TO
THE POUCH.

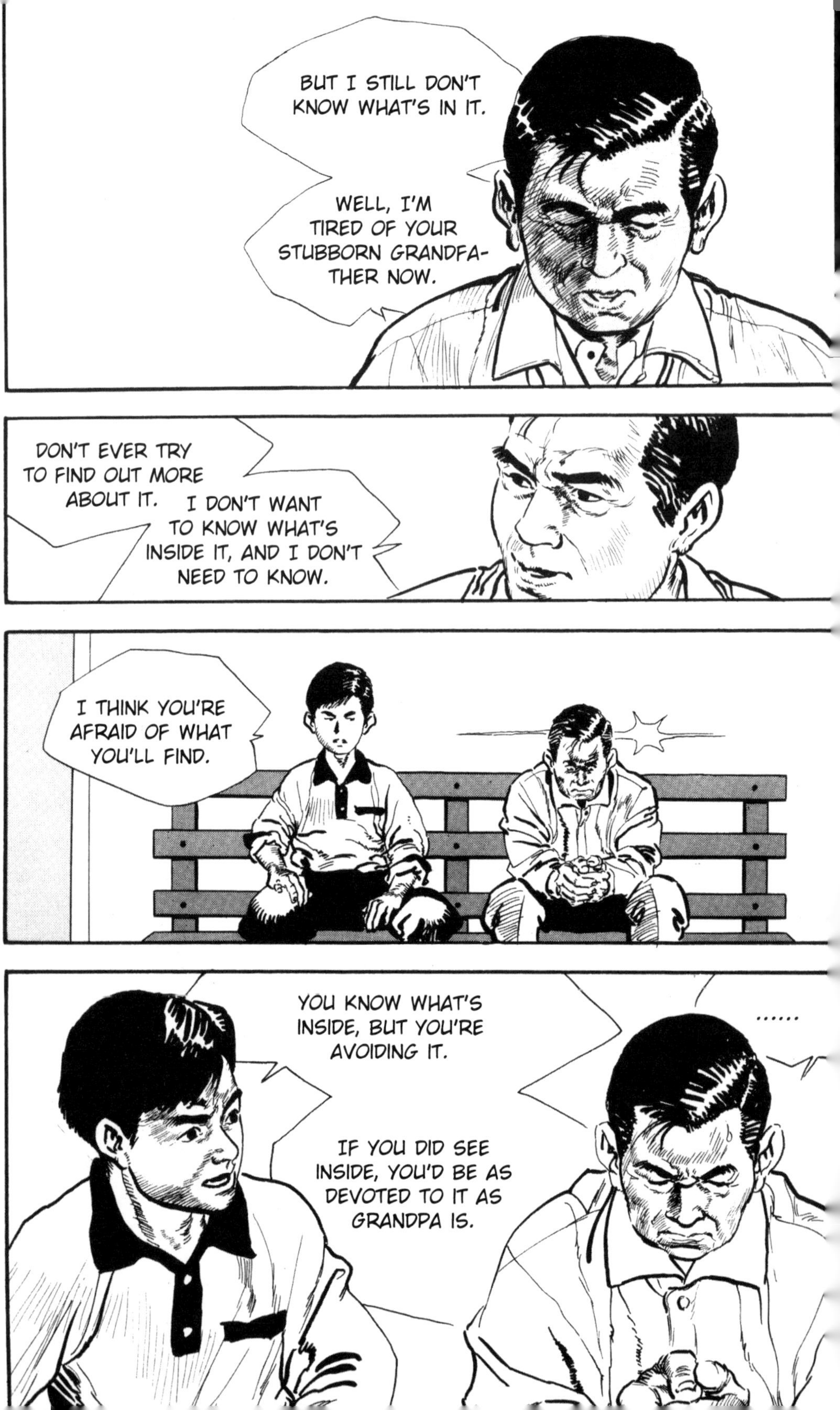

BUT I STILL DON'T KNOW WHAT'S IN IT.
WELL, I'M TIRED OF YOUR STUBBORN GRANDFA-THER NOW.
DON'T EVER TRY TO FIND OUT MORE ABOUT IT.
I DON'T WANT TO KNOW WHAT'S INSIDE IT, AND I DON'T NEED TO KNOW.
I THINK YOU'RE AFRAID OF WHAT YOU'LL FIND.
YOU KNOW WHAT'S INSIDE, BUT YOU'RE AVOIDING IT.
IF YOU DID SEE INSIDE, YOU'D BE AS DEVOTED TO IT AS GRANDPA IS.
......

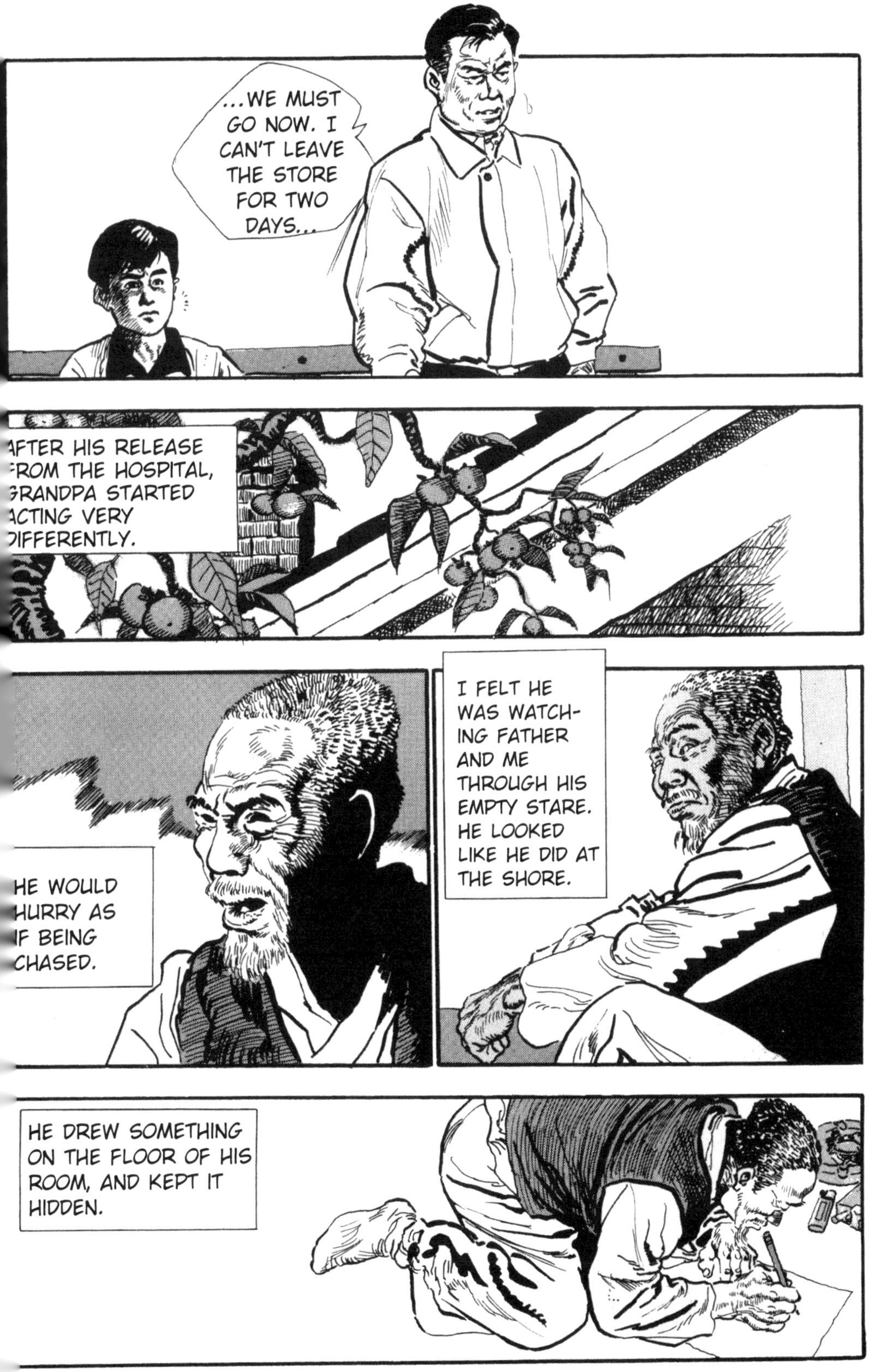
...WE MUST GO NOW. I CAN'T LEAVE THE STORE FOR TWO DAYS...
AFTER HIS RELEASE FROM THE HOSPITAL, GRANDPA STARTED ACTING VERY DIFFERENTLY.
HE WOULD HURRY AS IF BEING CHASED.
I FELT HE WAS WATCH-ING FATHER AND ME THROUGH HIS EMPTY STARE. HE LOOKED LIKE HE DID AT THE SHORE.
HE DREW SOMETHING ON THE FLOOR OF HIS ROOM, AND KEPT IT HIDDEN.

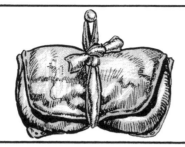

THE MARKS ON HIS POUCH WERE FINISHING TOUCHES.

HE ALSO GOT A SICKLE WITH A SHARP, GLEAMING BLADE.

HE WRAPPED THE BLADE IN TWISTED RAGS.

ALL THE WHILE, HE WAS MUTTERING TO HIMSELF...

...... FATHER, WAIT JUST A MOMENT......

... I AM COMING WITH MOTHER.

I WAS BECOMING FEARFUL.

THE SHADOW AROUND GRANDPA BECAME DARKER, LIKE SHADOWS CREEPING UP A WALL AT SUNSET.

... YES YOU HAVE TO BE BURIED TOGETHER...

HOWEVER, THERE WAS NOTHING I COULD DO.

... I'LL SEE YOU SOON I'M COMING SOON. SOON......

IT SEEMED LIKE A PRIVATE RITUAL IN HIS OWN SANCTUARY.

ONE COULD SENSE DEEP DESPAIR, WHICH KEPT PEOPLE OUT.

I FELT PITY FOR HIM AS THE SHADOWS LENGTHENED.

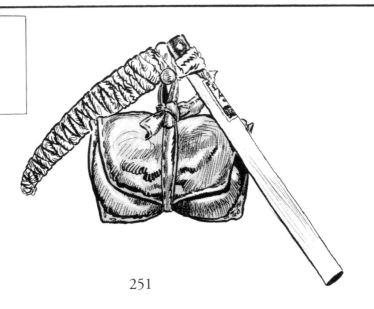

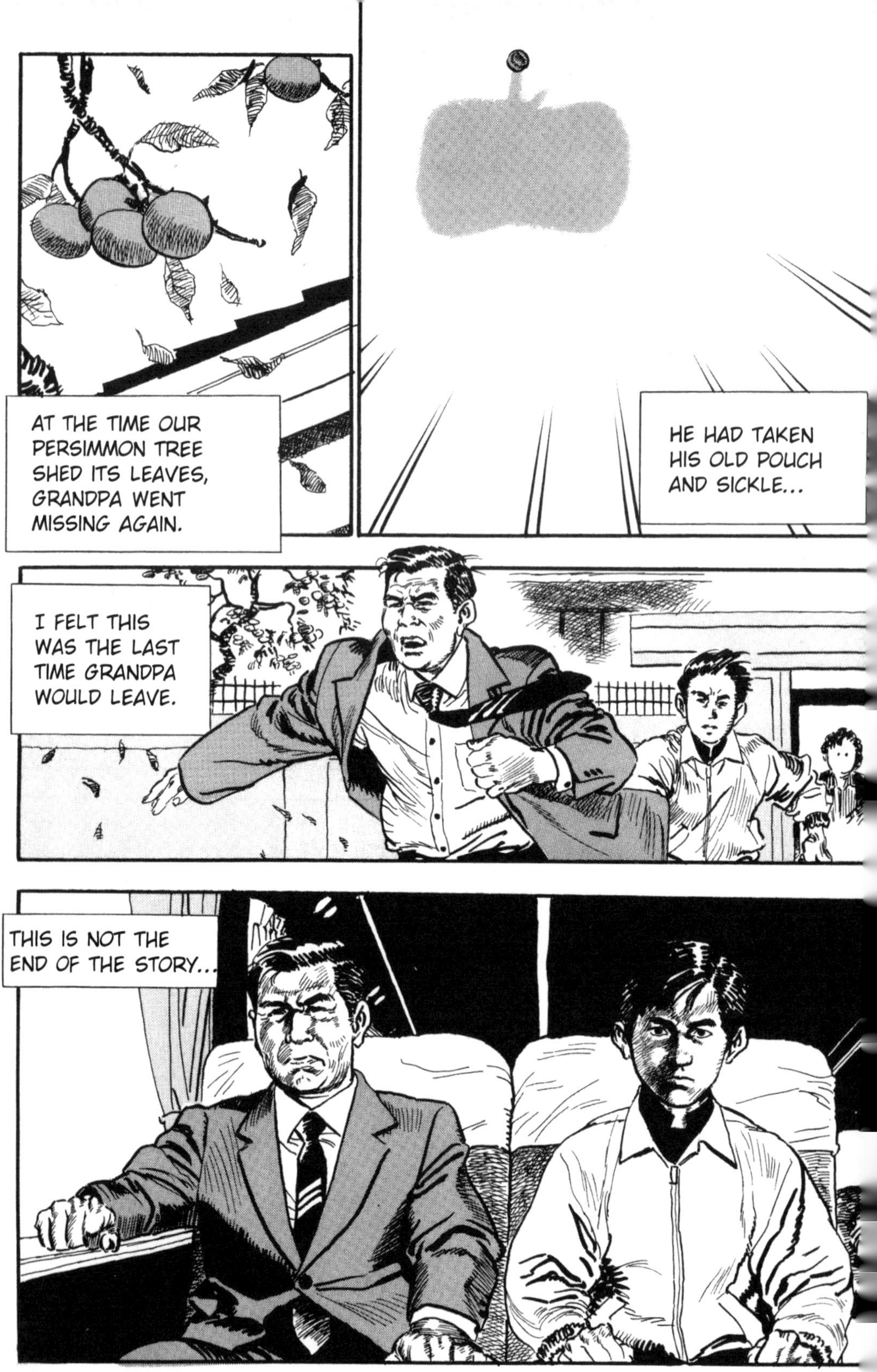
AT THE TIME OUR PERSIMMON TREE SHED ITS LEAVES, GRANDPA WENT MISSING AGAIN.
HE HAD TAKEN HIS OLD POUCH AND SICKLE...
I FELT THIS WAS THE LAST TIME GRANDPA WOULD LEAVE.
THIS IS NOT THE END OF THE STORY...

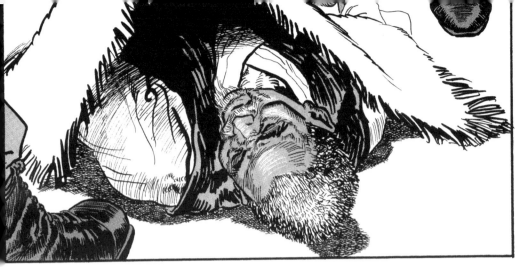

.... WELL, HE FINALLY DID IT. WHEN THEIR TIME COMES, OLD PEOPLE LIKE HIM TRY TO RETURN HOME LIKE THE SALMON. .TSK TSK TSK...

HE PROBABLY BROUGHT THE SICKLE TO CUT THE GRASS ON HIS FATHER'S GRAVE.

HE MUST HAVE BEEN CRAZY TO THINK HE COULD CROSS THE SEA AT HIS AGE.

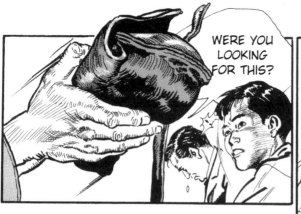

WERE YOU LOOKING FOR THIS?

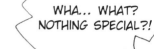

WHA... WHAT? NOTHING SPECIAL?!

IT WAS ON HIS BELT, BUT I DIDN'T FIND ANYTHING SPECIAL INSIDE.

THE POUCH CONTAINED A BALL OF WHITE HAIR AND A WORN-OUT RUBBER SHOE. I'M POSITIVE THEY WERE MY GRANDMA'S.

THERE WAS A TITLE FOR TWO TERRACED FIELDS,

Land Deed: 500 pyong* of land on the coast of Hwanghae Province, in the back of Jungchon Village.

*1 PYONG IS ABOUT 36 SQ. FT.

AND A ROUGHLY DRAWN MAP OF MY GREAT GRANDPA'S GRAVESITE.

To my children, Yemuk and Pyonggon: This is where my father is buried.

산지동   갈비봇

작연꼬개
너머가번질로
가다가 오른편/작은이/루가거하되
방앗간

GRANDPA KNEW HE COULDN'T DO EVERYTHING BY HIMSELF.

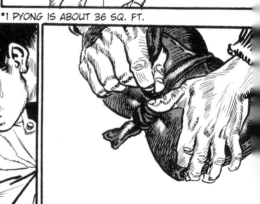

AFTER YEARS OF SUFFERING, HE THREW HIMSELF INTO THE SEA. THIS WOULD PASS HIS HEAVY LOAD ON TO THE FOLLOWING GENERATIONS.

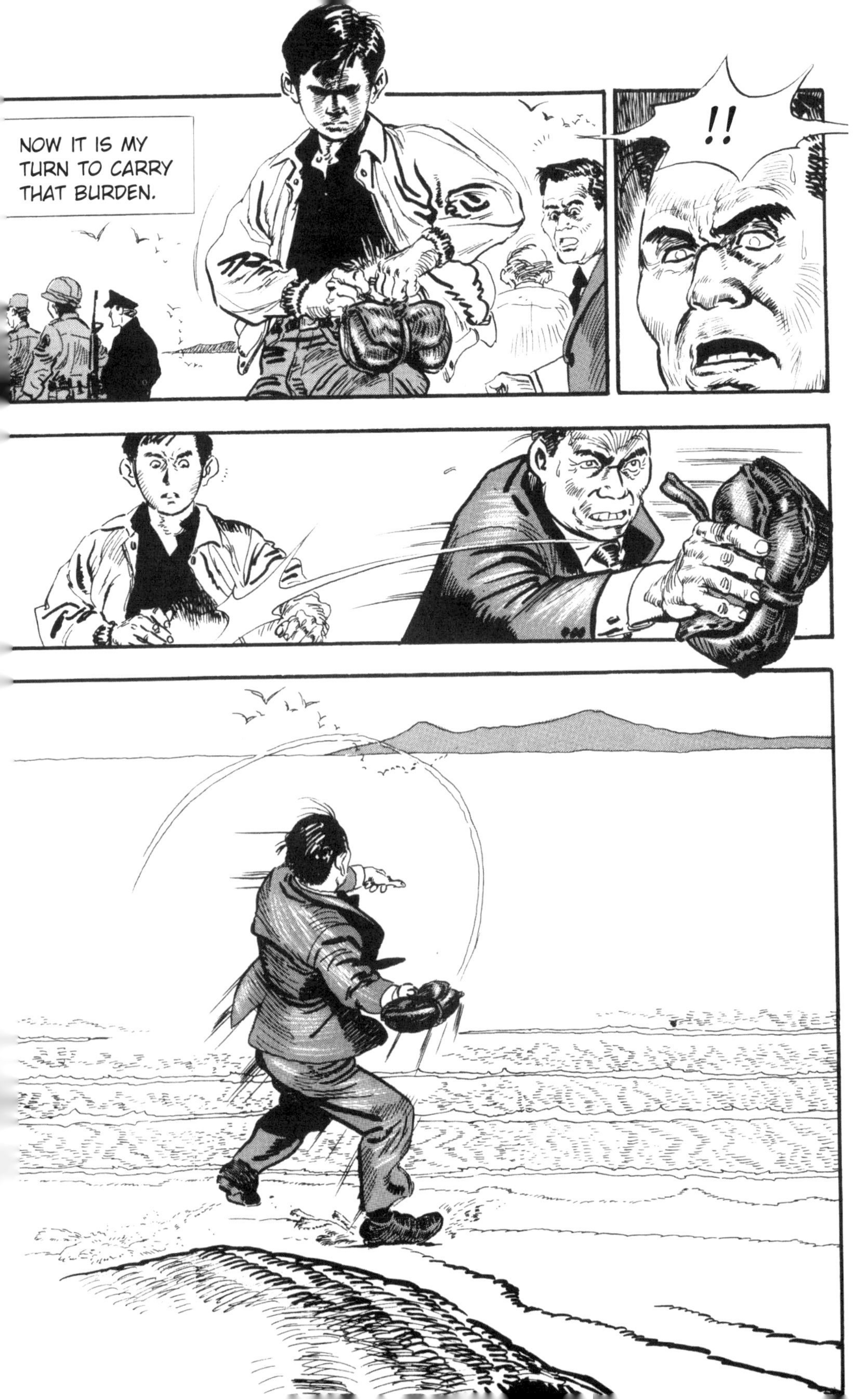
NOW IT IS MY TURN TO CARRY THAT BURDEN.
!!

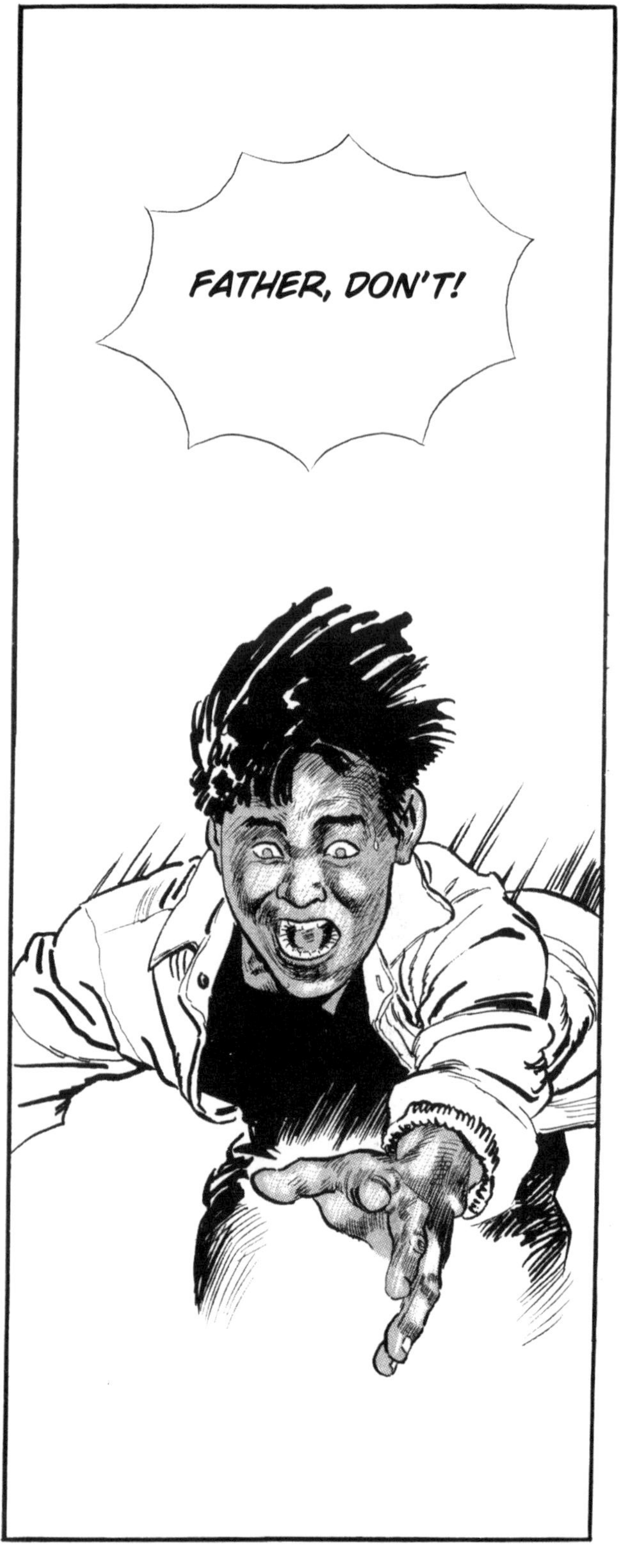
FATHER, DON'T!

BUJA'S PICTURE DIARY

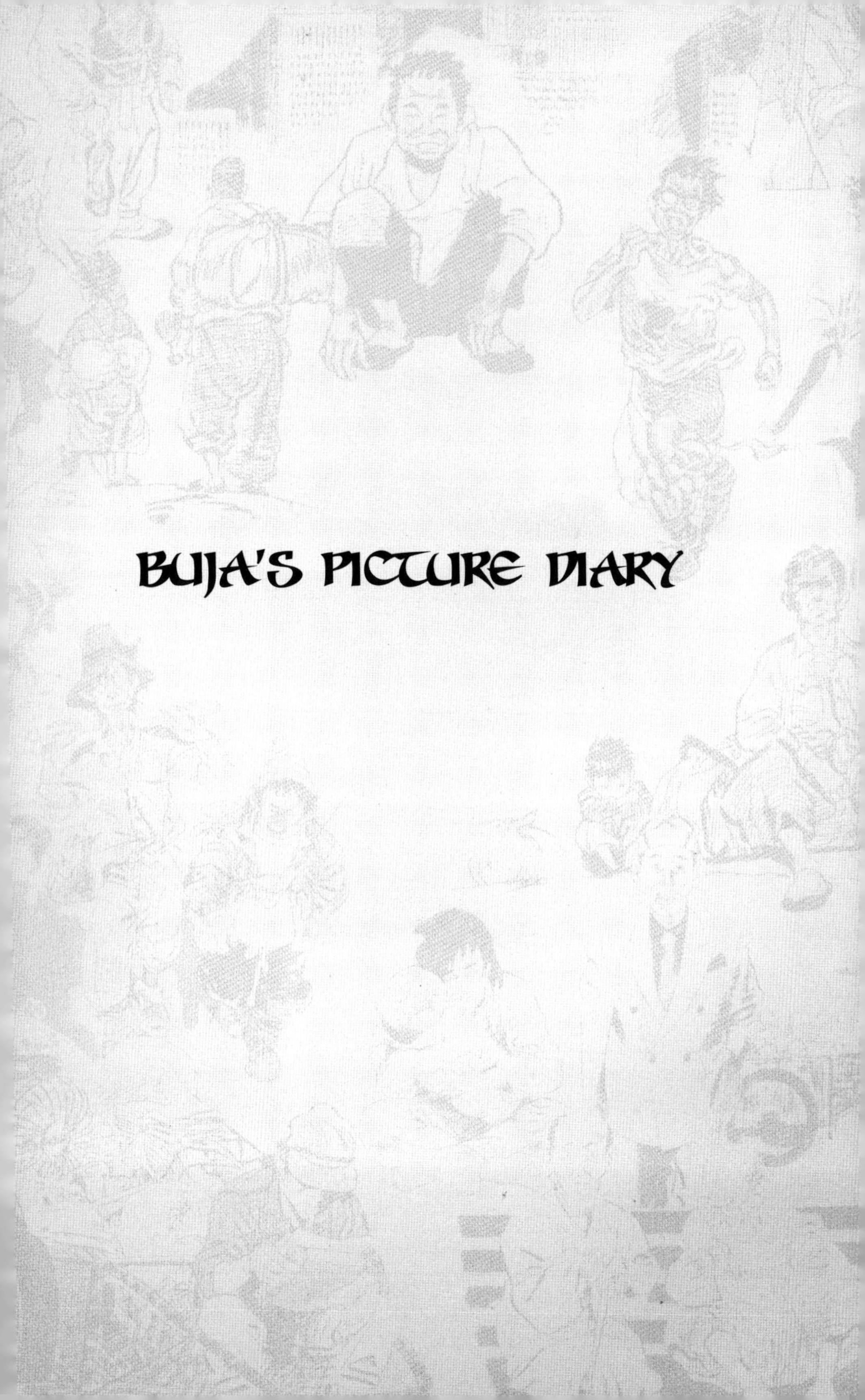

SEYEONG O
SEPTEMBER 1989

Friday, April 28th-Clear

Today, the other kids made fun of my name.
Aram teased me first by saying, "Buja*, Buja, poor Buja*".
Then the other kids started making fun of me, too.
I felt so bad I cried.
Aram's parents own the house we live in, but this is too much.
I don't know why Grandpa gave me this name.
If the teacher says my full name, Na Buja**, while checking attendance... The other kids laugh.
Being rich is a good thing, but I'm embarrassed.
Can't I change my name?

BUJA IS KOREAN FOR RICH.
*NA BUJA IS PRONOUNCED JUST THE SAME AS 'I AM RICH' IN KOREAN.

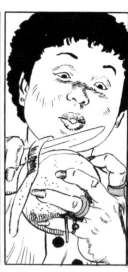

260

Monday, May 22nd Cloudy

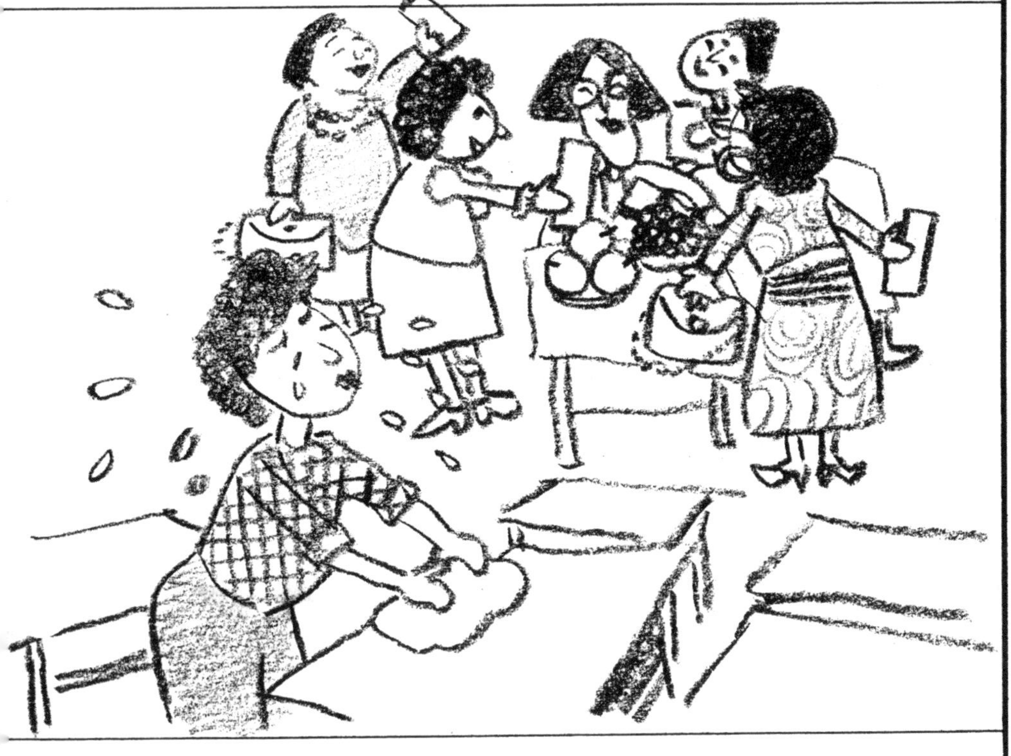

Today, some of our moms came to school.
They were in charge of cleaning the classroom.
The other moms came all dressed up, but my mom came in work clothes and slippers.
She must have been working at the apartment construction site.
The other moms were ~~flattering~~ buttering up the teacher so she would give their children special attention. My mom was cleaning. Her face was red and she was sweating.
I was mad and embarrassed.
The other moms handed the teacher white envelopes*, but my mom didn't give her anything.
She went home crying.

*THE ENVELOPES HAVE BRIBES IN THEM.

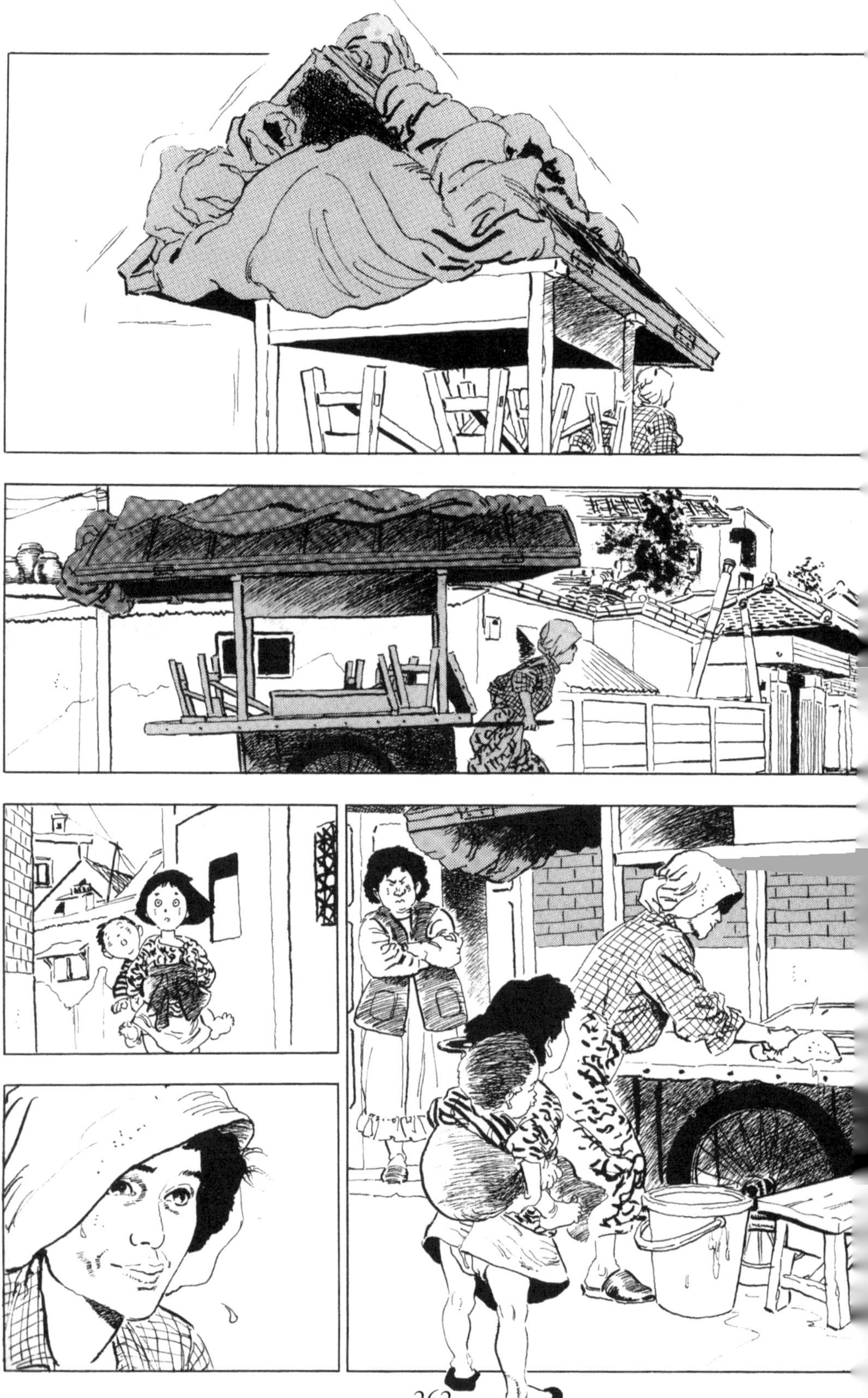

Thursday, June 29th Clear

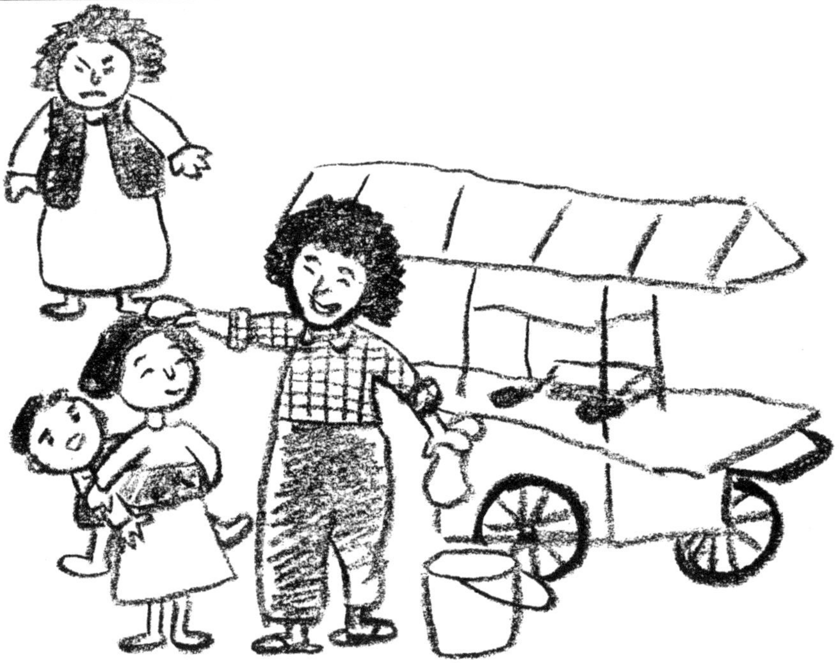

Today was a good day.
My mom got a vendor's cart from a carpenter's shop.
She ~~stands~~ stood it next to the front gate and kept wiping it, even though it wasn't dirty.
Aram's mom was getting upset about the house becoming dirty, and she was frowning, but my mom didn't seem to pay any attention.
She patted my head with a smile and said, Buja, this will solve our problems.
That was the first time she had smiled since my dad died.
My clothes got a little wet because my little brother peed on me, but I was still in a really good mood today.
I'm a little worried that Aram will tease me about the cart at school... But that's okay.

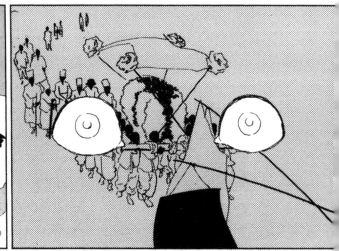

264

Wednesday, July 5th Rainy

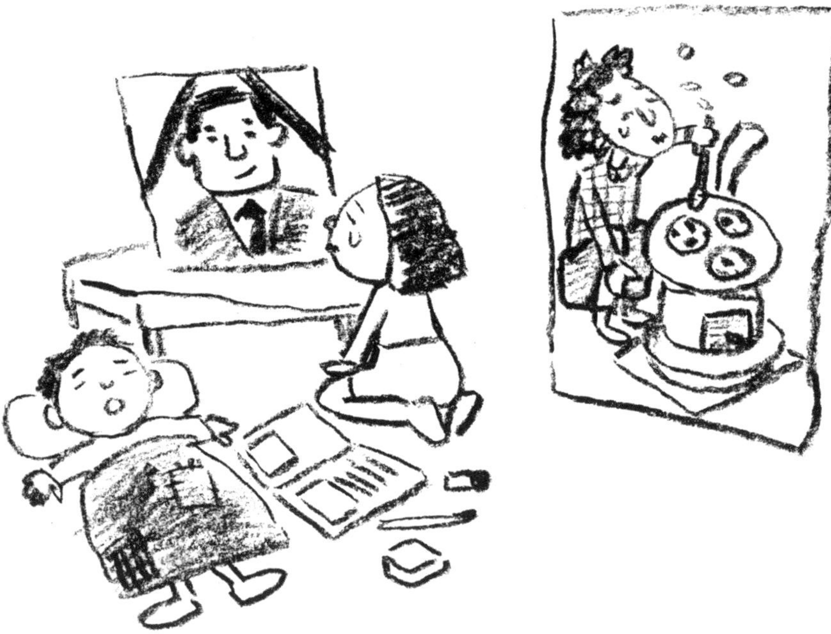

Today is my dad's memorial day.
He died one year ago today.
We lived in the country when my dad was alive.
We were very happy, until he was poisoned while spraying pesticides in the orchards.
He died, and so did my grandpa, a short time later.
My dad was strong and worked hard, but the poison killed him.
I don't know why people always have to spray pesticides on farms.
I really hate people who make pesticides.
Something smells good in the kitchen*, but I'm so sleepy.
My little brother already fell asleep.
I miss my dad.
I should say hello to him soon, but why am I so tired?

*HER MOM IS COOKING FOR THE MEMORIAL.

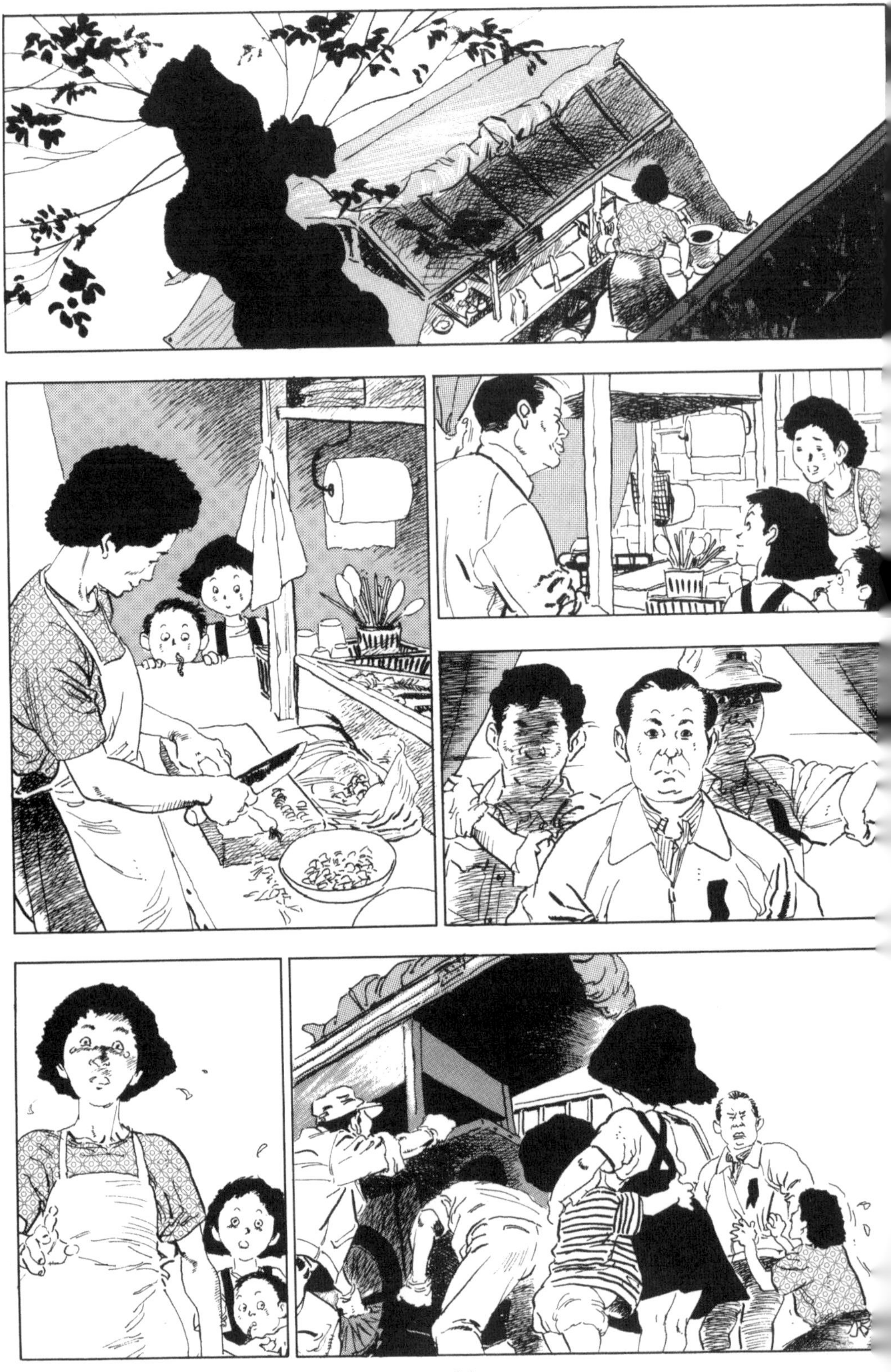

Monday, July 10th Clear

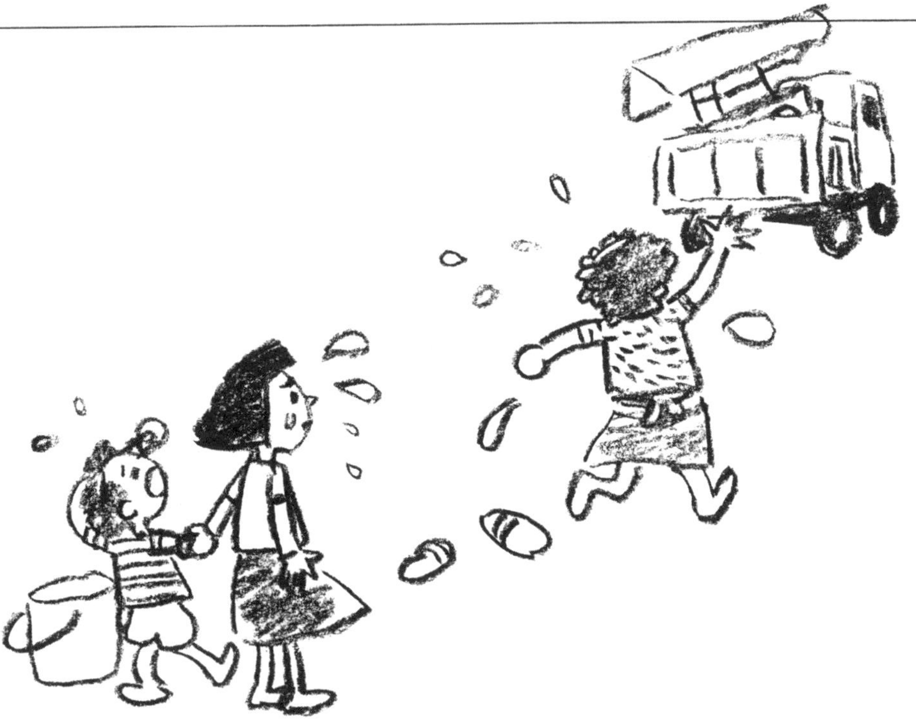

Today is a really sad day.
My mom set up the vendor's cart to do business, when some men came and hauled ~~the cart~~ it away in their truck*.
She cried and begged them not to, but they knocked her down and left.
I don't know what she did wrong. It's only been ten days since she started the business.
Some time ago, my ~~ma~~ mom was chased out of the marketplace while selling anchovies. She ended up working at an apartment building site. She went without lunches to buy that cart. The people who just took it away from her are really mean.
Can't the president do something about it?
My mom ran after them in her bare feet, and she still hasn't returned.

IN KOREA, YOU MUST HAVE PERMISSION TO DO BUSINESS IN CERTAIN AREAS. OTHERWISE, YOUR POSSESSIONS WILL BE CONFISCATED.

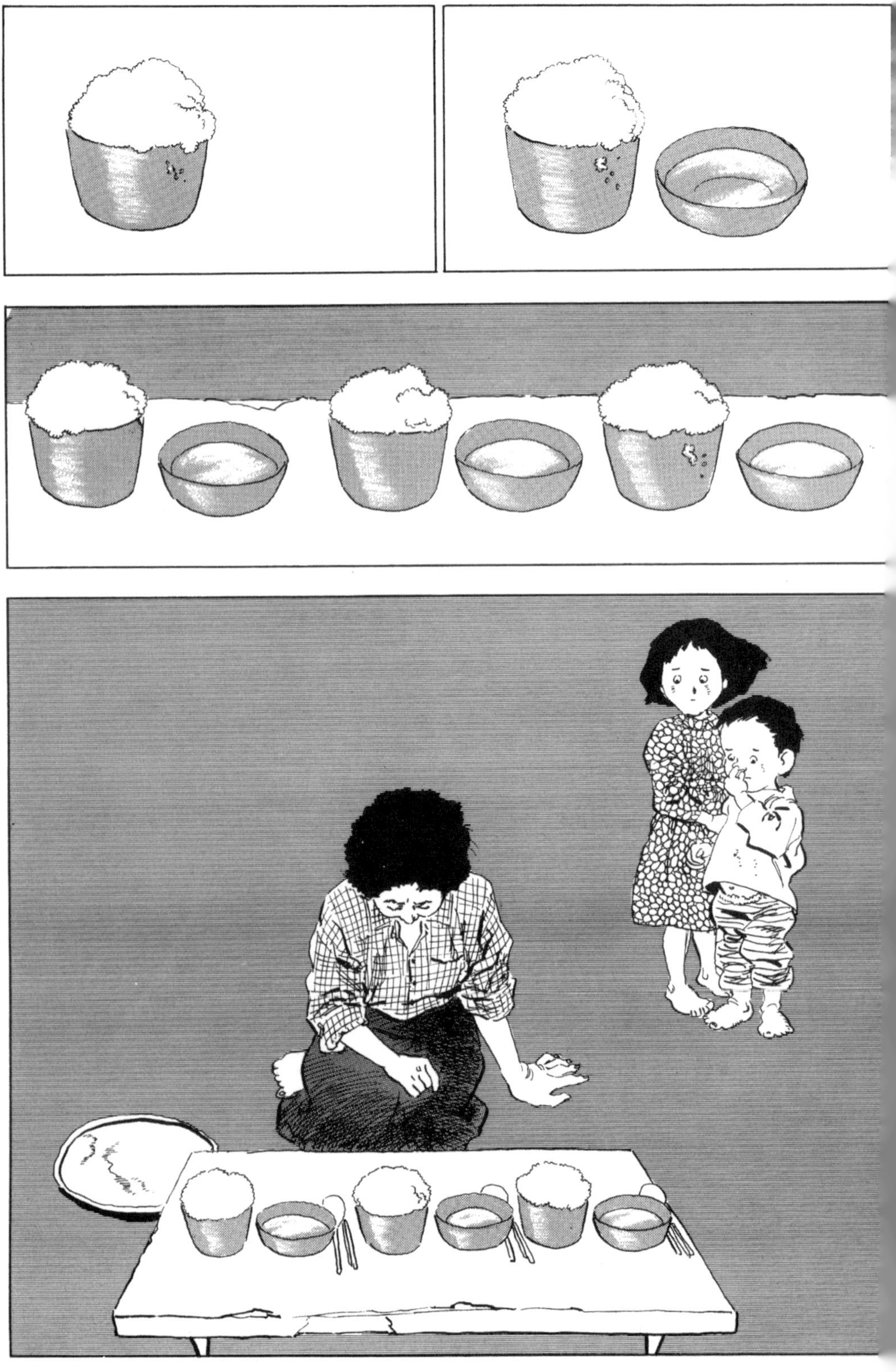

Thursday, September 14th Rainy

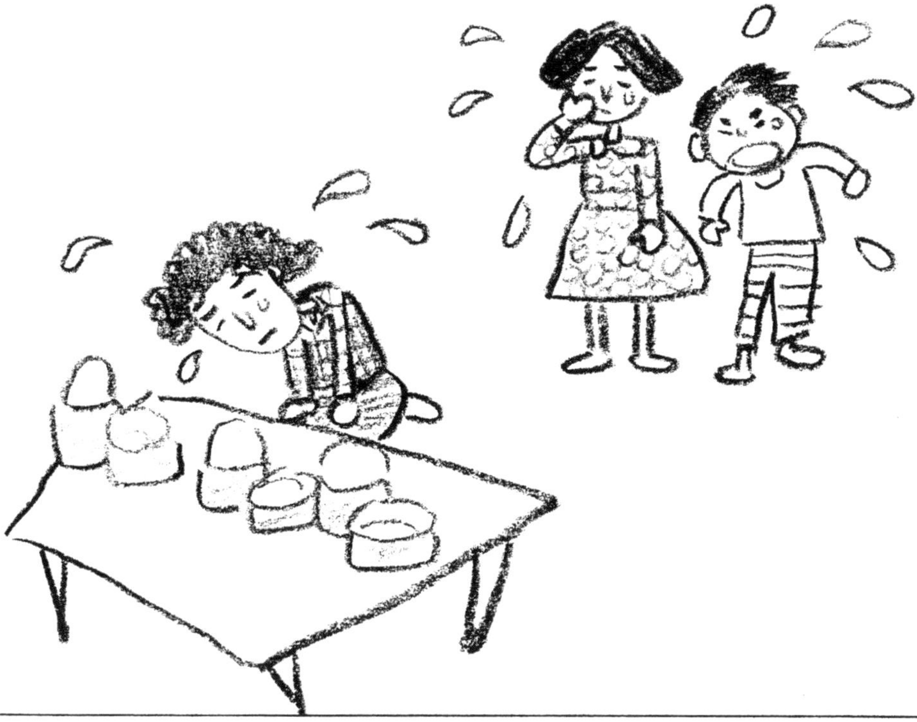

Today is Ch'usok, but I'm not happy at all.
I can't stop thinking about my dad and grandpa.
Aram's family, who owns this house, took off for their grandpa's place in the country.
I really envy them.
This morning, my mom put just rice and cold water on the table. She cried for a long time.
I cried too, and so did my little brother.

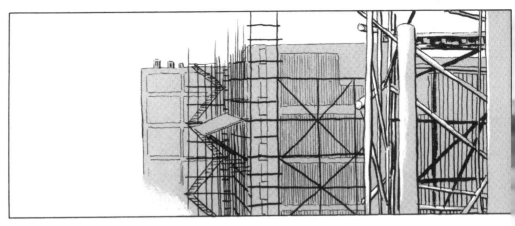

Monday, September 18th Clear

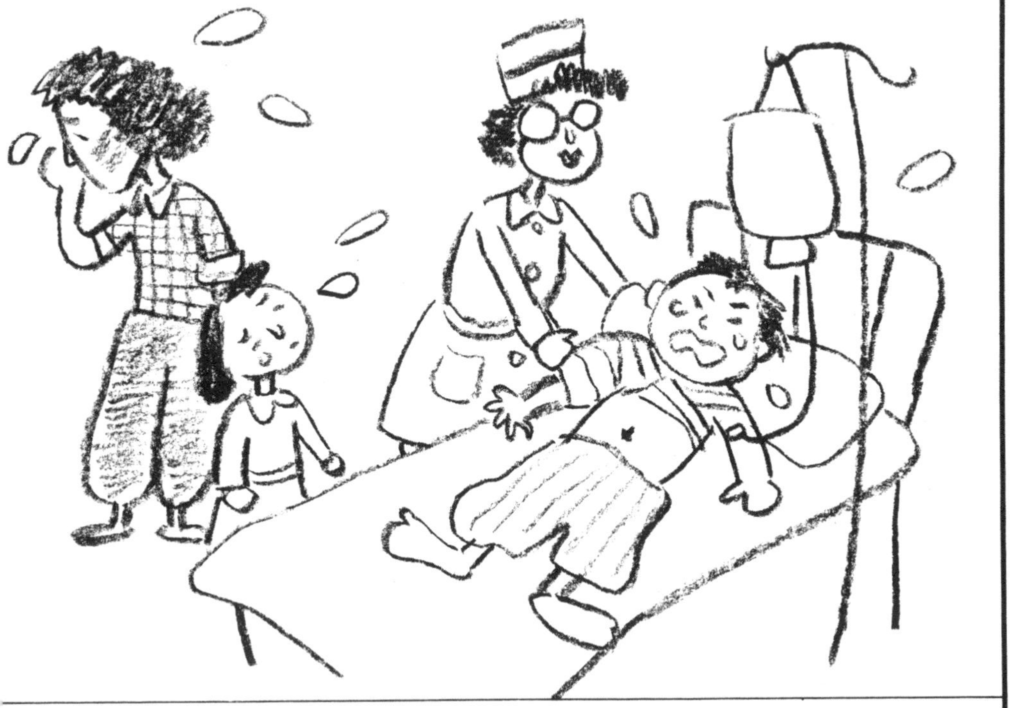

There was a big accident today.
This morning, Aram's mom said there was a job open for a housekeeper. But my mom went to the construction site, because she made more money there.
She only had a little to eat for breakfast. Then she put my little brother on her back, carried a bottle of water, and went out to work.
When my brother was playing at the construction site, a brick fell and broke his shoulder.
Other people said he was lucky his head wasn't hit, but I was sad because he had to have his shoulder tied up in the hospital. The pain made him cry.
Since that happened, my mom can't even go out to work anymore.
I'm really sad about my mom's thin and dark face.

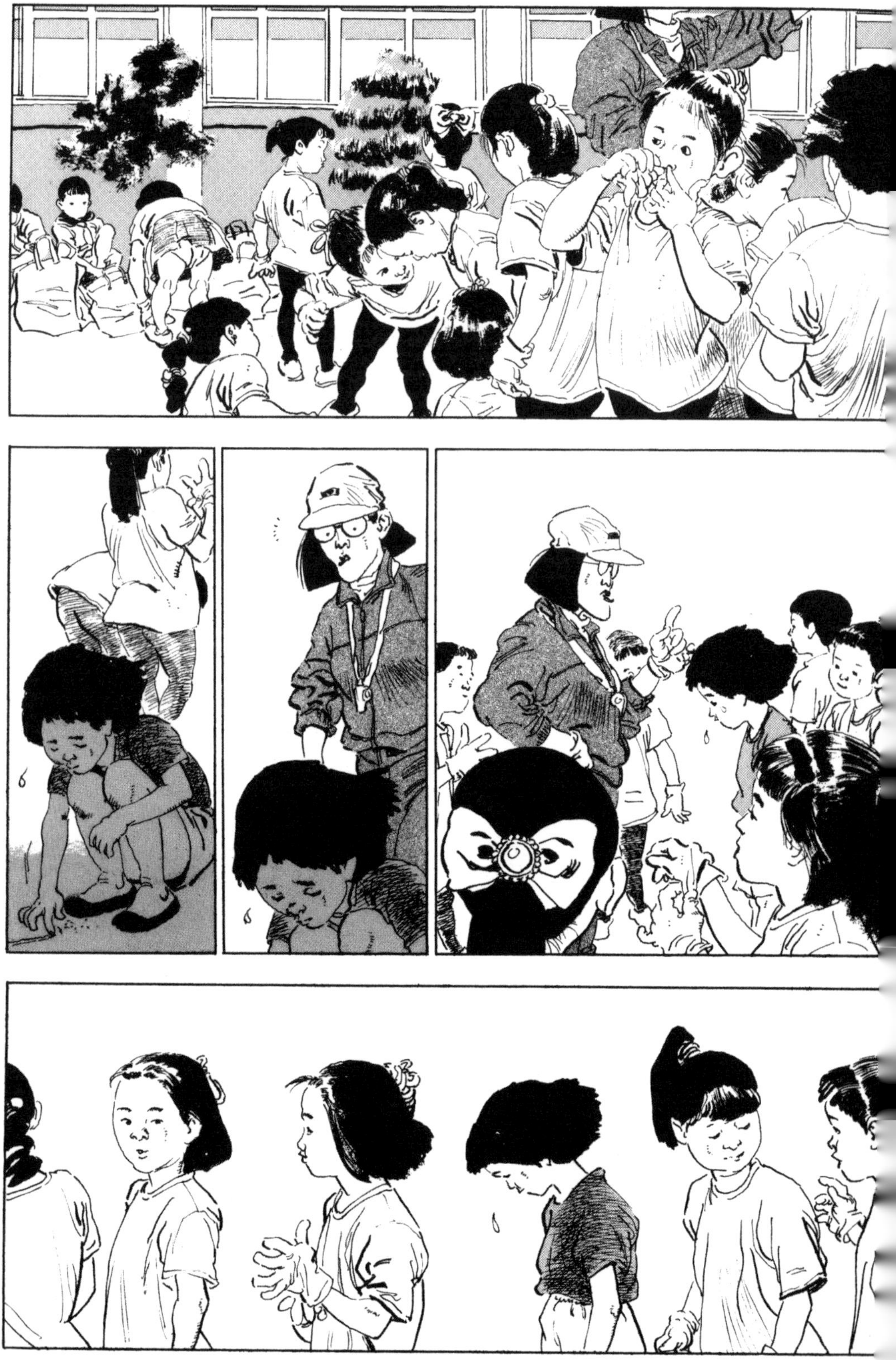

Wednesday, September 20th Clear

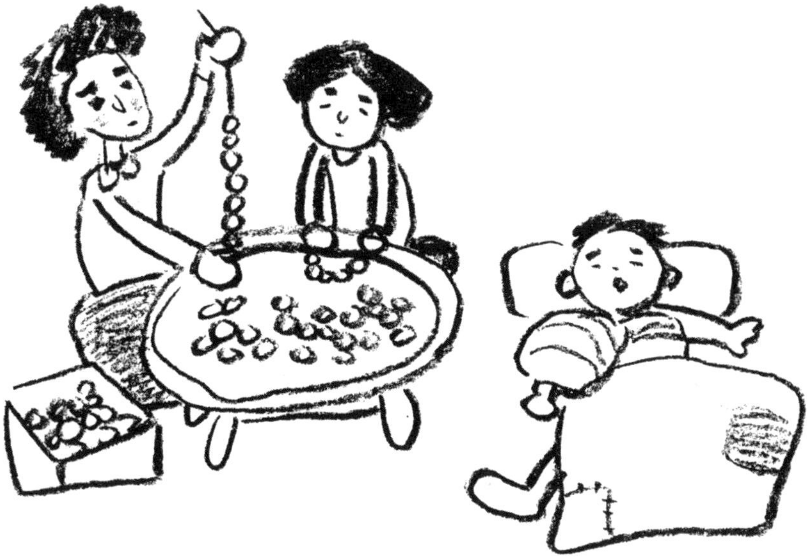

Today, we had final practice for the upcoming athletic festival.
My teacher scolded me.
When we were dancing, all of the other second graders were wearing dress uniforms, except for me.
My teacher told me I had to pack my dress uniform for the athletic festival that's coming up in a couple of days, but I still haven't told my mom about it.
The uniforms cost a lot of money, and I didn't want her to worry about it. I decided it was best not to say anything.
I still worry, though.
The other kids are all looking forward to the festival, but I'm not at all.
I wish there wasn't an athletic festival.

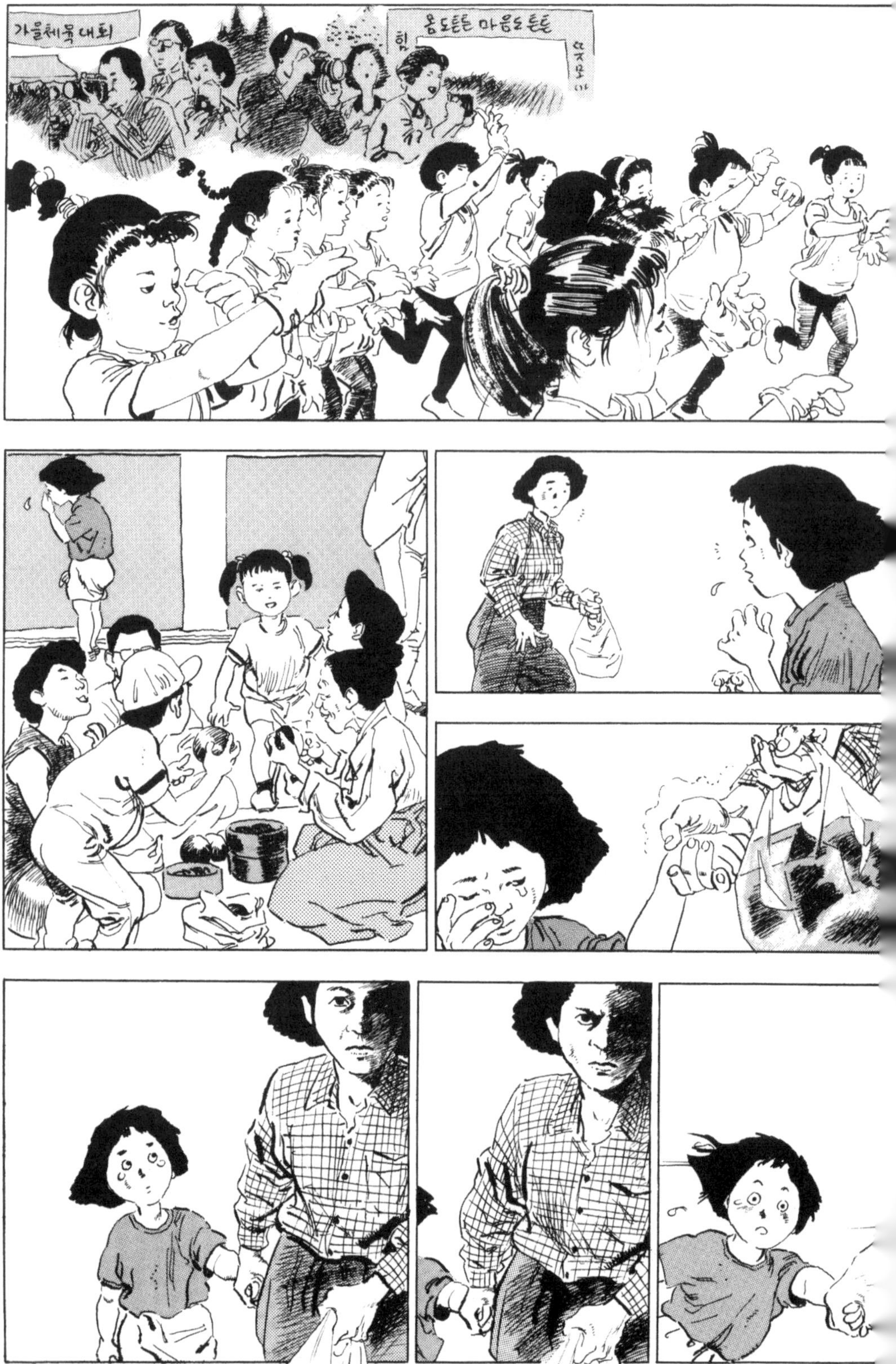
가을체육대회
몸도튼튼 마음도튼튼

Friday, September 22nd Clear

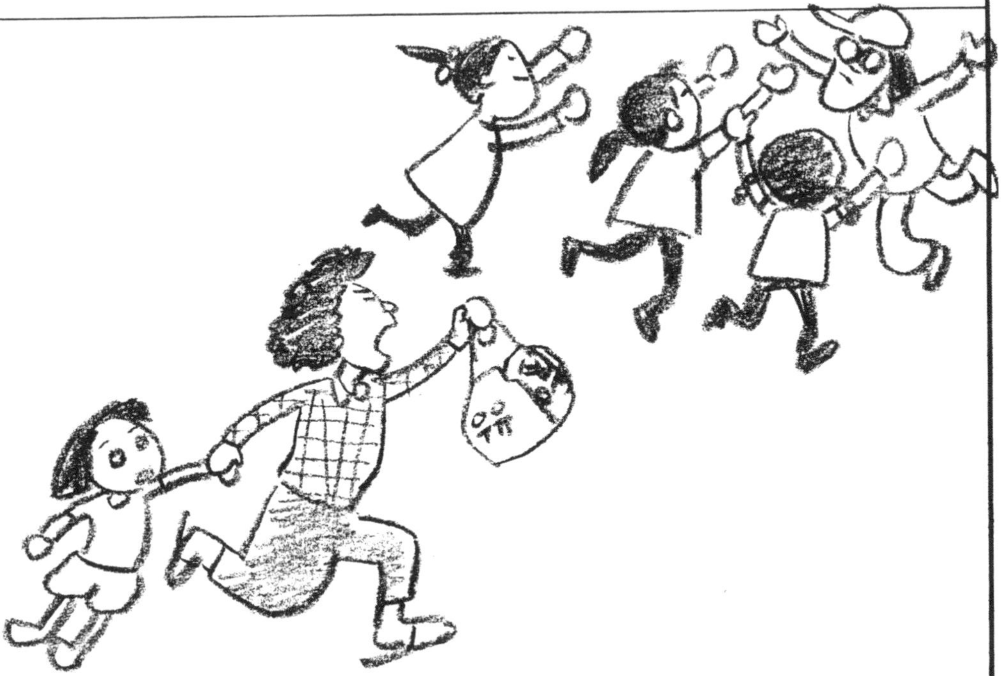

Today is our athletic festival.
All of the other children looked really happy. Their families brought lots of delicious things, took pictures, and ate. Everybody was happy.
I was alone and I worried. When it was our turn to dance, all of the other kids changed into their uniforms. I didn't.
My teacher yelled at me. She said, You didn't wear it during practice and you forgot to bring it again, so you'll have to be left out of the festival.
I had been crying alone in a corner when my mom came.
She held my hand and shook for a while. I thought she was crying again. She was always crying. I got even sadder thinking about it, so I looked up at her face. I was surprised she wasn't crying this time. Her face started to get scarier and scarier looking, and then she grabbed my hand and ran to the playground where the students were dancing.
She yelled, Second grade tenth class, where is the second grade tenth class? My child is also in the second grade tenth class! She still did not cry.

COMMENTS ABOUT SEYEONG O
WORKS OF AESTHETIC VALUE IN KOREAN GRAPHIC NOVELS
HAN CHANG-WAN

In the wrinkles of the torn and crumbling flesh,
The carved wrinkles held back from times past,
We look into the witness stand of the mirror that no one can avoid.
From Lim Dong-hwak's poem "How Are We Falling"

The strength in Seyeong O's graphic novels lies in his ability to move the reader. His ability to deliver emotion effectively while keeping an objective viewpoint is proof the work has surpassed a certain standard. Furthermore, the deep emotion felt through this objective viewpoint leads the readers to reflect upon themselves. The principles that allowed Seyeong O to attain an objective view can be condensed into three elements: transparency, consistency, and dramatic development; these elements are formal standards that are essential to establishing the beauty of realism.

Transparency is the number one device used by Seyeong O to capture human objectivism. It is closely related to Seyeong O's characteristic way of dividing scenes without any irregularity. His scenes are always highly geometrically refined. Through frames that have been molded into rectangles with no room for doubt, he has put into practice a kind of strict objectivism. The scene where the father and daughter are on the train going up to Seoul for the daughter's engagement in "Tear Gas" shows one method in which Seyeong O arranges the frames. The lengths are the same, side-to-side, but the panoramic scenes with different heights show a variety of elements around the main character, P'yong-hee. This composition functions as a decisive key to transparently show his agony. Also, his past stories are recollected with small broken square scenes. Even though temporal gaps like the present and past are expressed with different kinds of frames, one thing they have in common is that the background is faithfully objective.

The transparency of Seyeong O's graphic novels can also be found in the third-person storytelling. Seyeong O enjoys using narration without a hint of playfulness. Rarely, a speaker appears in the first person, in monologue, disassociating the reader from the main characters. Seyeong O does not control his characters; in that sense, his characters are independent. He merely gives them situations, and in that way they are existential.

This kind of non-meddling and existential setting is broken up into Seyeong O's transparent image construction. He is incredibly sharp when it comes to scene movement. The scene showing the side of the girl's head in "The Little Alley Watcher" starts with successive zoom-outs. A slow and calm narration moves at the same speed as the slowly progressing camera shots. The screen that centers on the back of the girl slowly pans to the right and tilts down to a puppy tied up in a corner of the yard. From here the screen zooms in once more, and finishes one scene with a full close-up shot of a puppy kicking away his dish out of anguish. Breath-stopping and slow but detailed, screen directions such as these continue on powerfully until the last scene. Elements such as the vacant countryside, a girl left all alone, and the natural environment which envelops all of this, spread their colorful feelings through Seyeong O's movie-like direction. At this point, the reader is enraptured by the arrangement typical of Seyeong O that both elaborately zooms in and out. When his work is finished, the reader can make sense of the entire story. This is the part where the reader is touched. Artistic inspiration is brought forth through transparency.

"Buja's Picture Diary" is the zenith of transparency. We can enjoy the author's wit through the fact that a poor child is called *Buja* ("rich" in Korean). A picture diary written from the view of a child is re-explained through illustrations without text. The readers can easily understand the situation, because it's already written in the diary. Why did Seyeong O adopt this style? To answer this question, we must read his thoughts as he deals with the subject of poverty. Being poor is only being poor, and that in itself cannot be disgraceful or a crime. But Buja's mother ends up having to fight a world that despises poverty. Here, the subject of poverty must be presented strictly objectively. So the type of form experimentation that he uses in the work is designed not no allow any sort of subjective opinion.

The strict use of frames, narration based on the third person, image arrangement that is stubbornly documentary-like, and the exclusion of subjective opinions explain the beauty of Seyeong O's graphic novels' depth. This beauty starts from none other than a formal point in realism called transparency.

The topics Seyeong O chooses are warm and familiarly humanistic. An issue he persists upon is reality itself in the land we live in. In other words, our reality as he sees it is full of the structural inconsistency that makes people unhappy. Therefore, the reality he presents in his graphic novels is comprised of specific and painful reflections upon fantasies and delusions. This is the second formal element we find in his work, which is the element of consistency. We see vivid consistency in the use of confrontation as the basis for his stories. The issue feared the most and most difficult to deal with is the object of confrontation, but without this confrontation we cannot look into human reality.

"The Secret of the Old Leather Pouch" deals with the issue of the division of North and South Korea, going down three generations from grandfather to father, and finally to "me." The leather pouch symbolizes the resentment that his grandfather, one who experienced the division personally, held all his life. Now, through "I" who picks up the leather pouch, which has become the only remnant of his grandfather along with his body, we remember our duty as a people to have a historical and noble reunification. On the other hand, the desperate motion of "my" father snatching the pouch away and preparing to throw it into the sea shows the grim reality we live in. The "red complex," which put his father's generation at a disadvantage just because their hometown and family were from the North, still goes on. The solution to division is not that simple. That is why the father wants to forget it all. He wants to avoid it. He cannot confront it. However, "I" disagrees with the father and confronts the biggest longstanding question in our era, which is division and reunification.

Park P'yong-hee, the main character of "Tear Gas," threw up twice in all his life: when his father, who was part of an anti-communist police force, was taken away by the communists, and when his son was beaten by the riot police while demonstrating. The historical irony, which is the distinct division of "anti-communists" and "anti anti-communists" is tragically personified by the closest direct bloodline, father and son. P'yong-hee eventually becomes entangled. It is a history he would like to go back and change completely. One individual's reasonable little wish is brutally broken up in time. Through his throwing up we cannot fail to see the chaos of modern society. We also realize that this chaos is the true form of our modern society. When we look at "Shoot! Shoot! Shoot! Shoot! Bang," which deals with the memories of Kwangju in the 80's, we read that Seyeong O's message to "confront modern history" goes further and rises to the rebirth of conscience and liberation of mankind. In this work, a reporter calmly covers the memory of a sin committed by a young man who shot someone. He escapes from himself, and his ability to judge is taken away. A firm message is expressed: "I must escape from the evil structure of society," which lies dormant in his mind.

The concerns that Seyeong O present are terrible. He invites us to the scenes of these concerns and does not provide a solution. They are about the sins of our era. As we know, they are sins without a solution. This point emphasizes the validity of his graphic novels. Also, in the sense that the cleansing of sins will take a very long time and may never disappear, his novels have crossover value as art. They scrutinize the heavy concerns of Korean society with an awareness that searches for a humanistic solution and greatly moves the reader. What makes Seyeong O's art exceptional is the timelessness of his work which in turn is rooted in his consistency.

Seyeong O's consistency is, on a technical side, shown through the documentary-like use of shots. His frames are very logical and grammatical. From whole to part, or from part to whole, none of the movements have a flaw in angle. To this, he adds the flow of time. The movement of space and time in this kind of moderation is well designed. So, the third element of Seyeong O's work is this documentary-like development. His graphic novels are extremely dramatic. His endings can even be brilliant. These characteristics usually originate from his background in literature. He is excellent at using backgrounds. In scenes he shows rather innocently, there is probably an underlying background set somewhere in a corner. This background eventually comes to life and strengthens the topic. This device puts images previously shown into focus. The scenes shown in the beginning seem to have nothing to do with the rest of the story. However, when the purpose of the story becomes clear, those seemingly unrelated scenes completely merge into the topic. At that point, the reader finally realizes what everything was about, and this process naturally strengthens the connection between the author and reader. The background in "Fire" is a scene of pigs mating. This rather disgusting scene is a device to symbolize the mother's debauchery. The "blackened can" in "The Snake Catcher Brothers' Dream" ends up being no different from the "white snake" they had hoped for. The can, which had been simply used as a piggybank, completed its symbolism through the contrast of black and white and came back to life brilliantly.

The materials Seyeong O uses as background are simple and placid. However, the shining emotion felt through the backgrounds is very deep. "Old Man Kim's Record" starts with a scene of a young trash collector passing by some old men who wearily sit on a bench. The story, which is told through a genealogy book and the writings stuck within it, ends much like the beginning, with a picture of some old men sitting on a bench. It moves us in a way that has us reflecting upon our own birth.

Directors like Nouvelle Vague (New Wave) flag bearers Leos Carax and Luc Besson were not formally educated in movie direction. That is why people in the movie industry discover the meaning of "resistance" in these directors' new and provocative movie worlds that dismantle the status quo. Seyeong O also did not learn how to draw or make graphic novels in a school. He didn't even go through the often-used apprenticeship system. Then do we also find signs of resistance in his novels? To answer this question we look for new elements in his novels. First, we read resistance in his social topics. However, this is a relational resistance in that it stretches the boundaries drawn by organizations and power. Relational resistance loses its power in an instant if the chain of oppression is loosened. On the surface, it is easy for resistance to only be lip service. Then in what kind of topic consciousness can an artist's absolute resistance be found? This is Seyeong O's challenge, as well as a new opportunity.

The analysis of Seyeong O's drawings shows clearly that he has a strong traditional background in literature, drawing, and the deliverance of images. Therefore, when it comes to the pictures, he is a traditionalist and a conservative.

Then is he not resisting any longer? On the contrary, his use of the graphic novel medium for mixing literature, drawings and imagery is his form of resistance. To set an example, he has made many experimentations. He tries hard to give each story its own form and style. This is how he resists the status quo.

Han Chang-wan is Head Planner for the Seoul International Comics Festival and a lecturer in the Department of Visual Arts at Sejong University.